Introduction to Leisure Services in North Carolina

Fifth Edition

Edited by
Paul L. Gaskill
Appalachian State University

Contributing Authors:

Aram Attarian
Delmar Bachert
Sarah Banks
Leandra A. Bedini
Erick Byrd
Robert B. Buerger
David A. Cardenas
Sharon E. Carter
Nelson Cooper
James P. Drummond
Eric Frauman
Nancy J. Gladwell
Diane G. Groff
Karla Henderson
Jim Herstine
Jeffery M. Hill
Tommy Holden

Susan A. McGhee
Maurice Phipps
Ed Raiola
Kevin Riley
James R. Sellers
H. Douglas Sessoms
Jim Sibthorp
Debby F. Singleton
Thomas K. Skalko
Glenn Ellen Starr Stilling
Charlsena F. Stone
Ben Tholkes
Roger Warren
Stephanie T. West
Wayne Williams
Beth E. Wilson

KENDALL/HUNT PUBLISHING COMPANY
4050 Westmark Drive P.O. Box 1840 Dubuque, Iowa 52004-1840

On the cover: Rafting, rock climbing, hiking, biking, and mountain images copyright © Corbis;
Speed skating and kayaking images copyright © PhotoDisc.

Copyright © 1990, 1993, 1997, 2001, 2006 by Kendall/Hunt Publishing Company

ISBN 0-7575-2529-6

Printed in the United States of America

10 9 8 7 6 5 4 3 2 1

Dedication

The fifth edition of *Introduction to Leisure Services in North Carolina* is dedicated to Dr. H. Douglas Sessoms, the editor of the first two editions of this text. Dr. Sessoms is Professor Emeritus at the University of North Carolina at Chapel Hill, and his influence on the development of both the leisure services and the preparation of leisure service professionals in North Carolina is unparalleled. This dedication is but a small token of the esteem that North Carolina leisure service educators hold for his tireless contributions to the discipline. Thank you, Doug, for all that you have done.

Editors Acknowledgement: Many thanks are due to all the contributing authors who made this text possible. Special recognition is due to Glenn Ellen Starr Stilling for her diligent work as a contributing author and for her extraordinary endeavors on the completion of the index for this text.

Contents

Chapter 1

A Brief History of Leisure Services in North Carolina

H. Douglas Sessoms and Roger Warren

Recreation and leisure services in North Carolina are major industries. They are a creator of jobs, a generator of revenue, and a provider of a basic human service: the provision of opportunities for meaningful leisure expression. These opportunities are made available through the efforts of thousands of professionals and volunteers working in a wide variety of agencies and organizations. Together they constitute the leisure service delivery system.

The leisure service delivery system is a term we use to describe those agencies and organizations that offer recreation opportunities to the public. The system is comprised of three major subsystems, each having its own characteristics and focus of service. The first, and perhaps most extensive, is the commercial system which is comprised of those agencies that provide services for profit. The programs are available to those who have the price of admission, and the agencies range in size from local billiard parlors to Paramount's Carowinds, from fishing piers to ski resorts and private camps. Although many of those working in these organizations do not consider themselves to be park and recreation professionals, the service they render is a recreation service.

The second major element of the leisure service delivery system is those agencies and organizations known as private recreation. This element is characterized by organizations having definable memberships, relying upon volunteers for leadership, and developing programs and services for a special interest or age group. Within the private sector there are organizations such as country clubs and neighborhood recreation associations as well as the Girl Scouts and the YMCA. Also included in this group are religious and industrial organizations since many churches and companies provide recreation services for their members. These groups are non-profit, and in some instances they are even quasi public; that is, they serve the public at large as does government and they draw upon the public for financial support through such efforts as the United Way.

The public sector is the third major element and the one most closely identified with the park and recreation profession. It includes all of those organizations and agencies that are supported through taxation or provided by government, including the therapeutic recreation services provided in our state hospitals. The range here is from local park and recreation systems to state and national parks and recreation areas. These programs are available to all and supported by all.

The leisure service delivery system in North Carolina has evolved over a period of time. Within this evolution different segments of the system have been dominant at different periods of history. In the early years of the state, the private sector was dominant. More recently, the commercial sector has become a central focus of the system. And, throughout the past eighty years, the public sector has been much involved. We begin the study of leisure services in North Carolina by reviewing the history of this movement and the profession that has evolved to provide these basic leisure services.

The Colonial and Antebellum Years

Like most southern colonies, North Carolina was settled by northern Europeans and slaves from central and west Africa. Unlike most other southern colonies, it was not a plantation state. It was a state of small land owners. Where there were plantations, the major crops varied from rice during North Carolina's earlier history to tobacco and cotton before the Civil War. Most of its major cities of commerce were located in the east; agriculture, forestry, and shipping were the state's major industries.

It is not surprising, therefore, that the leisure behaviors of colonial North Carolina would reflect the lifestyle of an agrarian population. Nor is it surprising that most of the earlier cultural and social programs began in its coastal plain communities. Among its more popular activities were cock fights, horse racing, and ring tournaments (an event that required riders on horseback to cover a designated course, spearing rings of various sizes, to see who could travel the course the quickest and capture the largest number of rings on his lance). There were few inhibitions of the common folk about gambling or drinking activities, as well as dancing. The English, Scottish, and Irish heritage were much apparent. Lotteries were operated by the state until 1834, and gambling was legal until 1835.

John Brickell, an Edenton physician, wrote in the 1730s that North Carolinians were fond of the dance, "relying heavily upon the fiddle or the bagpipe for their musick [sic] and that nearly every town had a race track since horse racing was popular with all social classes" (*North Carolina Illustrated, 1984*). In response to this interest in horsemanship and cultural activities, a good number of social clubs such as jockey clubs and thespian societies (drama) were organized throughout the state. The first thespian society was formed in Wilmington in the late 1700s, where one of the earliest constructed drama halls (Thalian Hall) still stands today. Theatrical groups would travel from one community to another, presenting plays in theaters supported by the thespian groups. Similarly, Lyceum societies were organized in the early 1800s, the first being in Fayetteville (1834), to promote public readings, orations, and declamation contests.

Early signs of tourism were also present. Nags Head, for example, began developing as a resort area in the early 1800s, and, with the discovery of several mineral springs in the west and the Piedmont, health spas became popular. It was recorded that in 1850 the Warm Springs Resort located near Asheville had 500 visitors, and, of that number, only fifty were North Carolinians. There were also successful warm springs resorts in Madison, Stokes, and Burke counties, as well as at Fuquay Springs in Wake county.

Just as music and dance were much a part of the North Carolina tradition so were the folk arts of pottery and quilting. It was not uncommon to have "dance frolics" twice a week in many communities as well as cotillions for the "Landed Gentry." Spirituals and ballads were shared by both slaves and non-slaves, and taverns and crossroads stores were popular meeting places for the common folk.

Although our forefathers seemingly enjoyed their leisure and had little sense of guilt in having fun, they did place certain restrictions on who could play and what activities were acceptable. Slaves were prohibited by law from playing any game of chance such as cards, dice and ninepins for any money, liquor or any kind of property (Johnson, 1937). Perhaps the best account of North Carolina's earliest behavior is contained in Guion Johnson's work, *Antebellum North Carolina—A Social History,* a history that changed with the advent of the War Between the States in 1861.

Turn of the Century

Although the Civil War radically altered the economic and political structures of North Carolina, it did not affect our leisure interests and behaviors nearly as much as did the growth of our factories, the expansion of our road and rail systems, and the development of steam and electricity as sources of power. As North Carolina urbanized and industrialized, it also entered the era of organized recreation, tourism, and mass entertainment. Fairs and traveling circuses were popular events. They reflected the folk activities of a rural society, but they also allowed participants to see and enjoy exotic animals, acrobatic groups, and dazzling costumes. One of the largest of these earlier fairs was the State Fair, which was held in Raleigh on a fifty five acre tract on Hillsborough Street, opposite where NC State University is now located. Begun in 1853, the NC State Fair was moved in the early half of the twentieth century to its present location.

> *The day was beautiful and the fair quite a success. Goods from the stores fill up very much, but on the whole the display except for cookery was very good The cookery (bread and cakes) was about 4 or 5 ft. on one shelf. There were many interesting machines which I did not have time to investigate—I saw one horse cultivator which I thought would suit my garden and vines exactly—The flowers were very pretty . . . . The display of vegetables was excellent . . . . The Grand Stand is an immense building and affords room for all to see the races easily. (An account of one day at the fair by William Tillinghast in 1875 from the Tillinghast Family Papers.) (Nathans, The Quest for Progress.)*

Urban parks also became popular in the late 1800s. Pullen Park was created in 1887 as a place where Raleighites could picnic, boat, skate, and enjoy nature. Commercial developers capitalized upon the interest of the public to have places they could go on an outing. The advent of electricity enabled them to create moving rides and fascinating light displays.

Interestingly, it was the power companies, such as Carolina Light and Power, who fostered the amusement park concept in North Carolina. Bloomsbury Park was built by the CPL in 1912 at the end of one of its trolley lines as an electric amusement park. Later, its most noticeable attraction, a carousel, was moved to Pullen Park in 1921 where it continued to operate. Today that carousel is valued as one of our state's historic artworks and is still in operation. Its hand carved animals, done by the Dentzel Carousel Co. of Philadelphia, are older than those exhibited at the Smithsonian.

The late 1800s was also when several of our state's major resorts were begun. James Tufts of Boston, a millionaire who had made his fortune through the invention of soda fountain equipment that made carbonated water, loved golf. When he learned of the "ideal" climate and terrain that existed in the Southern Pines region for golf, he decided in 1895 to build a resort that would bring people to that area to enjoy its beauty and recreation potential. As part of his plan, he bought 5,040 acres of land, built cottages, stores, streets, and hotels, and constructed a trolley line from his planned community, Pinehurst, to Southern Pines. The magnificence of the landscaping with winding roads and garden plantings can still be enjoyed today.

Golfing also brought us the Grove Park Inn. It was created in 1897 by E.W. Grove as a place for those who had "a lung condition" to come and enjoy the beauty of the fresh air. In doing so he made Asheville one of the "in places" for America's industrial and political leaders of that generation. Among those who partook of this hospitality and enjoyed the Inn's excellent golfing facilities were Henry Ford, Harry Forester, Herbert Hoover, Woodrow Wilson, and Thomas Edison.

Our mountain setting was also a factor in the development of camping and conference centers. The Baptist church established Bluemont, later to be known as Ridgecrest, in the late 1890s. Within a decade private camps began to appear, with C. Walton Johnson's Camp Sequoia being the first. Today, scores of camps and religious centers are located in the Blue Ridge and Black Mountain areas.

By 1900 team sports had become very popular. Promoted by textile companies as wholesome entertainment for their workers and by colleges and universities as a diversion for their students, baseball and football grew in acceptance. The first college football game played in North Carolina was between UNC and Wake Forest in 1888. Textile mills such as Bynum Mills and Franklin Manufacturing had baseball teams, playing semi professional ball, as early as 1910. Industrial YMCA's were developed in Hamlet, Durham, and Spencer; North Carolina's love affair with basketball was being nurtured by these fledgling programs. So was laid the foundation for current professional sports in the state: the Charlotte Bobcats, Carolina Panthers, and Carolina Hurricanes.

Public Recreation and Park Development

Following the nation's pattern of development for parks and recreation, most North Carolina municipalities developed their park systems before they established their recreation units. One of the earliest of our urban parks is the Tarboro Town Common. The five men who founded the town of Tarboro in 1760 set aside fifty acres as a "common for the use and benefit of the town." Although various encroachments have now reduced the size of the Common to nine acres, the park still exists and is included in the National Register of Historic Places.

The first municipal park and recreation department with full-time leadership was established in 1925 in Durham with C.R. Wood, a former YMCA director, as its head. The Charlotte department was established in 1927, while High Point created its public system in 1931. Although the 1940s were a period of growth for municipal departments (24 departments being established), most departments in that decade were created between 1946 and 1949, following World War II. The second major growth period of local recreation units came during the 1970s when fifty three new departments were established.

The rapid expansion of local recreation and park systems in the 1940s was largely due to two actions taken at the state level. One was the establishment of a state recreation committee, which evolved into the N.C. Recreation Commission. The other was the enactment of "the State Recreation Enabling Act" by the General Assembly. The State's first Recreation Committee was appointed by Governor J. Melville Broughton. Its primary purpose was to assist in alleviating some of the problems resulting from the influx of off-duty military personnel through recreation activities. The Committee was composed of forty members appointed by the governor to represent all segments of the recreation interests and activities of the state. Its goals were (1) to establish a permanent state recreation agency, (2) to establish a better recreation enabling act, and (3) to develop a strong professional recreation fellowship group. Within two years all three of these goals had been realized and North Carolina had established the N.C. Recreation Commission, the nation's first state recreation advisory service.

The Commission, as it was called, with Roy L. McMillan as the chairman and Harold Meyer as the director, was established to:

1. Study and appraise recreational needs of the state and assemble and disseminate information relative to recreation.
2. Cooperate in the promotion and organization of local recreation for counties, municipalities, townships, and other political subdivisions of the state, aid them in designing and laying out recreational areas and facilities, and advise them in the planning and financing of recreation programs.
3. Aid in recruiting, training, and placing recreation workers, and promote recreation institutes and conferences.
4. Establish and promote recreation standards.
5. Cooperate with state and federal agencies, the Recreation Advisory Committee, private member ship groups, and with commercial recreation interest, in the promotion of recreation opportunities.

Although it no longer exists, the Commission's functions are now carried out by the North Carolina Recreation Resources Service, administered by a grant to N.C. State University from the Department of Environment and Natural Resources.

North Carolina State Parks

In keeping with a national concern for the environment and its preservation at the turn of the nineteenth century, North Carolina in 1891 undertook a geological survey to examine its timber and mineral deposits. Reports prepared by the survey expressed concern over poor forestry practices and our state's lack of protection for the environment. As a result of Governor Craig's visit to Mount Mitchell in 1915 where he observed first-hand the devastation from poor timbering practices, the General Assembly established Mount Mitchell as our first state park. This was accomplished in 1916 with the acquisition of 795 acres. The park was administered under the Geological and Economic Survey until 1925 when the General Assembly passed the State Parks Act (GS 112-22) and created the Department of Conservation and Development.

In 1927 seven Coastal Plain lakes came under the jurisdiction of the Department, and, although it was given the responsibility for recreation management of these lakes, the state controlled only the water surface while the land around the lakes remained in private ownership. In later years some land was acquired for facility development, giving access to some of the lakes (for example, White, Jones, and Singletary Lakes).

A major growth period for state parks took place during the depression years as federally assisted programs created seven new state parks: Cape Hatteras, Crabtree Creek (later renamed Umstead), Hanging Rock, Jones Lake, Morrow Mountain, Pettigrew, and Singletary Lake. The Civilian Conservation Corps (CCC) constructed recreation facilities such as trails, lakes, picnic areas, and roads, and restored historical structures. The two early parks, Mount Mitchell and Fort Macon (North Carolina's second state park), also benefitted from the $2.25 million in federal funds that were spent in North Carolina during this period.

As the park system increased in size, the Branch of State Parks was created in 1935 under the Division of Forestry. Tom Morse became its first superintendent and supervised the work being done by the Civilian Conservation Corps. Following World War II the state parks movement regained momentum with the inclusion of Cliffs of the Neuse State Park in 1945. In 1948 State Parks was created as a division separate from Forestry.

During the decade of the 1950s, several management changes occurred: (1) Cape Hatteras State Park was deeded to the federal government in 1952 to become part of the Cape Hatteras National Seashore; (2) the Kerr Reservoir Development Commission was created (1951) to manage the recreation area leased from the Corps of Engineers at the newly built Kerr Reservoir; and (3) historic sites were transferred to the newly formed Department of Archives and History in 1955.

During the past thirty years, the state park system has added a number of park units, many of which came as the result of gifts or were purchased with matching monies from the federal government. Among them are Mount Jefferson, donated by the citizens of Ashe County; Hammocks Beach, a gift from the North Carolina Teacher's Association; and Duke Power, developed from land donated by the Duke Power Company. With grants from the Bureau of Outdoor Recreation and its Land and Water Conservation Fund, grants totaling over $15 million have been awarded to North Carolina since 1965.

As was the case for the development of local recreation and park systems, perhaps the decade of the 1970s was the most expansive decade for the state park system. Several legislative acts were passed, such as the 1971 Natural and Scenic River Systems Act, which encouraged park development. As a result of this act the New River and the Linville River were added to the North Carolina park and recreation system; a third river, the Horse Pasture River, was added in 1985. With money from the Babcock and Reynolds Foundation, the state created a natural heritage program in 1976 and added eight additional areas to the system. The North Carolina Trail System Act, passed in 1973, has provided a statewide system of trails for hiking, horseback riding, bicycling, and for small craft and motorized vehicle travel. One of the primary efforts of this act has been the creation of the mountains sea trail system. In total, park acreage in the 1970s increased from 5,173 acres to 116,978 acres. Unfortunately, appropriations for maintenance and development did not always keep up with the expansion of the system.

Aquatics seemed to be the focus of the 1980s. Jordan Lake, in 1981, and the Falls of the Neuse Lake, in 1983, became major recreation areas operated by the state park system.

They joined Kerr Lake which had come to the system in 1971, as some of our major recreation resources. A coastal aquatic area, Fort Fisher, was transferred from the Division of Archives and History in 1986 to the state park system. The decade ended on a high note when the General Assembly passed the State Park Act of 1987. The act defines the purpose of the state park system as protecting representative examples of North Carolina's unique biological, recreational, geological, scenic, and archaeological resources for future generations and providing for the public's enjoyment of those resources. The recreation division was directed to carry out the mission and to prepare a state park system-wide plan.

In 1994, the North Carolina General Assembly established the Park and Recreation Trust Fund (PARTF) (G.S. 113 44.15) as a non-reverting special revenue fund receiving 75 percent of the state's share of the excise tax on real estate deed transfers. A Park and Recreation Authority (G.S. 143B 313.1) consisting of eleven appointed members distributes these funds in three ways: 65 percent to the state park system for repairs, capital improvements, and land acquisition; 30 percent to a matching grant program for local government units for parks and recreation development, renovations, and land acquisition; and 5 percent to the coastal beach access program.

North Carolina's Federal Areas

No history of government's involvement in developing leisure opportunities for our citizens would be complete without mentioning the contribution of our federal government. It has played a significant role in the development of leisure services in our state. Among the major resources it has developed and still manages are the Blue Ridge Parkway, the Great Smoky Mountains National Park, the Cape Hatteras National Seashore, and our four national forests. Each of these areas, in its own way, has been an attraction for visitors as well as a favorite playground for Tarheels.

The Blue Ridge Parkway, a 469-mile linear park, was designed and built to connect the Shenandoah National Park to the Great Smoky Mountains National Park. Construction of the Parkway began in 1935 at Cumberland Knob and was completed in 1987 with the addition of the Linn Cove Viaduct. The route of the Parkway carries it through two states, six congressional districts, and twenty nine counties. It was designed as a Great Depression work project but evolved into a major recreation resource. In 1936 the U.S. Congress placed the Parkway under the jurisdiction of the National Park Service. Currently, over 30 million visitors travel portions of the Parkway each year.

Its counterpart at the other end of the state is the Cape Hatteras National Seashore. Established in 1937, it was the nation's first national seashore area and resulted from an extensive study by the National Park Service to identify beaches suitable for public use. It covers one hundred square miles and includes such historic sites as the Cape Hatteras Lighthouse, the Wright Brother Memorial, and the Pea Island National Wildlife Refuge.

North Carolina shares (with Tennessee) one of the nation's most heavily visited (over 10 million visitors annually) national parks. The Great Smoky Mountains National Park is the largest wilderness in the eastern United States and covers some 800 square miles. It was created in the early 1930s and identified in 1973 as a designated international biosphere reserve and part of the "Man and Biosphere Program." In 1983, the park was designated as a world heritage site by the United Nations. It is a unique resource in North Carolina.

North Carolina is also blessed with several national forests. The first was established in 1916 (Pisgah National Forest), followed by the creation of the Nantahala National Forest in 1920. Two others, the Croatan (1936) and the Uwharrie (1961), were added, providing North Carolinians with some 3 million acres of national forest lands. Of that amount, 100,000 acres have been set aside as wilderness areas. Perhaps most famous of those wilderness areas are the Linville Gorge and the Joyce Kilmer areas.

Other Significant Events

It is difficult to identify all the significant events that have enhanced the quality of life for our citizens. North Carolina is the cradle of the outdoor theater. Paul Green, a member of the faculty at UNC Chapel Hill, wrote the first outdoor drama, *The Lost Colony*. It was first produced on the Roanoke Island in 1937 and has provided hundreds of thousands of visitors with a unique view of North Carolina's early history. One of North Carolina's more famous actors, Andy Griffith, once starred in a *Lost Colony* production. Kermit Hunter, author of over forty outdoor dramas, wrote *Unto These Hills* (a play describing the plight of the Cherokee Indians) and the long-running *Horn in the West* (a saga about Daniel Boone). Both continue to be major attractions for summer visitors to Cherokee and Boone.

A few miles south of Boone is another North Carolina attraction, Grandfather Mountain. Developed by Hugh Morton in the 1950s, it contains many beautiful vistas. It is one of three developments of that decade that have brought millions of visitors to western North Carolina. The other two are more commercial: the Maggie Valley Cherokee Reservation area and the ski resorts in the Boone and Asheville areas. The ski resorts resulted from the technology that enabled developers to supplement natural snowfalls with artificial snow. Most of these were developed in the late 1960s, a time that also saw the creation of the North Carolina State Zoo near Asheboro. Complementing these developments were the more recent additions of major sporting arenas and museums in the Raleigh area. The multimillion dollar sports complex and the new North Carolina Museum of Natural Science have considerably expanded North Carolina's range of opportunities.

It is obvious from this historical account that many significant events have been omitted. The number is too great for any one discussion, but throughout the text more history is included. For example, in the chapter on professional development, the events that have influenced our programs of professional preparation are mentioned, as is a discussion of the development of, and role played by, the North Carolina Recreation and Park Association. More history is developed in the chapters on therapeutic recreation and recreation in the private sector as it pertains to those subjects.

One of the major pieces of history that is missing, however, is the specific leisure behaviors and contributions of Blacks and females, especially prior to the 1930s. This is due in part to the paucity of information about these two groups as groups prior to that time. We can speculate that much of the leisure and recreation interests of females centered on family, religion, and folk art activities. Traditionally, among the major events of our state and county fairs have been the displays of culinary and needle craft activities. Both females and Blacks have been involved in leadership roles since the earliest days of the playground movement, even though the system sometimes separated the races and the sexes. With the removal of these barriers in the 1950s, new roles were assumed. Mae Crandell was elected president of the N.C. Recreation Society in 1957, and Derick Davis became the first Black to hold that office in 1971 (Warren, 1989).

Summary

As we can see, our state is rich with natural resources and a colorful recreation heritage. Its leisure service delivery system is a configuration of its private, commercial, and public operations. North Carolina's heritage has given us historic cities, aided in the development of the NASCAR industry, and supported the development of folk crafts, pottery, woodcraft, and quilting. Legislative acts have encouraged the preservation and wise use of our natural resources and given the state a consulting service that has influenced the development of local governmental recreation programs. The state has benefitted from the wise leadership of many individuals and organizations, and, as the state once proclaimed on its automobile license tags, North Carolina is "Variety Vacationland."

Learning Exercises

1. Consult with the director of parks and recreation in your community or county to learn of the history of that department. See when it was begun, what conditions brought it into being, and who the leading advocates were for the creation of the department.

2. When discussing the history of the department, it would be well for you to also ask about changes that have occurred during the last decade and why those changes have occurred.

3. Talk with your grandparents or an elderly citizen about their recreation and play behaviors during their childhood. Also discuss with them their involvement with organized leisure services in scouting, recreation departments, amusement parks, etc. Ask them to compare what is available today with what they experienced in their youth.

4. Go to your local library and see if there are histories of your local community. In those histories, were there references to the citizens' recreational behavior? What were those behaviors? Who provided the opportunities for pleasure, and what types of facilities were available for general public gatherings?

References

North Carolina Illustrated. (1984). *1524* Chapel Hill: UNC Press, 54.

Johnson, G. (1937). *Antebellum North Carolina—A Social History*. Chapel Hill: UNC Press.

Nathans, S. (1983). *The Quest for Progress*. Chapel Hill: UNC Press, 85.

Warren, R. (1989). *History of the North Carolina Recreation and Park Society*. Unpublished paper; Raleigh, NC.

Chapter 2

Commercial Recreation

Nancy J. Gladwell and Erick Byrd

We begin our study of the leisure service delivery system in North Carolina by looking at the commercial, private-for-profit sector. It is the largest provider of recreation opportunities and the segment most often considered when the issues of travel and tourism are discussed.

It is estimated that Americans as a whole spend twelve cents of each disposable dollar earned on their pursuit of pleasure, and North Carolinians are no different. We enjoy having fun, have found it profitable to do so, and have developed an extensive system to provide us with the necessary leisure products and services. Commercial recreation is in the business of selling recreation. It is profit-driven and includes such enterprises as marinas, sport centers, resorts, bicycle shops, amusement parks, health clubs, travel agencies, water parks, golf courses, and movie theaters. Large commercial recreation enterprises, such as Walt Disney World and Carnival Cruise Lines, are commonly recognized by the public. However, it should be noted that the majority of commercial recreation agencies are classified as small businesses; this is certainly the case in North Carolina, where perhaps our largest single commercial recreation unit would be Paramount's Carowinds Park. Areas such as Maggie Valley or Nags Head, which are major resort destinations, are comprised of hundreds of small businesses.

Categories of Commercial Recreation

Commercial recreation organizations can be divided into five major categories or classifications:

1. Hospitality and food services;
2. Local commercial recreation industries;
3. Commercial recreation in the natural environment;
4. Retail sales; and
5. Travel and tourism.

This classification scheme is a combination of several other classification systems found in the commercial recreation and tourism literature. It is important to understand that these categories are not mutually exclusive. Even though each category has certain aspects that are unique, there is actually a great deal of overlap and interrelationship between categories.

Hospitality and Food Services

Hospitality and food services have as their primary functions the provision of lodging, food and beverages, and other related services for travelers, guests, and in some cases local residents. Hotels, bed and breakfasts, inns, restaurants, campgrounds, and resorts are examples of businesses that fall into this category. The following are examples of hospitality and food service organizations within North Carolina:

- **Pinehurst Hotel and Country Club** in Pinehurst
- **Grove Park Inn and Golf Club** in Asheville
- **Shell Island Resort Hotel** on Wrightsville Beach
- **Dosher Plantation House Bed and Breakfast** in Southport
- **The Hillsborough House Inn** in Hillsborough
- **Holiday Inn Four Seasons/Joseph S. Koury Convention Center** in Greensboro
- **The Angus Barn** in Raleigh
- **The Country Squire Steak House** in Kenansville
- **Fontana Village** in Fontana
- **The Salem Tavern** at Old Salem in Winston-Salem
- **The High Hampton Inn and Restaurant** in Cashiers
- **The Pilot House Restaurant** in Wilmington
- **The Sanitary Fish House** in Morehead City
- **The Catawba Queen** on Lake Norman
- **Barley's Micro Brewery and Pizzeria** in Asheville
- **Midway Campground and RV Resort** in Statesville

Even though the above-mentioned examples are uniquely representative of the hospitality and food service establishments of North Carolina, more commonly recognized organizations such as Red Roof Inns, Econo Lodges, Chuck E. Cheese/Show Biz Pizza, and Kampgrounds of America (KOA) also are representatives of this category.

The types of jobs within this industry are as diverse as the types of businesses themselves. Jobs in the hospitality industry include such positions as convention and meeting planner, director of guest relations, campground director, recreation/social director, general manager, banquet director, and marketing director. Students interested in working within this facet of commercial recreation should supplement their commercial recreation education with coursework in such areas as management, marketing, public relations, or hotel management. As is true with all leisure service careers, obtaining practical experience within the hospitality or food and beverage industries through internship and practicum experiences and/or part-time work will strengthen one's chances of gaining an entry-level position. To obtain a managerial position with most hospitality enterprises, it is frequently necessary to "pay your dues" by working up through the ranks of an organization.

The Local Commercial Recreation Industry

The local commercial recreation industry's primary function is to provide entertainment and leisure products, facilities, and services to the residents of a community and their guests. According to Crossley and Jamieson (1997), local commercial recreation can be divided into activities and programs, retail products, and entertainment providers. Recreation activity and programs are commercial recreation enterprises whose primary focus is on the provision of recreation programs and facilities. Examples of recreation activity and program providers are bowling alleys, fitness/health clubs, gymnastics studios, and golf courses. Examples of retail product providers are sporting goods stores, fishing and hunting equipment stores, and bicycle shops. Entertainment providers are commercial leisure businesses that provide the customer with opportunities to utilize facilities to view entertainment or be a passive participant in an activity. Movie theaters, amusement parks, and sports arenas are examples of entertainment providers. The following are examples of local commercial recreation businesses in North Carolina:

- **Sanderling Health Club** in Nags Head
- **The Wilmington Gymnastics and Dance Center** in Wilmington
- **The Barn Dinner Theater** in Greensboro
- **Greystone Swim and Racquet Club** in Raleigh
- **Shelby Aquatics Center** in Shelby
- **Kinston Indians Baseball Team** in Kinston
- **Paramount Carowinds Amusement Park** in Charlotte
- **The Dollar Theater** in Fayetteville
- **Johnson's Sports Corner** in Morehead City
- **Brunswick Triad Bowling Lanes** in High Point
- **Ericsson Stadium** in Charlotte
- **Spruce Pine Ice Skating** in Spruce Pine
- **ROC Ltd. Indoor Climbing** in Winston-Salem

As in the hospitality industry, the job opportunities within the local commercial recreation industry are as diverse as the businesses that comprise this category. Examples of positions in this industry are: owner, manager, instructor of activities (dance, swimming, tennis, bowling, etc.), sales manager, booking agent, concession operator, facility manager, and activity programmer. Supplementing one's recreation education with business courses, practical experience, and personal knowledge of the product or service being sold will enhance a student's chances of obtaining employment in this area of commercial recreation.

It should be noted that most commercial recreation businesses are classified as small businesses. The primary markets for such recreation organizations are the people who reside in the community within which the business is located and who have an interest in the leisure products and services being sold. Billiard parlors, magazine and book shops, movie theaters, and local pubs are illustrations of these services. Frequently their hours of operation, as is true with many recreation businesses, are determined by local "blue laws." The issues of the kinds of services rendered and the times these services can be provided are still debated in many of our communities, although less often in those areas promoted heavily as tourist destinations.

Commercial Recreation within the Natural Environment

Many commercial leisure opportunities take place within the natural environment. The owners of such businesses may have a true understanding of and appreciation for the conservation and protection of our natural resource base. In addition to their personal love of the out-of-doors, many owners recognize that if their businesses are to become and remain profitable and dynamic, they must protect the natural resources on which their businesses are dependent. Examples of commercial outdoor recreation businesses are marinas, golf courses, campgrounds, ski resorts, commercial swimming pools, river rafting businesses, resorts (seashore, mountain, or lake), residential camps, and wind-surfing operations. Their dependency upon the environment and the impact of their business on it are issues for both the environmentalist and the business sector. Perhaps no other component of the commercial sector is under the eye of the public as much as is this one, with the possible exception of some of the retail businesses which may be offering activities which some elements of the public might question as being in conflict with their values. Some commercial recreation businesses within the natural environment category in North Carolina are:

- **Fort Macon Marina** in Atlantic Beach
- **Island Passage** on Bald Head Island
- **French Swiss Ski College, Inc**. in Boone
- **Lochmere Golf Club** in Cary
- **Cross Country Campgrounds** in Denver
- **Pine Lake Stables and Tack Shop** in Mint Hill
- **Camp Seagull** in Oriental
- **Carolina Wilderness** (raft tours) in Hot Springs
- **Show Place Stables** in Brown Summit
- **Nantahala Outdoor Rafting** between Asheville and Boone

Those seeking career opportunities in this classification should consider combining a study in commercial recreation (to ensure an emphasis in business) and outdoor recreation (to ensure knowledge of natural resource management). Examples of job positions in this area are: camp director, aquatics specialist, golf instructor, publicity director, ski lift attendant, marina operator, and river raft guide.

Retail Sales

The retail sales component of commercial recreation is responsible for providing the recreation products used to participate in activities and programs provided by various recreation organizations. "Retailing is the means whereby services and products are delivered to consumers in a manner that is convenient to them" (Bullaro & Edginton, 1986, p. 74). Plus, for millions of North Carolinians, shopping is a favorite pastime.

There are two basic types of retail outlets: the store and the non-store (or catalog sales) operation. Store retail outlets are those where the consumer comes to the retailer to purchase the product or service offered by the business. This type of retail outlet includes bicycle stores, tennis pro-shops, golf pro-shops, athletic goods stores, outdoor equipment stores, equestrian supply stores, and surf shops, many of which are in retail and outlet malls. In recent years, there has been a mild explosion of outlet malls, taking advantage of the many textile and craft industries in the state that have traditionally operated company stores. Business at these locations has been brisk, and shopper holidays are numerous. Also popular are the renovated factories that are comprised of specialty shops and restaurants, such as Brightleaf Square in Durham. To some degree, malls and outlets have become the modern-day market square, the meeting place for neighbors. Some retail malls have even facilitated this concept by hosting school-age art shows, making the mall available to walkers prior to opening hours, and sponsoring local fairs and holiday shows for children or for special-interest groups, such as coin collectors. Many have even employed personnel to coordinate and promote such community events. The following are examples of stores, retail outlets, and malls in North Carolina:

- **Carr Mill** in Carrboro
- **Pedalpushers, Inc**. (bicycle shop) in Wilmington
- **Country Corner Marine Center, Inc.** in Mooresville
- **Tee to Green Golf Shop** in Eden
- **The Horse and Rider** in Greensboro
- **Great Outdoor Provision Company** in Winston-Salem
- **Overton Sporting Goods** in Greenville
- **Burlington Manufacturing Outlet Center** in Burlington
- **Marketplace** near the Raleigh-Durham Airport
- **Four Seasons Mall** in Greensboro
- **Crabtree Mall** in Raleigh
- **Barnes & Noble Booksellers** in Winston-Salem
- **The Bike Barn** in Corolla
- **The Gun Rack** in Greenville

Even though the primary function of store retail outlets is the sale of supplies for recreational activities, frequently these types of businesses also provide services such as bicycle maintenance, ski equipment rental, golf club repairs and tennis racquet restringing. In addition, it is not unusual to see such recreation businesses involved in the provision of recreation programs such as bicycle tours, ski trips, camping trips, and river rafting excursions.

The second type of retail outlet is termed the non-store retail outlet. The major difference between this type of retail outlet and the store outlet is that the recreation product or service is brought to the consumer directly through the postal service or other package delivery system. Most sales for non-store retail outlets are generated through mail order catalog sales. L.L. Bean, Lands End, and REI (Recreation Equipment, Inc.) are examples of nationally run non-store outlets. In recent years new forms of catalog sales have arisen. One is computerized shopping through the World Wide Web, where the customer uses a personal computer to locate the product or service of interest, determines the price, and then orders the desired item by entering a credit card number and shipping address. Shopping on the Web is gaining in popularity, particularly in the area of travel and tourism-related purchases such as airline tickets, hotel reservations, or rental car reservations. One problem that may affect the growth of this form of non-store sales is that there is a question of how secure an individual's credit card number may be. A last form of catalog sales is the home shopping programs found on cable television. Items and their prices are shown on the television screen. If an individual wishes to purchase a particular item, he/she simply picks up the telephone, dials the toll-free number on the television screen, gives his/her credit card number, and waits for the package to arrive. Catalog sales has excellent opportunity for continued growth, considering the fact that approximately 50 percent of homes in the United States have cable television (a commercial recreation business in its own right).

The Travel and Tourism Industry

The travel and tourism industry is responsible for accommodating, feeding, transporting, entertaining, and generally serving travelers and visitors. Smith (1977) defines a tourist as "a temporarily leisured person away from home to experience a change" (p. 2). Obviously, there is a tremendous amount of overlap between this industry and those previously discussed. For example, accommodating and feeding the tourist immediately links travel and tourism with the hospitality and food service industry. Likewise, entertaining the tourist is directly correlated with both the local commercial recreation industry and commercial outdoor recreation. Travel and tourism are not, however, solely the responsibility of the commercial sector. This industry also involves public recreation services, whether local, state, or national governments provide them. In 2003, visitor expenditures in North Carolina for travel-related activities were $12.6 billion. With 49.2 million people visiting North Carolina, providing the state with $1.1 billion in state and local tax revenues and nearly 200,000 jobs, North Carolina ranked sixth in person-trip volume by state (behind only California, Florida, Texas, Pennsylvania, and New York). This made tourism one of the largest economic sectors in North Carolina. Since travel and tourism impact the economy of North Carolina much more extensively than the other categories of commercial recreation, Chapter 3 provides a more detailed discussion.

Factors Impacting the Demand and Supply for Commercial Recreation

The number of commercial recreation enterprises located in a community can help determine its measurable economic vibrancy. Economic vibrancy can be defined as conditions that contribute to numerous economic indicators, such as the amount and quality of employment opportunities, tax revenues from the enterprise, real income, and the economic impact or influence of the commercial recreation venue in the community. In addition, the presence of wholesome commercial recreation businesses can enhance the quality of life in a community. The quality of life is improved because the range of leisure choices offered by governmental and non-profit recreation organizations is extended through the commercial enterprises.

The planned development of commercial recreation in a community may act as a catalyst for the rejuvenation of its physical environment, such as the restoration of buildings, improved landscaping, infrastructure improvement, or the addition of new and creative amenities to the existing commercial recreation inventory. In fact, when successfully developed, commercial recreation can put an obscure community on the map, as observed in Asheville, Boone, Gastonia, Kure Beach, Maggie Valley, New Bern, and Wilmington. Each of these small communities has been economically enhanced by the addition of commercial enterprises.

Thus, it is no surprise that many North Carolina communities are interested in encouraging the development of commercial recreation enterprises that will foster local economic growth. To create effective developmental policies, decision-makers need to understand the major forces that shape the demand and supply of commercial recreation enterprises. With this understanding, they will be able to capitalize on the potential economic growth the recreation enterprise might offer to the community.

Demand for Commercial Recreation

Demand for commercial recreation refers to the quantity of leisure offerings that may be purchased at a given price within a specified period of time. The proportion of purchase actually made in a given period of time is called *effective demand,* while the proportion that may occur is called *potential demand.* The demand for commercial recreation offerings is influenced by a number of interactive variables. These variables can be categorized into three basic types: buyer domain factors, seller domain factors, and mediating factors. Examples of buyer domain factors include the consumer's preferences, personality, income, mobility, lifestage, occupation, gender, religion, ethnicity, attitude, and experiences. Seller domain factors include the range of leisure opportunities offered, price of leisure offerings, quality of offerings, availability of recreation alternatives, quality and quantity of marketing efforts, location, and the ability to sell the product effectively. Mediating factors are those variables that affect demand in a general way. Examples of these include the total number of buyers and sellers in a community at a given time and the relationship to the number of people who are interested in or willing to purchase the product; predominant sociocultural beliefs and values; economic trends; governmental rules and regulations; and seasonality. These factors will affect consumers' confidence, demand for leisure offerings, and consumption.

Supply of Commercial Recreation

Supply, on the other hand, refers to the number of commercial recreation enterprises available in a community. In general, the supply of commercial recreation is contingent upon demand. The greater the demand for commercial recreation, the greater the supply, and vice versa. However, it is also possible that supply can create its own demand. For example, commercial recreation businesses may stimulate demand for their offerings by using innovative marketing practices. If successful, a demand-supply gap (disequilibrium) may be created, which may motivate other entrepreneurs to launch enterprises offering similar or modified offerings. The birth of new commercial recreation businesses in the community further enhances the attractiveness of the community, independently and collectively. If the new businesses continue to attract more consumers, another round of disequilibrium is created. When such a symbiotic scenario is achieved, a community is said to be in a *dynamic disequilibrium,* as seems to be occurring in Raleigh and Wilmington. In these communities there appear to be more users than there are opportunities for engaging in commercial recreation activities. An example of how this affects the consumer is that it becomes difficult to participate in the recreation experience because the waiting lines to gain entry are too long.

Like demand, the supply for commercial recreation is determined by a wide array of interacting variables. These variables can be categorized into two general types. The first is a community's supply of entrepreneurs. An entrepreneur (Crossley and Jamieson, 1997) is one who searches an environment (community) for trends and changes. The entrepreneur then locates, acquires, and manages resources (money, facilities, people, etc.) to exploit these changes as an opportunity. The second is the quality of the community's commercial recreation investment climate as perceived by the entrepreneurs.

Since commercial recreation enterprises do not evolve by themselves but are the product of entrepreneurial decisions, the greater the supply of entrepreneurs, the greater the likelihood that new commercial recreation businesses will be created. However, entrepreneurs' decisions to launch commercial recreation ventures are highly contingent on their perceptions of the quality of the relevant environments, such as: the level of demand; extent of competition; availability and cost of land, labor, and capital; quality of infrastructure; quality and quantity of supporting businesses; and legal hindrances. Accordingly, the supply of commercial recreation enterprises in a community can be described as the interactive function of a community's supply of entrepreneurs and the entrepreneurs' perceptions of the quality of the investment climate for commercial recreation within a particular community. The more favorable the two factors, the greater the likelihood that commercial recreation enterprises will be created, and vice versa.

How to Increase Supply and Demand for Commercial Recreation

How can communities in North Carolina stimulate greater demand and supply for commercial recreation so that they may enjoy the socioeconomic benefits associated with it? The most effective strategy that *can* be pursued is to initiate demand stimulation and supply stimulation strategies concurrently. Some practical demand stimulation strategies are to:

1. Publicize the benefits of leisure pursuits;
2. Encourage participation in the commercial recreation opportunities created by local providers;
3. Entice more leisure seekers to the community by utilizing innovative marketing strategies;
4. Emphasize the importance of delivering superior service to encourage repeat users who will spread positive word-of-mouth recommendations to others; and
5. Engage in creative pricing strategies and the promotion of the positive benefits of selected recreation programs so that consumers feel they are getting value for their money.

As for supply stimulation techniques, some practical strategies are:

1. Use fiscal, zoning, and development policies to entice local and non-local entrepreneurs to establish commercial recreation businesses in the community;

2. Establish research and development centers to collect and disseminate market information, such as how to package and sell the benefits of the locating commercial recreation development in the community. Organize annual events to recognize successful commercial recreation entrepreneurs;
3. Create community-wide apprenticeship/mentoring programs for entrepreneurship; and
4. Initiate and encourage joint public-private recreation enterprises.
5. In addition, it is imperative that communities enhance the quality of their general business investment environments, such as transportation, communication, utilities, housing, and streamlined tax and legal systems. Moreover, community residents and leaders must be in agreement that the development and growth of commercial recreation enterprises are desirable. In other words, there needs to be the understanding among community decision-makers, leaders, and residents that commercial recreation businesses that meet the philosophical beliefs of the community will enhance the quality of life of a community, not harm it.

The Future of Commercial Recreation in North Carolina

Successful organizations engage in research that will help them prepare for the future of their business. It is useful to project the future of a business because this knowledge will aid community leaders, entrepreneurs, managers, employees, or leisure studies students to make more informed decisions. Based on current and still unfolding demographic, economic, political, market, and technological information and events, some generally agreed future scenarios that will affect the demand and supply of commercial recreation in North Carolina are:

- Increased household incomes;
- Higher levels of education;
- Increased number of older adults;
- Influx of migrants from the northeastern and north-central states;
- Expansion of year-round schools;
- Growth in outdoor recreation participation;
- Increased demand for family-oriented leisure opportunities and non-tradinional recreation offerings;
- Higher demand for service and product quality;
- More support by government for local entrepreneurship; and
- Increased application of computer technology in the home, workplace, schools, and recreation settings.

Some implications of these predicated scenarios are:

- Market demand for commercial recreation will continue to increase in variety and quality;
- Opportunities for starting commercial recreation enterprises will be plentiful for the entrepreneur;

- Managers of commercial recreation businesses will need to be more efficient and effective in all areas of operations and in determining niche markets;
- Employment opportunities for commercial recreation students armed with the right attitude, skills, and experience are favorable; and
- Commercial recreation educators will need to monitor the industry's developments, needs, and trends closely.

Summary

The commercial recreation industry plays a major role in meeting many of the leisure desires and interests of the people of North Carolina and the tourists who choose to visit our state. It is a diverse industry that provides numerous recreation products and services. The characteristic that differentiates commercial recreation from the other sectors of recreation is its profit orientation. This is accomplished through the industry's ability to adjust its products and services to a rapidly changing marketplace and to successfully sell its products.

Those individuals who work in this sector are concerned about the quality of recreation experiences offered, as are their colleagues in the public and the non-profit sector. The implications of their concern are critical. If commercial recreation providers are not sufficiently concerned with the quality of the experiences provided by their business, it is unlikely that the business will succeed. There is a direct link between customer satisfaction and profit.

Learning Exercises

1. Choose a commercial recreation agency in the town in which you attend school, and ask the owner the following questions:

   ■ Why did you choose to open a commercial recreation business?
   ■ What skills, knowledge, and abilities are most important for a person who wants to work in a business like yours?
   ■ How did you go about opening your business?
   ■ What do you like **most** and **least** about owning your own commercial recreation business?
   ■ When you hire people, do you check to see if they have a degree in recreation?

2. Collect and bring to class any newspaper and magazine articles you read involving commercial recreation. Consult Chapter 18 for assistance in finding the articles. Do this for a two-week period.

3. **Small Group Assignment**

   Pretend you have $ 1,000,000 to invest in a commercial recreation business, and do the following:

   ■ Identify the kind of business you want to open.
   ■ Indicate the category of commercial recreation your agency fits into.
   ■ Determine where in North Carolina your business will be located.
   ■ Why did you choose this location for your business?
   ■ What products and/or services will your agency provide?
   ■ What clientele will you serve?
   ■ How many full-time, part-time, and seasonal employees will you need to operate your business?
   ■ Who will be your competition, and how will you meet and beat your competition?
   ■ What facilities will your business require?

4. In your hometown, check with your Chamber of Commerce to find out if the economic impact of commercial recreation has been calculated. If it has, what is the economic impact of commercial recreation on the community?

Sources of Further Information[GESS5]

Resort and Commercial Recreation Association
P.O. Box 1208
New Port Richey, FL 34656-1208

National Recreation and Park Association
22377 Belmont Ridge Road
Ashburn, VA 20148-4501

International Association of Amusement Parks
and Attractions
1448 Duke Street
Alexandria, VA 22314

References

Bullaro, J.J. & Edginton, C.R. (1986). *Commercial Recreation Services: Managing for Profit, Service, and Personal Satisfaction.* New York: Macmillan.

Crossley, J.C. & Jamieson, L.M. (1997). *Introduction to Commercial and Entrepreneurial Recreation.* (Rev. ed.) Champaign, IL: Sagamore.

Ellis, T. & Norton, R.L. (1988). *Commercial Recreation.* St. Louis: Times Mirror/Mosby College Publishing.

McIntosh, R.W. & Goeldner, C.R. (1999). *Tourism: Principles, Practices, Philosophies.* New York: John Wiley.

North Carolina Division of Tourism, Film, and Sport Development. *North Carolina 2004-2005 strategic plan.* Retrieved June 16, 2005 from, http://www.nccommerce.com/tourism/publications/NCT04-05.StrategicPlan.pdf

Smith, V.L. (1977). *Hosts and Guests: The Anthropology of Tourism.* Philadelphia: University of Pennsylvania Press.

Chapter 3

Tourism in North Carolina

Kevin Riley and Sarah Banks

Worldwide, tourism has become one of the largest industries, estimated to contribute nearly $3.5 trillion of economic activity and 207 million direct and indirect jobs (WTO, 2005). Although the industry was severely impacted after 9/11, most sectors have rebounded, and tourists appear to have become less fearful and as willing as ever to travel. For three years after 9/11, international travel had little growth, but in 2004, international tourism was again soaring, with hotspots such as Asia and the Pacific having a 29 percent increase and the Middle East experiencing a 20 percent increase. In fact, international travel overall has experienced the best growth rate in over twenty years (WTO, 2005). In the United States, new destinations emerge while traditional ones expand. Overall, North Carolina is the sixth most visited state in the country, with tourism now the state's largest industry.

Tourism is important to North Carolina for many reasons. In 2004, 49 million people visited North Carolina and spent nearly $13.2 billion on tourism related activities, an almost 5 percent increase from 2003. Domestic tourism expenditures support nearly 183,000 full-time employees, who earn nearly $3.5 billion in payroll income. In 2004, tourists spending money in North Carolina generated more than $2.1 billion in tax revenue for local, state, and federal governments. North Carolina residents make up about one-third of the state's tourism population, with the remainder coming from nearby states, including Virginia (10 percent), South Carolina (9 percent), Georgia (7 percent), Florida (6 percent), Pennsylvania (5 percent) and Tennessee (4 percent). Residents from Maryland, New York, and New Jersey each accounted for 3 percent of the North Carolina tourist population. The average spending per tourist group was $332, with out-of-state tourists typically staying at least four nights while in-state tourists accounted for almost 2.5 nights. Almost 50 percent of these visits required lodging in hotels, motels, and bed and breakfasts. For the past five years, the most popular recreation activities for these tourists were shopping, visiting beaches, outdoor activities, and visiting historic places/museums (www.nccommerce.com, 2005).

Tourism is not only an important industry economically but is also a multidisciplinary field of study, reflecting variations in individuals' leisure choices, changes in communities, and trends in society. The field of tourism focuses on subjects such as the geography of places, the history of attractions, the psychology of tourists, and the computer technology of information systems. As an industry, tourism is comprised of various sectors such as transportation, hospitality, recreation, and other human services. The World Tourism Organization identifies tourism as "the activities of persons traveling to and staying in places outside their usual environment for not more than one consecutive year for leisure, business and other purposes." As such, the study of tourism must consider the tourists, their travel activities, and the places they visit. The tourism system includes the tourist market, the travel and marketing linkages, and the destinations. People traveling away from home for business, visiting friends or relatives, or traveling for their personal business or pleasure are classified as tourists.

The destination or supply side of the system provides the tourists with accommodations, entertainment and attractions, and hospitality services. In 2004, North Carolina's nine Welcome Centers greeted over 9 million visitors. Welcome Centers and Visitor Centers facilitate the state's tourism by assisting travelers with directions and suggestions for local attractions, recreational activities, and final destinations. Marketing ensures an information flow among tourists, tourism organizations, and businesses. Modern technology heavily influences transportation and marketing linkages.

Attraction and service businesses, host governments, and communities of a destination area can all contribute toward developing a healthy tourism industry. In North Carolina, the Coastal, the Piedmont (also referred to as the Heartland), and the Mountain regions (Figure 3.1) all offer attractive tourism opportunities. The geographic characteristics are supported by modern and traditional urban and rural areas that provide many natural, cultural, and historical attractions. Even though skiing in the mountains or vacationing at the beach are the most visible recreation activities in North Carolina, the tourism industry has grown up to satisfy the more diverse interests of travelers. Product development and marketing ensure that North Carolina stays competitive for the special interest markets.

Attractions and destinations flourish only in functioning communities. State and local government, private enterprises and organizations, and the residents of the communities can cooperate to promote and support tourism. Most attractions work to promote their services to their particular markets, but cooperation between destinations will benefit the entire state as a tourism region and competitive market. Cooperative marketing and unified information systems in the form of Web sites, brochures, and conferences are examples of how the state can introduce less well known attractions to travelers. Several organizations, such as the North Carolina Division of Tourism, Film and Sports Development (within the Department of Commerce); the North Carolina Travel and Tourism Coalition; and the North Carolina Travel Industry Association (formerly the

Figure. 3.1 North Carolina Regions

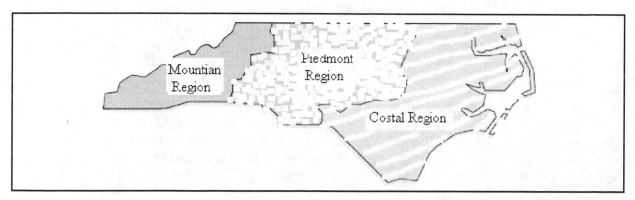

Travel Council of North Carolina) provide state-wide support for tourism. These organizations engage in marketing and lobbying activities, provide expert advice, support projects financially, and help communities develop their own resources. The Division of Tourism, Film and Sports Development coordinates the annual North Carolina Governor's Conference on Tourism. This conference brings together hundreds of leaders from the state's resorts, attractions, destination marketing organizations, hotels/motels, real estate rental companies, restaurants, and retail outlets to teach and learn about the latest trends and issues affecting the travel industry. Another service provided in part by this Division is the *North Carolina Travel Tracker,* a monthly report documenting tourism indicators and their economic impact on the Coastal, Heartland, and Mountain regions of North Carolina (www.nccommerce.com/tourism/). Such baseline data reveals trends, ongoing consequences, and upcoming challenges so that tourism resources and markets can be sustained and further developed.

Several state organizations assist and develop individual tourism attractions, organizations, and destinations. They believe that the strength of individual attractions enhances the overall vitality of the state's tourism industry. Within the North Carolina Department of Agriculture and Consumer Services is the Division of Agritourism. It helps farmers increase their economic opportunities through value-added, farm-related tourist activities while preserving the integrity of their farmland and heritage. Also within the North Carolina Department of Commerce is the Community Assist program. It houses the North Carolina Main Street Center (NCMSC) as well as the North Carolina Cooperative Extension Service. The latter's Tourism Outreach and Research Program provides education and development opportunities for state residents and entrepreneurs.

Many individual tourism destinations, communities, and/or regions have their own convention and visitors bureaus, destination management organizations, or tourism development authorities. These offices work to develop and market their local tourism attractions.

Tourism resources include facilities and services directly geared toward attracting more visitors, but the industry also relies on other support services such as grocery stores, medical facilities, and gas stations. Many tourism facilities such as hotels, resorts, airlines, and amusement or theme parks have developed a customer service attitude. Focusing on service quality and customer relations is important in an industry whose clientele is experienced, sophisticated, and can choose among many service offerings.

A customer orientation requires researching the needs and desires of the current and potential tourist markets. Visitors to North Carolina primarily wish to see the natural scenic beauty, experience the state's heritage, and encounter the friendliness of the local people. One third of visitors are from North Carolina, but the Division of Tourism, Film and Sports Development has expanded its marketing efforts and presence in overseas markets such as Canada, Great Britain, and Germany. Identifying the best potential market and developing a fitting travel product or destination for that market are keys to success in the tourism industry. North Carolina directly competes with the surrounding states of Florida, Georgia, South Carolina, Tennessee, and Virginia for the same tourism dollars. Similar interests draw visitors to the South, but unique attractions and destinations will lead them to North Carolina.

Many destinations in North Carolina have a clear understanding of their target market and have developed their resources accordingly. Some areas attempt to expand their limited attractions and become a destination where people spend more time and money at the location and perhaps visit again to explore even more. Other regions would like to become a tourism destination but have less to offer. These regions must evaluate their resources honestly before taking steps to development. Tourism development has many benefits for communities but many negative impacts as well. Responsible tourism development requires all members of the community to be aware of the impacts of tourism development and to participate in the decision-making process.

Benefits and Costs of Tourism

Much research has focused on identifying the positive and negative economic, social, and environmental impacts of tourism development. Depending on their level of involvement with the tourism industry or the stage of tourism development in their area, residents of host communities will likely have different perceptions of tourism. Residents of destination areas in early stages of tourism development have been shown to hold more positive attitudes toward tourism; however, a general ambivalence in the early stages of tourism development may also occur because it is too early for residents to have made up their minds. It has also been shown that while residents may initially hold high expectations for tourism development, support often diminishes over time. Indeed, it appears that locals who reside in tourist destinations have a social carrying capacity threshold, beyond which they will start to show their irritation and dissatisfaction with the outcomes of tourism development. Similarly, as growth and demand for tourism increase in an area, the impacts upon the community tend to become more apparent and more negative. At a certain point, attitudes will become much less favorable and community residents will no longer support such development. Because of this, tourism planners need to be well informed through ongoing data collection and research. They must work to make tourism a proactive force that maximizes the community's overall growth and minimizes costs to the environment and to resident culture.

Tourism is increasingly identified as a vehicle for regional and community development. Throughout the United States, state and local governments have become involved in tourism due to its potential as a means for economic development. As the importance of traditional industrial and agricultural economies fades in many regions, tourism is regarded as a panacea for the revival and renewed prosperity of rural as well as urban communities. In North Carolina, many communities rely on tourism dollars, although some counties are more heavily invested in tourism than others. In 2003, Mecklenburg, Wake, Guilford, Dare, Buncombe, Forsyth, and Durham counties generated half of the $683 million in state tourism revenue. However, in depressed economic times, nearly all regions of North Carolina have been affected by the loss of jobs and industry.

In the search for economic prosperity, however, communities must exercise caution in planning and developing new and existing tourism enterprises. Sometimes the allure of money and jobs, especially in economically depressed areas, obscures the costs of tourism for a community. Natives of the Outer Banks during the summer and Asheville during the fall tell stories of traffic congestion, pollution, crowding, and lack of access to restaurants, stores, and other local amenities. Unless their livelihood is directly related to the tourism industry, local people who live in tourism destinations (hosts) typically have little tolerance for tourists and often have derisive names for them. The problem is that planners, local government officials, and private entrepreneurs frequently fail to consider in advance the effects that tourism will have on their community. Moreover, people outside the field do not make distinctions among different types of tourists and the differential impacts they have on the community.

The importance of tourism to the economic well-being of many communities is particularly apparent when natural forces such as hurricanes threaten them during peak tourism seasons. The coastal counties were plagued by three hurricanes in 1996. Hurricane Bertha forced an evacuation of the beach communities during the middle of July; Hurricane Edouard threatened Labor Day weekend; and just a few days later Hurricane Fran hit, causing massive property damage and lost tourism revenue. In 1995, rain washed out the Martin Luther King weekend for North Carolina's ski areas. This weekend is traditionally the peak weekend for the state's ski areas, and an estimated $1.1 million in revenue earnings were lost (*Greensboro News and Record,* 1995). Periods of warm winter weather can be equally devastating for the ski industry. In late December 1996 and early January 1997, a warm-up caused the ski areas to close during the traditionally busy Christmas and New Year holiday period. In 1999, Hurricane Floyd and consequential flooding disabled North Carolina's major modes of transportation. Interstates 95 and 40 were closed in the eastern portion of the state, and train and air travel were also disrupted. Many tourism resources located in the flooded areas were destroyed, and millions of dollars were needed to repair the damage. Often, it is not until tourism is adversely affected by factors such as bad weather that communities realize the important role it plays in their economy. Therefore, overdependence on a single industry can have negative effects if this industry is threatened and the community has no other means of economic activity to replace it.

Negative social effects of tourism may include changes in family roles and relationships. In communities that have changed their economic base from agriculture or manufacturing to tourism, work-related traditions in families may change. This may be the first time family members have worked in a service-oriented industry that has different work conditions, work hours, and expectations than their previous occupations. Tourists also bring their own culture into a community. In small communities, an influx of new ideas and customs may be especially unsettling for the younger generations, who may be encouraged to leave home in search of new horizons. Additionally, the dress, demeanor, and customs of tourists may be offensive to locals. In a stable community, tourism can be particularly upsetting to the local culture. Then, as community relationships become more distant with the increase in the number of strange faces, crime rates tend to increase. Mass tourism can result in resentment against tourists and perceptions of a diminished quality of life for many inhabitants. Consequently, transportation officials need to plan strategies that effectively manage crowding and traffic congestion.

The number of attractions and accommodations available in a location may also influence the number of tourists visiting. By analyzing carefully the carrying capacity of their community and determining the best target segments of the tourist population, planners can reduce the number of visitors. They can focus on those who "fit" in their community, are most likely to have satisfying experiences, and will most likely return.

Environmental deterioration due to tourist traffic is another tourism management concern. Whether through erosion of steps and sidewalks or the effects of people's feet on trails, forests, or beaches, more visitors result in more damage and increased costs to maintain and repair such resources. Transporting, entertaining, and housing tourists inevitably increases a community's pollution, traffic, construction, and demands on infrastructure. In North Carolina, as people express an interest in nature-based tourism, environmentalists and tourism planners face the challenge of minimizing the effects of tourism on the natural environment before visitors destroy the very resources they have come to enjoy (Coastal Plain Nature-Based Tourism Workshop, 1997). For example, pollution due to automobile traffic within the Great Smoky Mountains National Park has greatly deteriorated the once clear and magnificent views of the landscape. Mount Mitchell State Park is being affected by acid rain and increased ozone exposure due to smog in the Asheville valley below it. Many North Carolina companies promote their ecotourism services and sustainable practices which, if successfully implemented, attempt to minimize resource impact and support environmental protection efforts.

Sustainable Development of Tourism

The concept of sustainable development is defined by the United Nations Department of Economic and Social Affairs as development that meets the needs of the present without compromising the ability of future generations to meet their own needs (http://www.un.org/esa/sustdev/). This ideal certainly applies to the development of tourism. No other industry so impacts and relies upon a host destination's population, natural environment, human services, modes of transportation, and related services and infrastructure. Impacts related to the influx of visitors have been shown to have social, environmental, and economic influences on a community. Tourism most often takes place within communities that are the "natural arenas" where local citizens play out their normal everyday lives and so can generate profound social concerns to them (Haywood, 1988). Tourism relies on the resident community to act not only as host and service provider but also as an additional attraction unto itself. The community contributes to the feel and aura of a destination, and even community members not affiliated with the industry must still contend with its impacts. As such, proper planning and input should be encouraged to ensure that all relevant stakeholders are allowed to voice their concerns and have their perspectives incorporated into future plans. It makes little sense for a community to develop and promote tourism if area residents' lack of support leads to negative feelings toward the industry and inappropriate reactions toward tourists. Instead, the first step in true community participatory development should be to involve all relevant and interested parties in an effort to heighten awareness, voice concerns, and learn more about the potential benefits and consequences of a growing tourism industry. It has been shown that those citizens who were better informed about both the positive and negative aspects of tourism development tended to view tourism in their community more favorably than those who were less informed (Koegh, 1990).

Planning for sustainable tourism should address quality of life for host communities, visitor satisfaction, and conservative use of natural and social resources. The goal of sustainability fits in well with tourism development and planning because most tourism development (which involves many stakeholders, such as tourists, government, businesses, and community residents) depends on attractions and activities related to the community's heritage, local culture, and natural environment. If these resources are degraded and overused, the industry itself will have destroyed the very factors that allowed its evolution in the first place. As tourism thrives on a community's resources, it must consider what can and should be put back into the community. Clearly, in order to continue to succeed, tourism should give back to the community in which it resides, because without any of its key components, such as host residents, government, and area businesses, the industry will fail.

A common negative societal impact of increased tourism development is a decline in local traditions and an increase in commercialization. However, with careful planning and zoning, the development of a homogenous culture may be prevented. For example, tourism can result in the designation of historic districts within a community, whereby old buildings are rejuvenated, new businesses are established, and even local crafts and customs are revived for the tourist trade. One example of this can be seen in Wilmington, where the Riverfront has been renovated and is once again alive and vibrant after lying neglected for years. North Carolina's Main Street program in particular works to stimulate economic development within the context of historic preservation. Since 1980, it has contributed more than $789 million in new investment to Main Street communities, leading to a net gain of 10,000 jobs in their downtowns, renovation of more than 2,400 buildings, and aid in establishing more than 5,400 new businesses across the state. Some of the North Carolina communities that have participated in this program include Morehead City, Brevard, Kinston, and Marion http://www.dca.commerce.state.nc.us/mainst/). Similarly, when the communities of Durham and Thomasville sought opportunities for increased economic development and tourism influx, they chose to capitalize on their own unique histories. Durham renovated a number of downtown buildings once used for tobacco production, and Thomasville centered its downtown rejuvenation on renovating a once-empty textile manufacturing plant.

Thus, when implementing plans to use tourism as a means of economic development, planners should be aware that the social and environmental costs to a community may be quite significant. Care should be taken to minimize the costs with long-term planning and sustainable development rather than concentrating on the immediate economic benefits. Destinations currently have to deal with all impacts of tourism development. With more pressure on our natural and cultural resources, more communities are rethinking their tourism development efforts. In the High Country, Mountain Keepers (formerly the Sustainable Tourism Council) works to bring awareness of sustainable tourism to the area and to promote farm tourism. Other regions, such as the coastal area, consider various forms of nature-based and ecotourism in their development efforts. Successful marketing in tourism requires a unique tourism product that protects and preserves the resources of the community.

Special Interest Tourism

The tourism system relies both on identifying and reaching a well-suited market and offering and developing suitable attractions. Tourism marketers work to match tourism products with interested travelers. Some of these products have been developed very recently, while others have a much longer tradition. The following sections describe some of North Carolina's special interest tourism sectors.

Cultural Tourism

Cultural tourism encompasses activities and destinations associated with arts, crafts, theater, and music. Some cultural tourism activities are year-round attractions, others are seasonal, and some may only be available for a few days, such as the many arts and music festivals staged around the state at different times of the year.

Figure 3.2 below depicts the various types of activities that cultural tourists engage in while visiting the state. Over 21 percent of tourists pursue cultural attractions or activities while on vacation in North Carolina (NCDTFSD, 2005).

Figure. 3.2 Selected Activities of North Carolina Tourists

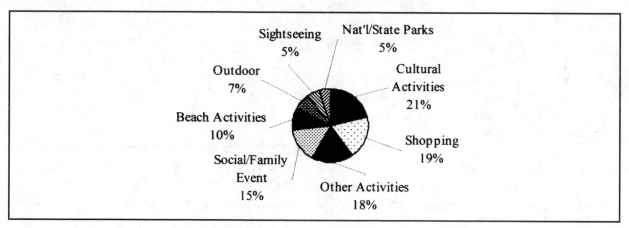

Rural sightseeing and visiting historic places account for 70 percent of the cultural activities pursued by North Carolina's tourists. The specific breakdown can be seen in Figure 3.3.

Figure. 3.3 Breakdown of Activities by Cultural Tourists

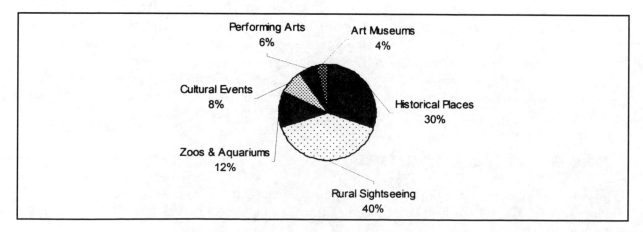

Theater and music attractions offered across the state include the Flat Rock Playhouse in Flat Rock and the State Theater in Charlotte. Outdoor music and drama attractions include *The Lost Colony* at Fort Raleigh National Historic Site, *Unto These Hills* in Cherokee, and *The Horn in the West* in Boone. Some arts and crafts attractions located in the state include the town of Seagrove, which has nearly a hundred potteries within a twenty-five-mile radius; and the Folk Art Center located on the Blue Ridge Parkway. Festivals providing music include Merlefest in North Wilkesboro, the Eastern Music Festival in Greensboro, the Mountain Dance and Folk Festival in Asheville, and the annual Craft Fair sponsored by the Southern Highland Craft Guild, also located in Asheville.

Heritage Tourism

Heritage tourism can be defined as travel that is motivated by a desire to experience the authentic natural, historic, and cultural resources of a community or region (www.nc-commerce.com). In North Carolina, heritage tourism is comprised of attractions that are preserved as a legacy for both present and future generations. North Carolina ranks ninth in the nation for attracting historic/cultural travelers, with this cohort spending more money on average ($623 vs. $289) than all other categories of tourists visiting the state. A major reason more money is spent is that these visitors stay longer in order to immerse themselves in their intended destination. The Travel Industry Association (TIA) of America maintains that heritage tourism is the fastest-growing segment of the travel market and has become a major element of economic development for both rural and metropolitan areas. The core of North Carolina's tourism industry has always been its rich history, natural scenic splendor, and exceptional cultural attractions (NCDTFSD, 2005).

Many of the state's historic sites and parks fall into this category, as do its national parks. North Carolina was first explored by Europeans in 1524 and became a crown colony in 1729. Thus, the state has a relatively long and varied history. Attractions for heritage tourists include sites related to the first colonists, the Revolutionary and Civil Wars, technological innovations, the settlements of various ethnic groups (including the Cherokee Indians and the Moravians), the achievements of notable North Carolinians, and the places inhabited by the tourists' personal ancestors. Examples of attractions in North Carolina for the heritage tourist include: The Biltmore Estate in Asheville, The Wright Brothers National Memorial, Chimney Rock State Park, USS North Carolina Battleship Memorial, Guilford Courthouse National Military Park, Cape Hatteras Lighthouse, The Cherokee Indian Reservation, Blue Ridge Parkway, Historic Hillsborough, Old Salem, Duke Homestead State Historic Site, and the North Carolina Transportation Museum.

Agritourism

Small, family-owned farms have become severely threatened with the importation of cheaper produce, more efficient "big-business" agriculture, and the demise of the tobacco industry in North Carolina. Still, farming is a major element of the heritage of North Carolina, and many people in this state are devoted to their land and the heritage of a farming upbringing. Agritourism offers a way for these farm owners to retain their land while expanding their economic options and providing a unique perspective to tourists on this disappearing way of life. Agritourism aims to preserve the cultural, natural, and historic uniqueness of farm and agricultural lands by protecting these resources through careful stewardship and sustainable use. At the same time, it generates economic development and tax base expansion by promoting North Carolina as a top tourist destination. Value can be added to a farm's overall earnings by providing various experiences to the farm visitor, capitalizing on unique ideas or skills inherent to the farm lifestyle, and knowing that customers generally pay more for specially packaged, high-quality and locally grown or crafted products. North Carolina now has all of the following forms of agrotourism: farm tours, crafts, equipment demonstrations, rural bed and breakfasts, fishing and hunting lodges or campsites, opportunities to learn about local food, classes in "country cooking," themed farms that offer harvest festivals and holiday activities, vineyard tours, and specialty cooking and historic tours.

Casino Tourism

The Indian Gaming Regulatory Act of 1988 allows Native Americans to operate whatever form of gambling a state will authorize. In North Carolina, table games of skill, such as blackjack or poker, are prohibited. However, video games such as video blackjack, video poker, and video dice are permitted. Harrah's Cherokee Casino and Hotel, the state's first casino, opened in November 1997. It is owned by the Eastern Band of Cherokee Indians and managed by Harrah's Entertainment, Incorporated. The casino is 60,000 square feet and has 2,400 gaming machines, three restaurants, and a nearly 1,500-seat auditorium for shows. The casino stimulates tourism and brings tourist-related revenue to the western region of North Carolina. In 2003, a $62 million hotel, accessed via an enclosed sky bridge, was added to the casino. The new hotel has 252 rooms, including 244 premium rooms, eight luxury suites, and 15,000 square feet of convention space with a seating capacity of 1,400. It is projected that the hotel will accelerate the growth of casino tourism. In 2004, nearly 3.5 million people visited Harrah's Cherokee Casino and Hotel. Of that number, 35 percent were from North Carolina. In 2004, the casino and hotel employed 1,734 people, with an average hourly rate of pay of $9.98 and an average salary of $49,161. In 2004, the casino and hotel paid over $64 million to the regional economy in salaries, wages, and employment taxes (personal Correspondence with Lynn Harland, 2005). Gaming profits have allowed the Cherokee tribal government to provide and expand needed programs and services such as health care, housing, recreation, and education.

Educational Tourism

Educational tourism is for individuals who wish to do more than simply relax during their vacations. While education is often a component of many types of tourism, indicated by the great interest in cultural, historic, and interpretative resources by most tourists, educational tourism offers a more specific learning element and outcome. For tourists who wish to attend workshops or learn something new while on vacation, North Carolina can provide a range of opportunities from day-long experiences to residential workshops. Elderhostel programs, hosted at campuses of the University of North Carolina System, provide residential learning for individuals aged fifty and above.

"Hands on Asheville, where you're not just a tourist, you're an artist" is an annual residential workshop series based in and around Asheville. Other educational opportunities include visits to The Morehead Planetarium, Chapel Hill; The North Carolina Museum of Natural Sciences, Raleigh; Discovery Place, Charlotte; Tobacco Farm Life Museum, Kenly; and the North Carolina Zoological Park, Asheboro.

Nature-Based Tourism

North Carolina is known for its varied, distinctive natural landscapes that include mountains in the west, rolling hills in the central part of the state, and ocean beaches in the east. It is not surprising that the top three tourist destinations in North Carolina are the Blue Ridge Parkway, the Great Smoky Mountains National Park, and Cape Hatteras National Seashore. Additionally, the Tar Heel State is home to 1.2 million acres of national forest land, 1,500 lakes over ten acres in size, and 37,000 miles of freshwater streams. There are several thousand miles of hiking trails, hundreds of designated mountain biking trails, excellent climbing and rappelling spots, rugged rivers with Class II and Class III rapids for kayaking and canoeing, and a number of limestone caves for spelunking.

Ocean adventure-based opportunities in the eastern portion of the state include sea kayaking, windsurfing, surfing, power boating, sail boating, and swimming. The lure of a beach vacation is still a major segment of the industry in North Carolina due to the state's sandy beaches and location on the Atlantic Ocean. The North Carolina beaches are divided into three areas: the Outer Banks, the Central Coast Beaches, and the Southern Coastal Beaches. The Outer Banks are a group of islands extending from the Virginia border to the southern tip of Ocracoke Island. Swimming is very dangerous here and is discouraged along the Cape Lookout National Seashore, but the views are extremely beautiful; and many visitors engage in fishing and boating. The Central Coast Beaches face south and are known as the Crystal Coast. Accessed from Beaufort, these beaches include Topsail Island (Jacksonville area), Wrightsville (Wilmington), and Pleasure Island (south of Wilmington). The Southern Coastal Beaches are often spoken of collectively as the Brunswick Island, or Brunswick County, beaches. Brunswick County has forty seven miles of coastline. Its beaches, from north to south, are: Bald Head Island, Oak Island (including Yaupon, Caswell, and Long Beach), Holden, Ocean Isle, Sunset, and Bird Island (the latter is undeveloped but accessible by land from Sunset Beach).

Winter adventure-based opportunities in the mountains include downhill skiing, snow tubing, cross-country skiing, and snowboarding. Snowboarding, a growing segment of the winter sports industry, brings new, young participants to the ski areas. This demographic change should ensure continued success for the ski resorts since traditional skiing by older skiers is predicted to decline (Crossley and Jamieson, 2001). The ski resorts in North Carolina include Beech Mountain, Hawksnest, Appalachian Ski Mountain, and Sugar Mountain Resorts. Although North Carolina's mountains may not be as tall or varied as those in other parts of the nation, the continued success of the ski industry here can be assured due to the close proximity of a strong market in Florida and Georgia.

Sport Tourism

One of the biggest growth areas in the travel and tourism industry in recent years has been sport tourism. Sport tourism consists of three major types: participatory, spectator, and nostalgia. North Carolina has many destinations that can accommodate all three types of sport tourists.

The participatory sport tourist takes part in a sport or physical activity while on vacation. The most popular vacation sports are golf, tennis, and skiing, although mountain biking, whitewater rafting, fishing, and hiking are becoming more popular. In North Carolina, destinations for the participatory sport tourist include: "The Golf Capital of the World"- Southern Pines in Pinehurst; Beech Mountain in Blowing Rock for snow skiing; Pinehurst Resort for tennis; Nantahala Outdoor Center for rafting, hiking, and biking; and Cape Hatteras for sport fishing.

North Carolina has a range of opportunities for people who like to spend their vacation as a sports spectator. The state is home to both professional and college sports, as well as host to a number of annual tournaments. Opportunities to watch professional sports while on vacation include: The Charlotte Bobcats, NBA basketball; The Carolina Panthers, NFL football; The Carolina Hurricanes, NHL Hockey; The Greensboro Grasshoppers, minor league baseball; and Carolina Dynamow, 'A' league professional soccer. A large market is also attracted by the NASCAR (National Association for Stock Car Auto Racing) industry to various race locations throughout the state. North Carolina has been called "NASCAR Valley" because most NASCAR teams are headquartered in Charlotte, Wilkesboro, Concord, Greensboro, High Point, Kernersville, Randleman, Huntersville, or Welcome. Appalachian State University's Belk Library and Information Commons houses an extensive stock car racing collection attempting to preserve the history of the sport. As the market for NASCAR continues to grow nationally, ongoing growth of this attraction in North Carolina shows no sign of slowing down.

North Carolina is also home to fifty four public and private junior and senior colleges and universities, many with their own intercollegiate sports. The biggest attractions in terms of the sport tourist are universities with NCAA Division One basketball and football teams playing in the Atlantic Coast Conference. The universities that fall into this category include: The University of North Carolina at Chapel Hill, Duke University, North Carolina State University, and Wake Forest University. The state also hosts a number of annual sport tournaments that often attract national and international visitors, including: The Greater Greensboro Open for golf, the U.S. Open for golf (held every couple of years at Pinehurst Number Two golf course), Atlantic Coast Conference Men's and Women's Basketball Tournaments, the Pinehurst Clay Court Tennis Tournament, and the Winston Cup NASCAR races.

The third type of sport tourist is the individual who is interested in nostalgia. Nostalgia seekers visit their favorite sport's hall of fame and other sports-related museums. North Carolina is home to the PGA World Golf Hall of Fame in Pinehurst. The Richard Petty Museum in Level Cross will attract those sport tourists who are interested in NASCAR and one of its heroes. Charlotte, North Carolina, is one of five cities being considered as home of the soon-to-be-built NASCAR Hall of Fame.

Employment Opportunities and Educational Programs

Since the early 1980s, the travel and tourism industry in North Carolina has been exhibiting a healthy growth trend, averaging a 6 percent increase annually. Forecasts project that the state will continue to increase in popularity at the regional, national, and international levels. If the recent past is a predictor of the future, then recreation and tourism students seeking a travel and tourism career in this state can confidently expect ample opportunities. In fact, the range of career options in North Carolina's travel and tourism industry is expansive. For students who feel entrepreneurial, opportunities to create and operate one's own tourism enterprise exist in all sectors of the industry. These may include tourism marketing, program facilitation, lodging, hospitality, commercial recreation, and transportation enterprises. Even without owning one's own business, career opportunities in the industry are limited only by one's attitude, skills, knowledge, and experience.

For students preparing to join the travel and tourism industry as employees, job opportunities exist in three broad categories: front-line personnel, support personnel, and management personnel. Front-line or customer contact personnel interact directly with the customers on a routine basis. Some examples of front-line personnel are travel agents, tour guides, flight attendants, front desk clerks, customer services representatives, park rangers, site interpreters, and food service hosts/ hostesses. Some of these employees' activities may be replaced by modern technology, but the tourism industry will need more people who can provide specialized knowledge and individual counseling. Support personnel, in contrast, do not come into direct contact with customers on a routine basis. Their primary function is to help ensure the effective and efficient functioning of tourism organizations. These positions include maintenance and housekeeping personnel, event coordinators, purchasing specialists, marketing specialists, accounts and financial personnel, consultants, and educators. The management personnel's primary role is to achieve the tourism organization's goals effectively and efficiently through its people. Depending on an organization's vertical and horizontal structure, management personnel can be further classified as junior, middle, and senior managers. Some examples of management personnel in the travel and tourism industry are directors of human resources, front office managers, marketing managers, accounts managers, restaurant managers, cruise directors, and directors of convention and visitor bureaus.

Presently, educational programs for travel and tourism in North Carolina are organized in three levels. Level one educational programs are those that teach students specialized skills for a specific sector in the industry. These institutions include community colleges, vocational/technical institutions, and proprietary schools. Upon successful completion of the prescribed course of study, students are granted associate degrees, diplomas, or certificates. Examples of level one institutions are Cape Fear Community College in Wilmington, Asheville-Buncombe Technical College, and Wilkes Community College. Level two programs are represented by four-year colleges and universities where the orientation is to provide career education rather than job training. Their aim is to produce "well-rounded graduates," students who are able to think conceptually and globally and are capable of seeking and sifting through complex information to improve decision-making. As such, students in the four-year travel and tourism programs are typically required to complete certain educational units from the following clusters: general education, specialized education, business education, collateral education, and applied education. Courses taken in completing the degree may include psychology, marketing, travel and tourism, tourism development, or internships in the field. Upon successful completion of the prescribed course of study, students receive a baccalaureate degree. Examples of level two institutions offering tourism-related degree programs are Appalachian State University, East Carolina University, North Carolina State University, University of North Carolina at Greensboro, and University of North Carolina at Wilmington. Level three programs teach students advanced management and educational skills and are divided into master's and doctoral studies. Master's degrees usually take between two and three years of full-time study, while doctoral degrees generally require another three to four years of full-time study after the master's degree. In general, doctoral studies are pursued by those who seek to become tourism educators and researchers. Currently, North Carolina has three institutions that offer level three tourism programs: the University of North Carolina at Chapel Hill, the University of North Carolina at Greensboro, and North Carolina State University. Master's and doctoral studies in tourism/hospitality may be pursued in allied disciplines, such as geography, business management, and leisure studies.

Is the Industry Right for You?

Although the mass media tends to depict jobs in the travel and tourism industry as fun-filled and enviable, students should be warned that the primary goal of tourism organizations is to please the customer. As such, unless one is really people and service oriented, a job in the travel and tourism industry could turn out to be a frustrating and unfulfilling one. Most tourism workers, including management personnel, must work evenings, on weekends, and holidays, as these are when customers are consuming touristic offerings. Moreover, during "tourist seasons," most tourism workers are required to work more than forty hours a week regardless of seniority and rank.

But for those who genuinely love to serve and enjoy interacting with people, the industry offers plenty of opportunities and challenges. In addition to intrinsic rewards like self-fulfillment and satisfaction, the industry also provides myriad opportunities for career growth, geographic mobility, chosen lifestyle, self-expression, creativity, and monetary success.

Summary

Travel and tourism is an exciting field of study and a growing and promising industry. With the help of educated professionals and community participation, and with cooperation from government, related organizations and businesses, North Carolina can expect a sustainable tourism future. Sustainability will also require an understanding of cautious development, service quality, and an appreciation of the many facets of its tourism markets and experiences.

Learning Exercises

1. Examine the varied components of the tourism industry in your hometown community.

2. Explore the functions of the North Carolina Division of Tourism, Film and Sports Development.

3. Choose three articles from professional journals (such as *Journal of Travel Research, Annals of Tourism Research,* or *Tourism Management*) and examine the issues they discuss. Consult Chapter 17 for help in finding these articles. Do the issues discussed in the articles have relevance for North Carolina's tourism industry?

4. Examine the curricula[GESS3] of different tourism programs in the state and discuss which dimensions of the field of travel and tourism will be discussed in the courses.

5. What do you expect tourism in the year 2010 will be like? How will tourism development in North Carolina be impacted in the future? Where do you expect the jobs to be?

Web pages to visit

North Carolina Department of Commerce. Tourism Division. http://www. commerce.state.nc.us/tourism/

North Carolina Cooperative Extension Service. Tourism Outreach and Research Program. http://www. ces.ncsu.edu/depts/tourism/optr

North Carolina. Department of Commerce. Division of Tourism, Film and Sports Development. http://www. visitnc.com

North Carolina Travel Industry Association. http://www. nctravelcouncil.com www. nttc.com

North Carolina Department of Agriculture & Consumer Services. *NC Agritourism.* http://www.ncagr.com/agritourism/.

North Carolina Department of Commerce. Community Assistance. *Main Street Program.* http://www.dca.commerce.state.nc.us/mainst/ .

North Carolina Cooperative Extension Service. *North Carolina Tourism: Resources in Education and Development.* http://www.nctourismresources.net/

References

Ahn, B.Y., Lee, B.K., & Shafer, C.S. (2002). Operationalizing sustainability in regional tourism planning: An application of the limits of acceptable change framework. *Tourism Management, 23*(1), 1-15.

Ap, J. & Crompton, J. (1993). Residents' strategies for responding to tourism impacts. *Journal of Travel Research, 32*(1), 47-50.

Coastal Plain Nature-Based Tourism Workshop. Mattamuskeet National Wildlife Refuge, Hyde County, NC, March 1, 1997.

Crossley, J.C. & Jamieson, L.M. (2001). *Introduction to Commercial and Entrepreneurial Recreation.* Champaign, IL: Sagamore.

Dogan, H. (1989). Forms of adjustment: Sociocultural impacts of tourism. *Annals of Tourism Research, 16,* 216-236.

Fridgen, J.D. (1990). *Dimensions of Tourism.* East Lansing MI: The Educational Institute of the American Hotel and Motel Association.

Haywood, K.M. (1988). Responsible and responsive tourism Planning in the community. *Tourism Management, 9*(2), 105-118.

International tourism obtains its best results in 20 years. (2005). Retrieved May 4, 2005, from http://www.world-tourism.org.

Johnson, J.D., Snepenger, D.J., & Akis, S. (1994). Residents' perceptions of tourism development. *Annals of Tourism Research. 21*(3), 629-642.

Koegh, B. (1990). Public participation in community tourism planning. *Annals of Tourism Research. 17,* 449-465.

Mansfeld, Y. & Ginosar, O. (1994). Determinants of locals' perceptions and attitudes towards tourism development in their locality. *Geoforum, 25*(2), 227-248.

McIntosh, R.W., Goeldner, C.R., & Ritchie, J.R. (1995). *Tourism: Principles, Practices, Philosophies* (7th ed.). New York: Wiley.

Murphy, P. (1983). Tourism as a community industry: An ecological model of tourism development. *Tourism Management, 4*(3): 180-193.

North Carolina Division of Tourism, Film and Sports Development (NCDTFSD) (2005). *Annual Report, 2004.* Raleigh, NC.

North Carolina Travel and Tourism Division (1995/1996). For a vacation you'll always remember, come to a state you'll never forget. *North Carolina Travel Guide.*

North Carolina International Task Force Report on International Marketing.

Peck, J. & Lepie, A. (1989). Tourism and development in three North Carolina coastal towns. In V. Smith (Ed.), *Hosts and guests. The anthropology of Tourism* (2nd Ed.) pp. 203-222. Philadelphia, PA: University of Pennsylvania Press.

Rain makes ski weekend a wash (1995, January 17). *Greensboro News and Record.*

Sauter, E. T., & Leisen, B. (1999). Managing stakeholders: A tourism planning model. *Annals of Tourism Research, 26*(2), 312-328.

Smith, V. (Ed.) (1989). *Hosts and Guests: The anthropology of Tourism* (2nd Ed.) pp. 203-222. Philadelphia, PA: University of Pennsylvania Press.

Taylor, G. (1995). The community approach: Does it really work? *Tourism Management, 16* (7): 487-489.

Tosun, C. (2001). Host perceptions of impacts: A comparative tourism study. *Annals of Tourism Research, 29* (1), 231-253.

United States Travel and Tourism Administration (USTTA) (1994). *Canadian Travel to the United States 1994.* Washington, DC.

Upchurch, R.S. & Teivane, U. (2000). Resident perceptions of tourism development in Riga, Latvia. *Tourism Management, 21*, 499-507.

Wall, G. (1996). Perspectives on tourism in selected Balinese villages. *Annals of Tourism Research, 23* (1), 123-137.

Chapter 4

The Private, Not-for-Profit Sector

Nelson Cooper and Karla Henderson

Numerous voluntary and not-for-profit agencies serve the leisure and recreational needs of North Carolina citizens. Not-for-profit agencies work cooperatively with tax supported parks and recreation departments and with commercial recreation businesses to provide a diversity of leisure services to residents in many communities. An essential characteristic of private not-for-profit agencies is a public service mission. They contribute to the common good through the promotion of altruistic, ethical, moral, or social values. These agencies were usually established by community members to meet significant social needs, and many predate public parks and recreation services in some communities. Programs and services offered by not-for-profit agencies are modified to meet the changing needs of society and clientele.

This chapter is concerned with not-for-profit agencies in North Carolina. Private not-for-profit agencies are distinguished from public or for-profit agencies generally due to their funding sources and their heavy reliance on volunteers for leadership. They are subsidized by a variety of sources such as voluntary contributions, the United Way, state and federal grants, fund-raising drives, membership fees, and foundation grants. Generally they are called "private" because they do not typically rely on any type of tax base funding or support. Additionally, not-for-profit leisure service agencies have definable memberships and many provide services exclusively for their members. Others offer services to the public in general. Not-for-profit agencies that are open to membership from the public are sometimes called quasi-public, semi-public, voluntary, or semi-private; and many of them have a strong youth service focus. Churches may also fall into the category of not-for-profit organizations. Legally, many not-for-profit agencies are tax exempt and subsequently have open membership policies. Participation is generally made available to all without regard to race, ethnic origin, or income level. Many of these agencies view recreation as a major component of the service they provide, rather than as an incidental activity.

Opportunities are abundant for employment in North Carolina through not-for-profit agencies. Some examples include Special Olympics, Boy Scouts, Girl Scouts, Young Men's Christian Association (YMCA), Young Women's Christian Association (YWCA), Young Men's Hebrew Association (YMHA), Young Women's Hebrew Association (YWHA), Muscular Dystrophy Association (MDA), American Red Cross, Children's Miracle Network, Arthritis Foundation, Easter Seals, Save the Earth, Ronald McDonald House

Charities, United Cerebral Palsy, North Carolina Rails-to-Trails, Sierra Club, Leukemia Society, the American Heart Association, and individual churches or communities of faith.

A discussion of the entire spectrum of not-for-profit agencies in North Carolina cannot be undertaken in this brief accounting. Therefore, we are selecting some common not-for-profit agencies that we label as voluntary special interest organizations that focus on serving youth, the environment, health, and sports.

Youth-Serving Agencies

Youth are one of the most highly served populations among not-for-profit agencies throughout North Carolina. Youth-serving agencies that have had a long tradition in North Carolina include the YMCA, YWCA, Boy Scouts of America, Girl Scouts of the USA, 4-H Clubs, Boys and Girls Clubs, Not-for Profit Camp Programs, and Special Olympics.

Young Men's Christian Association (YMCA)

The Young Men's Christian Association was founded in London, England in 1844. A group of workers in a London draper's shop, led by a young sales assistant named George Williams, organized the first YMCA to address the need for Bible study and prayer for people living in the unhealthy social conditions caused by the Industrial Revolution. Williams was a farm boy who had come to London after getting his start in the drapery trade in Bridgewater.

In England during the 1800s, the Industrial Revolution was bringing vice and corruption along with wealth and power to the cities. Hours were long and wages were low. Young clerks worked as many as seventeen hours a day. With no motion picture houses, swimming pools, football fields, lecture halls, or other constructive recreational facilities available during leisure hours, young men often turned to gambling, drinking, and immoral living. The YMCA began in these desperate conditions. The movement grew rapidly and established itself on a worldwide basis.

Today, 972 corporate YMCAs exist in the United States, operating 1,568 branches, units, and camps, and serving over 18 million YMCA members, including many youth. Over 100,000 full and part-time employees work for the YMCA, with 54,000 volunteer policymakers serving on YMCA boards and committees and more than 600,000 volunteer program leaders. Collectively, the YMCA is the largest not-for-profit community service organization in America.

The YMCA is for people of all faiths, races, abilities, ages, and incomes. No one is turned away for inability to pay. Although best known for health and fitness, YMCAs provide a variety of services, including swimming lessons, youth sports programs, massage therapy, residential and day camping, aerobics, child care, programs for people with disabilities, teen clubs, environmental programs, substance abuse programs, family nights, and international exchanges.

The organizational structure of a typical community YMCA relies heavily on a Board of Directors, an executive director, an operations director, and a financial manager. Because the YMCA is a "membership organization," a membership responsibility is identified within the traditional organizational structure. The YMCA recognizes that its quality is directly related to the training and experience of its employees; therefore, it uses a career ladder for employees. Professional Directors within the YMCA organization are members of an association and can transfer their employment from one YMCA to another.

In North Carolina, YMCAs are located in twenty nine cities and serve more than 100,000 people across the state. The YMCA offers practicum, internship, and professional career opportunities in a variety of settings.

Young Women's Christian Association (YWCA)

The Young Women's Christian Association began in London in 1855 as a Prayer Union. In 1858 the "Ladies" Christian Association was organized in New York City. The YWCA units joined together in 1906 and formalized a national movement. Many cities were faced with the need to provide low-cost housing, good nutrition, educational opportunities, and spiritual care for young women who came to the cities to work in factories spawned by the Industrial Revolution.

Today, YWCAs are located in 300 communities throughout the United States, operating at 1,778 different sites, and serving over 2 million YWCA members, including many youth. Over 18,000 full- and part-time employees work for the YWCA, along with more than 244,000 volunteers.

The YWCA's purpose is based on its creation as a women's membership movement nourished by roots in the Christian faith and sustained by the richness of many beliefs and values. Strengthened by diversity, the Association draws together members who strive to create opportunities for women's growth, leadership, and power to attain a common vision of peace, justice, freedom, and dignity for all people. The YWCA's one imperative is to use its collective power toward the elimination of racism where it exists and by any means possible. Core program themes address empowerment for women and their families by focusing on family life, youth development, health and wellness, and empowerment and community leadership.

Seven YWCAs are located in urban areas of North Carolina. Cities where YWCAs are located include: Asheville, Charlotte, Greensboro, High Point, Raleigh, Wilmington, and Winston-Salem. Each local community tailors its YWCA to meet the unique needs of that community. Programs offered by YWCAs in North Carolina include preschool-age and school-age child care on and off site, job training and job searches for low income people, displaced homemakers programs, fitness programs, and skill development opportunities for children and adults. The YWCA has taken a lead in North Carolina in developing the "Take Our Daughters to Work Program." Other YWCA annual programs include a "Day of Commitment to the Elimination of Racism" and a "Week without Violence."

Boy Scouts of America (BSA)

The Boy Scouts of America is the nation's largest organization for boys. Its roots are found in England in the life and work of Lt. General Robert Stephenson Smyth Baden-Powell, the founder of the worldwide scouting movement. Baden-Powell served a distinguished career in the British Army and was known for his courage, scouting skills, and tracking abilities. The Boy Scout movement came to America in 1910 with immediate success. The national program is disseminated through groups of states called regions and to local communities through councils and units (e.g., troops, packs, and posts).

Currently, the BSA provides four types of scouting programs designed to prepare young people to make ethical and moral choices over their lifetimes. Cub Scouting is a family- and home-centered program for first- through fifth-grade boys. Boy Scouting is a vigorous outdoor and peer group leadership program for sixth- through twelfth-grade boys. Varsity Scouting is an active, high adventure program for ninth- through twelfth-grade boys. Venturing is a high-adventure activities, sports, and hobbies program for boys and girls ages 14 through 20 years.

The purpose of the BSA is to build desirable qualities of character, train youth for responsible citizenship, and develop personal fitness. The Boy Scout program centers on local units (i.e., troops and packs) and subgroups (i.e., patrols and dens) within each local unit. Sponsoring organizations, such as community clubs or churches, provide trained adult leadership and facilities for weekly meetings. Skill development and leadership training are at the core of the program. Through an advancement program, boys progress through ranks and merit badge attainment while learning outdoor and life skills. In each community, the BSA is funded by the United Way, project sales, special events, registration fees, or various program and activity fees. Because outdoor experiences are at the core of its program, the BSA uses camping as a primary method of achieving its goals. Periodically, international jamborees are held throughout the world. Every four years, a national jamboree is held at Fort A.P. Hill in Virginia.

North Carolina has eleven BSA Councils that serve over 1,000,000 boys and girls. In addition, its eleven residential Boy Scout camps and reservations range in size from 300 to 3000 acres and include Camp Bowers, Camp John Barnhardt, Bonner Scout Reservation, Camp Durant, State Scout Reservation, and Daniel Boone Scout Reservation.

Career opportunities in the BSA exist in the career development program for entry-level district executives within council structures. In addition, employment opportunities are available in regional offices, camps, adventure base units, and in the national office.

Girl Scouts of the United States of America (GSUSA)

Girl Guides were established in 1910 in England as a result of the popularity of Boy Scouts. Agnes Baden-Powell, sister of the founder of Boy Scouts, spearheaded the movement. Within two years, Girl Guide or Girl Scout organizations were established in Australia, South Africa, Finland, Sweden, Denmark, Poland, Canada, and the United States. Girl Scouts spread to the US through the efforts of Juliette Gordon Low, a native of Savannah, Georgia. Low had become involved with Girl Scouts through her friendship with Agnes and Robert Baden-Powell while she was living in Europe. Although Girl Scouts has changed over the years, the emphasis on ecology and physical fitness has remained central to the movement.

The goals of GSUSA are to help girls develop to their full potential, relate to others with increasing understanding and respect, develop values to guide their actions, and contribute to the improvement of society. The Girl Scout program is offered to girl members through four program categories based upon age group: Daisy (grades K-1), Brownie (grades 1-3), Junior (grades 3-6), and Studio 2B (grades 7-12).

Over 50,000 girls are members in North Carolina. The state's seven GSUSA councils are located in Asheville, Charlotte, Colfax, Gastonia, Goldsboro, Hickory, and Raleigh. An eighth council, located in Virginia Beach, VA, also serves the northern coastal counties of North Carolina. Seven residential Girl Scout camps offer summer programs and are accredited by the American Camp Association. Girl Scout councils in North Carolina employ full-time staff and offer seasonal employment mainly at day and residential camps. Additionally, numerous volunteers are involved with GSUSA.

4-H Clubs

4-H is North Carolina's largest youth-serving organization. Historically 4-H has been a rural undertaking, but today 4-H programs are commonly found in metropolitan inner cities as well as rural areas. 4-H is a youth development program of the Cooperative Extension Service of the U.S. Department of Agriculture, North Carolina State University, and local counties. 4-H began in North Carolina in 1909, and since then thousands of North Carolinians have participated.

Unlike the other youth organizations discussed, 4-H receives a good deal of its funding from government sources. It involves a unique partnership among youth, volunteer leaders, state land-grant universities, the private sector, and federal, state, and county governments. Each county in North Carolina has a Cooperative Extension unit (including the unit on the Cherokee Indian Reservation) for a total of 101 units. The 4-H program is available to all youth aged 8-19 years. The overall mission is to assist youth in acquiring knowledge, developing life skills, and facilitating productive contributions to society.

In each unit, the Extension specialist recruits volunteers to provide the necessary leadership for the 4-H program. In North Carolina, over 18,000 volunteers provide youth services through 4-H programs to over 200,000 youth each year. The 4-H program has an equal number of males and females, with about one third of the members from minority racial/ethnic groups. Activities are undertaken through club meetings, after-school programs, camps, special events, and other programs. The 4-H interest areas include animal science, environmental science, cultural arts, energy and engineering, community development and careers, human development and communication, nutrition and family resources, health and safety, and horticultural sciences.

Boys and Girls Clubs of America

In 1860, several women in Hartford, Connecticut organized a club for boys to provide them with a positive alternative to roaming the streets. Other, similar clubs were formed throughout the United States, and eventually organized into the Boys Club Federation of America. In 1931 the name was changed to Boys Clubs of America. During the remainder of the twentieth century, the number of girl participants and members grew and became a significant part of the cause. In 1990 the organization's name was changed to Boys and Girls Clubs of America. Currently, more than 4.4 million boys and girls are served in 3,700 locations in the United States. More than 40,000 trained, professional staff are employed by the Boys and Girls Clubs of America.

The Boys and Girls Clubs provide young people with a means to develop everyday leadership and guidance. Participants receive information on health and develop physical fitness through a variety of programs. In North Carolina, Boys and Girls Clubs are a not-for-profit corporation under the state's statutes. The Salvation Army also sponsors some Boys and Girls Clubs in North Carolina. Forty-three Boys and Girls Clubs are located in North Carolina. Most clubs are governed by a Board of Directors made up of community citizens. Most clubs have a full-time executive director and other staff and volunteers. All clubs own or use a building that is open to all members during hours of operation. Each club is required to be available at least ten months of the year, five days a week, for a minimum of four hours each day. Members are aged 6 to 20 years.

Not-for-Profit Camping in North Carolina

The natural beauty and moderate climate of North Carolina have afforded many outdoor opportunities for its residents. Day and resident camps for children, youth, adults, and families abound in North Carolina and are sponsored by religious groups (e.g., Baptists, Methodists, Episcopalians), private independent owners, and (as described previously) by not-for-profit youth agencies (e.g., Girl Scouts, YMCA, 4-H). The purpose of these camps has remained constant over the years: Camp leaders seek to improve the lives of children and provide "character-building" opportunities. Many camp programs have also focused on youth from high- risk communities. Full-time employment and professional positions, as well as seasonal (i.e., mainly summer) openings, are always available.

Not-for-profit agencies in North Carolina as well as across the country, however, are under increased pressure to scrutinize the scope of their services concerning appropriateness, commitment, and economic viability. As organized camping becomes more market conscious, questions arise as to who will be able to go to camp, at what cost, under what external controls, and within what expectations for services and outcomes.

Strategically, not-for-profit camps are also recognizing the need for partnerships and collaboration as they seek to fulfill the needs of people in the state. One innovative example of a partnership is the work of Easter Seals. This organization, which serves people with disabilities, has gone to an inclusive model of camp programming. Instead of sending people with disabilities to a segregated camp, Easter Seals has partnered with over a dozen camps throughout North Carolina to enable people with disabilities to be mainstreamed into existing camp programs.

Not-for-Profit Agencies Focusing on the Environment

A number of private, not-for-profit agencies in North Carolina, both small and large, have a mission to promote, protect, and educate people about the environment and environmental resources. Three of the many organizations are highlighted in this section including: North Carolina Rails-to-Trails Program, Conservation Trust for North Carolina, and Sierra Club.

North Carolina Rails-to-Trails (NCRT)

North Carolina Rails-to-Trails (NCRT) began in 1988 as the offshoot of a Greenways Conference. NCRT monitors the state's rail system and actively pursues corridor preservation, retrieval, and conversion to public trails. The organization fosters local leadership and supports rail-trail initiatives throughout the state. The Rail-Trail staff provides coordination among local, state, and federal agencies, allied state and national organizations, and project funding sources.

The NCRT Board of Directors meet quarterly and represent a variety of interests including bicycling, hiking, equestrian, historic, conservation, preservation, and economic development. NCRT is a volunteer organization supported by dues, gifts, and grants. Public contact and project coordination offices are maintained by volunteers in Durham and Hickory.

Conservation Trust for North Carolina (CTNC)

The Conservation Trust for North Carolina (CTNC) is a not-for-profit organization with the mission of protecting and preserving land and water resources through conservation and through cooperation with landowners, local land trusts, and government agencies. The CTNC also serves as an umbrella organization for the local and regional land trusts throughout North Carolina. CTNC provides services such as grants and loans, legislative advocacy, public relations, contract management with state government, and information exchange, training, and planning. The work of CTNC helps protect natural resources, maintain rural character, and increase recreational opportunities.

Sierra Club

The Sierra Club is the oldest and largest grassroots environmental organization in the United States. The mission of the Sierra Club is to explore, enjoy, and protect the planet. The Sierra Club was founded in 1892 by John Muir, who believed, "Everybody needs beauty as well as bread—places to play in and pray in, where nature may heal and give strength to body and soul."

The North Carolina Chapter of the Sierra Club was formed in 1979. Currently almost 20,000 members are involved in thirteen local groups across North Carolina. Local groups offer monthly programs, projects, and social opportunities to enjoy nature.

Not-for-Profit Health Agencies

A variety of not-for-profit agencies in North Carolina promote and provide for general health, prevention, and rehabilitation. Two of these organizations are highlighted as health-related agencies: Easter Seals UCP North Carolina and Be Active North Carolina.

Easter Seals UCP North Carolina

Easter Seals UCP North Carolina provides diversified programs that enhance the quality of life of people with disabilities. The mission is to support people so they may achieve their personal outcomes of living, learning, working, and participating in their communities. An array of services are provided for people who have disabilities such as cerebral palsy, autism, spina bifida, mental retardation, muscular dystrophy, stroke, spinal cord injuries, and head injuries.

In 2004, Easter Seals UCP was established as a result of the merger of Easter Seals North Carolina with UCP of North Carolina. Easter Seals UCP's mission is to create opportunities, promote individual choice, and change the lives of children and adults with disabilities. Some of the services provided include child development centers, therapy, community inclusion services, residential living, supported employment, respite care, disability benefits counseling, advocacy, and recreational opportunities such as camping.

In North Carolina more than 30,000 children and adults are assisted annually through nine Easter Seals UCP service locations that support people in all one hundred counties. These nine service locations employ nearly 2,400 full-time staff, hourly direct care providers, and clinical professionals.

Be Active North Carolina

Be Active North Carolina is an advocacy organization dedicated to improving the health of all North Carolinians. The mission of Be Active North Carolina is to increase the physical activity levels and healthy lifestyles of all North Carolinians through people, programs, and policies. This strategy takes into account the social, political, cultural, environmental, organizational, and interpersonal influences that shape a person's habits regarding physical activity. Be Active North Carolina focuses on increasing awareness, creating and recognizing model programs, funding initiatives, and advocating for policy change. Be Active North Carolina provides information and resources for educators, health professionals, employers, communities, families, and individuals. In the summer of 2005, Be Active North Carolina opened a western office in the Department of Health, Leisure and Exercise Science at Appalachian State University in order to better serve citizens in the western North Carolina region.

Not-for-Profit Sports Agencies

Recreational sports programs and opportunities are typically found in public and commercial recreation venues. The demand for recreational sports has also resulted in private, not-for-profit agency development and growth in North Carolina. At the local level, many youth sports program groups have established themselves as private, not-for-profit groups to increase their potential for funding and members. Three statewide agencies are highlighted here that have continued to grow in providing sports services: Special Olympics North Carolina, North Carolina Senior Games, and North Carolina Amateur Sports.

Special Olympics North Carolina

Special Olympics is an international program of year-round sports training and competition for children and adults with mental retardation. In 1963 Eunice Kennedy Shriver started a day camp for people with mental retardation. Her experiences with her mentally retarded sister helped her to recognize that individuals with mental retardation were virtually ignored by society. She saw that people with mental retardation were far more capable in sports and physical activities than many experts thought. This day camp program demonstrated that individuals with mental retardation not only received benefits from participating in physical activity, but that they learned from participating in organized sports.

The first International Summer Special Olympics Games were held in Chicago in 1968 and attracted 1,000 participants from twenty six states and Canada. Today over 1 million participants and over 500,000 volunteers from 143 countries are involved in Special Olympics. The mission of Special Olympics is to provide year-round training and competition in a variety of sports for children and adults with mental retardation. In addition, Special Olympics creates continuing opportunities for them to develop physical fitness, demonstrate courage, experience the joy of achievement, be included in the community, build skills, and make friends. Families of persons with mental retardation become stronger through Special Olympics.

Special Olympics North Carolina provides year-round sports training and competition for more than 37,000 children and adults with intellectual disabilities in communities throughout the state. North Carolina has one of the largest Special Olympics programs in the world in terms of athlete participation. Special Olympics began in North Carolina in 1970 and is offered through eight areas that serve various regions in the state. Nearly every community in the state is served by Special Olympics. Annual athletic events in North Carolina include the Fall and Summer Games, Equestrian Championship, Alpine Skiing Games, Basketball Tournament, Bowling Tournament, and Ice Skating Games. Summer Games in North Carolina involve more than 1,500 athletes from over eighty counties. In 1999, the Special Olympics World Summer Games were hosted in Raleigh, Durham, and Chapel Hill. The World Summer Games event involved nearly 30,000 volunteers to enable 7,000 athletes from 150 countries to compete in nineteen sports.

Volunteer opportunities in Special Olympics include serving as coaches, chaperones, and fund-raisers. The major sources of funding for Special Olympics North Carolina are corporate foundations, contributions from individuals, and special events. Athletes are not charged any fees for their participation.

North Carolina Senior Games (NCSG)

North Carolina Senior Games (NCSG) is a wellness program designed for adults over the age of 55. This prevention program is focused on keeping the body, mind, and spirit fit while enjoying the company of friends, family, spectators, and volunteers.

NCSG began in 1983 with a vision to create a year-round health promotion and education program for older adults. Participants train all year, and each spring they participate in fifty three Local Games programs held across the state. Those individuals who qualify are invited to attend the State Finals each fall, which typically has about 3,000 participants. Every two years, some state games finalists qualify to represent North Carolina at the National Senior Games. Participants are divided into sex and age categories within five-year increments going from 55-59 to 100+ years. Events include sports such as archery, basketball, bocce, croquet, football throw, spin casting, and many more.

Opportunities are also available to participate in Silverarts, Silverstriders, and Silver Classic. Silverarts provides a heritage (e.g., basketweaving, quilting, woodcarving), visual (e.g., drawing, photography), performing (dance, vocal, line dance), and literary program (e.g., essays, poetry) along with a cheerleader program. Silverstriders is a national, award-winning walking program that includes log books for tracking progress; gifts; awards; and local Fun Walks. Silver Classic involves other types of special events targeted toward older adults.

The major sponsor of NCSG is the North Carolina Division of Aging and Adult Services, in partnership with Rex Hospital (Raleigh) and the Raleigh Parks and Recreation Department. Many other endorsing agencies work together to support local and state games. Numerous volunteers are used at the local level and at State Games.

North Carolina Amateur Sports (NCAS)

North Carolina Amateur Sports (NCAS) was established in 1983 to host the first sanctioned State Games of North Carolina in 1986 and the U.S. Olympic Festival in 1987. Today, NCAS operates with the goals of (1) promoting the spirit of amateur sports, physical fitness and health to all ages, and (2) skill development through participation in organized events, thus enriching the state of North Carolina. NCAS hosts the State Games of North Carolina, Cycle North Carolina (CNC), CNC Spring Retreat, the Be Active North Carolina Challenge, and the State Games Tobacco-Free Team., NCAS is staffed by six permanent, full-time employees and has a fourteen member Board of Directors. NCAS attributes its success to the thousands of volunteers who support the State Games and Cycle North Carolina. NCAS receives financial support from corporate sponsors, individual donors, and event revenues.

Other Not-for-Profit Recreation Opportunities

Other hobby organizations, special-interest groups, and club membership organizations are plentiful in North Carolina. Their primary purpose is to provide their members with opportunities for socializing and recreation. A wide variety of leisure interests are collectively represented in these types of organizations, such as running clubs, quilting groups, and community service organizations like Kiwanis or Lions. These organizations often provide extensive facilities, services, and programs for their membership and are often labeled as club, society, or civic associations. Usually members pay an initial membership fee and annual maintenance fee. Membership may be restricted, depending on the philosophy and purpose of the organization.

Additional examples of not-for-profit membership organizations in North Carolina beyond those previously mentioned (i.e., youth, environment, health, and sports) fall into categories such as social clubs, outdoor sport clubs, boat and vehicle clubs, biking and trail clubs, cultural and hobby clubs, and residential recreation associations. Although too numerous to list, the organizations are described in the *Annual Directory of North*

Carolina Organizations and *The Encyclopedia of Associations: National, State, and Local Organizations,* which may be available in the reference section of your library. Your local Chamber of Commerce or Recreation and Parks Department may have a list of the clubs and organizations that are available in your area.

Hundreds of private clubs and institutions operate tennis, golf, and swimming facilities for their members and families. Many of these organizations employ part-time help in their seasonal programs. Others have extensive facilities and employ a full-time staff. Many have dining facilities as well as activity centers. Career opportunities in management and professional instruction (e.g., tennis, golf) are available for those interested in this facet of leisure services.

Learning Exercises

1. Investigate a not-for-profit, youth-serving or membership organization in your hometown.

   a. Focus on the following factors: history/origin, organizational structure, facility/resources utilized, capital required for development, operating budget and sources of operating capital, membership fee structure, program/services provided, number of members served, and impact on local economy.

   b. After collecting this information, present an oral report/prepare a written report for in-class discussion.

   c. Compile a list of various special interest organizations in North Carolina that represent a specific leisure activity, and report your findings back to the class.

2. Visit a local YMCA/YWCA or other facility-based organization. Interview the executive director. Focus on changing needs of Y members and ways in which the Y attempts to respond within its mission and purposes. In your interview, include questions related to the Y's fund-raising methods, its impact on the local community, and its short- and long-range goals.

3. Write a paper that compares and contrasts the organizational structure and operating philosophy of a not-for-profit organization described in this chapter to those of a municipal parks and recreation agency.

4. Arrange to visit a cub pack, Boy Scout troop, or explorer post in you community or go to a girl scout meeting. You can contact your local Boy Scout Council or Girl Scout Council Office. As a result of your visit, prepare a report of your observations about the meeting, including how volunteers and youth interacted and the kinds of activities they undertook.

5. Interview a Boy Scout, Girl Scout, 4-H, or Boys and Girls Club professional. Ascertain the person's background and motivation for seeking a career in a youth-serving organization. What are the individual's long-term career development plans? What strategies will the individual employ to reach these goals?

References and Web Sites

Annual Directory of North Carolina Organizations, 29th ed. (1988). Raleigh: North Carolina Council of Women's Organizations. (Alphabetical index of all not-for-profit/service organizations in the state).

Encyclopedia of Associations: Regional, State, and Local Organizations. (2005). Detroit: Thomson Gale.

American Camp Association. http://www.acacamps.org/

Boy Scouts of America National Council. http://www.scouting.org

Girl Scouts. *Official Web site of the girl Scouts of the USA.* http://www.girlscouts.org

The Salvation Army International Home Page. http://www.SalvationArmy.org/

United Way of America: http://www.national.unitedway.org

YMCA: http://www.ymca.net

YWCA: http://www.ywca.org

Sierra Club, North Carolina Chapter: http://nc.sierraclub.org

North Carolina Senior Games: http://www. ncseniorgames.org

Easter Seals UCP North Carolina: http://nc.easterseals.com

DEPOT.HTM. North Carolina Rails-Trails information depot: http://www.ncrail-trails.org

Conservation Trust for North Carolina: http://www.ctnc.org

Be Active North Carolina: http://www.beactivenc.org/

North Carolina Amateur Sports (NCAS): http://www.ncsports.org/

Chapter 5

Local Government Park and Recreation Services

James R. Sellers and Stephanie T. West

Government, in the broadest sense, is the ordering of human relationships. Through government and through rational laws, it has been assumed that people can associate harmoniously and to their mutual benefit. Sessoms and Henderson (1994) state, "ultimately government does for people collectively what they are unable to do individually" (p.137).

Democratic government is government of the people, by the people, and for the people. It rests on a belief in the fundamental dignity and importance of the individual, the essential equality of human beings, and the individual's need for freedom. At the heart of democratic government are individuals, who have personal values, expectations, experiences, and problems. The welfare of the state, which operates through the process of government, has no meaning except the welfare of the individuals who comprise it. Another basic premise of democratic government is the ideal of the essential equality of human beings. People differ among themselves considerably in their personal values, interests, needs, and abilities. Democratic government affords people opportunities to pursue happiness according to their own ideals, to develop their own potentialities, and to participate in government according to their specific interests. A third basic premise of democratic government is that freedom is a basic need of human beings. The freedom to make choices and to act upon them is essential to an individual's growth and development. Only through the use of their freedom can individuals develop responsibility and self-restraint. Only by acting as free, responsible individuals can people develop their potentials fully.

A democratic government, dedicated to the well-being of its people, must provide programs and services to meet the needs and expectations of the people. There was a time when all levels of government, including local government, were relatively simple and provided few programs and services. Many programs and services that are currently considered essential local government functions were initiated and were provided for a period of time by agencies in the private sector. Education, police administration, fire protection, public works, health, and social welfare are outstanding examples of local government functions that passed through the stages from private to public support.

Park and recreation services evolved as a local government function under much the same circumstances as did other local government functions. Park and recreation services at the local or community level were, for the most part, considered to be a matter of private concern prior to the early 1900s. The primary providers of park and recreation services were voluntary youth-serving agencies, private membership associations, special interest groups, religious organizations, and commercial recreation enterprises. Since the early 1900s local governments have increasingly recognized parks and recreation as an essential function and have become a major provider of parks and recreation services designed to meet the leisure needs of their residents.

This chapter focuses on the role of local government in providing public park and recreation services in North Carolina. It presents descriptions of local government agencies offering park and recreation services as well as how these agencies make available the fiscal, human, and physical resources necessary to provide programs and services on a continuing basis. It also discusses career opportunities in local park and recreation agencies.

Mission and Functions of Local Government Park and Recreation Department Services

Park and recreation services as a function of government are first the responsibility of local government. Local government is closest to the people; it is at the local level where people live that recreation and leisure needs can best be determined and served. Local governments tend to adopt one primary philosophical orientation to the delivery of park and recreation services. Kraus and Curtis (2000) identify six leisure service orientations that are prevalent in the leisure services profession. These orientations are: 1) the quality of life or amenity approach, 2) the marketing approach, 3) the human services approach, 4) the prescriptive approach, 5) the environmental/aesthetic/preservationist approach, and 6) the hedonist/individualist approach. Most park and recreation departments adhere to the quality of life or amenity orientation. This orientation places emphasis on enrichment of the quality of life through the provision of park and recreation services that contribute to the social, physical, cultural, and general well-being of the community and its people.

Park and recreation departments in North Carolina most frequently perform the following five functions: 1) plan, develop, and maintain park and recreation areas; 2) provide park and recreation services on a continuing basis; 3) coordinate the use of existing human and physical resources; 4) provide special recreation services for persons with disabilities; and 5) cooperate with other government agencies. The extent to which park and recreation departments perform these functions is determined by local circumstances. A brief discussion of these functions is presented in the paragraphs that follow.

Most park and recreation departments in the state perceive that one of their primary functions is to plan, develop, and maintain a comprehensive system of park and recreation areas. Areas and facilities most frequently provided include playgrounds, tennis courts, athletic fields, basketball courts, golf courses, multipurpose recreation centers, swimming pools, picnic areas, beaches, outdoor theaters, stadiums, cultural centers, trail systems, nature centers, marinas, botanical gardens, and open-space settings. Such areas and facilities are developed for a variety of park and recreation uses and are enjoyed by local residents of all ages. More detail on areas and facilities is presented later in this chapter.

Park and recreation departments provide a wide variety of programs and services designed to meet the needs and interests of individuals and groups in the local community. Program activities tend to be classified under the following headings: cultural and performing arts; sports, games, and athletics; aquatics; literary activities; social recreation; outdoor recreation; arts and crafts; and volunteer services. Park and recreation departments strive to provide a diversified and continuing program that allow all local residents equal opportunity for participation and involvement. Such programs require good management, well-trained staff, and adequate financial support.

Many local agencies provide programs and services that supplement the efforts of public park and recreation departments. Cooperation and coordination between public park and recreation departments and private non-profit and commercial agencies is essential in order to avoid unnecessary duplication of facilities and overlapping of programs, to reduce financial costs, and to eliminate serious gaps in key areas of service. Park and recreation departments are the only local agencies responsible for and concerned with the leisure needs and interests of all residents and, therefore, should take the lead in promoting cooperation and coordination among the various local agencies providing recreation programs and services.

Many park and recreation departments in the state provide programs and services in conjunction with other local agencies. Such cooperative programming efforts have been dubbed "synergetic programming, " or the process combining the resources of two or more agencies to provide park and recreation services that could not be conducted by one agency acting alone. Sports and athletics, cultural events, and local festivals are most frequently the focus of synergetic programming efforts in North Carolina.

Park and recreation departments have become increasingly involved in providing specialized programming and services for persons with disabilities. Special recreation is the term traditionally used to describe programs and services offered for persons with disabilities. Additionally, specialized programs and services are often provided for other special population groups, such as youth-at-risk and senior citizens. Larger park and recreation departments are more likely than smaller departments to provide special recreation services designed to the needs, interests, and characteristics of persons with disabilities and other special population groups. Winston-Salem, Greensboro, Raleigh, Mecklenburg County, and Durham are examples of local governments with large park and recreation departments providing special recreation services.

Park and recreation departments work closely with other public agencies concerned with the well-being of local residents. Depending on local conditions, cooperative relationships are often developed with public school systems, youth-serving bureaus, social services and public health departments, housing authorities, libraries, museums, and the like. Cooperation among other local public agencies is essential to the delivery of leisure services designed to meet the needs of the total population.

Park and recreation departments also work closely with other local political subdivisions and with state and federal agencies. Cooperation between cities, counties, and other local political subdivisions, especially in large urban areas of the state, is essential if the best interests of the total population and a wide variety of park and recreation opportunities are to be provided. Cooperation with state and federal agencies affords local governments the opportunity to better utilize the programs and services provided by these agencies.

Legal Authority for Park and Recreation Services

Local government sponsorship of park and recreation services is dependent upon legal authority from state government. Local governments are political subdivisions of state government and must receive legal authority from state government under either general or special legislation in order to provide park and recreation services.

North Carolina's first municipal park and recreation department was established in 1925 in Durham with C. R. Wood, a former YMCA director, as its head. Charlotte established a park and recreation department in 1927, and High Point created its system in 1931. These pioneer park and recreation programs did not require special legislation from state government. Local government officials based their authority to provide park and recreation services on general welfare and police powers granted by the state constitution and on broad interpretations of existing park and school legislation. The need for specific recreation enabling legislation became apparent during the 1930s and 1940s with the growth of the organized recreation and park movement. Some local officials attempted to broaden existing general welfare and school legislation to include park and recreation services; other officials worked for the passage of state enabling legislation to allow local governments to establish and maintain park and recreation services. In 1946, North Carolina became the thirty fourth state to pass state recreation enabling legislation. All fifty states now have enabling legislation that authorizes one or more local government units to acquire, develop, and maintain property for park and recreation purposes and to conduct recreation programs and services under the direction of a professional staff.

Provisions in state recreation enabling laws can vary greatly. However, in order to be effective, state recreation enabling legislation should contain the following provisions:

1. Authorization for all local legal subdivisions to exercise the powers conferred, without hindrance or specification as to where such authority will originate in the structure of the government.
2. Provision for two or more subdivisional recreational service authorities to combine and otherwise coordinate the operation, administration, finance, and leadership of such recreational service.
3. Authorization for local recreational service authorities to acquire, build, construct, or otherwise develop such land and water areas or spaces as the local authorities deem adequate for the satisfactory provision of recreational service, as long as such measures are not inconsistent with public use or welfare.
4. Authorization for the expenditures of any funds, consistent with public welfare and local policy, which the local recreational service agency deems necessary for the most comprehensive recreational offerings and incidental services for the benefit of the public; and permission for said agency to receive any bequest, grant, or endowment of money, goods, services, equipment, or other real property which is in keeping with local policy and not inconsistent with any prescription as provided by law, as long as acceptance of such valuables does not require additional expenditures by the locality as a whole.
5. Authorization for the appropriation of funds from the general tax funds for the establishment and continued adequate operation of the most comprehensive recreational service program within the corporate or quasi-corporate boundaries, with

provision for issuance of bonds for the purchase of any real property, buildings, structures, or other facilities for recreational purposes within or outside of the boundaries of the local legal subdivision.

6. Permission for the local recreational service authority to utilize any of the buildings, grounds, structures, or facilities of other local legal subdivisions, agencies, bureaus, departments, or systems with the consent and agreement of said parties, or to utilize private property on mutually agreeable terms between the negotiating parties.

7. Authorization for the local recreational service system to conduct and otherwise operate activities, property, structures, and other facilities within or without the legal boundaries of the local subdivision for the maximum recreational services which might then be afforded to the citizens and public at large.

8. Authorization of metropolitan recreational districts or regions where the cooperation of local legal subdivisions proves inoperable so that such special governments, established to coincide with economic areas rather than with existing political boundaries, can provide comprehensive recreation services without regard to urban or rural lines of demarcation. Such governments are then empowered to organize, operate, and administer a complete program of recreational services with all the resources of land, water, real estate, structures, facilities, funds, and leadership necessary for the execution of this mandate (Hjelte & Shivers, 1978, pp. 37-38).

North Carolina's recreation enabling legislation contains most of these provisions and has proven to be highly effective over the past fifty years. More specifically, the state's recreation enabling law provides each city and county the authority to: establish and conduct a system of organized recreation; set aside land and buildings for parks and recreation purposes; acquire land by purchase, grant, gift, lease, or use of eminent domain, either within or outside the boundaries of the governmental unit for parks and recreation use; provide, acquire, equip, and maintain facilities for recreation use; appropriate funds to operate a parks and recreation system; and accept any gift, grant, lease, loan, or bequest of real or personal property for parks and recreation programs as long as the terms and conditions of the grantor or trustee do not require the governmental unit to discriminate among its citizens on the basis or race, sex, or religion. Additionally, this legislation permits cities and counties in North Carolina to establish joint park and recreation systems.

Governmental Jurisdictions and Managing Authorities

Local government is the term typically used to describe any political unit of government such as a city, township, village, borough, county, or special district. Cities, townships, and counties are the most frequently found local government units in North Carolina. Cities and townships are referred to as municipalities for discussion purposes. In 2004-2005, the North Carolina Recreation Resources Service reported 216 recognized local government park and recreation departments in North Carolina

There is no specific relationship between the political subdivision (municipality or county) and the organizational structure utilized to deliver park and recreation services. However, when a local government unit decides to provide park and recreation services, it is faced with deciding which type of managing authority is best suited for local conditions. Jensen (1995) asserts that local governments generally consider the following factors when deciding on type of managing authority: 1) which options are available under the state's enabling legislation, 2) which managing authority could provide the best financial support, 3) which organizational option is preferred by the public, and 4) which arrangement would be best for availability of facilities (p.134).

There are several possible approaches to organizing park and recreation services within the framework of local government. The five most prevalent types of managing authorities at the local level are as follows: 1) parks and recreation administered as separate departments; 2) recreation administered under a parks department; 3) recreation administered under a school board or district; 4) park and recreation services administered in a department as one of several responsibilities; and 5) park and recreation functions administered in a combined department. In North Carolina, the most prevalent type of managing authority is the combined park and recreation department.

The post-World War II period witnessed significant expansion of the organized recreation and park movement in municipalities in North Carolina. Between 1940 and 1950, twenty four municipalities established park and recreation services as a local government function. Most municipalities establishing park and recreation services during this period continued the pattern of administering parks and recreation as separate, independent departments. Proponents of separate parks and recreation departments point out that: 1) parks and recreation are unique functions that merit having separate departments under the direction of professional staff; 2) separate departments give the direct and expedient attention necessary to provide quality programs and services; 3) separate departments are more likely to receive adequate financial support; 4) separate departments are smaller and more efficient; and 5) separate departments are more accountable because of their single function. Chatham County, Iredell County, Hamlet, Southport, and Alexander County are examples of local governments that continue to offer recreation services as a separate function.

The chief arguments against having a separate recreation department and a separate parks department are: 1) separate departments add to the complexity of local government and generally result in duplication of programs and unnecessary expense, 2) separate departments are likely to compound problems associated with coordination and long-range planning, and 3) separate departments are in competition for funds.

Since the early 1960s, the most prevalent type of managing authority has been the combined parks and recreation department. Many North Carolina municipalities with separate parks and recreation departments combined parks and recreation into a single administrative unit during the 1960s. During the 1970s, fifty three local government units in North Carolina initiated park and recreation services. These new departments were predominantly combined park and recreation departments. Local officials saw little need for establishing separate parks departments and separate recreation departments. Combining parks and recreation in a single department allowed both functions to be carried out with one major objective in mind-meeting the leisure needs of local residents.

The trend toward combined park and recreation departments in North Carolina has continued since the 1970s. For example, Archdale established a combined park and recreation department in 1982 and Matthews initiated its park and recreation department in 1995. The strongest points in favor of a combined park and recreation departments are: (1) combining park and recreation services under one department avoids conflicts that may arise between park management and recreation programming; (2) combining park and recreation services in a single agency results in financial savings and improved services by reducing overlapping services, simplifying operating procedures, and coordinating maintenance and program schedules; (3) combined park and recreation departments have a broader base of public support and are in better position to develop a more comprehensive and diversified program; and (4) combined park and recreation departments are in a better position to facilitate long-range planning and to develop broad, cooperative relationships with other public and private agencies concerned with recreation.

Nearly all park and recreation departments in North Carolina operate as line departments within the framework of local government. Directors of park and recreation departments typically report to a city or county manager (depending on the governmental unit offering the service) and utilize the services of an advisory board or committee. Advisory boards are purely advisory and can only make recommendations; therefore, they cannot speak or act with any legal authority. Advisory boards encourage citizen involvement with professional staff. Advisory board members may be either elected or appointed, and boards usually consist of five to seven members. Board membership is typically representative of the various social, economic, and cultural components of the local community. Advisory boards provide opportunities for citizen involvement in policy making, planning, program development, and facility development. They provide a meaningful channel of communication between the park and recreation department and local residents.

Parks, Programs, Services, and Facilities

The variety of programs and services available through park and recreation departments in North Carolina is nearly infinite. Programs range from the elementary to the intricate, from the highly structured to individual freedom of choice, and from the intellectual and artistic to the physical. Local interests and needs dictate the variety of programs and services desirable for each municipality or county. People's needs and the human, physical, and financial resources to meet those needs vary among geographical areas. It is for this reason that each department differs in design and operation. When viewing the numerous innovative municipal, county, and joint municipal/county park and recreation departments that are relatively new or evolving, one cannot help being impressed with the fluidity of park and recreation services in North Carolina.

The space in this chapter does not allow for a comprehensive analysis of this subject; such an undertaking would require a massive publication in itself. Being fully aware of the fact that some excellent departments may not be named, the authors have elected to proceed with a brief synopsis of a sampling of outstanding municipal, county, and joint municipal/county park and recreation departments in North Carolina. In addition, a summary of the most recent trends among North Carolina's parks and recreation departments will conclude the chapter.

Municipal, county, and joint municipal/county park and recreation departments depicted in this chapter are summarized according to their size and distinctive elements. North Carolina's Municipal and County Parks and Recreation Services Study, Fiscal Year 2004-2005 grouped departments into the following population categories: A) departments serving populations greater than 100,000; B) departments serving populations between 99,999 and 50,000; C) departments serving populations between 49,999 and 25,000; D) departments serving populations between 24,999 and 10,000; E) departments serving populations between 9,999 and 5,000; and F) departments serving populations less than 5,000.

The City of Raleigh Parks and Recreation Department, Wake County Parks and Recreation Division, and Onslow County Parks and Recreation Department are Category "A" departments serving populations greater than 100,000. The City of Raleigh has a well established Department of Parks and Recreation. The Department's purpose is to actively encourage, provide, promote and protect quality leisure/recreation, and cultural opportunities, facilities, and environments which are essential to the enhancement of the lives of citizens of all ages. Residents and visitors alike may enjoy more than 5,400 acres of park land, twenty nine community centers (including two art centers), four major lakes, 108 tennis courts, fifty seven ball fields, and eight public swimming pools.

Pullen Park, which is one of Raleigh's most popular facilities, attracts over 1 million visitors each year. The historic Dentzel carousel, a C. P. Huntington miniature train, paddle boats, and kiddie rides provide a special flavor of old-fashioned fun and tradition. Other unique parks feature two disc golf courses, a BMX course, two historic properties (the Tucker House and the Borden Building), Theater in the Park, the Raleigh Little Theater, Durant Nature Park, the All Children's Playground at Laurel Hills, the Walnut Creek Softball Complex (which is a ten-field facility), and the Pullen Aquatic Center.

The Raleigh Department of Parks and Recreation received the National Gold Medal Award for Excellence in Special Recreation in 1994 and the National Gold Medal Award for Excellence in Parks and Recreation Management in 1990. Raleigh's nationally acclaimed Capital Area Greenway System is a continuous network of corridors following streams and paths throughout the city that provides over forty one miles of greenway trails. The Raleigh Parks and Recreation Department is a model of a department that has grown with its city, meeting the increasing demands for quality leisure, cultural, social, and recreational services.

Wake County Parks and Recreation Division is an excellent example of how county parks and recreation departments have expanded to meet growing urban and suburban needs. This impressive system, which includes the City of Raleigh, was formed in 1976 by the Board of County Commissioners. The Division's mission is to acquire and maintain a system of natural areas, open spaces, historic sites, and recreational facilities created to enhance the natural environment so as to provide resources that will meet the leisure and recreational needs of the residents of Wake County.

The Wake County Parks and Recreation Department serves citizens in three ways. One is through large, resource-based facilities that put nature study, boating, hiking, sports, and educational activities within the reach of every citizen. Secondly, it serves citizens of Wake County through cooperative efforts with Wake County Public Schools in developing schools/parks that enhance the play facilities available to students while school is in session and also serve the needs of neighborhood residents during weekends, holidays, and vacations. Third, citizens are served through the grant-in-aid program that assists municipalities and non-profit organizations with funding to develop facilities to meet the needs expressed in the county's Parks and Recreation Master Plan. The partnership formed through the grant-in-aid program fosters community involvement in providing a network of quality recreation opportunities. The program is open to all municipalities and non-profit organizations in Wake County. Each applicant is required to match grant requests on a 50:50 basis. The County Board of Commissioners currently allocates $200,000 annually for this program.

The Wake County Parks and Recreation Department has direct involvement with county parks, district parks, school parks, and special use areas. County parks are land and/or water-based sites, scenic in character, and large enough to serve the needs of the county on a regional level. These are resource-oriented parks. District parks are user-based parks reserved for special recreational activities. These parks may include active and/or passive recreational activities such as picnic shelters, playgrounds, soccer fields, or hiking trails. School parks are park and recreation areas that are built in conjunction with an elementary, middle, or high school. There are three categories of special use areas: nature preserves/underdeveloped areas designed for minimal impact usage; historic areas that may be as small as one house or as large as an entire battlefield; and special use areas, which center on a particular theme or use.

Onslow County Parks and Recreation Department is a NACO (National Association of Counties) and NACRPO (National Association of County Park and Recreation Officials) award winner. This coastal county includes the City of Jacksonville. Onslow County Recreation and Parks Department was established in 1976. Onslow County has a diverse and transient population as it is home to several Marine Corps bases: Camp Lejeune, Camp Johnson, Camp Geiger, and the New River Marine Corps Air Station. The high volume of military personnel gives the county a unique atmosphere and presents some programming challenges.

The Parks Division operates an outstanding network of parks and beaches. It maintains over 367 acres of park land within the county. This includes four regional county parks (fifty five acre Onslow Pines Park, thirty seven acre Hubert By-Pass Park, fifty six acre Stump Sound Park, and 195-acre Richlands/Steed Park), four public beach access sites, thirteen public beach access crosswalks, and the New River Waterfront Park.

The Recreation Division provides numerous special programs for all ages. A sampling of the activities provided includes the July 4th Freedom Festival, the New River Music Festival, a summer day camp program, a Saturday with Santa, an annual Easter egg hunt, Onslow Senior Games, Hershey Track and Field Meet, nature programs, and a variety of organized sports programs.

The Asheville Parks and Recreation Department and the Greenville Recreation and Parks Department are Category B departments serving populations of 50,000 to 99,999. Asheville's Parks and Recreation Department holds the unique distinction of being the first municipal park and recreation department to be nationally accredited from the Commission on Accreditation of Park and Recreation Agencies. The department received its accreditation in February 1994 and was re-accredited in February 1999. The department provides a network of eleven neighborhood recreation centers, thirty-six parks and play areas, two swimming pools, twenty-two tennis courts, and twenty-six ball fields. The department also maintains and operates the eighty seven acre historic Riverside Cemetery as well as all city-owned public facilities. In addition to more than 600 acres of park land, Asheville's Parks and Recreation Department offers highly diversified recreation programs for preschoolers, children, teens, adults, and senior adults. The department offers a wide variety of athletic programs, cultural arts activities, centers and playground activities, and special events such as the Father-Son/Father-Daughter Golf

Tournament and the City of Asheville Open Tennis Court Championships. The department also sponsors or co-sponsors several cultural festivals and special events, including Shindig on the Green, the Greek Festival, Light Up Your Holidays, and the Bele Chere Festival.

The Greenville Recreation and Parks Department is a fine example of a department that is expanding to keep pace with the ever-changing recreational needs of a growing community in North Carolina. The department encompasses over twenty parks and facilities to serve its citizens. River Park North is a unique 309-acre park where activities are offered that appeal to all age groups. Its facilities and activities include picnic areas, pedal boats, hiking, fishing, and the Walter L. Stawavich Science and Nature Center. The Town Commons Park, a scenic park located beside the Tar River, contains an outdoor stage for concerts and outdoor events. Summer in the Park is a free outdoor concert series held at the Town Commons Park during the months of June and July. Music for the entire family ranges from blues to jazz to country. The Greenville Recreation and Parks Department provides many athletic and cultural programs for children, including baseball leagues, day camps, arts and crafts, drama, swimming lessons, soccer, basketball, and cheerleading. The Teen Center is a friendly, well supervised recreation center where teens in grades 7-12 meet on weekends to enjoy music, large-screen television, and movies. Special events include dances, beach volleyball, and talent shows.

Greenville's outdoor recreation facilities include city swimming pools, a skateboard park, several lighted tennis courts, a tennis center, and golf courses for public play. On the 1.5-mile Green Mill Run Greenway, walkers and bikers can discover a variety of birds, plants, and animals.

The Greenville Aquatic and Fitness Center offers an indoor swimming pool, aerobic and fitness classes, and a full fitness center. The Special Programs Office manages training programs for youth and adult athletes with disabilities. Some of the athletic programs offered for special populations include swimming, powerlifting, gymnastics, tennis, basketball, and soccer. Citizens over 55 have the opportunity to keep active and train for participation in the annual Senior Games events. Senior Games include such activities as shuffleboard, ping-pong, horseshoes, and bridge, as well as more active events such as basketball, aerobics, and line dancing.

The Burlington Recreation and Parks Department and Forsyth County Parks and Recreation Department are examples of Category C departments serving populations between 25,000-49,999. The Burlington Parks and Recreation Department has an interesting combination of historical attractions blended with modern facilities. The department was established in 1928 and now has use of more than 1,000 acres of park land and a variety of unique facilities.

City Park is a special park that provides more than seventy seven acres of activities and entertainment for the entire family. One of the three municipally operated amusement areas in the state is located in City Park. One of the highlights of the amusement area is the fully restored Dentzel carousel, which is part of the National Register of Historic Places. The annual Burlington Carousel Festival attracts thousands of visitors each year. Other City Park events include a concert series and baseball and softball tournaments.

Other public parks offer championship golf courses; a nationally recognized BMX (bicycle motorcross) track, where several national races have been held; athletic fields for youth athletic tournaments; indoor gymnasiums and multipurpose rooms; a branch library; and the Burlington Athletic Stadium, which seats more than 3,500 spectators for the city's professional baseball team, the Burlington Indians. The Historic Burlington Depot is a treasure of the Burlington Recreation and Parks Department; it serves as an attractive multipurpose facility for indoor and outdoor events year-round. Several municipal lakes provide water sports, fishing, and relaxation in an aquatic setting. The Burlington Recreation and Parks Department continues to acquire and develop park land and park resources needed to provide quality leisure services for the entire community.

Forsyth County Parks and Recreation Department was founded in 1975. The recreation programs are typical of many county parks and recreation departments in that they use various school facilities for their financially self-sufficient recreation program. The department's park system encompasses 1,300 acres at thirteen sites. Forsyth County parks range in size from the one-acre River Park to the 492-acre Horizons Park. Each park has its own special flavor, ranging from athletic complexes like Union Cross Park with lighted fields, tennis courts, and basketball courts to a large regional park such as Horizon Park.

Triad Park is jointly owned and funded by Forsyth and Guilford counties. This regional park is a great example of cooperation between county governments. It is a flagship of cooperation and dedication, showing the best of what communities can do when they work together for the common good. A total of 414 acres have been bought by the counties as a regional centerpiece park that has nature-based park facilities nestled in the woods and meadows. The park plan leaves the majority of the park land in its natural state. This park, which is currently being developed, will feature an amphitheater, picnic facilities, eighteen acre lake, disc golf course, orienteering course, hiking trails, horse trails, mountain bike trails, mountain bicycle area, natural wetlands and interpretive area, agricultural and equestrian area, a 15,000-square-foot multipurpose building, camping, and active play areas. In August 1994, Triad Park was awarded a national honor from the National Association of Counties that cited the cooperation of the Forsyth and Guilford County Commissioners in making this joint-county park a reality. The American Society of Landscape Architects presented their merit award to the Triad Park Master Plan in September 1995.

The Tarboro Parks and Recreation Department is an example of a Category D department serving populations of 10,000 to 24,999. Tarboro provides its citizens two multipurpose community centers that include a gymnasium, meeting rooms, fitness center, and a game room; the E. L. Robertson Center for Senior Citizens; and Town Commons, which consists of twelve acres in the heart of downtown and boasts one of two original commons in the United States. Tarboro has six additional parks, including the seventy five acre Western Boulevard Park and the fifty two acre Indian Lake Park. The latter provides a pavilion, an outdoor stage, a seven-acre lake, nature trails, and a nature center. Tarboro provides a full array of quality recreation programs to ensure that all segments of its population are served.

The Southern Pines Recreation and Parks Department is a Category E department serving populations of 5,000 to 9,999. Southern Pines' Recreation and Parks Department is a testimony to the fact that one can live in a small community and still be enriched by excellent programs. Although the department offers a full complement of recreation activities, it specializes in athletic programs, programs for senior citizens, and special events.

The city's six public parks include the 165-acre Reservoir Park, the Camble House Grounds, and the Douglas Community Center. The city is in the process of developing a site master plan for a fifty acre park and is planning new neighborhood parks.

The Zebulon Parks and Recreation Department is representative of a Category F department serving a population of less than 5,000. Zebulon's Parks and Recreation Department features a strong youth sports program providing baseball, softball, basketball, soccer, and karate. Its adult sports program emphasizes men's softball, coed softball, church softball leagues, men's basketball, and an aerobics program. Other children's programs include Sports for Tots and a children's summer activities camp. Special events such as Arts in the Park and special concerts are an important part of Zebulon's programming.

Zebulon provides leisure opportunities at four city-owned parks. Little River Park provides natural areas, two baseball/softball fields, basketball courts, fitness trails, a tot lot, and picnic shelters. The department utilizes school and National Guard facilities for its programs.

Financing Park and Recreation Services

Park and recreation services provided by local governments require broad, continuing support. Public park and recreation services designed to meet the leisure needs of local residents can no more be self-supporting than can education, health, fire protection, law enforcement, welfare, or any other public service. Funds are needed to acquire and develop land for park and recreation purposes, to employ full-time and part-time personnel, to purchase equipment and supplies, and to maintain the areas and facilities needed to support a diversified leisure services program.

Funds allocated for the provision of park and recreation services by local governments in North Carolina vary considerably depending upon the nature and scope of programs and services provided. The measure of per capita spending provides a means of budget comparison between local government units providing park and recreation services. Per capita spending is calculated by the division of the total park and recreation budget by the total population of the local government jurisdiction.

Based on its annual survey of municipal and county expenditures for park and recreation services, the North Carolina Recreation Resources Services reported that in 2004-2005, municipalities with populations of 100,000 or more spent an average of $85.83 per capita, compared with $182.43 for municipalities between 50,000 and 99,999, $86.89 for municipalities between 25,000 and 49,999, and $78.56 for municipalities between 10,000 and 24,999 in population. Raleigh spent more for park and recreation services than any other municipality in North Carolina; its park and recreation department's total budget was in excess of $31 million. Mecklenburg County's park and recreation budget was nearly $28,600,000, and Greensboro's was nearly $22,326,000. On a per capita basis, Raleigh spent $116.42; Mecklenburg County, $45.92; and Greensboro, $128.65.

Municipal park and recreation departments tend to spend more per capita than either joint municipal-county park and recreation departments or county park and recreation departments. The differences in per capita spending reflect, to a great extent, the nature and scope of programs and services provided by municipal and county departments.

Municipal park and recreation departments tend to stress recreation programming and minimize land preservation and resource management. County park and recreation departments tend to function as stewards of the land and place less emphasis on direct provision of programs and services. Because many of the recreation opportunities offered by county departments are of an outdoor nature—camping, hiking, fishing, boating, picnicking, nature trails, walking paths, open space areas, etc., which require little supervision of professional staff—the lower per capita spending is not surprising. It is expected that per capita spending by county park and recreation departments will increase over time as new programs and services are initiated.

Funds needed to support park and recreation services may be classified as either current operating expenditures or capital expenditures. Current operating expenditures include personnel salaries and benefits, materials and supplies, contractual services, communication and transportation expenses, rent, insurance, and other regularly occurring expenditures. Capital expenditures include expenditures for non-expendable equipment, major renovation projects, and acquisition and development of areas and facilities of a substantial nature. Current operating funds generally come from general fund appropriations and user fees and charges. Funds for capital expenditures most often come from bonds, gifts and donations, and government grants.

According to the North Carolina Recreation Resources Service, the most frequently reported current operating expenditures by local park and recreation departments in North Carolina during 2004-2005 were personnel, contracted operations, materials and supplies, maintenance and repairs, contracted personnel, travel and training, and a category called other operations. By far the largest current operating expenditure reported was *personnel. Contracted services* are the second most reported current operating expenditure. Increased usage of contractual services and contracted personnel tends to be cost efficient and enhance departmental flexibility in the delivery of programs and services.

New development, land acquisition, revitalization of existing areas, and equipment purchases were the most frequently reported capital expenditures by park and recreation departments in North Carolina during 2004-2005. Emphasis on new development and land acquisition suggests the park and recreation and parks departments recognize the need for additional park and recreation resources and are relying more heavily on local revenue sources to fund such projects, since federal and state grants are no longer readily available to support capital developments. Revitalization of existing areas and facilities may indicate that some local governments have experienced deterioration of existing park and recreation infrastructures and that more emphasis is being placed on local revenues to deal with the problem. It seems likely that local governments will rely even more on local revenues to maintain park and recreation infrastructures unless new sources of federal and state assistance become available.

Local governments in North Carolina use a variety of revenue sources to fund park and recreation services. Revenue sources may be categorized as either "own-source" revenues or "intergovernmental revenues." The major sources of own-source revenues are property taxes, non-property taxes, user fees and charges, and debt proceeds. Intergovernmental revenues consist of federal and state assistance to local governments to support the provision of public services, including parks and recreation.

Local governments primarily fund park and recreation services through their own sources of revenues. State law permits local governments to appropriate local tax funds for park and recreation services. Most funds used to support park and recreation services offered by local governments come from the general appropriation fund; all other revenue sources are supplementary. The general appropriation fund is a non-restricted fund into which most self-generated revenues are placed. All local governments in North Carolina have a general fund. General fund revenues are derived primarily from local taxes. There are a number of different types of local taxes, including property taxes, general and selective sales taxes, and special product and service taxes. The property tax, which is usually levied on real estate and personal property, continues to be the major source of funding for park and recreation departments in North Carolina. Local non-property taxes (e.g., general and selective sales taxes) generate a relatively small portion of total department budgets; however, local non-property taxes appear to be increasing in importance as a revenue source for some park and recreation departments in the state. Non-property taxes provide local governments with a source of revenue diversification. Specifically, non-property taxes allow local governments to collect revenue from nonresidents and to generate revenue from residents who do not own real property.

Fees and charges represent a major revenue source for park and recreation services at the local level. Using fees and charges to supplement general fund appropriations has become a common practice in park and recreation departments in North Carolina. Some park and recreation departments choose to collect fees and charges as a source of revenue diversification to improve the quality of their programs and services. Some local governments even mandate that park and recreation departments recover specific percentages of their general fund allocations through user fees and charges. Both the number of park and recreation departments using fees and charges and the revenue generated by fees and charges have significantly increased since the much-heralded tax revolt movement of the late 1970s.

Most park and recreation authorities in North Carolina agree that basic park and recreation services should be provided without charge to local residents when sufficient funds are available from general fund appropriations. With the current focus on reducing local taxes and maximizing government efficiency, few if any park and recreation departments can provide quality programs without charging user fees for some services. Fees and charges are most frequently made for: 1) specialized facilities such as golf courses, swimming pools, and tennis courts, which require intensive maintenance; 2) services involving special privileges; 3) programs requiring higher than average costs for materials used; 4) rental of specialized equipment such as cameras, golf clubs, and ski equipment; 5) programs requiring additional or highly specialized instruction; 6) exclusive use of a facility by an individual or group; and 7) use of facilities, programs, and services by non-residents.

The use of fees and charges to support park and recreation services depends, to a large extent, on local conditions: demand for programs and services, general fund appropriations available, ability of residents to pay, and the general philosophy of professional staff and local officials. As would be expected, revenue generated by fees and charges varies considerably. Some parks and recreation departments generate a relatively small percentage of their operating budgets through fees and charges, while other park and recreation departments generate a significant percentage.

Local governments in North Carolina have the authority to issue bonds to finance capital acquisitions and improvements. Bonds represent a form of deferred payment that allow local governments to spread the cost of large-scale capital projects over a number of years. State law places a limit of bond indebtedness on local governments. General obligation bonds are the type of bonds most often used to finance the acquisition and development of large local parks and the construction of major areas and facilities such as golf courses, swimming pools, and community centers. General obligation bonds are payable from general fund appropriations of the municipality or county issuing the bonds. Voter approval at either a general or special election is generally required before local governments issue general obligation bonds for park and recreation functions.

Gifts, donations, and requests have played a major role in the provision of park and recreation services in many municipalities and counties in North Carolina. Park and recreation departments often receive gifts of land, buildings, structures, etc. from civic-minded individuals or groups, industries or business firms, and philanthropic organizations. Such gifts, donations, and bequests afford local governments the opportunity to acquire and develop property for park and recreation purposes without overburdening taxpayers. Greensboro and Forsyth County are two examples of local governments that have benefitted significantly from gifts, donations, and bequests. Greensboro's Bryan Park features two eighteen hole championship golf courses complete with practice facilities and a fully-equipped pro shop and grill. The Bryan Enrichment Center offers spacious conference rooms, recreation areas, and scenic terraces. The soccer complex, operated by the Greensboro Youth Soccer Association, features eleven fields designed for seasonal and tournament play. Additional park facilities include picnic shelters, miniature golf, volleyball courts, tennis courts, horseshoe pits, a playground, and the Lake Townsend Marina. Much of the land acquisition and facility development at Bryan Park resulted from contributions from Joseph M. Bryan and his family to the City of Greensboro. Tanglewood contains two eighteen hole championship golf courses, a swimming pool, hotel accommodations, a campground, horse stables and riding trails, miniature golf, and many other recreation facilities. Tanglewood hosts numerous special events annually, including the Vantage Golf Tournament and the Festival of Lights. Tanglewood, which is operated by the Forsyth County Park Authority, Incorporated, was acquired by Forsyth County from the Reynolds Foundation. Financial assistance from the Z. Smith Reynolds Foundation helped to make the acquisition possible. Careful consideration should be given to special restrictions placed on gifts of real or personal property. Only those gifts permitted by state law may be accepted.

Local governments in North Carolina have traditionally received substantial financial support from the federal government to finance capital developments for park and recreation services. The Land and Water Conservation Fund, Community Development Block Grants, and the Urban Parks and Recreation Recovery Program were major federal programs providing funds to support capital improvements for park and recreation purposes during the 1960s and 1970s. Federal funding has been reduced significantly in recent years. Some federal revenue sources have been eliminated, while others have experienced significant reductions. For example, the Land and Water Conservation Fund, established in 1965 to provide matching funds to the states and their political subdivisions for the acquisition of land and development of outdoor recreation areas, has been virtually eliminated. Federal appropriations for state and local assistance have slipped over the past decade to less than 10 percent of total Land and Water Conservation Fund appropriations.

Federal cutbacks in funding to the state and its political subdivisions had a significant impact on land acquisition and park development during the 1980s and 1990s. To assure the provision of park and recreation services, the 1995 General Assembly established the North Carolina Park and Recreation Trust Fund, which became a permanent, dedicated funding source for state parks and local governments to acquire and develop park and recreation areas. The number of dollars deposited in the trust fund will continue to fluctuate each year according to revenue generated from the states' share of the deed transfer tax. The North Carolina Parks and Recreation Trust Fund is discussed in greater detail in Chapter 6.

Career Opportunities

Career opportunities in North Carolina's county and municipal park and recreation departments are numerous and varied. Careers in park and recreation services in North Carolina are listed in two major categories: recreation program services and park/natural resource management. Recreation program services are concerned with the delivery of recreation programs. Examples of positions in recreation include superintendent of recreation, recreation supervisor, center director, dance specialist, athletic supervisor, and teen supervisor. Park/natural resource management deals with the design, construction, and maintenance of outdoor facilities, parks, and natural areas. Examples of positions in this area include superintendent of parks, park supervisor, area planner, maintenance supervisor, and landscape architect.

The following are listings of typical staff positions in North Carolina, with brief descriptions and estimated median salaries that accompany the positions:

1. Director of Parks and Recreation: The chief executive officer (CEO) is responsible for the organization's philosophical direction, policies and procedures, and organization of human, physical, and financial resources. The administrator directs a comprehensive recreation program for the municipality/county and evaluates all resources and programs. The median salary for this position varies by county and municipality size, ranging from $32,026 to $92,421.
2. Assistant Director of Parks and Recreation: A general assistant to the director of recreation and parks. The assistant director often acts for the director in his/her absence and heads many special projects, such as budget planning and in-service training. This person ensures that policies and procedures are carried out properly and handles personnel, public relations, evaluations, finance, and legal details. Median salary for this position varies by county and municipality size, ranging from $36,297 to $59,218.
3. Supervisor of Recreation: Accountable for all recreation programs, services, and facilities for a district or large geographic area; or responsible for the planning, organization, marketing, supervision, and evaluation of a specialized activity grouping such as sports, teens, dance, outdoor recreation, or senior citizens at a city/county-wide level. Median salary for this position varies by county and municipality size, ranging from $19,000 to $50,829.
4. Supervisor of Parks: Manages the operation of a park district or geographic area; supervises educational and interpretive programs; works with community groups in

horticulture-related activities; directs personnel in job assignments, conducts training sessions and monitors work crews; and promotes and assists in environmental protection, land acquisition, and conservation stewardship of ecosystems and natural resources at the local level. Median salary for this position varies by county and municipality size, ranging from $23,766 to $49,221.

5. Athletic Director: Responsible for the planning, organization, supervision, evaluation, and implementation of a comprehensive municipal/county-wide sports program. The program may include daily and seasonal recreational sports programs such as leagues, tournaments, and special events. Median salaries for these positions vary by county and municipality size, ranging from $20,697 to $51,358.

Recent Trends in Local Government Parks and Recreation

A number of trends have emerged in the provision of parks and recreation by local governments in North Carolina in recent years. Selected trends are highlighted in the following paragraphs.

Greenways and walking trails: Greenways provide a scenic and environmentally friendly walkway and bike path for the enjoyment of walkers, runners, bicyclists, in-line skaters, and nature enthusiasts. Most cities/towns in North Carolina now either have a greenway or plan to develop one. In addition, many municipalities have a proposed plan for the growth and development of a comprehensive trail system as part of a greenway master plan. Greenway trails in Raleigh connect many of its parks. In addition, many of Raleigh's major ecological features can be experienced in their natural state along the greenway. The Capital Area Greenway in Raleigh became a reality in 1974, after the city became concerned over rapid growth and urbanization. The Parks and Recreation Department responded with a greenway master plan that permitted urban development while preserving Raleigh's characteristic natural beauty. A forty six mile, 3,000 acre system now exists and continues to grow.

Skate/BMX parks: After receiving a petition in the early 1990s from over one hundred parents and children complaining that the children had nowhere to ride other than the streets, the Greenville Recreation and Parks Department built its first skate ramp. Since the construction of this small wooden ramp, participation in skateboarding and BMX (bicycle motorcross) bike freestyle riding has grown considerably all over the United States. On the cutting edge of skate/BMX parks since the beginning of their popularity, Greenville has attracted some of the nation's best BMX riders, leading ESPN commentators to call Greenville Pro Town USA for BMX bikers. Skate parks and multi-use skate/BMX parks are now practically a standard in most North Carolina cities.

BMX tracks: While many parks and recreation departments allow BMX bikers to use their skate parks, some departments provide facilities geared specifically to BMX bikes. Their rationale is that parks that allow BMX bike use need to be structurally designed to withstand potential damage to the concrete and/or ramps. For instance, a higher psi concrete is needed, as well as protecting exposed concrete edges with steel to limit the chipping and chunking in the concrete that occurs when a bike peg hits the concrete. In addition, thicker gauge steel is needed for coping; and all coping and edge plates must be tightly secured with anchors spaced more frequently than needed in skate-only facilities.

The BMX track offered at Wilkes County's The Edge Skate Park and BMX Bike Track provides a dirt track as well as dirt mounds designed specifically for BMX bikes.

Disc golf: To accommodate demands for one of the fastest-growing sports in America, disc golf courses have grown at an average of 17 percent between 1980 and 1999 (Siniscalchi, 2005). Disc golf courses allow departments to provide recreational opportunities with limited financial resources while protecting valuable natural and cultural resources. An advantage to disc golf over ball golf is that disc golf courses are usually incorporated into existing landscape, rather than designed and artificially landscaped. In addition, maintenance needs beyond what would need to be done to maintain the parkland are negligible. For participants, the major advantages of disc golf are that there is usually no charge to play and equipment costs are minimal. Courses can be found in parks across the state, including an eighteen hole course operated by the New Hanover County Parks and Recreation Department and a nine hole course at Stumpy Creek Park, operated by the Iredell County Parks and Recreation Department.

Dog parks: Stricter enforcement of leash laws has led to a rise in the development of off-leash dog parks. Charlotte opened its first off-leash dog park in 2002 to over 500 dogs on the first day (Leschin-Hoar, 2005). A local dog park association, FiDO-Carolina (Fellowship in Dog Ownership), was instrumental in providing political allies, additional funding, maintenance, and support for the new park. To address the needs of residents in different areas of the county, all wanting off-leash areas in their district, FiDO-Carolina and the Mecklenberg County Park and Recreation Department created an Off-Leash Dog Area Advisory Council (OLDAAC). The council, chaired by a park commissioner, consists of nine appointed citizens and serves as a liaison between the department and county residents by advising on issues of marketing, memberships, partnerships, programming, and long-range planning. The department has committed to building nine off-leash areas.

Open space acquisition and land conservation: Recent research suggests that open space, or undeveloped land, contributes to the environmental and financial well-being of an area by helping it avoid problems associated with development, including: water drainage, soil erosion, air and water pollution, the destruction of animal habitats, and the congestion-related issues of traffic, noise, safety, and increased taxes needed to sustain the additional burdens on existing infrastructure (Crompton, 2004). Several cities and counties (Wake County, Guilford County, Town of Cary) have included the acquisition of open space as one of the top priorities in their parks and recreation master plans. Multiple bond referenda have passed to bring this goal to fruition. According to the Guilford County Open Space Report, voters considered 148 separate referenda in 1998 regarding the acquisition of open space, 84 percent of which passed, resulting in about $5.28 billion dollars in funding (Guilford County Community Development Department [GCCDD], 2000). In 2000, Wake County voters passed a $15 million bond referendum to establish the Wake County Open Space Preservation Program (wakegov.com, 2005). Between 2000 and 2005, Wake County spent approximately $12 million to acquire or partner in the acquisition of more than 1,800 acres of open space at a cost to its partners of about $11 million. In 2004, voters passed a second bond referendum for $26 million, to be earmarked for the continuation of the Open Space Preservation Program, with the county's long-term goal to protect 30,000 acres of open space. Types of land most frequently considered appropriate for acquisition and preservation include:

- Suitable properties adjacent to existing parks and open space lands
- Wetlands, meadows, and mature forests
- Creek, stream, and river corridors
- Groundwater recharge areas
- Buffers for drinking water supply, lakes, and streams
- Corridors connecting parks, open spaces, schools, neighborhoods
- Sites of geologic or historic importance
- Sites providing significant plant or wildlife habitat
- Sites providing significant water quality protection
- Additional sites as indicated by an open space program map or master plan (GCCDD, 2000)

Use of natural landscaping: According to Greco (2005), public park designers in America are beginning to reexamine their design principles to adopt more natural, sustainable environments. Three benefits of this trend include opportunities to provide parks with "historically accurate aesthetics, environmentally desirable habitats and financially appealing budgets" (Greco, 2005, p. 71). When natural flora is present, local fauna is more attracted to the park; and maintenance costs are lower due to decreased needs for irrigation and mowing. The biggest challenge to providing natural landscapes is that they are often less colorful or exotic than what visitors to parks expect. An example of the use of natural landscaping in a park can be found at Fayetteville's J. Bayard Clark Park.

Learning Exercises

1. Contact a local recreation and park manager. Discuss several of the current issues that are confronting this individual and the agency. Are any of these concerns reflected in this chapter?

2. Compare the recreation and park offerings of your home town or county with those of a nearby town or county. What are the similarities and differences? Draw some conclusions about the quality of leisure services provided in each area.

3. Review the Web sites of several North Carolina parks and recreation departments. Do you notice any of the trends identified in the trends discussion at the end of this chapter? Are any other trends evident?

References

Crompton, J.L. (2004). *The Proximate Principle: The Impact of Parks, Open Space and Water Features on Residential Property Values and the Property Tax Base.* Ashburn, VA: National Recreation and Park Association.

Greco, J.A. (2005). It's only natural. *Parks & Recreation, 40* (4), 70-73.

Guilford County Community Development Department. (2000). *Guilford County open space report.* Retrieved May 31, 2005, from http://www.co.guilford.nc.us/government/planning1/devord/open_spa.html.

Hjelte, G, & Shivers, J. (1978). *Public Administration of Recreational Services.* (2nd ed.). Philadelphia: Lea & Febiger.

Leschin-Hoar, C. (2005). Fighting for Fido. *Parks & Recreation, 40* (1), 32-36.

North Carolina Recreation Resources Service. (2005). *North Carolina Parks and Recreation Services study, fiscal year 2004-2005.* Raleigh, North Carolina: Author. Retrieved June 19, 2005, from http://natural-resources.ncsu.edu/rrs/mcprss_05.pdf

Jensen, C.R. (1995). *Outdoor Recreation in America.* (5th ed.). Champaign, Illinois: Human Kinetics.

Kraus, R.,& Curtis, J. (2000). *Creative Management in Recreation, Parks and Leisure Services.* (6th ed.). St. Louis, Missouri: McGraw-Hill Higher Education.

Sessoms, H..D. & Henderson, K.A. (1994). *Introduction to Leisure Services.* (7th ed.). State College, Pennsylvania: Venture Publishing, Inc.

Siniscalchi, J. (2005). Flying saucers. *Parks & Recreation, 40* (1), 42-47.

Chapter 6

State and Federal Recreation Service

Wayne Williams and James P. Drummond

Federal Agencies in North Carolina

All levels of government are involved with provision of leisure services. Each level enacts laws regulating public behavior, provides programs and activities, and manages resources. Local governments tend to be more concerned with programming and provision of services while state and federal governments tend to focus on resource management and legislation.

The National Park Service, U.S. Forest Service, U.S. Fish and Wildlife Service, U.S. Army Corps of Engineers and Tennessee Valley Authority are responsible for managing a collection of scenic, historic and natural recreation resources in North Carolina.

National Park Service

National parks have been described as a nation's "crown jewels" and "living museums." The National Park Service (NPS) preserves, protects, and provides for appropriate recreational use of these unique natural and cultural resources. Ten operational areas typical of NPS diversity are found in North Carolina. The Great Smoky Mountains National Park straddles the Tennessee-North Carolina border and encompasses over 500,000 acres. A greater number of plant and animal species dwell within its boundaries than within the entire continent of Europe. This park provides opportunities for camping, biking, fishing, and trail hiking (including access to the Appalachian Trail, America's first national trail). Given its natural beauty and central location in the eastern United States, it is not surprising that the Great Smoky Mountains National Park annually experiences more visitation than any national park with more than 10.3 million visits in 1999.

Unique also is the Blue Ridge Parkway, this nation's first recreational roadway, which connects Shenandoah National Park in Virginia with Great Smoky Mountains National Park. Much of this scenic drive is above 3,000 feet in elevation, providing numerous scenic vistas. Utilization of the Parkway generates an estimated $2 billion annual economic impact in adjacent communities in North Carolina and Virginia.

Other firsts include the original English settlement in North America on land that is now designated Fort Raleigh National Historic Site. Wilbur and Orville Wright achieved the first sustained flight in a heavier-than-air machine in 1903; Kill Devil Hill is now enshrined as the Wright Brothers National Memorial.

Cape Hatteras Lighthouse, the tallest brick lighthouse in America, was reopened in May 2000 after being moved 2,900 feet inland from its original site due to threatening erosion. Other national parks in North Carolina include Moore's Creek National Battleground, Guilford County Courthouse National Military Park, Carl Sandburg Home National Historic Site, and Cape Lookout National Seashore.

The National Wild and Scenic Rivers Act and the National Trails System Act

Congress passed the National Wild and Scenic Rivers Act in 1968. The act protects rivers from dam construction, channelization, and mining while recognizing them for their outstanding scenic, recreational, geologic, historical, cultural, or other natural values. Based upon how much development has taken place along their flow, rivers are designated as wild, scenic, or recreational. Rivers are added to the system by an act of Congress, or by the secretary of the interior upon a request from a governor. Four North Carolina rivers have been designated as scenic or recreational.

The New River in the northwestern part of the state was one of the first rivers in the nation to receive this protection. The New is a state- protected river, indicating that its shoreline is primarily private property rather than state or national property. The New features pastoral and wooded hillside scenery, fishing, and canoe-in camping at three state park units. The 26.5-mile designated portion of the river runs from Dog Creek to the Virginia state line. The Lumber River, in southcentral North Carolina, is also state managed and has a mixed designation of eighty one miles of scenic and recreational waters that offer canoeing, fishing, and wildlife viewing.

The Horsepasture in the Nantahala National Forest has the shortest length of any designated river in the system, at only 4.2 miles. However, that short stretch contains five major waterfalls including Rainbow Falls with 125 feet of vertical drop. The headwaters of Wilson Creek are at the base of Grandfather Mountain in the Pisgah National Forest, and 15.8 miles of its length are designated as a mix of scenic and recreational waters. This mountain stream provides whitewater canoeing/kayaking and excellent trout fishing.

The National Scenic Trails System Act, also passed in 1968, created a two tiered system of trails. The Appalachian Trail, established in 1921, was officially recognized as a national scenic trail in the 1968 act. National scenic or historic trails are designated by an act of Congress, and must be of national interest.

North Carolina includes parts of two other trails in this category, the Trail of Tears National Historic Trail (TTNHT) and the Overmountain Victory National Trail (OVNHT). The TTNHT is a memorial to members of the Cherokee Tribe who were forcibly removed from their ancestral lands in the Southeast to Oklahoma. Thousands died in the process of making the 2,200-mile land and water trip across what is now nine states. The OVNHTcommemorates the route taken by Revolutionary War patriots from the Appalachian Mountains frontier to the battle of Kings Mountain on the North Carolina-South Carolina border. There, the patriots were victorious, setting in motion a series of battles in the South that led to the surrender of the British at Yorktown and independence for the colonies.

More local in character, national recreation trails are far too numerous in the state to list here. These trails are on federal, state, local and even private property. No act of Congress is required, but these trails must meet quality standards as approved by the National Park Service and be open to the public. They include trails in national forests, national parks, state parks, city and county parks, greenways, and trails on Grandfather Mountain. This trail recognition program has spurred the development of hundreds of local exercise, recreation, and nature trails across the nation.

U.S. Forest Service

The U.S. Forest Service (USFS) is dedicated to multiple-use and sustained yield management of water, rangeland, wildlife, timber and recreation resources. Under this mandate, a management policy structure provides a combination of public uses while ensuring productivity of the natural resource base.

Modern American forestry began in North Carolina on land that was once part of the 100,000-acre Biltmore Estate. In 1892 George Vanderbilt hired Gifford Pinchot to manage his forest lands. Pinchot later became the first director of the USFS under President Theodore Roosevelt and subsequently directed a phenomenal growth in national forest holdings.

Pinchot was succeeded by Dr. Carl Schenck as manager of Biltmore forests. Dr. Schenck established the nation's first school of forestry in 1898 on land that is now home to the Cradle of Forestry museum and historic site near Brevard. Frederick Law Olmsted, who designed New York's Central Park with Calvert Vaux, served as original landscape architect for the Biltmore Estate.

Sale of a large portion of the Biltmore Estate to the USFS provided the nucleus of Pisgah National Forest, America's first eastern forest. Along with Pisgah are three additional national forests in North Carolina, Croatan, Nantahala and Uhwarrie, totaling more than one million acres.

Located within these forests are sixty three recreational areas with opportunities for boating, fishing, camping, hunting, biking, picnicking, whitewater boating, and swimming. A 1,700 mile network of trails including 200 miles of the Appalachian Trail and portions of the North Carolina Mountains-To-Sea Trail lie within these national forests, along with eleven designated wilderness areas encompassing 100,000 acres and the Horsepasture National Scenic River.

U.S. Army Corps of Engineers

Although not as extensive in operation as the National Park Service and U.S. Forest Service, the Army Corps of Engineers has influenced development of outdoor recreation through a series of reservoir impoundments. Upon completion of John H. Kerr Reservoir in 1953, recreation lakeshores were leased to North Carolina's Kerr Reservoir

Development Commission. In 1971, this commission was merged with the North Carolina State Parks and Recreation Commission.

Thirty years later, shorelines of two very popular Corps reservoirs, Lake Jordan and Falls Lake, were added to the North Carolina State Park system under ninety nine year leases to be used as recreation areas. W. Kerr Scott Reservoir near Wilkesboro is operated independently by the Corps and offers opportunities for camping, hunting, picnicking, fishing, swimming, and boating. In addition, boating access, fishing, and picnicking are available at Cape Fear River locks and dams.

Tennessee Valley Authority

Similar to the Army Corps of Engineers, the Tennessee Valley Authority (TVA) provides water-based recreation opportunities through an extensive series of reservoirs, including Fontana and Chatuga Lakes in North Carolina.

Formed as a federal government corporation in 1933, TVA administers reservoirs and surrounding lands primarily for flood control, navigation, and hydropower generation. Included in its management plan are extensive recreation facilities and natural resource based recreational opportunities.

U.S. Fish and Wildlife Service

A system of eleven refuges encompassing approximately 257,000 acres of land and water is managed by the U.S. Fish and Wildlife Service. This network of resources provides habitat for hundreds of species of plants and animals, including approximately sixty endangered species. Among these endangered animals is the red wolf, which has been reintroduced at Alligator River and Pocosin Lake refuges.

Management plans for refuges allow for wildlife observation, photography, boating, hiking, fishing, and controlled hunts. Cooperative agreements at some locations allow farmers to plant and harvest crops with an understanding that some portion will remain for wildlife.

Department of Defense

Each military installation in North Carolina offers special services operations providing leisure activities to active and retired military personnel and their families. Programs at Fort Bragg, Camp Lejune, Seymour Johnson, and Pope Field offer a full range of recreation facilities and programs. Military bases such as Fort Bragg and Camp Lejeune cover thousands of acres, providing habitat for wildlife and filtration areas for water quality, as well as outdoor recreation opportunities for military personnel, their families, and guests.

Other Federal Agencies

In addition to those federal agencies mentioned above, others such as the Department of Education offer educational grants and training venues for therapeutic recreation specialists. The Department of Health and Human Services provides programs for senior citizens, public housing playgrounds and community center grants. It has been estimated that as many as seventy federal agencies are involved directly and/or indirectly in some aspect of recreation and park services.

Cherokee Land Reservation

Under the Treaty of New Echota in 1835, the Cherokee Tribe was forcibly removed from its ancestral lands and marched on a "Trail of Tears" to an Oklahoma reservation. Treaty articles provided that tribe members who chose to remain in North Carolina might do so, but without U.S. citizenship. Approximately 1,100 stayed and became known as the Eastern Cherokees with limited self government power granted by the North Carolina legislature.

In 1816 federal legislation mandated that a 5,600-acre reservation be held in trust for the Eastern Cherokees. That reservation is located in parts of Cherokee, Graham, Jackson, and Swain counties in western North Carolina.

Tourism is the primary economic producer on and near reservation lands. Outdoor activities such as hiking and fishing attract visitors, as does "Unto These Hills", an outdoor drama that portrays removal of the Cherokees to Oklahoma.

In late 1997, Harrah's Cherokee Casino opened as a 275,000-square-foot facility featuring 60,000 square feet of gaming area with 2,400 video-based gaming machines. Contained within are three restaurants, extensive entertainment/meeting space and child care facility open twenty four hours per day seven days per week. Tribal Bingo is currently being relocated to casino premises in order to access available amenities there; both operations are enterprises of the Eastern Band of Cherokee Indians.

Contemporary Federal Legislation

The Intermodal Surface Transportation Efficiency Act (ISTEA) -1991 and TEA 21- 1998 are administered by the U.S. Department of Transportation. This legislation provides funding for pedestrian and bicycle trails, acquisition of scenic easements, historic preservation and recreation utilization of abandoned railroad corridors. While focused on projects that enhance commuting and travel by means other than automobiles, one of the results of this legislation has been to expand and improve recreation trails and greenways. The East Coast Greenway, a proposed 2,600- mile bicycle trail from Maine to Florida, has received over $500 million from this grant program. See www.greenway.org for information on this new bike trail.

State Agencies in North Carolina

Protecting, conserving, and preserving native flora and fauna of North Carolina is founded on game laws from the Colonial past. Today, the many divisions and bureaus of the Department of Environment and Natural Resources play major roles in the conservation of North Carolina's natural resources. A brief description of state agencies and programs involved in parks and recreation in North Carolina follows.

Department of Environment and Natural Resources

The North Carolina Constitution and State Parks Acts (1925 and 1987) gave the **Division of Parks and Recreation** a twin charge of managing natural resources for present use and enjoyment while preserving these natural treasures as part of a heritage that will be passed along to future generations.

A concern for natural resource quality late in the nineteenth century led to establishment of Mount Mitchell as North Carolina's first state park in 1916. Currently twenty nine parks and four recreation areas along with twenty five other operational units on over 170, 000 acres comprise a diverse state park system. A historical perspective and other related issues are provided in more detail in the introductory, outdoor recreation, and camping chapters.

Gorges State Park, located in Transylvania County west of Asheville, is the newest addition to the system. Covering 7,100 acres of parkland adjoining 2,900 acres of north Carolina Wildlife Resources Commission gamelands, it is a significant natural area with a 2,000 foot change in elevation and numerous rare and endangered species. The park master plan is still in development as of this writing.

The Division of Parks and Recreation, in cooperation with North Carolina State University (NCSU), offers technical and planning assistance to recreation and leisure agencies through **Recreation Resources Service** (RRS). With headquarters on the NCSU campus, RRS supports regional consultants throughout the state who provide advice on design, grants, accessibility, and safety to local recreation agencies. RRS produces publications on recreation and park design, playground safety, and grantsmanship, and maintains a list of job openings in the field. RRS staff present regional workshops and distance learning programs as well. For more information, visit their web site at www.cfr.ncsu.edu/rrs/.

Through a comprehensive **State Trails Program**, the Division of Parks and Recreation assists organizations in planning, developing and managing a statewide system of trails including greenways; hiking, biking and horse trails; river trails; and off-highway vehicle trails. The State Trails Program originated in 1973 with passage of the North Carolina Trails System Act and employs a staff of three regional trails specialists.

State and federal legislation, including North Carolina's Adopt-A-Trail Grant (1996) and the National Recreational Trail Funding Program, provided approximately $1.3 million in 2000 for trail development. Perhaps the most ambitious project is a 700-mile "Mountains to Sea Trail" extending from Clingman's Dome to Jockey's Ridge on the coast.

The North Carolina Natural and Scenic Rivers System is a program intended to preserve and protect outstanding free-flowing rivers, river quality and adjacent lands for the benefit of present and future generations. Four rivers have been designated since 1971. In 1985, the General Assembly passed the **Natural Heritage Program** with the following mandate:

1. Conduct biological inventories through statewide identifications and evaluations.
2. Sponsor county-based natural area inventories in cooperation with local

governments and local land trusts. Significant natural areas are identified and incorporated into the local land-use and conservation-planning process.

3. Maintain biological and mapping system databases.
4. Disseminate information on rare plants and animals.
5. Maintain a priority protection list of significant natural areas.
6. Assist and encourage landowners in voluntary protection of significant   natural areas, plants, and animals.

The Division of Parks and Recreation coordinates the Land and Water Conservation Fund, a federal funding program established in 1965 to assist in acquisition, planning and development of outdoor recreation resources nationwide. Currently six full-time consultants employed by the Department of Environment and Natural Resources coordinate new and ongoing LWCF grants. Many scholars have declared LWCF legislation as one of the most significant events in the development of public parks and recreation in America.

As a result of LWCF "abolition" in 1989, many states sought stable funds for park and recreation planning and development. Thus in 1994, the North Carolina General Assembly created the **Parks and Recreation Trust Fund** (PRTF). Seventy-five cents of each dollar of "deed transfer tax" (state's share) is dedicated to the Parks and Recreation Trust Fund. In 2005, this fund provided approximately $10 million with 65 percent for state parks, 30 percent for local parks on a dollar per dollar matching basis and 5 percent for coastal and beach access programs. The maximum matching grant for municipalities and counties was increased to $500,000, and thirty six communities benefited from this program in 2005.

Another fiscal milestone was passage of a $35 million State Park Bond Referendum in 1993. These funds were utilized for land acquisition and capital improvements at new and existing park and recreation sites. Through these expenditures, a trend in which North Carolina state parks ranked forty ninth nationally in per capita expenditures for operation and maintenance was reversed.

Several other grant programs are administered under the Department of Environment and Natural Resources. **The Clean Water Management Trust Fund** was created by the General assembly in 1996 to clean up pollution in the state's surface waters and to protect and conserve those waters not yet polluted. From 1997 to 2004 the fund provided $485,633,003 for projects that enhance water quality throughout the state. Local governments, state agencies, and non-profit organizations received funding that was used to acquire waterfront property, purchase conservation easements, and restore lake and river shorelines. In addition to improving water quality, canoeists, anglers, hikers and campers benefit from the environmental improvements made possible by this legislation.

The North Carolina Natural Heritage Trust Fund, established in 1987, is funded from the sale of personalized license plates and a portion of the deed stamp tax. These funds are used for acquiring natural lands for state parks, preserves, wildlife conservation areas, coastal reserves, natural and scenic rivers, historic site properties and other outdoor recreation and natural areas. In 2004, $12 million was made available to state agencies under this program.

In 1999, citizens expressed concern about preservation of open space to the Smart Growth Commission. As a result, the North Carolinia General Assembly created the

Million Acre Initiative (MAI) in 2000. The MAI is a collaborative endeavor to protect an additional one million acres of open space in the state by the end of 2009. The Department of Environment and Natural Resources is coordinating this massive effort. Not a new grant program, the MAI is funded through existing federal, state, local and private sources. If successful, the program will conserve an additional 3.4 percent of the state's total land area.

The North Carolina Division of Forest Resources works cooperatively with private land owners to develop and protect more than 16.8 million acres of forest land. Three nurseries provide 30-35 million seedlings at cost for annual reforestation projects. A series of six "educational forests" offer various environmental education and outdoor recreation opportunities. Demonstration projects and interpretative trails with "talking trees" provide hiking and nature study with picnic shelters and walk-in tent campsites offering additional recreation choices. Timber products, watersheds and soils, habitat for wildlife, and outdoor recreation areas are all influenced by quality and quantity of well managed forest lands in North Carolina.

North Carolina Aquariums are located on Roanoke Island, Pine Knoll Shores (near Atlantic Beach), and Fort Fisher. Programs and activities are designed to promote an awareness, understanding, conservation and appreciation of coastal North Carolina's diverse cultural and natural aquatic resources. Recent expansions doubled the size of all three aquariums.

The Division of Water Quality conducts comprehensive planning and management of surface and groundwater resources. This division issues pollution control permits, evaluates environmental quality, and carves out enforcement actions for violations of environmental regulations.

The Division of Air Quality serves to conserve and protect air resources. This is accomplished by establishing ambient air quality standards, monitoring air quality, permitting and inspecting stationary air emissions sources, and establishing inspection programs for motor vehicles.

A controversial issue in North Carolina, and all other coastal states, is coastal management. To some degree this issue was addressed by the General Assembly in 1974 with passage of the Coastal Area Management Act administered by the **Division of Coastal Management**. The purpose of this legislation was to strike a balance between use and preservation of coastal resources, taking into consideration conflicting needs and interests of private and public users of coastal lands and waters. In order to establish policies and standards for coastal development, this act created the Coastal Resource Commission (CRC) and Coastal Resources Advisory Council. Fifteen governor-appointed citizens comprise the Commission while representatives of local government, marine science, and other government agencies compose the Council.

One effort administered by the Division of Coastal Management is the Public Beach Access Program begun in 1982. It has been legally established that every citizen has a right to beach access and that beaches are common property. A controversial issue is how visitors can gain access to beaches upon arriving at coastal destinations. More than $2.1 million appropriated by the General Assembly, combined with $2.5 million from federal grants and $2.5 million in local funds, created a system of vitally needed public parking lots, restrooms, dune crossovers, and other related facilities. This action helped guarantee public access to the ocean without infringing upon property rights of those who own beachfront property. Ongoing financing for these projects is provided in the Park and Recreation Trust Fund.

The North Carolina Zoological Park is the first state-supported zoo in America and has benefited from both private and corporate sources as well as state appropriations. Corporate benefactors include Hardee's Food Systems, Pizza Hut Restaurants, R. J. Reynolds Industries, North Carolina Jaycees, and the North Carolina Zoological Society. Public funding has been provided through the General Assembly, Land and Water Conservation Fund, and National Park Service.

Recognized as one of the nation's finest, a primary mission of the zoo is to make visitors aware of connections between humans and animals and plants from throughout the world. This is accomplished with exhibit regions covering more than 500 acres containing 30,000 tropical plants and 1,100 exotic animals featured in exhibits focused on Africa, the Great Plains, North Carolina, etc.

Founded in 1897, **The North Carolina Museum of Natural Sciences** opened its new facility in April 2000. Located in Raleigh, its mission is to collect and preserve state biological diversity, promote environmental awareness, and relate natural sciences to everyday life. This is accomplished through state-of-the-art museum exhibits, outreach programs, and school programs.

North Carolina Wildlife Resources Commision

The North Carolina Wildlife Resources Commission is a "special fund" agency responsible for conservation of state wildlife resources as well as administration of safe boating laws. A significant portion of the funding for this agency is derived from the sale of hunting and fishing licenses. The NCWRC establishes and enforces hunting and fishing seasons and regulations, and conducts wildlife and fisheries research and management programs. The commission manages 2 million acres of public and private lands for public hunting and fishing under the State Game Lands program. Educational programs offered to the public include: environmental and wildlife education workshops, hunter and boater safety education, and boating and fishing access development. The commission publishes the award-winning *Wildlife in North Carolina* magazine and other educational literature.

In 2002 the State Wildlife Grants program was created by the federal government. In 2004 the program provided $75 million to the states for wildlife related projects. In North Carolina, these funds are administered by the NCWRC, and they have supported research on urban wildlife, non-game species, etc. The NCWRC is currently preparing a Statewide Comprehensive Wildlife Conservation Strategy as mandated by the federal government.

Department of Human Resources

Within this unit of state government is the **Division of Mental Health-Developmental Disabilities and Substance Abuse Services**, an agency that oversees state mental hospitals and education-care facilities for those with severe learning disabilities. Each of these facilities provides recreation services for residents. They also employ both therapeutic recreation professionals such as therapists and supervisors as well as recreation assistants and activity specialists. Much of the professional development in therapeutic recreation services has come from leadership provided through these facilities and programs.

Department of Transportation

Since 1987, the Department of Transportation's **Division of Bicycle and Pedestrian Transportation** has allocated funds for independent bicycle projects through the annual Transportation Improvement Program (TIP). More than 2,500 miles of local bike routes and 3,000 miles of cross-state "Bicycling Highway" routes have been mapped. Thousands of bike parking spaces, "share the road" signs, and safe drainage grates have been installed.

Funding for TIP projects increased from $250,000 in 1987 to $3 million in 2000. These funds also provided for completion of a major statewide bicycle safety education and facility development initiative. The Basics of Bicycle curriculum and other companion programs provide training for more than 50,000 elementary school children annually. Joint federal funding from ISTEA and TEA 21 have been prominent in statewide trail projects.

A 1996 publication, "Bicycling and Walking in North Carolina: A Long Range Transportation Plan", articulated the following goals:

1. Provide the bicycle and pedestrian facilities necessary to support mobility needs and economic vitality of communities throughout North Carolina;
2. Provide a comprehensive program of education and enforcement strategies that will improve the safety of all bicyclists and pedestrians;
3. Institutionalize bicycling and walking consideration to enhance current transportation practices at the state, regional, county, and local level;
4. Identify and promote new and innovative ways to advance bicycle and pedestrian safety and enjoyment through research and needs assessment; and
5. Encourage bicycling and walking as viable transportation alternatives.

Department of Public Instruction

Leisure programs conducted by the **Department of Public Instruction** include: Arts Education, Dance Education, Health Education, Physical Education, Sports Medicine, and Middle School Athletics. A general purpose of these programs is to enhance and strengthen lifetime fitness skills for children to be safe, healthy, and physically active. This mission includes providing accurate and timely information and technology for youth to grow into informed adults.

Although not directly involved in the provision of interscholastic sports, the State Board of Education recognizes and works with the **North Carolina High School Athletic Association** (a non-profit voluntary corporation) as the organization responsible for administering high school athletic programs. This association currently has 340 member schools with more than 130,000 student athletes actively involved in interscholastic athletic activities annually. A primary commitment is ". . . to provide a wholesome athletic environment . . .".

Department of Cultural Resources

Several divisions of this department enrich culture and recreation in North Carolina, including the following.

The Division of Archives and History is responsible for preserving and maintaining records of twenty two state historic sites. Its **Archaeology and Historic Preservation** unit assists private citizens, private institutions, local government and agencies of state and federal government in identification, evaluation, protection, and enhancement of properties significant in North Carolina history and archaeology.

Responsibility for promoting and safeguarding the documentary heritage of the state resides with the **Archives and Records** unit. **Historical Publications** generates books, documentary volumes, archival guides, posters, maps, charts, and facsimile documents that relate to North Carolina history. This unit produces the *North Carolina Historical Review*, which is this state's journal of history.

Through cooperative programs with other libraries and organizations, **The State Library** serves government agencies, businesses, and all citizens of the state. In statutory compliance, the State Library provides resources, services, and programs to function as an information distribution system and resource center to promote knowledge, education, commerce, and business.

Supporting excellence and providing opportunity for public experience in arts are responsibilities of the **North Carolina Arts Council** and **North Carolina Museum of Art**. Grants are offered annually to support dance, folklife, literature, music, theater, and interdisciplinary programs.

More than sixty concerts are performed each year by the **North Carolina Symphony** orchestra, a major professional orchestra founded in 1932. In addition, approximately 170 adult and children's performances are sponsored annually to encourage and discover emerging musical talent. A more complete description of arts programs may be found in Chapter 7.

The Governor's Crime Commission has several programs and grants directly related to recreation. It has been shown that recreation intervention and reaction are indeed effective in dealing with juvenile delinquency.

Department of Commerce

The stated mission of the **Division of Tourism, Film and Sport Development** is "to strengthen state's tourism, film and sport industries in order to enhance the economic well being and quality of life for all North Carolinians." This industry accounted for more than $12 billion in 1999.

A system of local grants is administered by the **Division of Tourism** to promote Heritage Tourism throughout North Carolina. In addition, this organization maintains eight welcome centers on interstate highways to assist incoming travelers.

The Sports Development Agency promotes North Carolina as a venue for major amateur and professional events. An estimated $240 million dollars was generated by the

1999 U.S. Golf Open Championship held at Pinehurst. This event was so successful that a decision has been made to return this championship to Pinehurst in 2005.

Television, motion picture, and advertising production locations are promoted by the North Carolina Film Office. This office offers location scout services to producers and supports the state's four regional film commissions in their efforts to increase film production in North Carolina.

Regulatory Functions of State Government

In addition to managing a wide range of recreation resources, the state of North Carolina plays a major role in regulating the formation and functions of municipalities, counties, recreation businesses, and non-profit corporations. These regulatory laws are integral parts of the North Carolina legal statutes. For example, Article 18, SO 160A-354 (known as the "Administration of Parks and Recreation Programs Act") gives city and county governments power and authority to create and operate park and recreation systems as a legitimate function of local and county government. Other statutes enacted by the General Assembly govern such actions as:

1. Creation and operation of recreation-oriented corporations such as ski resorts and commercial campgrounds;
2. Establishment and operation of non-profit corporations such as country clubs, yacht clubs, and rod and gun clubs;
3. Regulation of residential camps;
4. Regulation of swimming pools, amusement park rides, and restaurants including sale of alcoholic beverages;
5. Creation of regional boards and commissions which promote travel and tourism;
6. Cooperative efforts with federal agencies such as the National Park Service and U.S. Forest Service.

Learning Exercises

Information on state and federal recreation services in North Carolina is available on a number of Web sites. Visit the sites below and answer the questions for each.

1. http://www.enr.state.nc.us/
   Click on Divisions/Agencies for information on how the North Carolina Division of Environment and Natural Resources is organized. Next, click on Division of Parks and Recreation to learn about specific state parks in your region of North Carolina. Click on Grant Programs, and answer the following questions about the Parks and Recreation Trust Fund: How are funds divided among state parks, community recreation, etc.? Check the list of current year grants to learn about projects in your community. Also under Grant Programs, click on NC Trails Program and Natural Resource Heritage Trust Fund for information on monies available through these grant programs.

2. http://www.2.ncsu.edu/ncsu/forest_resources/recresource/index.html
   Click on Resources for general information about Recreation Resources Service. Then click on Teleconferences & Workshops, and Publications for listings that might be useful to you.

3. http://www.nps.gov
   Click on Visit Your Parks, By State, and North Carolina for information on National Park operations in North Carolina.

4. http://www.cs.unca.edu:80/nfsnc/
   Click on Forest Facts and Figures for introductory information on national forests in the state. For information on campgrounds, trails, hunting, fishing, boating, etc., click on Outdoor Recreation. Click on Roadless Areas for an update on the ongoing issue of designated roadless areas in national forests in North Carolina.

5. Most college and university libraries have a set of the North Carolina Statutes. Ask a reference librarian for instructions in the use of the statutes and answer the following questions:
    a. What topics are covered in the State Parks System Plan?

    b. How is the principle of eminent domain applied to state parks and forests in North Carolina?

    c. What are the purposes of the North Carolina National Park, Parkway, and Forests Development Council?

6. Locate the nearest reservoir open to public recreation in your region of the state. What agency manages the reservoir, and what recreational opportunities does it offer?

Sources for Further Information

U.S. Government Webmaster
www.lib.lsu.edu/cgi-bin/search.cgi

U.S. Forest Service in North Carolina
PO Box 2750
Asheville, NC 28802
Telephone: (828) 257-4200

National Park Service
Southeast Regional Office
100 Alabama Street S.W.
Atlanta, GA 30303
Telephone: (404) 562-3100

Tennessee Valley Authority
Recreation Resources Program
Forestry Building
Norris, TN 37828

U.S. Army Corps of Engineers
South Atlantic District
P.O. Box 1890
Wilmington, NC 28402
Telephone: (910) 343-4827

U.S. Fish and Wildlife Service
P.O. Box 33096
Raleigh, NC 27636
Telephone: (919) 856-4520

North Carolina Webmaster
www.state.nc.us

NC Department of Commerce—Division of Tourism, Film and Sports Development
Telephone: (919) 733-7651
www.commerce.state.nc.us/tourism

NC Department of Crime Control and Public Safety
Telephone: (919) 733-4564
www.nccrimecontrol.org

NC Department of Cultural Resources
Telephone: (919) 733-5722
www.dcr.state.nc.us

Archives and History	(919) 733-7305
Museum of History	(919) 715-0200
Museum of Art	(919) 839-6262
Arts Council	(919) 733-2111
Symphony	(919) 733-2750
State Library	(919) 733-2570

Department of Environment and Natural Resources
www.enr.nc.us

Division of Parks and Recreation
Telephone: (919) 733-4181
http://ils.unc.edu/parkproject/ncparks.html

NC Zoological Park
Telephone: 1-800-488-0444
www.nczoo.org

NC Aquariums
www.aquariums.state.nc.us

Forest Resources
Telephone: (919) 733-2162
www.dfr.state.nc.us

Wildlife Resources Commission
Telephone: (910) 288-5738
www.wildlife.state.nc.us

Department of Public Instruction
Telephone: (919) 715-1000
www.dpi.state.nc.us

North Carolina High School Athletic Association
Telephone: (919) 962-1686
www.nchsaa.unc.edu

Department of Transportation
Bicycle and Pedestrian Transportation
Telephone: (919) 715-2340
www.dot.state.nc.us/transit.bicycle

Others:

Cherokee Indian Reservation
Telephone: 1-800-357-2771
1-800 438-1601
www.cherokee-nc.com

Chapter 7
Cultural and Community Activities
Nancy J. Gladwell, Beth E. Wilson, and Charlsena F. Stone

Two of the most basic forms of leisure expression, which are sometimes overlooked by students of recreation and parks management, are cultural arts and community activities. These are, respectively, activities that express and explore our heritage and activities that give us a sense of community. Examples include: theater productions performed by community members for community audiences; local museums and art galleries that display exhibits making us more aware of whence we came; Fourth of July celebrations; festivals that celebrate the ethnic roots of North Carolinians; trips to the North Carolina Zoological Park; and neighborhood block parties with food, games, song, and fellowship.

Given the independent spirit of North Carolinians and the diversity of ethnic, racial, and religious groups in our state, the need for cultural events and community activities is considerable. These activities help us express what we are, what we have been, and what we want to be. They serve as a counterforce to the independent, competitive, and aggressive activities that are so much a part of our popular culture.

The personal and social benefits derived from involvement in cultural and community activities can be substantial. Examples of such benefits are enhanced self-esteem for the participants in a flower festival, cultural pride derived from visiting a historical museum, mental growth and development for the observer of a living history display, social enhancement for the revelers at a madrigal dinner, satisfying entertainment for the audience at the performance of a community brass band, and increased physical fitness for participants in a dance performance. In addition to the personal benefits, it would be hard not to argue that these activities also help make us more caring, compassionate, and tolerant as a society.

Although most people have an understanding of what is meant by community activities, the term "culture" can cause a good deal of confusion. Although culture is a broad term, in this chapter it will be used in a limited sense. We will discuss only those aspects of culture that involve bringing people together to express a shared sense of heritage and community. We will not discuss aspects of popular culture such as mass spectator sports, television, popular music, films, books, and videos.

A new study from the John Walker College of Business at Appalachian State University reveals that North Carolina's non-profit arts industry provides $723 million annually and nearly 7,000 full-time jobs. Undoubtedly, the for-profit sector (including artists, education, the film industry, the informal arts, and festivals) will add billions of dollars to complete the picture of the economic impact of the creative industry in North Carolina. Cultural tourism is the fastest-growing segment of the tourism industry, up 13 percent between 1996 and 2002, according to the Travel Industry Association of America. In July 2003, North Carolina was named one of the top ten states for cultural and heritage tourism. In addition, more than one million North Carolinians- nearly one of every eight citizens- are active arts supporters, members, or volunteers. The economic value of cultural volunteerism is an impressive $130 million. Meanwhile, arts funding is dynamic. Each grant dollar invested by the North Carolina Arts Council is matched by $24 of other local funding.

Cultural activities in North Carolina provide multiple benefits to individuals, families, communities, and the economy. Park and recreation professionals should have an understanding of and appreciation for the importance of these benefits, as well as an awareness of the resources available to provide quality programs and services.

Government Involvement

Local park and recreation agencies, as well as some state and federal agencies, play a key role in the provision of cultural and community activities. Park and recreation agencies must be aware of the resources available at the local, state, and national level in order to take advantage of the technical and financial assistance opportunities that exist.

Community Resources

Most park and recreation professionals think of municipal and county departments as the foundation for community leisure services. The extent to which these agencies provide cultural programs and resources will vary greatly across the state. Some departments provide mainly sports and athletic programs while others offer broader opportunities in cultural programs, events, festivals, and arts facilities. For example, the Cary Parks, Recreation and Cultural Resources Department changed to its current name to recognize the strong cultural programs component that exists in its delivery of leisure services. Many park and recreation departments have cultural resource divisions and supervisors within their organizations and offer programs and instructional classes in music, dance, drama, arts and crafts, and other hobbies. They also offer festivals, concerts, and a variety of cultural events. These departments often cooperate with other local arts organizations to provide these opportunities.

Interagency Cooperation

The trend today is toward interagency cooperation. Rarely is one agency the sole sponsor for a cultural arts program or community event. Smaller communities must rely upon combining resources with other government agencies, non-profit organizations, and commercial businesses to continue providing high-quality cultural opportunities. In addition, there is considerable pressure for these programs to be financially self-sufficient; and many departments are engaging in corporate and business fund-raising to supplement departmental resources and program fees.

Chapter 7

A major cooperating agency for many departments is the local arts council/commission. There are approximately 103 local arts councils in the state, and each is an important player in interagency cooperation. Arts councils provide a significant resource for local park and recreation departments, primarily in terms of arts expertise. Arts councils are also a good resource for technical assistance, volunteers, judges, and facilities. Many councils are also the designated local funding agency for grants for the arts. Funding opportunities are available from the North Carolina Arts Council to local arts councils, and park and recreation departments can take advantage of these matching grants and incentive programs.

An example of interagency cooperation is Silver Arts, an arts program created by North Carolina Senior Games, Inc. for adults aged 55 and better. Designed as "a celebration of the creative expression of seniors in North Carolina," this program has provided a stage for the creative talents of visual, heritage, literary, and performing artists. Silver Arts is offered through the fifty three local Senior Games held throughout the state and complements the traditional sports and athletic events.

Each local Senior Games is sanctioned by North Carolina Senior Games, Inc. (NCSG), and a primary requirement for sanctioning is the demonstration of interagency cooperation. The Silver Arts showcases and competitions are usually presented by a variety of agencies: park and recreation departments, senior centers, arts councils, community schools, cooperative extension, schools and universities, libraries, and local businesses.

In Davie County and Winston-Salem, the park and recreation department and the local arts council are equal partners, utilizing the public library and a private art gallery for their shows. In Greenville, the community schools program and the local arts council are cooperating partners. New Hanover County and Wake County combine the resources of senior centers and park and recreation departments.

Agencies that have never worked together before are discovering that the Silver Arts program creates a spirit of cooperation and a sharing of resources beneficial to all involved. Older adults benefit by having a quality arts program, and the community and the agencies benefit by combining efforts rather than competing for resources and participants. The only program of its kind in the nation, Silver Arts is truly a model of quality arts programming.

Other cultural events and community activities are used for fund-raising for educational, charitable, health-related, and social service programs. For example, each December the Greensboro Symphony performs holiday concerts in the Triad where food donations are taken in lieu of admission fees. The food is distributed to the hungry through the Salvation Army in the Piedmont Triad. WGHP-Fox TV and WMAG Radio organize the event, which is co-sponsored by Sealy, Inc. and Old Dominion Freight Lines.

State Resources

In a previous chapter we described some of the leisure services provided by our state government. Our discussion focused on agencies involved with regulatory and land management responsibilities. In this chapter we discuss state agencies that are primarily concerned with cultural programs.

Department of Cultural Resources

The Department of Cultural Resources provides significant cultural and historical opportunities throughout the state. The mission of the Department of Cultural Resources is to "enrich the cultural, educational, and economic well-being of North Carolina's citizens and visitors. We do this by working to enhance the availability and quality of our state's historic, library and artistic resources" (http://www.findnc.org/deptcultural.html). This is the agency that oversees the work of the North Carolina Museum of Art, the North Carolina Museum of History, the North Carolina Symphony, the North Carolina Arts Council, the Division of Archives and History (which is responsible for the state's historic sites), and the State Library of North Carolina.

The **North Carolina Museum of Art**, located in Raleigh, receives direct funding from the legislature and has attracted the attention of individual contributors and corporate sponsors. The museum's paintings and sculpture represent more than 500 years of artistic heritage. The museum also presents changing exhibits, lectures, workshops, family festivals, films and videos, outdoor theatre, and performing arts events. In addition, the museum has established, on approximately 164 acres of land, an Art and Nature Park. The park's purpose is preserving open space, restoring various ecosystems, and introducing creative and accessible programs of art, education, and recreation to the public. Park and recreation students and faculty at North Carolina State University are collaborating with museum staff on interpretive trail design, signage, and special events. The Art and Nature Park is unique in the United States and will be a model demonstration of the blending of parks and art in nature.

The **North Carolina Museum of History**, also located in Raleigh, features exhibits on all aspects of the state's history. The North Carolina Historical Time Lines provide visitors with education and entertainment concerning the important events in North Carolina's rich history. The Sports Hall of Fame gallery is a treat for sports enthusiasts. The museum captures the cultural significance of the state's history and exhibits the music and heritage arts of our past.

Although the **North Carolina Symphony** is a private, non-profit corporation, it receives direct funding from the legislature. The sixty five member orchestra, founded in 1932 as the first state-supported symphony, uses Meymandi Center Hall (in Raleigh) as its home base but spends most of the year touring the state, providing concerts and performing for school groups.

The **North Carolina Arts Council** provides both technical and financial assistance to organizations and individual artists throughout the state. The majority ($6.2 million) of its $7.8 million budget is made available to local non-profit organizations through matching grants for arts programs and events. Local parks and recreation departments may qualify for funding under its Grass Roots Program. The impacts of the Arts Council in 2002-2003 were:

- ■ Over 9.5 million people participated in projects funded by the Arts Council.
- ■ Projects were funded in ninety eight counties in North Carolina.

- Grants went to 826 organizations, of which 448 were arts organizations and 334 were schools and community and civic groups. Grants also went to 145 individuals.
- Each dollar awarded by the Arts Council was matched by twenty four other dollars, many generated directly by the Council's grant.

The Department of Cultural Resources is also responsible for twenty seven state historic sites. These are special sites that have significant historical and cultural value and need to be interpreted to the public and preserved. The following are some examples:

- **Tryon Palace** in New Bern served as the capitol and the residence of Governor William Tryon when North Carolina was a colony.
- **Alamance Battleground** near Burlington was the site of a 1771 battle between Royal militia and Regulators (armed backcountry farmers).
- **Bennett Place** near Durham is where General Joseph E. Johnston and General William T. Sherman met and signed surrender papers for Confederate armies in the Carolinas, Georgia, and Florida.
- **Brunswick Town** near Southport was a colonial seaport burned by British troops in 1776.
- **Fort Fisher**, located three miles south of Kure Beach, was the site of the largest land-sea battle fought during the Civil War until the fort fell in 1865.
- At **Reed Gold Mine**, located near Concord, gold was discovered in 1799. The site includes underground mine tunnels and a reconstructed ore-crushing mill.
- **Historic Bath**, located near Washington, was the first incorporated town in the colony and was the home of the pirate Blackbeard.

The Department of Environment and Natural Resources

The Department of Environment and Natural Resources administers such resources as the North Carolina Aquariums, the State Park System, and the North Carolina Zoological Park, all reflections of North Carolina's rich history and culture. The **North Carolina Aquariums**, located on Roanoke Island near Manteo, at Pine Knoll Shores, and at Fort Fisher on Kure Beach, are designed to enhance people's understanding and appreciation of North Carolina's coastal areas and marine resources. Educational opportunities allow visitors to see, touch, and experience North Carolina's unique coastal ecosystems and marine wildlife. Displays include sea turtles, horseshoe crabs, sea otters, sharks, and moray eels, to name a few. Also available are gift shops featuring items with a coastal theme and coastal craft workshops.

The mission of the **North Carolina State Park System** is "to conserve and protect representative examples of the natural beauty, ecological features and recreational resources of statewide significance; to provide outdoor recreational opportunities in a safe and healthy environment; and to provide environmental education opportunities that promote stewardship of the state's natural heritage" (http://ils.unc.edu/parkproject/nc-parks.html).

The North Carolina Zoological Park, located in Asheboro, was the nation's first state-supported zoo. In addition, it is the largest walk-through natural-habitat zoo in the

United States. The zoo owns an additional 900 acres of land for future development within the Uwharrie Mountains, which are considered to be one of the oldest mountain ranges in the world.

Department of Agriculture and Consumer Services

The Department of Agriculture and Consumer Affairs administers the **State Fairgrounds** (site of the State Fair held each October) as well as shows, craft fairs, and concerts throughout the year. Today the State Fair educates the public on the importance of agriculture in their daily lives and in North Carolina's economy. In addition, the State Fair provides the opportunity to experience music and crafts that reflect the state's rich heritage. The **North Carolina Farmers Markets**—located in Asheville, Charlotte, the Piedmont Triad, Lumberton, and Raleigh—offer a variety of local fruits, vegetables, and flowering plants in addition to seasonal events and activities (such as pumpkin carving, spinning and weaving demonstrations, and wreath-making workshops).

The University of North Carolina System

The cultural arts and community activity contributions of the sixteen campuses of the UNC System are varied. In addition to being a major provider of sports and sports entertainment, our universities and colleges contribute significantly to the cultural life of the state. They provide concerts, plays, and art shows as well as serving as local "parks" with their gardens and walkways. The following are examples of some of the activities, events, and facilities provided by the various campuses of the University of North Carolina that enhance the cultural environment of the State:

- **The Botanical Gardens**, set aside by the University of North Carolina at Asheville, are ten acres of indigenous plants and trees native to the Southern Appalachian Mountains. The Botanical Gardens serve as a laboratory for students, a wildlife refuge, and source of enjoyment for visitors.
- On the campus of North Carolina A & T University, the **Mattye Reed African Heritage Center** houses one of the finest collections of African artifacts in the United States.
- At the **Morehead Planetarium and Science Center**, located on the University of North Carolina at Chapel Hill campus, astronauts were once trained in celestial navigation. The planetarium offers a variety of programs, shows, and exhibits to educate the public about astronomy.
- At North Carolina State University, the **Craft Center** offers classes, materials, equipment, and work space for students and area residents. With looms, woodworking equipment, pottery wheels, a kiln, and a photographic lab, the Craft Center provides instruction for beginners and a place for advanced craftsmen to work.
- Each summer the School of Music at The University of North Carolina at Greensboro offers the largest university music camp in America. The two-week **Summer Music Camp** offers programs in band, mixed chorus, orchestra, and piano to students from around the country and world.

The North Carolina School of the Arts (NCSA) in Winston-Salem, a member of the University of North Carolina System, deserves special attention. This campus, serving both high school and college students, exists primarily for the purpose of developing artists and fostering the performing arts. To be admitted, students must pass an audition in one of the school's primary areas: dance, music, theater, or drama. The School of the Arts has a commitment to touring and outreach. Its programs enrich the cultural life of many areas of the state and the region while providing its students with valuable performance experience. Through its Community Public Performances program, NCSA students perform at community colleges, historic sites, art museums, and other venues. NCSA has an ongoing relationship with several North Carolina communities to perform chamber music concerts. Some of these communities include: Chapel Hill, Hendersonville, Wilmington, Davidson, Raleigh, and Charlotte. NCSA's dance students tour eight to ten North Carolina schools each year to perform, its music students visit thirty elementary schools per year, and more than 100 students and faculty participate in over seventy performances during the summer at the Illuminations at Roanoke Island Festival Park in Manteo, North Carolina.

Although this section has focused primarily upon the contributions of the UNC System, a number of private universities in North Carolina also contribute to our cultural heritage and resources. For example: the internationally acclaimed **Eastern Music Festival** takes place at Guilford College in Greensboro for six weeks each summer; Mars Hill has the **Rural Life Museum** and features a fall music festival; Louisburg College annually hosts the **Franklin County Folk Festival**; and at Duke University, one can tour **Duke Chapel** and the **Sarah P. Duke Memorial Gardens**.

Federal Resources

The federal government is involved in making cultural arts and activities more widely available to millions of Americans and in preserving our cultural heritage for present and future generations. The major federal resource for cultural arts funding to the state has been the **National Endowment for the Arts** (NEA). The NEA supports and invests in hundreds of artistic endeavors in cities and towns throughout the country. The North Carolina Arts Council receives about $702,300 from the NEA to support its Partnership Agreement activities. The NEA's Folk Arts grants support state, regional, and local folk arts positions and their related activities, including statewide apprenticeship programs, documentation initiatives, and arts learning projects. Access to Artistic Excellence grants support the creation and presentation of work in the disciplines of dance, design, folk and traditional arts, literature, local arts agencies, media arts, multidisciplinary, museums, music, musical theatre, opera, presenting, theatre, and visual arts. In 2005, nineteen North Carolina organizations were awarded $1,114,800 in NEA grant awards.

The following sites demonstrate the federal government's contribution to our understanding and appreciation of North Carolina history, culture, and heritage:

- **Great Smoky Mountains National Park** offers a Pioneer Homestead that depicts pioneer life through reconstructed log buildings and exhibits.
- **Cape Hatteras National Seashore** on the Outer Banks includes the village of Ocracoke (where Blackbeard was slain) and the historic lighthouse.

- **Wright Brothers National Memorial** (near Kitty Hawk and Kill Devil Hills) commemorates the work of Orville and Wilbur Wright, who made the first powered aircraft flight on December 17, 1903.
- **Moore's Creek National Military Park**, about twenty miles northwest of Wilmington, is the site of a battle fought in 1776 by patriots against British loyalists.
- Marching bands from **Camp Lejeune Marine Base** and **Fort Bragg Army Base** give concerts and participate in local festivals, parades, and celebrations.
- **Guilford Courthouse National Military Park** in Greensboro was the site of a pivotal Revolutionary War battle in 1781.

The Link with Commercial Recreation and Travel and Tourism

In many cases, cultural events and community activities generate revenue and are closely associated with commercial recreation. In some cases, a cultural activity is intended to serve only the local community, while in other situations, it is intended to attract visitors from other sections of the state or nation. In this way, these events not only provide local community recreation but also support tourism. In fact, tourism dollars may provide the financial support to keep the event alive and growing. In this way, a community event and a tourist attraction become melded, thereby providing an experience for everyone.

Festivals and special events are held to celebrate many aspects of the life of a community. They may celebrate a religious or secular holiday, historic event, or person of significance in the life of that area. There may be an annual fair held as an outgrowth of agricultural harvests or to highlight local manufacturing. Events may be seasonal, perhaps tied to nearby sporting contests or hunting seasons. The event will quite likely reflect the ethnic or religious heritage of the area or celebrate its cultural diversity. Some events are created for educational or recreational purposes, the enjoyment of local citizens, or to raise money for a charitable reason. Others are intended to promote the community to people outside the area. Hosting a fair, festival, special event, or local celebration reflects the cultural face of a community and demonstrates its vitality and livability.

While festivals and events may have been started for a number of reasons, many began as small, local celebrations and have grown to be large events attracting numerous locals and community visitors. Local communities are realizing the importance of these events and celebrations in terms of community cohesiveness, positive public relations, regional awareness, and economic impact. The number of events continues to grow each year, and at this time the events held annually in North Carolina are in the thousands. The **North Carolina Division of Tourism, Film, and Sports Development** helps to publicize such events statewide through its annual publication, *North Carolina Calendar of Events*. People can request this booklet and other travel materials by calling their toll-free number (1-800-VISITNC).

The following selective list of these events and activities is divided in to the following categories: local festivals, ethnic heritage programs, outdoor dramas, arts and crafts shows, living histories, community gardens, historic preservation, and Elderhostel.

Local Festivals

- **Carolina Dogwood Festival** in Statesville
- **Bull Durham Blues Festival** in Durham
- **North Carolina Strawberry Festival** in Chadbourn
- **Honeybee Festival** in Kernersville
- **Firefly Festival** in Boone
- **Blessing the Fleet Festival** in Hobucken
- **National Hollerin' Contest** in Spivey's Corner
- **Mayberry Days** in Mount Airy
- **Wright Kite Festival** in Kill Devil Hills
- **Azalea Festival** in Wilmington
- **Barbecue Festival** in Lexington
- **Spot Festival** in Hampstead
- **North Carolina Shakespeare Festival** in High Point
- **Riverfest** in Bryson City
- **Grape Escape Art & Wine Festival** in North Wilksboro
- **Woolly Worm Festival** in Banner Elk

Ethnic Heritage Programs

- **African American Heritage Festival** in Sedalia
- **Old Time Fiddler's & Bluegrass Festival** in Union Grove
- **3 King's Day Festival (traditional Spanish celebration)** in Goldsboro
- **Oktoberfest** in Hickory
- **International Family Folk Festival** in Burlington
- **Native American Heritage Festival and Powwow** in Charlotte
- **Annual Multi-Cultural Festival** in Lexington
- **North Carolina Celtic Festival and Highland Games** in Winston-Salem

Outdoor Dramas

- *The Lost Colony* in Manteo
- *Unto These Hills* in Cherokee
- *Horn in the West* in Boone
- *Listen and Remember* in Waxhaw
- *Worthy Is the Lamb* in Swansboro
- *From This Day Forward* in Valdese
- *First in Freedom* in Halifax

Music, Arts, and Crafts

- **Annual Storytelling & Crafts Festival** in Beech Mountain
- **Dew in the Valley Arts and Crafts Festival** in Maggie Valley
- **Lazy Daze Arts & Crafts Festival** in Cary
- **Music of the Mountains** in Lake Toxaway
- **Tar Heel Craftsman's Fair** in Kill Devil Hills
- **Christmas Fantasia Arts and Crafts Show** in Wilmington
- **Flat Rock Music Festival** in Flat Rock
- **Arts & Crafts on the Run** in Banner Elk
- **Annual Gospel Singing by the Lake** in Waynesville
- **Art in the Park** in Blowing Rock

Living Histories

- Since 1925 the **John C. Campbell Folk School**, located in Brasstown, has been teaching students about traditional folk art, music, crafts, and dance.
- Pan for gold at **Reed Gold Mine State Historic Site**, just southeast of Concord. You can also see the mine's operating ore-crushing mill and walk its underground tunnel.
- A tour on the **USS North Carolina Battleship Memorial** or attending the Battleship's summer evening light show takes one back to World War II, when the USS North Carolina proudly sailed the seas. This battleship was considered the greatest sea weapon of its day.
- In **Historic Cherokee** one can experience the culture and history of the Eastern Band of Cherokee Indians through their art, dances, and language.
- A living history encampment, weapons demonstrations, and skirmishing take place at the **Bentonville Battleground State Historic Site** on the anniversary of this significant Civil War battle.
- **Old Salem** is a living history restoration of the Moravian community called Salem that was started in 1766. One can tour the buildings, museums, and gardens to experience how the Moravians lived during the sixteenth century.
- **The International Civil Rights Museum**, opening in Greensboro in 2005, will feature numerous exhibits, including the lunch counter from Woolworth's where four North Carolina A&T University freshmen were refused service. Many believe the Woolworth's Sit-In launched the civil rights movement in North Carolina and was a defining moment nationally.

Community Gardens

- **Sarah P. Duke Memorial Gardens** on the west campus of Duke University provides a variety of spectacular gardens and a lily pond.
- **Elizabethan Gardens** on Roanoke Island are an imaginative recreation of a sixteenth century Elizabethan pleasure garden.

- Wilmington's **Airlie Gardens** provide the visitor with a chance to stroll around and through its spacious lawns, gardens, lakes, and centuries-old live oak trees. It is particularly magnificent during the spring when the azaleas, camellias, and dogwoods are at their peak.
- **Daniel Boone Native Gardens** in Boone offers six different garden areas with native plants and rustic architecture.
- **Tanglewood Park Arboretum and Rose Garden** in Clemmons showcases a variety of plants from around the world. It features an accredited All American Rose Garden that has 800 rose bushes. The Arboretum has audio stations to enhance the experience for individuals with visual impairments.
- **Waterworks Visual Art Center's Hamlin Sensory Garden** in Salisbury enables visitors to experience the various scents, textures, colors and shapes of plants during all four seasons of the year. Descriptions of plants are labeled in both English and Braille.

In addition to these and other formal gardens, numerous garden or house and garden tours are conducted in many communities throughout the state.

Cultural Diversity and Ethnic Heritage Programs

North Carolina has a culturally diverse population, and many groups across the state celebrate their diversity annually. Native Americans, African Americans, Moravians, Quakers, and Scottish Americans offer a variety of programs and resources designed to entertain and educate the public about their ethnic heritage. Examples of Native American offerings include:

- **Charlotte Nature Museum** in Charlotte offers collections of historic materials and an Indian Studies Program.
- **Guilford Historical Museum** in Greensboro and the **Schiele Museum** in Gastonia offer Native American artifacts, dioramas, and interpretive workshops.
- The outdoor dramas *Unto These Hills* at the Cherokee Indian Reservation.
- **Lumbee Homecoming** during the week of July 4th in Pembroke.

Examples of African American cultural attractions include:

- **St. Phillip's Church** in Winston-Salem, the oldest standing African American house of worship in North Carolina.
- **Somerset Place**, near Albermarle, where reunions are held for descendants of property owners and slaves.
- **Historic Stagville**, near Durham, preserves elaborate cabins and a mule barn built by highly skilled slave carpenters.
- **Diggs Museum**, in Winston-Salem, exhibits paintings, sculptures, photographs, and other crafts.
- **National Black Theater Festival** in Winston-Salem attracts thousands of spectators and participants from all over the world.
- **Carolina's Black Family Reunion** in Charlotte.
- **The International Civil Rights Museum** in Greensboro houses artifacts and exhibits of the civil rights movement.

Moravian history in the state is recreated in many locations, including:

- **Old Salem**, a living history village in Winston-Salem that provides tours, lectures, art exhibits, and interpretive programs in a faithfully restored eighteenth century town founded in 1776. Interpreters dressed in period costumes demonstrate historic activities and trades.
- **Bethabara Park** in Winston-Salem, the first Moravian settlement in North Carolina. This park features a museum and a reconstructed colonial community and fort. A reenactment of a Revolutionary War encampment happens here each May.

Quaker historic sites in the state include:

- **The Cane Creek Quaker Meeting** was established in Alamance County in 1751.
- **The New Garden Meeting House** in Greensboro was founded in 1754.
- **Guilford College**, founded in 1837 as a Quaker institution, houses an extensive library collection of Quaker publications and historical materials.
- **Mendenhall Plantation** near Greensboro, a restored plantation and a part of the Underground Railroad that helped slaves escape to freedom.

Scottish clans host gatherings in several parts of the state to celebrate their heritage. These include the **Highland Games and Gathering of Scottish Clans** at Grandfather Mountain near Linville in July of each year; the **Lake (Loch) Norman Games** near Charlotte; and the **Red Springs Games** in Red Springs (Robeson County). These games feature athletic events, music, and dance, all in celebration of participants' Scottish ancestry. In addition, Franklin is the home of the **Scottish Tartans Museum**, the first built outside of Scotland.

In the last decade, North Carolina has seen a significant growth in the number of Asians and Hispanics/Latinos who have chosen to call North Carolina home. **The Asian Chess Tournament** held in Charlotte, the **Hung Gar Kung Fe Academy** in Mooresville, and the **Turku** (which features rhythms of cultures along Central Asia's fabled Silk Road) in Brasstown are examples of how Asians are beginning to showcase their culture within the state. Examples of Hispanic cultural opportunities include **Out of Bounds: Contemporary Hispanic & Latino Art** (held in Boone) and the **La Fiesta Del Pueblo**, North Carolina's biggest Latino festival (held on the State Fairgrounds in Raleigh).

Historic Preservation

In a number of communities throughout the state, concerned people have worked to preserve the historically and architecturally significant structures that reflect North Carolina's heritage. Some examples include Old Salem, Thalean Hall in Wilmington, historic Halifax, the Dentzel Carousel in Raleigh's Pullman Park, historic Hillsborough, Charlotte's Spirit Square, the Elizabeth City historic district, the Carolina Theatre in Greensboro, the Biltmore Estate in Asheville, and the USS North Carolina (docked at Wilmington).

Elderhostel

Elderhostel, a national non-profit organization, offers adults age 55 and older a chance to visit an educational institution for a week and take classes on a variety of topics and interests. Programs are held in classrooms, museums, environmental education centers, boats, trains, and forests. The first Elderhostel programs in North Carolina were held in 1977 at Appalachian State University, UNC-Chapel Hill, and UNC-Charlotte. Current locations include Appalachian State University, Blue Ridge Community College, College of the Albermarle, Guilford College, John C. Campbell Folk School, Lees-McRae College, Mars Hill College, Montreat Conference Center, Old Salem, Inc., Pamlico Community College, the Summit Episcopal Center, Trinity Conference Center, UNC-Wilmington, UNC-Chapel Hill, and Western Carolina University. North Carolina was the first state to offer multi-generational programs for grandparents and grandchildren and was the first state to offer programs sponsored by a craft/folk school (John C. Campbell Folk School in Brasstown, North Carolina).

Summary

Cultural and community activities help us express our heritage and feel a sense of community in a fast-paced, competitive world. Local park and recreation agencies are involved with these activities by directly providing them (direct provision approach) or by supporting the sponsoring agencies and organizations (facilitator approach).

The North Carolina Department of Cultural Resources—through the Museum of Art, the Museum of History, the North Carolina Symphony, the state Arts Council, and the state's twenty-seven historic sites—is a significant provider of historic and cultural events and facilities. It should be mentioned that many cultural or heritage events, celebrations, or attractions are offered through partnerships between public and private agencies. Many events (including craft fairs, folk music festivals, military reenactments, outdoor dramas, and contests) take place at the community level and reflect a high degree of personal involvement.

Learning Exercises

1. Assume that a family of four just moved to your hometown. The father would like to be involved with a Civil War reenactment group, the mother would like to find a group with whom to play Mah Jongg, the 15-year-old daughter wants to learn to salsa dance, and the 13-year-old son wants to play in a competitive soccer league. List all possible places in your home town where each member of the family could go to seek his or her leisure experiences.

2. Evaluate the cultural and community activities currently offered in your hometown. (1) List two that you have attended or participated in. (2) List two that you have not participated in, and explain why. (3) List two that are not offered but would interest you if they were.

3. How many of North Carolina's twenty-seven state historic sites have you visited? How many can you name?

4. During the semester, attend a cultural event or community activity that you have never before experienced. Report your experience to the class.

Sources for Further Information

North Carolina Arts Council
Department of Cultural Resources
Raleigh, NC 27699-4632
(919) 733-2111
ncarts@ncmail.net
http://www.ncarts.org/

North Carolina Museum of Art
Street Address
2110 Blue Ridge Road.
Raleigh, NC 27607-6494
Mailing Address
4630 Mail Services Center
Raleigh, NC 27699-4630
(919) 839-6262
http://ncartmuseum.org/

North Carolina Division of Tourism, Film, and Sports Development
North Carolina Department of Commerce
301 North Wilmington Street
Raleigh, NC 27601
(919) 733-4151
http://www.nccommerce.com/tourism/

North Carolina Historic Sites
NC Division of Archives and History
Dobbs Building
Street Address
430 N. Salisbury Street
Room 2050
4620 Mail Service Center
Raleigh, NC 27699-4620
(919) 733-7862
http://www.ah.dcr.state.nc.us/sections/hs/default.htm

North Carolina Museum of History
Street Address
5 East Edenton Street MSC 4650
Raleigh, NC 27699-4650
MailingAddress
4650 Mail Service Center
Raleigh, NC 27699-4650
(919) 807-7900
http://ncmuseumofhistory.org/

North Carolina Zoological Park
4401 Zoo Parkway
Asheboro, NC 27205
1-800-488-0444
http://www.nczoo.org/

North Carolina Division of Parks and Recreation
North Carolina Department of Environmental and Natural Resources
Street Address
512 N. Salisbury Street, Archdale Bldg
7th Floor, Room 732
Raleigh, NC 27699-1615
Mailing Address
1615 MSC
Raleigh, NC 27699
http://ils.unc.edu/parkproject/ncparks.html

North Carolina Aquariums
Raleigh Administrative Office
417 North Blount Street
Raleigh, North Carolina 27601
1-800-832-FISH (3474)
admin@ncaquariums.com
http://www.ncaquariums.com/

Chapter 8

Therapeutic Recreation

Susan A. McGhee, Thomas K. Skalko, and Sharon E. Carter

Therapeutic recreation, also known as recreational therapy, is a health-related field in which recreation activities are used to assist individuals with special needs in gaining or redeveloping the skills and abilities necessary to access and participate in normal life activities. People with special needs are those whose physical, psychological, intellectual, or social functioning is impacted in some way that affects their independent functioning and/or participation in meaningful life experiences. Therapeutic recreation (TR) is a process whereby each individual's special needs are assessed and identified. Then, a program of activities is prescribed and implemented to improve the individual's functional abilities and thus enhance the quality of the individual's life.

This chapter provides an overview of therapeutic recreation in North Carolina and a discussion of its importance for persons with special needs. Readers should also gain knowledge of various service delivery settings, professional service delivery guidelines, credentialing of personnel, professional organizations, and employment opportunities.

Historical Development: A North Carolina Perspective

North Carolina has a well-documented history of leadership in promoting the recreation profession; however, the documented history of therapeutic recreation in the state is somewhat sketchy. The early history of therapeutic recreation in North Carolina was recorded as bits and pieces of information handed down in a haphazard fashion to the North Carolina Recreation and Park Society (which is now the North Carolina Recreation and Park Association). What is known is that much of the early leadership resulted from the work of Harold Meyer and the Hospital Division of the North Carolina Recreation Society. Recreation programs for North Carolinians with illnesses, disabilities, or handicapping conditions began at Dorothea Dix Hospital during the late 1930s. Even though no concrete evidence exists, it is assumed that the development of therapeutic recreation in North Carolina likely occurred in the state hospital system during the 1940s to such a level that on June 14, 1949, Hospital Recreation became the third division of the North Carolina Recreation Association (Brendle, 1964). In 1953, the Hospital Recreation Division, along with several other organizations (including the North Carolina Recreation Commission), assisted the University of North Carolina at

Chapel Hill in conducting the first hospital recreation institute ever held in the southeastern United States. The institute, a brainchild of Meyer, stimulated the growth of therapeutic recreation in clinical settings.

With the social changes of the 1960s came a new awareness of the needs of persons with impairments, disabilities, and handicapping conditions. The passage of several federal laws, such as the Community Mental Health Centers Act of 1963, initiated the decentralization of the state hospital system and increased the responsibility of communities to care for their citizens with chronic impairments. These social changes also provided greater visibility to and increased awareness of human rights for persons with disabling conditions. Recreation for persons with disabling conditions was no longer just the responsibility of long-term care hospitals. Throughout the 1970s and well into the next decade, community mental health day treatment programs, group homes for persons with mental retardation, and nursing homes and adult day centers for senior citizens with disabling conditions sprang up in communities across the state. Often, the daily structure in these agencies was provided through therapeutic recreation services. During this same time period, therapeutic recreation services evolved from providing diversional recreation activities that were modified to permit participation by persons with disabling conditions to a focus on providing prescriptive treatment interventions.

A number of other events attest to the growth, development, and recognition of therapeutic recreation as a viable component of the health and human services system in North Carolina:

- In 1963, North Carolina's first community-based recreation program for persons with special needs opened in Greensboro through the joint efforts of the Joseph P. Kennedy, Jr. Foundation and the Greensboro Parks and Recreation Department.
- Although no specific date or reason can be found in the minutes, the Hospital Recreation Division of the North Carolina Recreation and Park Society (formerly the North Carolina Recreation Association) changed its name to the Therapeutic Recreation Division around 1969.
- During the 1970s and 1980s, several of North Carolina's colleges and universities added a therapeutic recreation option or emphasis to their existing recreation curricula.
- In 1982, North Carolina state government established a therapeutic recreation position classification series for personnel providing treatment-oriented therapeutic recreation services. Prior to this, therapeutic recreation personnel were often hired within state facilities as rehabilitation therapists, assistants, technicians, or aids.
- The Therapeutic Recreation Division of what became the North Carolina Recreation and Park Association adopted an official, operational definition of therapeutic recreation in 1983.
- North Carolina therapeutic recreation professionals joined with professionals from other southern states to form the Southeast Therapeutic Recreation Symposium, Inc. (STRS), a private, non-profit organization whose sole purpose is to provide continuing education for therapeutic recreation practitioners. The STRS was incorporated in 1985.
- A landmark event in the history of the state's therapeutic recreation movement occurred in 1986 when the North Carolina General Assembly passed the Therapeutic Recreation Personnel Certification Act (Senate Bill 24). This act prohibited individuals

from representing themselves as qualified to deliver therapeutic recreation services unless certified by the North Carolina Therapeutic Recreation Certification Board (TRCB).

- The incorporation of the North Carolina Recreation Therapy Association (NCRTA) on June 23, 1988, provided the state with a second therapeutic recreation professional organization. NCRTA became an affiliate chapter of the American Therapeutic Recreation Association in 1989 and published its definition statement in 1992.

- In 1995, the North Carolina Therapeutic Recreation Practice Competencies Task Force, comprised of representatives from both state professional organizations and the Therapeutic Recreation Certification Board, examined the practice competencies for therapeutic recreation specialists in North Carolina (West, 1996). These 217 entry-level practice competency items were verified in separate statewide and regional Delphi technique surveys.

- The TRCB voted in 1995 to implement an examination as a criterion for certification and require continuing education as a criterion for recertification. Based on a unique agreement with the National Council for Therapeutic Recreation Certification (NCTRC), the national examination is utilized in North Carolina for assuring professional competency of state-certified therapeutic recreation specialists. The first administration of the exam for state certification was in November 1996.

- In 1996, North Carolina state government incorporated special consideration of regulatory or accreditation agency requirements for employment. For therapeutic recreation, this recognized state TRCB certification as a requirement above the minimum training specified for state therapeutic recreation positions.

- A 1998 curriculum survey identified eleven colleges and universities providing baccalaureate coursework in therapeutic recreation; however, only ten of these academic institutions identified a specific therapeutic recreation degree or option (McGhee, 1999). Although Shaw University added an option in therapeutic recreation to its baccalaureate curriculum in 2003, the therapeutic recreation baccalaureate program at the University of North Carolina at Chapel Hill, the oldest program in the state, was discontinued in 2004. There are eleven baccalaureate degree and two associate degree TR programs in the state. In addition, there are three masters degree programs (East Carolina University, University of North Carolina-Chapel Hill, and University of North Carolina-Greensboro).

- In the 2005 session of the General Assembly, an amendment to the existing TR Personnel Certification Act (Chapter 90C) was introduced. This amendment, entitled *An Act to Update the Laws Regulating the Practice of Recreational Therapy*, proposed to replace the existing system with licensure for recreational therapists and recreational therapy assistants. The bill was passed by the House on May 23, 2005 and approached Senate consideration. As of mid-July 2005, the Assembly was still in session and the bill was still under consideration.

Today, therapeutic recreation in North Carolina is a dynamic and expanding allied health field. From its meager beginnings with only a handful of hospital recreators, therapeutic recreation has grown into a respected health service profession. North Carolina has approximately 517 state-certified therapeutic recreation specialists and assistants. Initially practiced only in state hospitals, therapeutic recreation services are now available to persons with illnesses and disabling conditions in a variety of settings, including acute medical care, physical rehabilitation, mental health, long-term care, residential care, schools, and community recreation and health agencies.

Basic Concepts and Definitions

Perhaps the most noteworthy evidence of the role that North Carolina therapeutic recreation professionals play in the national evolution of therapeutic recreation is in defining the field and its primary mission. From the early meetings of the regional institutes on hospital recreation to today, the organized therapeutic recreation movement in North Carolina has been a focal point in defining the field and reflecting its diverse perspectives.

The basic concepts and definitions of therapeutic recreation in North Carolina parallel the evolution of the field at the national level as well as the competing philosophical orientations for the field (i.e., therapy and/or special recreation and leisure). The two professional organizations representing therapeutic recreation interests within North Carolina are affiliated with the two national professional organizations. The North Carolina Recreation Therapy Association (NCRTA) is a chapter affiliate of the American Therapeutic Recreation Association (ATRA), while the North Carolina Recreation and Park Association (NCRPA) is an affiliate of the National Recreation and Park Association (NRPA). In turn, the affiliation between NCRPA and NRPA enhances the cooperation and communication between the TR Division of NCRPA and the National Therapeutic Recreation Society (NTRS), a branch of NRPA. Each state organization adopts a mission and definition for therapeutic recreation and recreational therapy consistent with these affiliations.

According to the North Carolina Recreation and Park Association- Therapeutic Recreation Division, therapeutic recreation is defined as:

> . . . the use of recreation to improve, develop, and/or maintain physical, psychological, emotional, and/or social behaviors and to assist individuals in establishing and expressing a more independent lifestyle. Therapeutic recreation includes treatment, leisure education, and voluntary recreation participation. These specialized programs are individualized and may be provided in clinical, residential, or community settings (NCRPS-TR, 1988).

This definition of therapeutic recreation directly parallels the definition adopted by the NTRS Board of Directors in 1994 and continues to be consistent with the NTRS's current definition of therapeutic recreation that states that:

> therapeutic recreation uses treatment, education and recreation services to help people with illnesses, disabilities and other conditions to develop and use their leisure in ways that enhance their health, functional abilities, independence and quality of life (NTRS, 2000).

The definitions promoted by both NCRPA-TR Division and NTRS identify and utilize treatment, education, and recreation services to promote an independent lifestyle and leisure functioning. These foci are consistent with the missions of the affiliate national organization (i.e., NRPA) and adopt a broad-based approach to the therapeutic recreation profession.

The emergence of the North Carolina Recreation Therapy Association, in 1988, paralleled the continuing struggle of the field with regard to its philosophical orientation. Departing from the terminology of therapeutic recreation adopted by NTRS in the 1960s and returning to the use of the term "recreation therapy," the North Carolina Recreation Therapy Association developed a definition of services emphasizing the treatment orientation of the field. Based on a treatment or therapy orientation, the NCRTA defined recreation therapy as:

> . . . *the provision of planned treatment or therapy (i.e., health restoration, remediation, habilitation, rehabilitation), which uses recreation and activities as the primary medium of treatment for persons who are limited in their functional abilities due to illness, disability, maladaption, or other conditions (NCRTA, 1992).*

As an ATRA chapter affiliate, the NCRTA definition for recreation therapy parallels the recreational therapy component of the ATRA definition for therapeutic recreation. As presented by the American Therapeutic Recreation Association (1988), therapeutic recreation is:

> *the provision of treatment services and the provision of recreation services to persons with illness or disabling conditions. The primary purpose of treatment services, which are often referred to as recreational therapy, is to restore, remediate, or rehabilitate in order to improve functioning and independence as well as reduce or eliminate the effects of illness or disability. The primary purpose of recreation services is to provide recreation resources and opportunities in order to improve health and well-being. Therapeutic recreation is provided by professionals who are trained, certified, registered, or licensed to provide therapeutic recreation.*

Although the ATRA definition identifies both recreational therapy services and recreation services, the primary philosophical orientation of the organization focuses on therapeutic recreation as a treatment modality. This is consistent with the therapy/treatment orientation of the North Carolina Recreation Therapy Association.

Another term that is associated with the therapeutic recreation field is *recreation for individuals with disabling conditions* (or inclusive recreation), which replaced outdated terms such as special recreation, adapted recreation, and recreation for special populations. All of these terms do not adequately represent the concept of therapeutic recreation as defined by the professional organizations. *Recreation for individuals with disabling conditions* refers to the provision of recreation opportunities that have been modified to enable successful participation by persons with disabling conditions. Such services may include learning new activities and adaptive skills, as well as using adaptive equipment and modified rules to assist these individuals to meet their recreation and leisure needs as independently as possible. Therapeutic recreation professionals have varying opinions as to whether recreation for individuals with disabling conditions (inclusive recreation) is a component of therapeutic recreation or of the broader field of recreation and leisure.

Through the years, North Carolina therapeutic recreation professionals have continued to influence the defining of the field at the national level. Despite the lack of one unified definition and philosophical perspective, therapeutic recreation in North Carolina is a strong and vibrant profession, providing services across the spectrum of health care, social, educational, and community settings. The positive influence of recreation and leisure on an individual's life and the use of activities as interventions to enhance the individual's health and overall well-being continue to be basic concepts common to North Carolina therapeutic recreation professionals.

Service Delivery Settings

While therapeutic recreation is provided in a diversity of settings, it is administered through a process to which the profession has long ascribed. The therapeutic recreation process is a systematic approach to services consisting of four steps: assessment, treatment/individualized program planning, implementation, and evaluation (APIE). Assessment is the gathering of information regarding the participant's functional skills and abilities, particularly in relation to independence and life activities. Since the assessment data identifies problem areas that can be treated through therapeutic recreation interventions, it serves as the foundation for development of the treatment/individualized program plan. These individualized plans consist of specific goals and objectives targeting increased functioning and minimizing identified problems. Specific intervention strategies and activities are also components of the treatment/individualized program plan. Implementation is the actual delivery of the therapeutic recreation interventions to the participant. During evaluation, the participant's progress toward achieving the predetermined goals and objectives is monitored and modifications to the interventions are identified in order to enhance the individual's outcomes. This process (assessment, planning, implementation, and evaluation) is fundamental to the delivery of therapeutic recreation services, regardless of the setting where therapeutic recreation is practiced.

The provision of therapeutic recreation services takes place in a variety of agencies that serve persons with illnesses and disabling conditions. Dependent upon the mission of the agency and the needs of each specific participant, therapeutic recreation may encompass treatment, illness and disability prevention, and health promotion through use of specific interventions and facilitation techniques. In medical-based settings, the certified therapeutic recreation specialist collaborates with the interdisciplinary team in designing the overall treatment program. The certified therapeutic recreation specialist then designs the participant's therapeutic recreation/recreational therapy treatment program and determines the interventions to be used. The scope of therapeutic recreation services is as diverse as the individual's needs and interests, availability of resources, and each therapeutic recreation specialist's competencies and level of skill. Therapeutic recreation services are provided in acute medical, physical rehabilitation, psychiatric/behavioral health, mental health, long-term care, residential, community, school, and correctional settings.

Acute Medical Care Settings

In medical care settings, services are based on a medical model in which treatment of disease and functional limitations is the primary purpose of all care. Medical settings may provide in-patient services where the person resides in the agency for the duration of the treatment, or acute care services that provide in-patient treatment for relatively short periods of time). Medical settings also include out-patient services, where the individual comes into the agency only for a few hours to receive treatment.

Many acute care medical settings exist in North Carolina and serve a wide range of persons with illnesses or disabling conditions. Numerous city and county hospitals, private hospitals and clinics, and university medical centers, as well as some psychiatric hospitals and Veteran's Administration hospitals, are types of acute care settings. Therapeutic recreation in acute care is typically provided in medical specialty units that serve persons who are experiencing life-altering illnesses. Such medical specialty units include oncology, transplant units, pediatrics, burn units, substance abuse units, and acute psychiatry/behavioral health.

Physical Rehabilitation

Agencies providing physical rehabilitation services are often managed as medical settings, although their missions are not always based solely on the medical model. Many physical rehabilitation centers use a combination of the medical model (treatment of disease and functional limitations) and the education/training model (teaching of adaptive techniques and resources) to facilitate maximum independence. Physical rehabilitation centers are often affiliated with acute medical care agencies, typically admitting patients into the rehabilitation center as acute medical care needs are resolved and the care focus shifts to rehabilitation. Physical rehabilitation centers, once called convalescent hospitals, provide either in-patient or out-patient care, depending on the needs of the individual. Within North Carolina's physical rehabilitation settings, therapeutic recreation is typically provided for persons who have experienced a cardiac crisis, cerebrovascular incident (stroke), traumatic brain injury, spinal cord injury, or orthopedic injury.

Psychiatry/Behavioral Health and Mental Health

Psychiatry is one of the oldest clinical service delivery settings in which therapeutic recreation practitioners have served. Today in North Carolina, many acute care agencies provide in-patient psychiatric/behavioral health treatment, as well as out-patient or day treatment programs. Additionally, private psychiatric facilities provide out-patient services and/or partial hospitalization programs. These facilities offer a range of mental health services, including individual and family therapy, substance abuse counseling and education, and interpersonal skills development.

Depending on the specific needs and characteristics of the individual, therapeutic recreation services in psychiatric settings typically address social skills development, interpersonal skills, coping and adjustment capacity, decision-making skills, anger management, stress management, and appropriate expression of emotions. Such functional skills enable the individual to interact effectively in the community setting. Individuals who need more extended services than these short-term psychiatric agencies provide are referred to long-term care or residential facilities.

In 2004, North Carolina underwent a transformation of the community mental health system. In the past, community mental health centers offered a range of direct mental health services. Today, community mental health centers have divested their direct service functions and operate as Local Management Entities (LME). In turn, the LME now refs appropriate mental health services to approved private mental health providers within the system. This has changed the way in which mental health services, including therapeutic recreation services, are provided. Independent, self-supporting mental health providers deliver services designed to achieve specific outcomes with the individual. The LME system allows for approved providers, including therapeutic recreation specialists, to engage in the delivery of quality mental health services either as self-employed independent providers or as employees of a larger private agency.

Long-Term Care and Residential Settings

As the term implies, long-term care and residential facilities provide extended placement, typically from three or six months and longer. Long-term care includes skilled nursing facilities or nursing homes, state institutions (either psychiatric/behavioral health or mental retardation/developmental disability focused), and total care communities that provide educational, custodial, and nursing care for extended periods of time for persons with chronic illnesses or disabling conditions. While many long-term care facilities target services for individuals with disabling conditions due to age-related illnesses, more facilities are incorporating services regardless of age to persons using ventilators and individuals with chronic/terminal illnesses or in need of extended rehabilitation services. These individuals are not in need of acute medical or nursing care and are medically stable but require some care or supervision that prevents them from living independently in the community. Some nursing homes also maintain sub-acute care units that provide selective rehabilitation services. These sub-acute care units serve as a transitional step between expensive hospital and rehabilitation centers and the minimal supervision of independent living.

The term *residential setting* generally refers to an interim placement between acute medical or rehabilitation settings and independent community living. Residential facilities are community-based homes that provide supervision and some assistance with activities of daily living. Intermediate-care homes, board and care homes, retirement homes, transitional homes, group homes, and halfway houses are considered residential facilities. In North Carolina, residential settings typically serve individuals who cannot live independently due to some disabling condition. Residential care settings often provide services for persons who are partially disabled due to age-related illnesses, persons with mental retardation or developmental disabilities, and/or persons with acquired immunodeficiency syndrome (AIDS).

Therapeutic recreation services for persons living in long-term or residential care facilities may be provided in the facility itself or may be accessed through community-based therapeutic recreation and recreation programs. Accessing existing community-based TR and recreation services is more common for residential care facilities. Since the long-term care facility becomes the individual's home, perhaps less so for residential care facilities, diversional leisure activities are provided as well as prescriptive therapeutic recreation services. The scope of therapeutic recreation services for persons living in long-term and residential settings is extremely diverse but generally emphasizes maintaining functional abilities and enhancing existing abilities. Promoting independence is important in both settings; however, preparation for independent community-based living is emphasized in residential care facilities. This focus supports the continued trend of decreasing the numbers of persons residing in long-term state institutions.

Community-Based Services

Community-based therapeutic recreation services are provided to persons with disabling conditions in the town, city, or neighborhood where these individuals reside. The majority of the community-based programs are sponsored through city or county recreation and park agencies; however, private and non-profit community organizations frequently offer community-based therapeutic recreation services. Many of the agencies and services described elsewhere in this book provide either therapeutic recreation services or access for persons with disabling conditions to general recreation programs.

Community-based therapeutic recreation services may focus on the provision of treatment or recreation opportunities for persons with special needs. Prescriptive interventions, or recreational therapy services, are emphasized in medical and residential facilities but are only provided as needed in community agencies. In addition, recreation opportunities are provided for the broad range of persons with special needs who reside in the community. Through modifying facilities, using adaptive equipment, altering rules and strategies, teaching adaptive skills, and educating for leisure, therapeutic recreation specialists ensure that persons with special needs have recreation opportunities equal to those of the general population within their home communities.

The national trend toward home and community care for persons with illnesses and disabling conditions has led to innovative service settings for the therapeutic recreation profession. Programs that provide supervised independence for persons with mental retardation or chronic mental illness, adult day programs for senior citizens with disabling conditions, and hospice services for persons who are terminally ill are several examples of new community settings where therapeutic recreation is practiced. In addition, therapeutic recreation service providers are finding unique service delivery options for addressing obesity and modified programs of physical activity for all persons.

One unique approach to increasing independence in meeting leisure needs is the Independent Living Rehabilitation Programs that were initiated in the mid-1980s. The Center for Recreation and Disability Studies at the University of North Carolina at Chapel Hill received a demonstration grant to provide therapeutic recreation services for recently discharged rehabilitation patients in Greenville and Fayetteville. The therapeutic recreation specialist conferred with the client and staff at the rehabilitation facility prior to discharge and delivered leisure education-focused services in the client's home after discharge. The success of this project resulted in the Vocational Rehabilitation Program (Department of Human Resources) incorporating a therapeutic recreation specialist on the staff of each new independent living program.

School Settings

The provision of therapeutic recreation services in the public school system is based on the Education for All Handicapped Children Act of 1975 (Public Law 94-142), which identified recreation as a "related service" in meeting the needs of children with disabilities. As specified in the law's regulations, recreation as a related service includes four specific elements: assessment of leisure functioning, therapeutic recreation, recreation in schools and communities, and leisure education. Within North Carolina, only a few such programs existed in the public schools in the late 1970s, such as in Stanly County. Although not presently included, leisure education for adults with mental retardation was once a component of the Compensatory Education Program at the community college level. The Center for Recreation and Disability Studies was a guiding force in accomplishing this. Grant-funded pilot projects in the early 1990s, such as the School-Community Leisure Link and Leisure Education for Compensatory Education, opened the doors for the practice of therapeutic recreation in North Carolina's school systems. Professional preparation efforts have included preparing therapeutic recreation specialists to work in the public schools and incorporating therapeutic recreation and leisure education into special education and teacher preparation programs.

Correctional Settings

Adult and youth offenders in North Carolina's prison system can certainly be identified as a population with unique needs. The emphasis for the general prison population, however, has been on recreation services rather than on therapeutic recreation services. The first recorded correctional recreation program was established in Raleigh's State Prison in 1961, although some forms of informal recreation opportunities existed prior to that date. In the state prison units, some type of recreation service is provided for inmates; however, only the larger state institutions provide a recreation program managed by professional recreation personnel.

Recreation services in North Carolina's prisons are unique to each prison unit. For example, the Western Carolina Correctional Center, serving male youth offenders, provides general recreation programs for all inmates but only provides therapeutic recreation for a selected segment of the prison population. Throughout the state prisons, over 10 percent of inmates have disabling conditions, including learning disabilities, mental retardation, emotional or behavior disorders, personality disorders, or persons with physical disabling conditions. Although some other prisons provide services similar to Western Carolina's program, most of North Carolina's prisons deliver general recreation programs rather than formal therapeutic recreation. Therapeutic recreation in correctional settings may well be an area for further development in the future. This is evidenced by new initiatives to develop programs that address functional skills in interpersonal communications, emotional control, group cooperation, stress management, and anger management. All of these outcomes can be delivered through therapeutic recreation services.

North Carolina has a wide range of delivery settings in which therapeutic recreation is practiced and a broad scope of services is provided for persons with varying levels of impairment or disability. Whether practiced in medical, rehabilitation, community, long-term care, residential care, school, or correctional settings, therapeutic recreation contributes to the functional performance of the individual and promotes the quality of care and life of North Carolina's citizens with disabling conditions or special needs.

Practice Delivery Guidelines

Therapeutic recreation adheres to practice delivery guidelines that are generated both internally and externally to the profession. These guidelines of practice fall into three distinct areas: professional codes of ethics, professional standards of practice (both internal standards), and healthcare accreditation (external standards). In combination, these standards provide the framework for the delivery of therapeutic recreation services and are designed to promote the best possible practice in the interest of protecting the therapeutic recreation consumer.

Code of Professional Ethics

Therapeutic recreation as a profession adopted codes of ethical conduct and practice very early. Like medicine or law, therapeutic recreation specialists and assistants are bound to ethical principles. Principles that govern the conduct of the professional include: to act on behalf of the individual and to not cause harm, to be honest and fair, to ensure equity in the distribution of services, to respect the rights of individuals to make their own choices, to protect the consumer's identity and information, and to continue to learn and develop as a professional service provider. The professional's conduct is driven by a commitment to uphold these ethical principles and to act in the best interest of the consumer, the public, and the profession.

Therapeutic recreation professionals in North Carolina accept these ethical principles and use them to direct their practice. Although not dictated by law, North Carolina's Therapeutic Recreation Personnel Certification Act stipulates that therapeutic recreation professionals adhere to these principles. Should an individual be found in violation of these ethical principles, the North Carolina Therapeutic Recreation Certification Board and the National Council for Therapeutic Recreation Certification may withdraw the individual's state and/or national professional or paraprofessional credential. The anticipated modification of the state certification process into a licensure process will further strengthen the role of the professional credentialing board in addressing ethical violations.

Professional Standards of Practice

Unlike codes of ethics that offer direction for ethical practice, professional standards of practice offer guidelines for delivering services. The first standards of practice for therapeutic recreation were established by the National Therapeutic Recreation Society in the early 1980s. After several revisions during the 1990s, the current National Therapeutic Recreation Society's standards are entitled *Standards of Practice for a Continuum of Care in Therapeutic Recreation*. Today, the field has two separate standards of practice documents. In 1991, the American Therapeutic Recreation Association published *Standards for the Practice of Therapeutic Recreation*, which when revised in 2000 added a Self-Assessment Guide to assist therapeutic recreation departments in monitoring their own service delivery.

Despite emerging from different professional organizations and possessing different formats, both sets of standards of practice promote similar outcomes. These outcomes are centered on promoting the highest quality of service for the consumer. The professional standards of practice for therapeutic recreation set a benchmark or standard for quality therapeutic recreation services, including how services should be delivered, who is qualified to deliver these services, and what types of outcomes or results indicate that quality services were provided.

The standards of practice documents help the therapeutic recreation practitioner and administrator provide quality services, protect the interests of the consumer, and help the profession set uniform expectations in practice. They are the backbone of professional service delivery and the road map for providing quality services.

Healthcare Accreditation Standards

Professional standards of practice are established internally by a profession, but healthcare accreditation standards are developed by agencies outside the profession. In health care and social service delivery systems, private and public agencies assume the responsibility for ensuring that quality services are delivered to the consumer. These agencies are categorized as either public regulatory agencies or private healthcare accreditation agencies. Public regulatory agencies include the Centers for Medicare and Medicaid Services (formerly the Health Care Financing Administration). Private healthcare accreditation agencies include the Joint Commission on Accreditation of Healthcare Organizations and the Commission on the Accreditation of Rehabilitation Facilities. Although there is some overlap, each agency has a distinct function.

The Centers for Medicare and Medicaid Services (CMS) is the federal agency responsible for the administration of federally-funded Medicare and Medicaid programs that serve persons who are elderly, disabled, or poor. The CMS sets standards of care for hospitals, nursing homes, and rehabilitation facilities in order to ensure that agencies receiving federal funds to serve elderly persons (Medicare) and persons of low income (Medicaid) provide the highest quality of services, at the most reasonable cost to the public. These standards offer guidelines for service delivery for the entire agency as well as for individual disciplines. Agencies that do not meet these standards of care are subject to the loss of reimbursement for services provided to Medicare and Medicaid-eligible patients.

Like the Centers for Medicare and Medicaid Services, the Joint Commission on Accreditation of Healthcare Organizations (JCAHO or the Joint Commission) and the Commission on Accreditation of Rehabilitation Facilities (CARF) also set standards for the delivery of health care services by hospitals, rehabilitation facilities, alcohol and substance abuse agencies, home health care services, and long-term care facilities. These organizations, however, are privately operated, independent entities that engage in the voluntary accreditation of health care agencies. Their primary goal is to offer a mechanism for health care delivery programs to voluntarily review their programs and services. The Joint Commission and CARF both set standards of care and then offer their expertise to the hospital or health care agency to review programs and services in order to be designated as an independently accredited health care agency. Although there are no financial penalties for failure to meet the accreditation standards, a positive accreditation review is an indication of the quality of services delivered by the individual agency. These healthcare accreditation reviews are similar to a Good Housekeeping Seal of Approval for hospitals and other healthcare providers and serve as assurance to the public that the agency provides safe and dependable health care services of the highest quality.

These external reviews include standards that must be met by therapeutic recreation programs at individual agencies. Therapeutic recreation professionals (administrators and therapists) are charged with ensuring that their services meet the standards set by these external agencies.

Credentialing of Therapeutic Recreation Personnel

Just as practice delivery guidelines promote quality therapeutic recreation services, credentialing of therapeutic recreation personnel promotes the delivery of quality services by identifying individuals who are competent to provide those services. Some form of personnel credentialing for therapeutic recreation has existed since 1956. Whether in the form of registration, certification, or licensure, protecting the consumer is the ultimate purpose of credentialing programs. By assuring that personnel delivering services possess at least the minimum knowledge for competent practice, quality therapeutic recreation services are promoted.

National Credentialing

In the earliest credentialing program, hospital recreation personnel were identified through the registration plan of the Council for Advancement of Hospital Recreation. These individuals were then absorbed into the voluntary registration program that the National Therapeutic Recreation Society established in 1968. This voluntary program evolved to become the National Council for Therapeutic Recreation Certification (NCTRC), which was established in 1981 and accepted some 3,000 registered therapeutic recreation personnel from the existing program. Initially NCTRC awarded two credentials: the certified therapeutic recreation specialist (CTRS) at the professional level and the certified therapeutic recreation assistant (CTRA) at the paraprofessional level. In 1998, NCTRC discontinued awarding the CTRA certification; this level of certification disappeared in 2000, when the existing certifications expired. While national certification is not mandatory, the credential has been identified by health care accrediting organizations and governmental regulatory groups as denoting "qualified" personnel. Additionally, position advertisements and job descriptions commonly specify certification as a therapeutic recreation specialist among the minimum qualifications for therapeutic recreation positions.

Initially, NCTRC awarded certification based on a review of the applicant's education and experience. An important milestone in assuring protection for the TR consumer was the 1990 implementation of a national certification examination for the CTRS credential. Passing the examination, which is offered three times per year (January, May, and October), is now the final step in obtaining initial CTRS certification. This certification is for a five-year period and requires payment of an annual maintenance fee. Recertification requires proof of continued competence as evidenced by a combination of two of the following: TR professional experience, continuing education, and/or retaking and passing the CTRS examination. As of April 2005, NCTRC reported over 16,000 active CTRS certificants nationally. Approximately 728 of those certificants lived in North Carolina.

North Carolina Credentialing

State therapeutic recreation licensure processes were established in Utah (1974) and Georgia (1975) to restrict persons from performing therapeutic recreation tasks without first obtaining a professional license in the state. The 1986 Session of the North Carolina General Assembly passed the State of North Carolina Certification Bill (Senate Bill 249), which established the first mandatory state-level title protection process for therapeutic recreation. This law became effective on June 30, 1987, and is administered by North Carolina's Therapeutic Recreation Certification Board (TRCB) under the provisions of the *Therapeutic Recreation Personnel Certification Act* (Chapter 90C) and the *Administrative Procedure Act* (Chapter 150B). This statute protects the North Carolina public from persons who might misrepresent themselves as certified in the field of therapeutic recreation. The law requires that persons delivering therapeutic recreation services in North Carolina become certified through the TRCB prior to identifying themselves as certified in the profession. In North Carolina, only individuals who obtained certification under Chapter 90C could use the term "certified" with the titles "therapeutic recreation specialist" (TRS), "recreation therapist" or "recreational therapist" (RT), "therapeutic recreation assistant" (TRA), or any combination or derivation of such. In April 2005, TRCB reported a total of 517 state-certified TR personnel (474 TRS and forty three TRA).

Since state law takes precedence over national certification, persons who are nationally certified through NCTRC cannot use the CTRS designation in North Carolina without first obtaining the state credential. The Professional Conduct Committee of TRCB is responsible for investigating any misrepresentation of status or other suspected violations of the Therapeutic Recreation Personnel Certification Act. Depending on severity, violations may result in a letter of reprimand; remedial education requirements; denial, suspension or revocation of certification; fines up to $500.00; and/or imprisonment for up to sixty days.

An Executive Director serves as a liaison between the TRCB and the state government and general public, promotes awareness and compliance with regulations, and coordinates the ongoing business of the TRCB. The TRCB is comprised of seven members, including three practicing therapeutic recreation specialists, one therapeutic recreation specialist engaged in training, one practicing therapeutic recreation assistant, and two public members. Each member is appointed by North Carolina government officials to a three-year term and can serve a maximum of two consecutive terms. The TRCB meets three times a year (typically January, June, and September) to review applications and conduct other business.

Since its origin in 1987, the TRCB has continued to evolve. Initially, applicants who were working in therapeutic recreation as a therapeutic recreation specialist or assistant were awarded certification through a grandfathering clause. When this clause expired on March 1, 1991, all certifications were then awarded based on a review of academic background and experience. In 1995, the TRCB entered into a significant agreement with the National Council for Therapeutic Recreation Certification to use the national certification examination to test all new North Carolina therapeutic recreation specialist applicants. The first administration of the national certification exam for North Carolina TRS certification was on November 9, 1996. North Carolina benefitted by gaining access to a valid and reliable examination and establishing closer ties with national certification requirements. In turn, the National Council benefitted by establishing its first formal relationship and examination agreement with a state credentialing board. Such a relationship has potential for replication with other states. Additional evolution of TRCB included implementation of continuing education and experience requirements for both TRS and TRA certification renewal, beginning with the January 1997 review.

The next phase in the evolution of therapeutic recreation credentialing in North Carolina was presented to the General Assembly on March 10, 2005 as an amendment to the TR Personnel Certification Act. This amendment, entitled *An Act to Update the Laws Regulating the Practice of Recreational Therapy*, proposed replacing the existing certification system with licensure for recreational therapists and recreational therapy assistants. The outcome of the Recreational Therapy Licensure Act will be determined during the 2005 legislative session. An update on the status of the amendment may be obtained through the North Carolina Legislature's Web site (www.ncleg.net). The TRCB's Web site (www.trcb.org) is a reliable resource for any changes in state credentialing.

In summary, implementation of the original components of the Therapeutic Recreation Personnel Certification Act required a great deal of time and effort to negotiate. The continued refinement and upgrading of the standards and procedures used to identify qualified therapeutic recreation personnel represents a commitment to refining the evaluation of competency and enhancing protection of the public. An amended North Carolina credentialing system that brings licensure to the profession will represent another milestone in this commitment.

Professional Organizations

Therapeutic recreation professionals in North Carolina have the opportunity to contribute significantly to the therapeutic recreation profession through involvement with two state organizations that address therapeutic recreation concerns. Although each organization has identified a specific focus and set of priorities, the two organizations communicate openly and work together on common issues such as marketing, professional competencies, and credentialing. It is not unusual for North Carolina therapeutic recreation professionals to maintain membership in both organizations.

North Carolina Recreation and Park Association Therapeutic Recreation Division

The Therapeutic Recreation Division is one of ten divisions within the North Carolina Recreation and Park Association (NCRPA). Since its founding, the TR Division, formerly the Hospital Recreation Division, has reflected the strong recreation emphasis of the NCRPA and its affiliation with the National Recreation and Park Association. The TR Division addresses issues related to comprehensive therapeutic recreation services in clinical, residential, and community settings. Members of the TR Division participate in the NCRPA and in the TR Division's regional or standing committees. The TR Division has organized smaller interest groups based on specific clientele or service delivery setting, such as mental health/psychiatry, rehabilitation, clinical, community based, pediatrics, aging, and mental retardation/developmental disabilities. Opportunities for professional development are available to TR Division members through specialty interest group workshops, sessions at the NCRPA Annual Conference each fall, and a specific therapeutic recreation-focused conference provided each spring by the TR Division. Members also receive therapeutic recreation news in NCRPA News, published quarterly. Additionally, the TR Division sponsors research projects by its members on issues that impact therapeutic recreation service delivery and the professional.

North Carolina Recreation Therapy Association

The North Carolina Recreation Therapy Association (NCRTA) was incorporated in 1988 as an independent organization to address the specific needs of therapeutic recreation professionals in health care and human service settings. NCRTA focuses on advocacy for recreation therapy as a treatment modality and on providing an alternative to the recreation and leisure focus of the NCRPA- TR Division. In 1989, NCRTA became the sixth chapter affiliate of the American Therapeutic Recreation Association (ATRA) and received the first ATRA Chapter Affiliate of the Year Award in September 1996. The organization's Web site and its quarterly publication, *NCRTA Update*, emphasize upcoming events and relevant professional information, as well as networking opportunities. Professional development opportunities are provided through the annual fall NCRTA conference and the spring Student/Professional Issues Forum. NCRTA also provides funding for efficacy research.

Therapeutic Recreation Employment Structure and Trends

Therapeutic recreation services are delivered by professionals and paraprofessionals trained and credentialed in therapeutic recreation. The professional therapeutic recreation specialist or recreational therapist is credentialed as a certified Therapeutic Recreation Specialist (TRS). The paraprofessional is referred to as a Therapeutic Recreation Assistant (TRA) and possesses the state credential at that level. Both levels work cooperatively in the interest of the consumer. Each, however, has distinctly different levels of training and responsibility.

Therapeutic Recreation Specialist/Recreational Therapist

The professionally trained and credentialed therapeutic recreation specialist is generally charged with the development of the overall therapeutic recreation program, including preparation of the treatment or care plan for the consumer. In turn, the specialist is responsible for the assessment of consumer needs, development of the plan of care, direct service delivery or oversight of the services, documentation, evaluation, and discharge/transition planning. In addition, the TRS develops the programs designed to meet the physical, social, cognitive, and emotional needs of the recipient. The professional-level specialist is also responsible for supervision of the therapeutic recreation assistant, practicum students, and volunteers.

Therapeutic Recreation Assistant/Recreational Therapy Assistant

The therapeutic recreation assistant works under the supervision of the therapeutic recreation specialist. Since the delivery of quality therapeutic recreation services is a multifaceted, complex, and demanding array of duties, the TR assistant plays an important role in working with the TR specialist to ensure that a comprehensive range of services is provided to the consumer. Working under the supervision of the TRS, the TRA might assist in assessing needs and outcomes, implementing interventions designated on the plan of care, and providing recreation opportunities designed to meet the psychosocial needs of the consumer. In addition, the TRA may assist the TRS with setting up for intervention sessions, post-session clean-up, patient transport, and group leadership. Although TRAs provide multiple services, they are not credentialed to work independently in therapeutic recreation service delivery.

Employment Settings and Populations Served

The therapeutic recreation specialist/recreational therapist and the therapeutic recreation assistant/recreational therapy assistant play a vital role in the care and treatment of persons with disabling conditions. The April 2005 data from the North Carolina Therapeutic Recreation Certification Board illustrates that the employment settings and populations served by therapeutic recreation are indeed diverse.

Approximately 45 percent of the TR specialist positions and 40 percent of TR assistant positions are in acute medical care or hospital settings. The second largest number of certified personnel works in long-term care such as nursing homes, accounting for 14 percent of TR specialist positions and 26 percent of TR assistant positions. Physical rehabilitation facilities employ 13 percent of the certified TR specialists and 10 percent of the TR assistants. Community-based settings provide about 12 percent of the positions for persons who are classified as a TRS and 6 percent for those who are a TRA, with parks and recreation agencies being the largest community employer (followed by schools as the second largest). A few therapeutic recreation specialists and therapeutic recreation assistants work in other settings, such as the military, hospice, public health, group homes, and corrections.

According to the TRCB employment data, persons with mental illness and persons with age-related illnesses (geriatrics) are identified as the individuals most often served by both therapeutic recreation specialists and therapeutic recreation assistants. Persons with developmental disabilities and persons with physically disabling conditions are served by about 22 percent of certified TR specialists and 14 percent of TR assistants. Therapeutic recreation specialists also work with pediatrics (children), persons with severe burns, and persons admitted to medical/surgical units in hospitals with such illnesses as heart attacks, diabetes, or cancer.

Employment in therapeutic recreation in North Carolina is robust; however, employment trends continue to evolve. The increased presence of recreational therapy in pediatrics and medical/surgical units, as well as the expansion into school, public health, community mental health, and hospice settings during the last few years demonstrates the potential therapeutic recreation has for growth in the future.

The Shifting Healthcare System

Increasingly, the roles and responsibilities of both the therapeutic recreation specialist and the therapeutic recreation assistant are changing. With the changing health care system and the move toward managed care with its emphasis on cost-containment and cost-efficiency, professionals will be required to expand their capabilities.

The state healthcare system in North Carolina is undergoing significant changes during the first decade of the twenty first century. As a result of a 2001 legislative act mandating system reform for state-operated mental health, developmental disabilities, and substance abuse services, the state implemented a plan to privatize services for these consumers. Currently many individuals served in state hospitals and residential care facilities are being moved to small, privately owned care facilities in their home communities. Additionally, the role of community-based state mental health services is changing from providing direct care to facilitating private care. The result of these changes will ultimately be a decrease in state-sponsored services that will precipitate a need for more private and local services, including therapeutic recreation.

The managed care system of health services is a nationwide movement toward standardized guidelines of care. One of the profound effects of managed care on hospital-based therapeutic recreation services is the dramatic decrease in the length of time allotted for in-patient treatment. Often clinical therapeutic recreation professionals have only enough time to assess an individual's needs, develop a discharge or transition plan, and refer the individual to out-patient or partial hospitalization services. Unfortunately, persons who are transitioned to home health care often lose the opportunity to receive therapeutic recreation services unless they are referred to a community therapeutic recreation program.

The changing health care environment at both the state and national levels certainly creates challenges for therapeutic recreation professionals, but it can also provide many opportunities. One of the greatest assets therapeutic recreation specialists and therapeutic recreation assistants have for charting the future of the profession is their ability to "think outside the box."

Charting the Future: Opportunities and Challenges

As with many allied health professions, therapeutic recreation has a promising future. The aging of our society and the changing health care system will emphasize health promotion, illness prevention, and outcome-based practices. Therapeutic recreation professionals will find themselves in a position to become invaluable service providers. The outcome of this scenario will be based on the profession's ability to embrace the evolving system of service delivery.

The challenge confronting all allied health professions is to function effectively in a managed care system of health services. The managed care system places emphasis on a defined set of services that are cost-effective and efficient in treating persons with a range of illnesses, disabilities, and diagnoses. As with all allied health professionals, therapeutic recreation professionals must offer the kind and quality of services that will respond to the needs of the consumer within the financial confines of the managed care system. In addition, the services must produce the desired outcomes in functional performance for the individual. This trend is considered to be both a challenge and an opportunity for all health care service providers and professions. It will be incumbent upon the therapeutic recreation profession to investigate and implement innovative, yet effective, service approaches to meet the health care needs of the future.

The future will require the therapeutic recreation profession to continue incorporating progressive practices and strategies. It will be essential to increase research on the effects of various therapeutic recreation interventions and the outcomes of specific services. Both the American Therapeutic Recreation Foundation (an affiliate of the American Therapeutic Recreation Association) and the National Therapeutic Recreation Society have established research support grants for the implementation of efficacy research. In addition, the North Carolina Recreation Therapy Association and the North Carolina Recreation and Park Association- Therapeutic Recreation Division have also invested a portion of revenue in efficacy research, as has the Southeast Therapeutic Recreation Symposium, Inc. These research funds are a proactive means to address the challenges of the future.

The therapeutic recreation profession is positioning itself for a range of approaches in order to respond to the changing environment. With managed care and an emphasis on out-patient services, partial hospitalization, and home health services, professionally trained therapeutic recreation specialists have opportunities to integrate their services into this evolving healthcare system. Carefully developed therapeutic recreation services can be designed to meet the health care, health promotion, illness prevention, and rehabilitative needs of a wide variety of persons no longer in need of hospitalized services but in need of continued rehabilitation, prevention, and health promotion services.

The therapeutic recreation entrepreneur is in a strong position to offer a multitude of home health services as an independent contractor or as a member of a home health service agency. In addition, opportunities for co-treatment systems with other allied health and social service providers exist.

Notwithstanding efforts to address the changing health care environment, the profession is accepting the challenges presented within the public policy arena. The American Therapeutic Recreation Association and the National Therapeutic Recreation Society have both been active in shaping public policy. Recent efforts to clarify language under the Centers for Medicare and Medicaid Services (CMS) Guidelines will be instrumental in positioning recreational therapy services as a recognized and acceptable service under the Medicare prospective payment system (PPS) and will open opportunities for consumers to better access recreational therapy services in skilled nursing facilities, in-patient psychiatric hospitals, and in-patient rehabilitation units. It will be through continued efforts of the national and state organizations in public policy and involvement with regulatory agencies that therapeutic recreation professions will continue to be in a position to meet the challenges ahead.

As in the past, the present and future supply and demand for therapeutic recreation services is strong. According to the Bureau of Labor Statistics, U.S. Department of Labor (2004), employment in therapeutic recreation overall is expected to grow more slowly than the average for all occupations through 2012. However, slightly faster employment growth is predicted in residential (community care) facilities and out-patient settings that serve persons with disabling conditions, the elderly, or persons diagnosed with mental retardation, mental illness, or substance abuse problems. This trend is consistent for North Carolina and the southeastern region of the country. With concerted efforts on behalf of the state's professionals and the efforts of the state and national organizations, the future for therapeutic recreation practice is positive despite the changing health care and human services landscape.

Summary

North Carolina has a long and rich history of leadership in the therapeutic recreation movement and continues to be an innovative force in the development of the profession. The creation of specific therapeutic recreation positions, state use of the national certification examination in 1996, the Task Force investigation of practice competencies, and the proposed 2005 Recreational Therapy Licensure Act attest to North Carolina's commitment to ensuring quality therapeutic recreation services for persons with disabling conditions.

In the initial years of the twenty first century, therapeutic recreation specialists and assistants statewide are keeping abreast of the sweeping changes in the healthcare system. Therapeutic recreation programs today are continually adjusting to encompass society's desire for wellness education, preventive medicine, health care cost containment, and the philosophy of promoting the independence and basic human rights of persons with illnesses or disabling conditions. Whether practiced in medical, rehabilitation, community, long-term care, residential care, school, or correctional settings, therapeutic recreation promises to be an exciting and challenging field of health care service in the twenty first century.

Learning Exercises

1. Within the chapter, the term *therapeutic recreation* is defined in several ways. What are the common elements of these definitions? What are the key concepts that are consistent with other allied health professions? What concepts are unique to therapeutic recreation?

2. Identify three ways in which TR practitioners in North Carolina have been leaders in the field of therapeutic recreation.

3. Identify the service delivery settings in your community that provide therapeutic recreation services. What types of therapeutic recreation services are being provided? To what degree are persons with disabling conditions being served?

4. Describe how North Carolina's credentialing process works in conjunction with the national certification process.

5. Visit a local community recreation and park department's therapeutic recreation program and the recreational therapy program at a local hospital. How are the services provided similar and how are they different? How are the participants in each program different?

6. Interview a practicing therapeutic recreation professional. Ask what prompted the professional to enter the field. Ask what skills and abilities are most important to success as a TR practitioner.

7. Identify two ways therapeutic recreation monitors the quality of services and the quality of personnel delivering those services.

8. Visit the Web sites of the professional TR associations (their URLs are listed below). Also visit the Therapeutic Recreation Directory (www.recreationtherapy.com) and see what is there. Identify two things that you learned from these Web sites.

Resources

Credentialing Organizations

National Council for Therapeutic Recreation Certification (NCTRC)
7 Elmwood Drive
New City, NY 10956
Phone: (845) 639-1439   Fax: (845) 639-1471
www.nctrc.org

State of North Carolina- Therapeutic Recreation Certification Board (TRCB)
P.O. Box 67
Saxapahaw, NC 27340
Phone: (336) 212-1133
www.trcb.org

National Professional Organizations

National Recreation and Park Association (NRPA)
National Therapeutic Recreation Society (NTRS)
22377 Belmont Ridge Road
Ashburn, VA 20148-4501
Phone: (703) 858-0784   Fax (703) 858-0794
NRPA: www.nrpa.org
NTRS: www.nrpa.org/content/default.aspx?documentId=530

American Therapeutic Recreation Association (ATRA)
1414 Prince Street, Suite 204
Alexandria, Virginia 22314
Phone: (703) 683-9420   Fax (703) 683-9431
www.atra-tr.org

North Carolina professional organizations

North Carolina Recreation and Park Association (NCRPA)
(formerly the North Carolina Recreation and Park Society)
Therapeutic Recreation Division
883 Washington Street
Raleigh, NC 27605-3251
Phone: (919) 832-5868   Fax (919) 832-3323
www.ncrps.org

North Carolina Recreation Therapy Association (NCRTA)
P.O. Box 1307
Chapel Hill, NC 27514-1307
www.ncrta.org

References

American Therapeutic Recreation Association. (1988). ATRA Definition Statement of Therapeutic Recreation. Hattiesburg, MS: Author.

American Therapeutic Recreation Association. (2000). Standards for the Practice of Therapeutic Recreation and Self-Assessment Guide. Alexandria, VA: Author.

Brendle, J.H. (1964). A History of the North Carolina Recreation Society. Unpublished master's thesis. University of North Carolina, Chapel Hill.

Bureau of Labor Statistics, U.S. Department of Labor. (2004). Recreational therapists. *Occupational Outlook Handbook*, (2004-05 ed.). Retrieved on May 12, 2005, from: http://stats.bls.gov/oco/ocos082.htm

McGhee, S.A. (Spring 1999). Status report: North Carolina therapeutic recreation academic programs. *North Carolina Therapeutic Recreation Certification Board Newsletter, 10* (2): 3.

North Carolina Recreation and Park Society- Therapeutic Recreation Division. (1988). Definition Statement of Therapeutic Recreation. Raleigh, NC: Author.

North Carolina Recreation Therapy Association. (1992). Definition statement of Recreation Therapy. Chapel Hill, NC: Author.

National Therapeutic Recreation Society. (2000). Therapeutic Recreation Definition. Retrieved on May 12, 2005, from: http://www.nrpa.org/content/default.aspx?documentId=949

National Therapeutic Recreation Society. (2003). Standards of practice for a continuum of care in therapeutic recreation. Retrieved May 15, 2005 from http://www.nrpa.org/content/default.aspx?documentId=1446

West, R. (Winter 1996). Past chair's message. *North Carolina Therapeutic Recreation Certification Board Newsletter, 4* (1): 3.

Chapter 9

Professional Preparation
and Development

David A. Cardenas, Diane G. Groff, and Leandra A. Bedini

With our understanding of the delivery system of leisure services and an awareness of the issues and programs in the specialty services, our focus turns to the growth of recreation and parks as a profession. In addition, this chapter will look at the future of leisure services in North Carolina.

The professionalization of the leisure service delivery system in North Carolina began shortly after the formation of the Playground Association of America in 1906. North Carolina responded in a variety of ways to the Playground Association's promotion of the "right to play of every child" and the urging of municipalities to develop playgrounds for children. By the early 1920s several municipalities such as Winston-Salem and Durham had employed full-time persons to direct their playground programs, the state legislature had established our state park system operated by professional personnel, and the University of North Carolina at Chapel Hill had appointed Harold D. Meyer, an Associate Professor in Sociology, to teach courses in the sociology of leisure. The pattern of growth continued throughout the 1930s as more municipalities created community recreation programs. Many of these recreation programs resulted from the efforts of the Works Projects Administration (WPA) and the strong advocacy of Meyer who was a field consultant for the WPA during the Depression. By the middle of the 1940s North Carolina had emerged as a leader in the development of the parks and recreation profession.

History of Professional Preparation in North Carolina

No formal degree program in recreation and parks existed in the state until 1941 when The University of North Carolina at Chapel Hill (UNC-CH) created a recreation leadership option within the Department of Sociology. However, The University of North Carolina actually began preparing recreation personnel as early as 1921. At that time, Harold Meyer came to the University at the invitation of Howard W. Odom to develop a sociology of leisure course. By 1924, the University was offering three courses dealing with play and community recreation. Throughout the 1920s, Meyer urged school systems to establish extra-curricular programs, and he worked with communities to create local youth-serving agencies and public recreation services. In tribute to his effort and the work of the University, UNC-CH was chosen in 1938 as the location for the second annual conference on the design of curricula to prepare recreation leaders. At this time,

Meyer and a select number of local recreation administrators joined the newly formed Society of Playground Workers, later known as the American Recreation Society, to promote professionalism.

By the mid-1940s, the University of North Carolina at Chapel Hill was unable to meet the increased demands for recreation leadership in the state. North Carolina State College (now North Carolina State University) stepped forward in 1946 to help meet this demand by creating a Department of Industrial and Rural Recreation within the School of Education. For the next 30 years, Thomas Hines directed the program dedicated to the development of recreation leaders.

The third and fourth curricula established in North Carolina were developed at institutions with special missions. In the early 1950s, programs were developed at the Women's College of the University (now UNC-Greensboro) and at one of the predominantly black institutions, North Carolina Central College (now North Carolina Central University). Dorothea Davis was the key leader in the creation of the Greensboro program while A.E. Weatherford was the driving force behind the program at Central.

In 1975 North Carolina mandated the development of community colleges to meet the local educational needs of North Carolina citizens. Since that time, associate degree programs in recreation have been established at a number of community colleges. Caldwell and Carteret Community Colleges were among the first to establish two year curricula that trained recreation students to meet specific needs in the profession.

Development of the Profession

A major concern since the 1930s has been the need for recognition and visibility of parks, recreation, and leisure services as a profession. Professions are, by definition, occupations aligned with specific social functions (i.e., education, health, and organized religions) that follow standards for educational development and practice that assure the public proper service and care. This stance is evident in the "Education for Leisure" statement given by the Society of Park and Recreation Educators (SPRE, 1975) and reflects the attitude of recreation and park practitioners as they implement programs for accreditation, certification, and professional preparation.

In 1995, the Sessoms Professional Leadership Institute was held at the University of North Carolina at Chapel Hill to honor H. Douglas Sessoms as he retired from 41 years of teaching in Leisure Studies and Recreation Administration at UNC-CH. The proceedings from that Institute are summarized in the 1995 *Schole* with three papers that address the development of the profession and professional leadership. Participants at that Institute defined professional leadership broadly to include all efforts that practitioners and educators provide for quality park and recreation opportunities that serve all people. Their belief was that park, recreation, and leisure service professionals have a role to play in enhancing the quality of human and environmental life (Henderson, 1995).

In his reflections on the development of the profession, Sessoms (1995) noted that the profession has returned to a mission first articulated at the turn of the century with concerns for the poor, immigrants, our cities, crime and delinquency, and burgeoning social issues. He noted that the roles of recreation professionals are complex and challenging (Sessoms, 1990). He stated that these issues require the professional to bring to any situation knowledge and expertise that allow the creation of physical and attitudinal environments to facilitate the recreation experience. Such skills and knowledge include an understanding of participant interests and desires, an assessment of the resources available and needed, and the activities and services that result in participant satisfaction.

Professions are concerned with the preparation of future practitioners and their abilities to meet the expectations required by the job. Accreditation, the body of knowledge based upon research, and certification are emphasized as defining elements of any profession. The following sections specifically address the development of these professional concerns.

Accreditation

One of the essential criteria specified for identification and recognition as a profession is the authority of the occupation to acknowledge through accreditation special professional preparation (Sessoms, 1993; Shapiro, 1977). Accreditation is seen as one way to ensure educational and professional standards by stimulating institutional self-improvement and monitoring. North Carolina State University (NCSU) led the way in accreditation when, in 1977, they became the first program in the country to be accredited by the National Council on Accreditation (now known as the National Recreation and Park Association/American Alliance of Leisure and Recreation Council on Accreditation). The following year, the program at UNC-Chapel Hill was accredited. Today, Appalachian State University, East Carolina University, North Carolina Central University, North Carolina State University, University of North Carolina at Greensboro, University of North Carolina at Wilmington, and Winston-Salem State University have accredited baccalaureate degree programs. Our state is also recognized for national leadership in accreditation provided by many professionals who have served on the Council of Accreditation or as accreditation visitors for the Council.

The establishment of accreditation was begun in the 1960s with concern for developing a "foundation of understanding and skills" necessary for all majors (Sessoms, 1993). An "in-house" accreditation process was begun in 1975 that focused on general education and professional education experiences. Two areas of specialization (Recreation Program Services and Recreation Resource Management) were offered in addition to the general accreditation that was applied to the undergraduate and graduate curricula. However, during the next decade the accreditation of graduate programs was dropped and the desire for more specializations materialized in the accreditation of dozens of curriculum-specific options. The "in-house" voluntary approach to accreditation changed in 1986 when the Council on Post-secondary Accreditation approved the NRPA/AALR procedures.

In 1988 the Council on Accreditation reversed the decision to allow for accreditation of specializations. Recreation and park education had become fragmented and practitioners and educators feared that the field of parks and recreation would be negatively affected. A concern was felt that students identified more with their special interest area rather than with the profession. NRPA took action to remedy this concern by approving a national certification exam as part of certification and the Council on Accreditation returned to only accrediting the four original option areas: Recreation and Park Administration, Recreation Resource Management, Recreation Program Supervision, and Therapeutic Recreation. The Council took an additional step when they mandated a curriculum must demonstrate not only the linkage between general education requirements and professional emphasis requirements, but also between the general educational requirements and the option. These actions were consistent with the recommendations of the Carnegie Commission report that stated additional course work in the liberal arts should be taken as a prerequisite for course work in a discipline or profession (Sessoms, 1993). Today, many students in professional preparation programs throughout North Carolina see directly the influence of these professional developments on the courses they take and the experiences considered to be critical to their development as recreation professionals.

Body of Knowledge through Research Activities

Research is often viewed as a benchmark of professional development as an occupation searches for answers to theoretical inquiries and improvements in professional practices. People often assume that research is done by academics in various colleges and universities. While their input is often critical, the involvement of practitioners in their own professional settings and programs is imperative. The links between research and practice have become ever more important as educators struggle to provide students with relevant learning based upon the most recent research findings. The demand for applied research to meet the needs of practitioners has also resulted in collaborative research efforts. These projects team practitioners and educators in an effort to bring about findings that will inform practice, add to the body of knowledge in recreation and leisure, and provide direction for ways in which the profession can influence social change within our society. In addition, North Carolina is a leader in the dissemination of applied research as evidenced by the work of Drs. Rob Stiefvater and Shirley Harper who established *LARnet*, an on-line cyber journal dedicated to applied leisure and recreation research. The journal is sponsored by North Carolina Central University. The journal can be accessed at http://www.nccu.edu/larnet/.

North Carolina is nationally known for our "cutting edge" research. The topics generally reflect an interest in advancing the theoretical aspects of parks, recreation, and leisure studies, but they also provide practical research findings and implications for use by practitioners. The following list provides a general perspective to the breadth of recreation research undertaken by educators as well as practitioners in the state:

- historical research (e.g., therapeutic recreation; pioneers in recreation; the intersection of gender, race, and class through leisure)
- ethics and aesthetics (e.g., environmental and animal rights; religion/spirituality and environmental attitudes)
- community reintegration for people with disabilities
- recreation as a related service in the schools for students with disabilities
- consumer behavior and its economic impact
- accessibility in recreation facilities, spaces, and programs
- management practices in recreation service delivery
- fiscal practices within parks and recreation agencies
- outdoor recreation trails studies
- liability and risk management

- environmental perceptions and outdoor ethics
- personnel preparation in therapeutic recreation
- family recreation
- leisure for underserved and diverse populations (e.g., women, immigrants, older adults, family caregivers, ethnic groups, people with disabilities, lesbian/gay/bisexual individuals, youth-at-risk, cultural competency)
- tourism (e.g., lifespan, sustainability, stakeholder analysis, marketing, social/economic/environmental impacts)
- inclusive volunteering
- health promotion and prevention of disease and disability
- active living (facilitating health and wellness through the built environment)
- community involvement (e.g., levels of participation, perception, satisfaction)
- service learning
- experiential education

All of these research interests attest to the wide variety of issues that face the profession of parks, recreation, and leisure services. Professionals are continually challenged to find the most relevant information and improved practices that allow them to provide the programs and facilities that contribute to the quality of life to all members of their communities.

Certification

Accreditation and certification are two basic elements of professionalization. Park and recreation professionals in North Carolina have been strong advocates and promoters of these efforts. As indicated earlier, North Carolina State University was the first university to have its baccalaureate degree program accredited by the NRPA/AALR Council on Accreditation. While the act of accreditation verifies that an institution has met certain standards of professional preparation, certification is an act of verifying that the individual professional has met the minimum requirements to practice as a professional. North Carolina was among the first to develop a credentialing plan for its recreation and park professionals. The initial plan was created by the North Carolina Recreation and Park Society in 1954. Currently, the North Carolina Certification Model plan is conducted as part of the National Recreation and Park Association's certification program. Through this voluntary plan, a professional can become credentialed as a Certified Park and Recreation Professional.

North Carolina has also been a leader in certifying therapeutic recreation professionals. Recognizing the value of certification in the medical arena, both in the hospitals and the community, therapeutic recreation professionals in North Carolina responded to issues of liability and technical competency by drafting legislation for consideration by the state legislature.

In July of 1986, North Carolina Senate Bill 249, the Therapeutic Recreation Personnel Certification Act, was ratified making North Carolina one of only two states in the U.S. to credential therapeutic recreation specialists. As indicated in the chapter on Therapeutic Recreation, this law was enacted to assure persons who represent themselves as Therapeutic Recreation Specialists or Therapeutic Recreation Assistants meet certain standards as set forth by the State of North Carolina. Any person who uses the credentials without being certified by the state could be fined up to $500 and/or be imprisoned for up to 60 days.

In the Fall of 2000, the Therapeutic Recreation Certification Board developed a task force to review the Therapeutic Recreation Personnel Certification Act. The task force examined the law to see if the language and standards outlined were adequate to address the changing needs of practitioners working in health care. After conversation with practitioners and educators throughout the state, the task force suggested pursuing state licensure. Citing the need to better protect consumers of TR services and stay current with changes in health care, TRCB submitted House Bill 613 to the North Carolina House of Representatives on March 10, 2005. The "North Carolina Recreational Therapy Licensure Act" differs from previous legislation in that the bill, "includes licensure, expands Board composition to include a licensed Medical Doctor, authorizes the Board to discipline or revoke privileges to those found in violation of ethical and disciplinary standards of practice, and allows the board to change the fee structure" (Garrett, n.d.). At the time of publication, the bill had received support from the majority of the House of Representatives and had been passed on to the Senate for review. A bill does not become law until it is passed by both the House and Senate and, if required, signed by the Governor.

As of February 2005 there were 460 TRSs and 38 TRAs certified by the North Carolina Therapeutic Recreation Certification Board. For more information about TRCB contact them at http://www.trcb.org/.

Institutes and Continuing Education

Realizing that learning is a lifelong process and that the honing of professional skills occurs throughout one's career, the universities and colleges of North Carolina have made a concerted effort to offer a variety of continuing educational activities for recreation professionals. Many of them have taken the form of institutes, the proceedings of which have added significantly to the professional literature of the field.

Institutes have traditionally been the outgrowth of findings and implications of research conducted in the state. These institutes often address critical continuing education needs of practitioners for information and practices necessary for optimal recreation and leisure services delivery systems. The earliest of these occurred at UNC-Chapel Hill and North Carolina State University. Beginning in the 1950s, UNC-Chapel Hill conducted national and regional institutes on recreation services to those with special needs and recreation in community and medical settings. For example, UNC at Chapel Hill and UNC Hospitals co-hosted the Recreation Therapy Institute from 1989 to 1992.

Consistent with its earlier mandate, the Department of Recreation Resource Management at NC State University limited its continuing education programs to two subject areas during the 1950s: industrial recreation and park management. However, as interest in recreation management grew, and given the unique resources of a land grant college, the faculty at NC State in the 1960s directed its attention to developing a series of professional schools in conjunction with the National Recreation and Park Association. Most of these have been at Wheeling, West Virginia, and have dealt with finance, facilities and maintenance, and program supervision. The Park and Recreation Maintenance

Management School, Revenue Sources Management School, School for Zoos and Aquarium Personnel, Supervisors' Management School, and National Institute of Golf Management, School of RV Park & Campground Management, and Revenue Development and Management School were designed for executives and supervisory personnel. Their focus, as their names imply, is management and the application of new technologies and concepts to enhance the fiscal administration and operation of parks and recreation systems. For more information about this programs visit the Oglebay National Training Center Website at http://www.oglebay-resort.com/schools/.

Graduate Education

An important and growing aspect of professional development is graduate education. The reason for this growing importance is need for advanced learning and training in a specialized area of study, such as but not limited to Graphic Information System (GIS), Park Management, Budget Analysis, Planning and Policy Development, Therapeutic Recreation Administration, and Natural Resource Management. Graduate school provides this and also increases skills in such areas as critical thinking, problem solving, writing, research, oral and written communication, and technological advances. Currently, North Carolina has five institutions that offer master degree programs in recreation (East Carolina University, North Carolina Central University, North Carolina State University, University of North Carolina at Chapel Hill, and University of North Carolina at Greensboro) which focus on the areas of therapeutic recreation, commercial recreation, recreation management, park management, tourism management, and sport management. In addition, in 2000 North Carolina State University began the first doctoral program Recreation in North Carolina.

Current Continuing Education Opportunities

Municipal and County Park and Recreation Directors Conference

North Carolina State University and Recreation Resources Services sponsors this yearly two-day workshop for part and recreation directors designed to update information and provide and opportunity for networking, sharing, and exploring issues of mutual concerns. The conference is directed by its members and their executive committee and is open only to administrators of local parks and recreation systems. Since 1948 it had been hosted by UNC at Chapel Hill. In the spring of 2005, Recreation Resources Services took over coordination of the conference.

Revenue Sources Management School

The Revenue Sources Management School is a two-year educational program for park and recreation administrators, managers, and supervisors. Its purpose is to teach new concepts and technologies that enhance fiscal administration and the operation of revenue producing programs and facilities. This school is offered through North Carolina State University.

The Supervisors Management School

North Carolina State University sponsors this two-year education program for park and recreation executives and supervisory personnel. The instructional program is designed to serve park, recreation and conservation personnel whose responsibility it is to manage park and recreation maintenance programs.

Recreation Resources Services Programs

These continuing education opportunities are operated by the State of North Carolina for park, recreation, and leisure services professionals. These programs, often conducted jointly with other North Carolina universities or the North Carolina Recreation and Park Society, provide educational experiences that help practitioners stay current with changing issues and technologies. These programs include risk management, festivals and special events, playground safety, environmental issues, computer technology, conservation and law enforcement, and therapeutic recreation. The North Carolina Recreation and Park Society also offers continuing education courses and workshops on National Playground Safety Institute Certification, Park and Recreation Advisory Board Training, Athletic Field Maintenance, and other topics offered through their teleconference series. A current listing of opportunities can be found at their website: http://www.cnr.ncsu.edu/rrs/

State Recreation and Park Conferences

Each fall, the North Carolina Recreation and Parks Association (NCRPA) hosts a two and a half day conference that contains many continuing education opportunities related to programming, social issues, technology, and administrative practices.

The individual divisions and regions also sponsor throughout the year a variety of continuing professional education conferences and workshops located around the state. For example, every spring, the Therapeutic Recreation Division of NCRPA sponsors a two-day conference that specifically focuses on issues relevant to practitioners in therapeutic recreation such as managed care, innovative therapeutic techniques and interventions, and serving diverse populations with disabilities.

Similarly, the North Carolina Recreation Therapy Association hosts its annual two-day conference each fall with a wide variety of continuing education programs and topics. In addition, in the spring of each year, NCRTA hosts a Student Forum, a one-day workshop, oriented solely to issues and concerns of therapeutic recreation students.

North Carolina Area Health Education Centers (AHEC)

In 1970, the Carnegie Commission recommended the development of a nationwide system of Area Health Education Centers to address the needs of provision and retention of quality health care workers. By 1975, nine AHECs were operational in the state of North Carolina. NCAHEC provides information and resources to both students and practitioners working in health care. In particular, it provides continuing education workshops, a digital library, and publications on-line to allied health professionals throughout the state. For more information, go to http://www.ncahec.net/welcome.htm

Scholarship Opportunities

Several organizations provide scholarships to recognize achievement as well as provide opportunities for students and professionals to attend their workshops. The following are examples of some of these scholarships:

- Richard Hatfield Student Scholarship (North Carolina Recreation Therapy Association) is a "working" scholarship with the conference planning committee to assist with registration, room monitoring and student networking. The scholarship recipient will receive free conference registration, one year free NCRTA membership and room accommodations for the conference.
- North Carolina Recreator's Foundation provides financial assistance in the form of scholarships to qualified and deserving students who are pursuing an education for a career in the recreation and parks profession and professionals seeking continuing education. Three scholarships are awarded each year: one to an undergraduate student, the Fletcher Graduate Scholarship, and Professional Development Grant Application Scholarship.
- NCRPA - Therapeutic Recreation Division awards two Student Scholarships to defray the cost of attending its annual Spring conference.
- Tourism Education Foundation Scholarship has developed a combination of undergraduate and graduate scholarships to recognize the current students in tourism or hospitality management programs at North Carolina colleges and universities, as well as individuals employed by the tourism or hospitality industries wanting advanced study in tourism management at a North Carolina college or university offering such programs. In addition to the honorarium, recipients will receive complimentary registration to a tourism or hospitality conference
- North Carolina Alliance for Athletics, Health, Physical Education, Recreation, and Dance awards two undergraduate scholarships: the June P. Galloway Undergraduate Scholarship and the Nathan Taylor Dodson Undergraduate Scholarship.

International Study Opportunities

Several of the colleges and universities in North Carolina provide opportunities to study abroad in a variety of countries. For example, the following countries have programs associated with colleges and universities in North Carolina:

Appalachian State University	Poland, Italy, Costa Rica
East Carolina University	Australia
Elon College	Australia
North Carolina Central University	Italy
North Carolina State University	Costa Rica, Spain, England, Finland
University of North Carolina Greensboro	Australia, Scotland, England, Finland
University of North Carolina Wilmington	England
Western Carolina University	England

Many schools also have extensive Study Abroad opportunities offered through their University's International Study Offices. These programs help link students interested in recreation with other academic centers around the world.

Distance Learning

Another form of regular and continuing education is through distance learning. While none of the universities and colleges has established specific distance learning programs, several opportunities have existed for distance learning opportunities. For example, UNC-Chapel Hill, N.C. State University, and UNC-Wilmington offered a cooperatively taught course on park planning and facility design through the state satellite system. The course was open to campus-based students as well as practitioners throughout the state. The satellite system continues to be a valuable learning venue that periodically is used by various schools to reach professionals throughout the state.

Another opportunity to reach beyond the physical bounds of the campus exists through internet opportunities. For example, East Carolina University offered the first web-based introduction course and continues to develop online courses. N.C. State University and UNC-Greensboro have also developed valuable online learning opportunities a variety of concentrations to help students and professionals learn advance their education. Learning experiences enhanced through technological advances will likely continue to offer a wide variety of continuing and professional education.

State Societies and Professional Organizations

Professional development of practitioners is also promoted through the activities of the professional associations and organizations. These professional societies meet varying needs of the professionals in the field such as continuing education, legislative efforts, networking, and professional assistance. The organizations described in the following section provide information about select professional associations of interest to North Carolina recreation professionals.

North Carolina Recreation and Park Association

Historically, North Carolina has led the way toward a strong commitment for a united association to promote the role of recreation for individuals and communities. The North

Carolina Recreation and Park Association (formerly Society) has been a major force influencing legislation, providing financial assistance for students pursuing careers in parks and recreation, developing programs of in-service and continuing education, and promoting accreditation and certification for curricula and professionals in North Carolina.

Formed in Charlotte in 1944, the North Carolina Recreation Association, as it was first known, was established with Jesse Reynolds, Director of Parks and Recreation in Wilmington, as its president. Its first annual conference was held in Raleigh in the fall of 1945 and had 62 members. It was decided by the early leadership of the state society that it should be affiliated with the American Recreation Society (ARS) as one of its chapters. When the ARS merged with four other organizations to form the Nation Recreation and Park Association in 1965, the North Carolina Recreation and Park Society became an affiliate of NRPA.

Recognizing the need to address the special interests of its membership, the Society created various special interest divisions to reflect a more specific focal point of a particular group of professionals. For example, the first division was the Industrial Division in 1948. A year later the Municipal Division and the Hospital Division were added. Also in 1949, the Student Division was added as a result of a petition from students at North Carolina State College, the University of North Carolina at Chapel Hill, and the Women's College of North Carolina at Greensboro (Warren, 1989). Presently, the North Carolina Recreation and Park Association has over 2400 members in the divisions of Athletics, Commission Boards, Conservation And Enforcement, County Recreation, Educators, Municipal Recreation, Senior Programs, Students, And Therapeutic Recreation. Its newest division is the Culturally Diverse Programs Division that was instituted to aid in the development of recreation programs that address the needs of a diverse citizenship of the state of North Carolina. NCRPA publishes the *NCRPA News* and is directed by Mike Waters at 883 Washington Street, Raleigh, NC 27605-3251. Their website is www.ncrps.org.

North Carolina Recreation Therapy Association

The North Carolina Recreation Therapy Association (NCRTA) was founded on June 23, 1988. This independent non-profit organization was incorporated by the state of NC. It is an autonomous, state organization for professionals who provide services with a treatment focus to people with disabilities. The organization serves as an advocate for Recreation Therapy in order to promote the health and well being of the public through services and the development and enforcement of standards. Services provided by NCRTA include education/training opportunities, legislative and health care monitoring, research support, student support and networking, professional communication network, an association newsletter, and liaisons with other allied health professionals. To promote opportunities for collaboration with other professionals, NCRTA has been invited to appoint a member of the organization to represent them on the Council for Allied Health in North Carolina. The council represents over 18,000 allied health professionals from 26 professions and is a unique statewide body designed to provide information and support for the expanding number of professionals in NC. For more information about the council contact them at http://www.alliedhealthcouncilNC.org/. NCRTA, a chapter affiliate of the American Therapeutic Recreation Association, has approximately 255 members as of May 2005. Contact NCRTA at http://www.ncrta.org/.

Recreation Resources Service

Recreation Resources Service (RRS) is a clearinghouse and resource center providing technical materials, information, a networking system, continuing education applied research and administer the Parks and Recreation Trust Fund and Land and Conservation Fund for all park and recreation providers in North Carolina, public and private. It is a revised version of a concept originally put forth by the Department of Health, Environment and Natural Resources that was mandated by the North Carolina General Assembly many years ago. RRS provides these services at little to no cost to municipal, county, state and federal governments and public or private agencies or individuals engaged in or contemplating activity in parks and recreation in North Carolina. All one-hundred counties have requested and received service and almost all cities with parks and recreation departments have requested and received service. Specific services include publications distribution, financial grants, technical assistance bulletins, a online-job bulletin, in-service continuing education workshops and short courses, and conceptual planning. A current listing of opportunities and resources can be found at www.cnr.ncsu.edu/rrs.

Professional Societies and Organizations Contact Information

Listed below are some of North Carolina's professional societies and organizations and their respective Web-sites. Periodically check their websites for upcoming professional conferences, meetings, and continual educational programs.

North Carolina Recreation Therapy Association (http://www.ncrta.org/)
North Carolina Alliance for Athletics, Health, Physical Education, Recreation and Dance http://www.ncaahperd.org/)
North Carolina Recreation & Park Association (http://www.ncrps.org/)
North Carolina Association of County Commissioners (http://www.ncacc.org/)
North Carolina League of Municipalities (http://www.nclm.org/)
North Carolina Association of Convention and Visitor Bureaus (http://visit.nc.org/)
North Carolina Travel Industry Association (http://www.nctravelcouncil.com/)
North Carolina Restaurant Association (http://www.ncra.org/)

Summary

This chapter has highlighted some of the points for consideration for understanding professional preparation and development in North Carolina. As suggested throughout this chapter, North Carolina has a proud tradition of being in the forefront in the development of parks, recreation and leisure academic curricula in higher education. This interest in the development of well-educated, highly qualified individuals has also been a major focus to the professional associations. These organizations have contributed greatly to the wide variety of continuing education opportunities as well as to the development of the profession in North Carolina through their activities and interests. In addition, its progressive quality and growth assure that North Carolina will continue as a leader in the field of recreation, parks, and leisure studies for many years to come.

Learning Exercises

1. Pick one recreation professional association or society and explore its website. From the website find the following information, mission, annual conference (date and location), publications, membership information, and scholarship information.

2. Visit the Recreation Resources Service (RRS) Website www.cnr.ncsu.edu/rrs. What is the purpose and mission of RRS and what types of services and assistance do they provide our profession?

3. Arrange a visit to one of the listed universities to discuss curricula and program focus.

4. Interview graduates from several different curricula in North Carolina. Compare and contrast your findings in terms of curriculum, preparation, and accreditation.

5. Interview a recreation professional and discuss her or his perceptions of the certification process and its contribution to the recreation profession.

6. Go to one of the professional association or society websites and identify a resource that would help you become more involved in your profession (e.g., lending library, job lists, internship guides, related organizations).

7. Identify 5 jobs that you would like to have when you graduate. Identify competencies required to obtain this position. Consider education, experience, credentials, specific knowledge base, etc. Identify your own strengths and weaknesses for this position and outline a plan to meet these competencies by graduation.

References

Goodrich, K. (1981). The new pro-accreditation activists, accreditation's hope. *Parks and Recreation*, *16*(4), 51-54.

Henderson, K.A. (1995). Professional leadership in recreation, parks, and leisure services: Past, present, and future. *Schole: A Journal of Leisure Studies and Recreation Education, 10*, 88.

Sessoms, H.D. (1995). Reflections of a recreation educator. *Schole: A Journal of Leisure Studies and Recreation Education, 10*, 89-96.

Sessoms, H.D. (1993). *Eight decades of leadership development: A history of programs of professional preparation in parks and recreation, 1909-1989*. Arlington, VA: National Recreation and Park Association.

Sessoms, H.D. (1990). On becoming a profession- Requirements and Strategies. *Journal of Park and Recreation Administration, 8* (4), 33-42.

Shapiro, Ira. (1977). The path to accreditation. *Parks and Recreation, 12* (1), 29.

Society of Park and Recreation Educators. (1975). Education for leisure. A position statement contained in D. Weiskopf (Ed.) *Proceedings of the 1975 Dallas SPRE Institute.* Arlington, VA: National Recreation and Park Association.

Garrett, B. (n.d.). TRCB: *Frequently Asked Questions, available from the* Therapeutic Recreation Certification Board, PO Box 67, Saxapahaw, NC 27340

Warren, R. (1989). *History of North Carolina Recreation and Park Society*, Raleigh, N.C.: North Carolina State University.

Sources for Further Information

Name of College/University: Appalachian State University
Curriculum Name: Recreation Management
Address: Holmes Convocation Center, Boone, NC 28608
Phone: 828-262-6335/3140
Fax: 828-262-3138
E-MAIL: willwe@appstate.edu
Web Site Address: http://www.hles.appstate.edu/www_docs/depart.hles/leisure.html
Department Head: Dr. Wayne Williams, Program Director
Degrees offered: Bachelor of Science in Recreation Management
Options/Concentrations: Commercial Recreation & Tourism Management, Recreation and Park Management, Outdoor Experiential Education
NRPA Accredited: Yes

Name of College/University: Belmont Abbey College
Curriculum Name: Therapeutic Recreation
Address: 100 Belmont, Mt. Holly Road, Belmont, NC 28012
Phone: 111-888.BAC.0110
Fax:
E-MAIL: kimberlyrobertson@bac.edu
Web Site Address: http://www.belmontabbeycollege.edu/Academics/therarec.shtml
Department Head: Dr. Kimberly Robertson, Program Coordinator
Degrees offered: Bachelor of Science
Options/Concentrations: Therapeutic Recreation,

Name of College/University: Carteret Community College
Curriculum Name: Therapeutic Recreation
Address: 3505 Arendell St., Morehead City, NC 28557
Phone: 252-247-6000
Fax: 252-247-2514
E-MAIL: cef@carteret.edu
Web Site Address: www.carteret.edu/education/academicprograms/
therapeuticrec/trsite/htm
Department Head: Charlotte Ferris, Program Coordinator
Degrees offered: Associate
Options/Concentrations: Therapeutic Recreation,

Name of College/University: East Carolina University
Curriculum Name: Recreation and Leisure Studies
Address: 174 Minges Coliseum, Greenville, NC 27858 - 4353
Phone: 252-328-4640
Fax: 252-328-4642
E-MAIL: fridgenj@mail.ecu.edu
Web Site Address: http://www.ecu.edu/rcls/
Department Head: Dr. Joseph Fridgen
Degrees offered: Bachelor of Science, Master of Science
Options/Concentrations: Management of Recreation Facilities and Services,
Recreational Therapy, Management of Recreation Facilities and Services
Administration, Recreational Therapy Administration
NRPA Accredited: Yes

Name of College/University: Elon College
Curriculum Name: Leisure/Sport Management
Address: Campus Box 2233, Elon University, Elon, NC 27244
Phone: 336-584-2559
Fax: 336-584-2443
E-MAIL: drummond@elon.edu
Web Site Address: http://www.elon.edu/e-web/academics/education/lsm/
Department Head: Dr. James Drummond
Degrees offered: Bachelor of Science

Name of College/University: Mars Hill College
Curriculum Name: Recreation and Leisure Services
Address: Chambers Gym, 100 Athletic St., Mars Hill College, Mars Hill, NC 28754
Phone: (828) 689-1369
E-MAIL: ledsall@mhc.edu
Web Site Address: http://www.mhc.edu/physed/index.asp
Department Head: Lura Edsall
Degrees offered: Bachelor of Science
Options/Concentrations: Sports, Physical Education and Recreation

Name of College/University: Mount Olive College
Curriculum Name: Recreation and Leisure Studies
Address: 634 Henderson St., Mount Olive, NC 28365
Phone: (919) 658- 7878 or 1-800-653-0854 ext. 1175
Fax: E-MAIL: scarter@exchange.moc.edu
Web Site Address: http://www.mountolivecollege.edu/request.cfm?Section= academics&pagename=Recreation%20and%20Leisure
Department Head: Dr. Sharon Carter
Degrees offered: Bachelor of Science
Options/Concentrations: Therapeutic Recreation, Sport Management, Leisure Service Management, and Athletic Training

Name of College/University: NC A&T State University
Curriculum Name: Health, Physical Education and Recreation
Address: 201 Corbett Gym, Greensboro, NC 27411
Phone: 336-334-7712
Fax: 36-334-7258
E-MAIL: deborahc@ncat.edu
Web Site Address: http://www.ncat.edu/~schofed/SOE%20hper.htm
Department Head: Dr. Deborah J. Callaway
Degrees offered: Bachelor of Science
Options/Concentrations: Therapeutic Recreation

Name of College/University: North Carolina Central University
Curriculum Name: Physical Education and Recreation
Address: Campus Box 19542, Durham, NC 27707
Phone: 919-560-6332
Fax: 919-560-5012
E-MAIL: politano@nccu.edu.
Web Site Address: http://www.nccu.edu/artsci/pe/pe.html
Department Head: Dr. Beverly Allen
Degrees offered: Bachelor of Science, Master of Science
Options/Concentrations: Recreation Administration, Therapeutic Recreation
NRPA Accredited: Yes

Name of College/University: North Carolina State University
Curriculum Name: Department of Parks, Recreation, and Tourism Management
Address: Box 8004, 4008 Biltmore Hall, Raleigh, NC 27695 - 8004
Phone: 919-515-3276
Fax: 919-515-3687
E-MAIL: Doug_Wellman@ncsu.edu
Web Site Address: http://www.cfr.ncsu.edu/prtm/html
Department Head: Dr. J. Douglas Wellman
Degrees offered: Bachelor of Science, Master of Science, Master of Natural Resources Master of Parks, Recreation and Tourism Management, Doctorate of Philosophy
Options/Concentrations: Program Management, Tourism and Commercial Recreation, Sport Management, and Park and Natural Resources Recreation Management.
NRPA Accredited: Yes

Name of College/University: Southeastern Community College
Curriculum Name: Park Ranger Technology
Address: PO Box 151, Whiteville, NC 28472
Phone: 910-642-7141 ext. 329
Fax: 910-642-5658
E-MAIL:
Web Site Address: www.southeastern.cc.nc.us/park.htm
Department Head:
Degrees offered: Associate of Applied Science
Options/Concentrations:

Name of College/University: Shaw University
Curriculum Name: Recreation, Therapeutic Recreation
Address: 118 East South St Raleigh NC, 27601
Phone: 919-546-8205
Fax: 919 743-4693
E-MAIL: jsmieth@shawu.edu
Web Site Address: http://www.shawuniversity.edu/ap_cgps_dept_allied_health.htm
Department Head: Dr. Gaddis Faulcon
Degrees offered: Bachelor of Science in Recreation, Bachelor of Science in Therapeutic Recreation
Options/Concentrations: Recreation, Therapeutic Recreation

Name of College/University: University of North Carolina at Chapel Hill
Curriculum Name: Recreation and Leisure Studies Specialization in the Department of Exercise and Sport Science
Address: CB 8700 Chapel Hill, NC 27599
Phone: 919-962-0534
Fax: 919-962-6325
E-MAIL: groff@email.unc.edu
Web Site Address:
Department Head: Kevin Guskiewicz
Degrees offered: Bachelors of Science in Recreation Administration, Therapeutic Recreation; Master of Science in Recreational Administration
Options/Concentrations: Recreation Administration, Therapeutic Recreation
NRPA Accredited: Yes

Name of College/University: University of North Carolina at Greensboro
Curriculum Name: Recreation, Tourism and Hospitality Management
Address: PO Box 26170, Greensboro, NC 27402
Phone: 336-334-5327
Fax: 336-334-3238
E-MAIL: sjs@uncg.edu
Web Site Address: http://www.uncg.edu/rth/
Department Head: Dr. Stuart J. Schleien
Degrees offered: Bachelors of Science in Recreation and Parks Management, Bachelors of Arts in Tourism and Hospitality Management, Master of Science in Recreation and Parks Management
Options/Concentrations: Therapeutic Recreation, Commercial Recreation, Leisure Service Management, Hotel and Restaurant Management, and Travel and Tourism
NRPA Accredited: Yes

Name of College/University: University of North Carolina at Wilmington
Curriculum Name: Parks and Recreation Management
Address: 601 S. College Rd., Wilmington, NC 28403
Phone: 910-962-3250
Fax: 910-962-7073
E-MAIL: kinneyt@uncw.edu
Web Site Address: www.uncw.edu/hahs
Department Head: Dr. Terry Kinney
Degrees offered: Bachelor of Arts
Options/Concentrations: Therapeutic Recreation, Leisure Service Management
NRPA Accredited: Yes

Name of College/University: Western Carolina University
Curriculum Name: Health and Human Performance
Address: Reid Gym, Cullowhee, NC 28723
Phone: 828-227-7332
Fax: 828-227-7645
E-MAIL: Claxton@email.wcu.edu
Web Site Address: http://www.ceap.wcu.edu/hhp/HHPHome.html
Department Head: Dr. David Claxton
Degrees offered: Bachelor of Science
Options/Concentrations: Parks and Recreation Management, Recreational Therapy, Physical Education, and Sport Management

Name of College/University: Western Piedmont Community College
Curriculum Name: Therapeutic Recreation
Address: 1001 Burkemont Ave., Morganton, NC 28655
Phone: 828-438-5577
Fax: 828-438-6015
E-MAIL: cindyk@wp.cc.nc.us
Web Site Address: www.wpcc.edu
Department Head: Cynthia Konarski, Program Coordinator
Degrees offered: Associates
Options/Concentrations: Therapeutic Recreation

Name of College/University: Winston-Salem State University
Curriculum Name: Therapeutic Recreation Program
Address: Therapeutic Recreation Coordinator, Department Of Physical Education, Winston Salem State University, C.B. 19386, Winston Salem NC 27110
Phone: 336-750-2590
Fax: 336-750-2591
E-MAIL: gopalanh@wssu.edu
Web Site Address: http://gorams.wssu.edu/soe/HPSS/tr.htm
Department Head: Dr. Himanshu Gopalan, Coordinator
Degrees offered: Bachelor of Science
Options/Concentrations: Therapeutic Recreation
NRPA Accredited: Yes

Chapter 10

Outdoor Recreation and the Environment

Aram Attarian, Tommy Holden, Jim Sibthorp, and Delmar Bachert

North Carolina's varied topography, temperate climate, and diverse natural resources provide a range of opportunities for outdoor enthusiasts. The state's resources stretch from the mountains, through the piedmont, to the coastal plain, and finally to the tidewater region and the Atlantic Ocean with its beautiful barrier islands. These exceptional resources and the people who use them frame the study of outdoor recreation in the state.

The jurisdiction and stewardship of the land and water resources of North Carolina are entrusted to the state. *The North Carolina Constitution*, Article XIV, Section 5, recognizes the importance of the state's unique natural resource heritage:

> *It shall be the policy of this State to conserve and protect all lands and waters for the benefit of all its citizenry, and to this end it should be a proper function of the State of North Carolina and its political subdivisions to acquire and preserve parks, recreational, and scenic areas, to control and limit pollution of our air and water, to control excessive noise, and in every other appropriate way to preserve as a part of the common heritage of this state its forests; wetlands, estuaries, beaches, historical sites, and open lands, and places of beauty.*

The primary objectives of this chapter will be to investigate the outdoor recreation opportunities in the Old North State. First, the climate and geography that give North Carolina its diversity will be examined. Secondly, an overview of outdoor recreation activities that are resource dependent (lakes, mountains, rivers, etc.) will be explored, followed by human-made resource dependent activities (i.e., golf courses and ski resorts). Finally, the concept of supply and demand as it relates to the future of outdoor recreation in North Carolina will be discussed.

Resource–Dependent Opportunities

North Carolina's humid subtropical climate and varied geography combine to form unique environments allowing recreationists to pursue a variety of outdoor recreation activities. North Carolina's geography consists of a mountain region located in the western part of the state that contains the highest elevations in the eastern United States. Found in this region are 200 peaks with elevations reaching 5,000 feet and forty nine peaks with elevations more than 6,000 feet. This region also contains valleys, deep gorges, and swiftly moving rivers and streams (Drake & Bromley, 1997; Ellis, 2000).

The piedmont region is located in the central part of the state. The mountains to the west and the fall line of the coastal plain to the east are its bounds. This 150-mile wide area contains the primary urban areas of the state and much of the state's population. Rolling terrain, large rivers, and reservoirs contribute to the character of the region (Newman, 1995).

The coastal plain encompasses over one-fourth of the state's land. The rolling hills of the piedmont to the west and tidewater to the east mark its boundaries. This naturally diverse area is approximately one hundred to 140-miles-wide and includes slow-moving rivers and the only natural lakes found in the state (Drake & Bromley, 1997; Gade, Rex, & Young, 2002). The state's easternmost region, the tidewater, is characterized primarily by low-lying terrain. This region extends from the barrier islands to approximately thirty to eighty miles inland and includes 4,000 miles of beaches, sounds, offshore barrier islands, tidal flats, and wetlands (Gade et al., 2002).

There are many outstanding outdoor recreation resources located within these regions. North Carolina has thirty state parks, sixteen state natural areas, seven state lakes, four state recreation areas, four state natural and scenic rivers, and two state trails. Together these total 168,455 acres of land and water (North Carolina Division of Parks and Recreation, 2005). The state is also home to four national forests, managed by the United States Department of Agriculture- Forest Service and ten federally designated Wilderness areas. The Department of Interior's jurisdiction in North Carolina is comprised of ten National Park Service units that consist of national parks, seashores, parkways, wild and scenic rivers, trails, historic sites, memorials, and cemeteries. Unique among these resources is the nation's most visited national park, Great Smoky Mountains National Park, and Cape Hatteras, the nation's first national seashore, is a continuing source of pride. Additionally, the United States Fish and Wildlife Service manages ten National Wildlife Refuges.

Land- Based Activities

During 2004 some of the most visited attractions in the state were the Blue Ridge Parkway, Cape Hatteras National Seashore, Great Smoky Mountains National Park, and North Carolina state parks (North Carolina Department of Commerce- Tourism, Film, and Sports Development, 2004a). North Carolina's land based resources support a variety of outdoor activities. Some of activities these are presented below.

Camping

Camping is a popular outdoor recreation activity in the state. According to the Outdoor Industry Foundation (2003), over 1,000,000 North Carolinians participated in overnight camping during 2002. To support camping, more than 15,000 tent and trailer campsites are available statewide through more than 300 privately owned campgrounds. An additional 4,000 public campsites are also available (Drake & Bromley, 1997).

Hiking and Backpacking

Hiking and backpacking are popular outdoor recreation activities with over 45 million participants nationwide (National Sporting Goods Association, 2004). Found in North Carolina are over 1,000 trails covering more than 3,000 miles, including more than 300 miles of the Appalachian Trail (deHart, 2005). The state lends itself to a variety of hiking and backpacking opportunities. City, county, and state parks, national forests, national park areas, and private land holdings are the primary hiking and backpacking resources found in the state.

The North Carolina mountains are a popular destination, especially during the spring wildflower and rhododendron bloom, and during the fall color spectacular. Among the more popular destinations are the rugged peaks of Grandfather Mountain, the trails along the Blue Ridge Parkway, and the hundreds of trails found in the Pisgah and Nantahala National Forests. Trails found in this region range from ridge tops and valleys, streams and high elevation spruce-fir forests, to low elevation hardwood forests. The biologically diverse Great Smoky Mountains National Park is also popular, as are the Shining Rock and Linville Gorge Wilderness areas. Several state parks with well-marked and maintained trails are also found in this area.

Surprisingly, a variety of quality hiking and backpacking areas can be found in the piedmont region close to the state's urban and population centers. Dominating this region are state, county, and municipal parks, some with extensive greenway systems. Large reservoirs such as Kerr Lake, Falls Lake, Jordan Lake, Lake Norman, and others have established trail systems. The Uwharrie National Forest, located in the South Central portion of the state, provides a "close to home," semi-primitive outing experience for the adventuresome.

Like the piedmont region, the coastal and tidewater areas contain municipal, county, state, and federal areas to pursue hiking and backpacking. National Wildlife Refuges and the Croatan National Forest contain diverse estuary and pocosin areas. Cape Hatteras and Cape Lookout National Seashores provide over one hundred miles of combined undeveloped beach.

Currently under construction is the Mountains to Sea Trail (MST). When completed it will be a 900+ mile trail consisting of footpaths, roads, river, and state bike routes that will connect Clingman's Dome in Great Smoky Mountains National Park with Jockey's Ridge State Park on the coast. Currently, more than 400 miles of the MST have been completed. The MST trail got its start in 1973 when the North Carolina General Assembly passed the North Carolina Trails System Act to establish trails throughout the natural, scenic, and urban areas of the state.

Other resources for hiking and backpacking include North Carolina state parks and components of the National Trails System (NTS) established by Congress in 1968. The NTS in North Carolina includes a number of important trails located in the state's mountain region. These trails include the Overmountain Victory Trail, Bartram Trail, Grandfather and Daniel Boone Scout Trail, Whiteside Mountain Trail, and the Trail of Tears.

Rock Climbing

Participation in rock climbing has been projected to grow faster than the population over the next half-century, especially in the southern United States (Cordell, 1999). Newer, safer, and more available equipment, growth of instructional programs and guide services, indoor climbing walls, and more media visibility are some of the factors contributing to this projected growth (Attarian, 1993). Rock climbing has been an outdoor recreation activity in North Carolina since the early 1940s when exploration of the cliffs in Linville Gorge began (Kelley, 1995). The sport slowly grew through the 1950s and 60s. Development continued through the 1970s and 80s with the exploration of new areas and more difficult ascents.

Recently, bouldering has become a popular climbing activity, especially in North Carolina's High Country. Bouldering is climbing close to the ground where falls are short and usually inconsequential and without the use of a rope or anchors for protection. Bouldering areas around Grandfather Mountain have been described as "bouldering's holy grail" (Young, 2001, p. 70). John Sherman (1994), America's bouldering "guru," once referred to the Blowing Rock Boulders "as the best boulderfield of its size in America" (p. 89).

North Carolina climbing areas have become popular year-round destinations for climbers throughout the Southeast and the nation. Mild winters, sound rock, access, and a variety of climbing environments from well established top rope areas near urban centers to climbing in remote wilderness areas have contributed to its popularity. Dominating the climbing landscapes are the unique granite domes, or plutons, formed when molten lava hardened underground. Over time, the action of wind, water, and other erosive forces eroded the softer layers of rock on top of the hard granite, exposing the rock visible today. Stone Mountain, Looking Glass Rock, and Cedar Rock are good examples of this type of rock. Steep quartzite and granite walls are also common throughout the state and vary in height from one pitch in length (<165') to over 900 foot big walls.

The *Climber's Guide to North Carolina* (Kelly, 1995) and *Selected Climbs in North Carolina* (Lambert & Shull, 2003) have identified fourteen different climbing areas on public land. These areas include four state parks (Hanging Rock, Pilot Mountain, Stone Mountain, and Crowder's Mountain), documenting over 30,000 climbers visits in 1999 (North Carolina Division of Parks and Recreation, 2000). Climbing areas are also located in Pisgah and Nantahala National Forests, and along the Blue Ridge Parkway's Grandfather Mountain Corridor. National publications including *Climbing* and *Rock and Ice* have featured many of these climbing and bouldering areas.

Rockhounding (Gem and Mineral Collecting)

There are more than 400 different varieties of minerals and gems found in North Carolina. Minerals of value can be found in many counties, and North Carolina has a worldwide reputation for its mineral wealth. The first significant discovery of gold in the United States was made in North Carolina in 1799.

The most popular minerals among collectors include: agate, aquamarine, barite, beryl, calcite, chalcedony, corundum, epidote, feldspar (North Carolina leads the nation in the production of feldspar), galena, opal, horneblende, magnetite, muscovite, olivine, pyrite, quartz, tourmaline and zircon, rubies, sapphires, and emeralds. North Carolina has more precious and semi-precious gems than any other state in the nation and is the only state where emeralds are found. A large emerald known as the "Carolina Emerald," valued at $100,000.00, was found in Hiddenite, North Carolina. It became recognized as the largest and finest cut emerald in North America (North Carolina Travel and Tourism Division, 1996).

Gemstones such as rubies and sapphires have been found in the western counties, and emeralds have been found in Alexander and Mitchell counties. Cabarrus and Stanley counties contain sites for panning gold. Other semiprecious gems that are found in the state include: moonstone, peridot, rhodolite, kyanite, and hiddenite, just to name a few. Many of these minerals can be "mined" in commercially operated "gem mines" throughout the state, especially in the mountain region.

Mountain Biking

According to the International Mountain Biking Association (IMBA), mountain bike participation continues to grow. Most reliable estimates put the number of regular U.S. mountain bikers at about 9-10 million (Blumenthal, 2001). The Outdoor Industry Foundation (2003) reports that over 16% of North Carolinians participated in mountain biking during 2001 to 2002.

There are over 2000 miles of trails available to Tarheel mountain bike enthusiasts (Muth, 2003). All four of the state's national forests are open to mountain biking, with over eighty five trails open year-round. While designated wilderness areas prohibit use of mechanized equipment including mountain bikes, cyclists may travel all closed roads in non-wilderness areas unless posted. Examples of popular riding areas include the nationally known Tsali Recreation Area located in the Nantahala National Forest, Woods Run in Uwharrie National Forest, and the Bent Creek area in Pisgah National Forest (Setzer, 2000).

In addition to national forests, Umstead and South Mountain State Parks allow mountain biking on bridle trails and access roads only. Dupont State Forest and the Dark Mountain Trails at W. Kerr Scott Reservoir are also popular destinations. Many municipal parks also provide maintained trails for mountain biking. Some of these parks include Wake County's Lake Crabtree and Harris Lake Parks, Bur-Mill Park in Greensboro, San-Lee Park in Sanford, and Little River Park in Orange and Durham Counties.

Horseback Riding

The horse industry has a significant impact on North Carolina's economy. The North Carolina Department of Agriculture reports that 65,000 horse producers own over 225,000 horses. This generates over $704 million of gross revenue from training, showing, boarding, and breeding facilities in addition to agri-business sales of horse-related products (North Carolina State University Cooperative Extension- Horse Husbandry, 2005). Of the horse owners in North Carolina, 75 percent prefer trail riding as their primary activity (Holden, 1999).

Equestrian related activities encompass more than thirty events each year and include rodeos, steeplechase events, horse shows, and trail riding on public and private lands. Ranches and stables offer instruction, rentals, and guided trail rides. Many of these facilities can be found throughout the state.

Hunting

North Carolina hunting expenditures totaled 458 million dollars in 2001 (International Association of Fish and Wildlife Agencies, 2002). This activity is managed by the North Carolina Wildlife Resources Commission (NCWRC) who oversee over 2 million acres of public game lands. The commission is charged with managing the wildlife resources in the state including the state's hunting, fishing, and trapping regulations. Since its inception in 1947, the Commission has monitored and managed wildlife populations throughout the state and has been a model for other states to follow (Wildlife in North Carolina, 1999). The NCWRC is also responsible for educating the public on hunting safety and the environment, and works with landowners to manage wildlife on private lands. The Commission has an extensive big game program that oversees the harvest and other management activities of a statewide deer population that numbers more than 900,000 animals, a wild turkey project that includes more than 100,000 birds, and an extensive black bear range (Wildlife in North Carolina, 1999). Small game species (two of the state's most important small game species are the cottontail rabbit and bobwhite quail) and waterfowl are also important wildlife resources managed for hunting.

Watchable Wildlife

North Carolina wildlife is diverse and includes 120 species of mammals, 200 species of birds, seventy species of reptiles, eighty species of amphibians, and 245 species of freshwater fish (Drake & Bromley, 1997). Each year over 2.4 million people enjoy wildlife through activities such as bird watching and photography (Jahn, 2002). Watching wildlife is a popular form of outdoor recreation in North Carolina, accounting for over $827 million in expenditures for 2001 (United States Department of the Interior, Fish and Wildlife Service, 2003). Bird watching attracted 1.3 million North Carolinians during 2001. The majority, 73 percent, observed wild birds around their homes, while 40 percent took trips away from home to watch birds (United States Department of the Interior, Fish and Wildlife Service, 2003).

Watchable Wildlife is a national initiative that has emerged as the percentage of consumptive sportsmen has declined across America. Watchable Wildlife is a program that does not consume wildlife but brings people closer to nature. Program goals are to provide opportunities for the public to enjoy wildlife on public and private lands, contribute to local economic development, promote learning about wildlife and habitat needs, and encourage active public support for resource conservation.

North Carolina is home to the Charles Kuralt trail, which links eleven wildlife refuges through 300 miles of trails in Virginia and North Carolina. The North Carolina Wildlife Viewing Guide (Roe, 1992) has been produced to help people find and observe our state's abundant wildlife.

Off Highway Vehicles (OHV)

A number of opportunities exist state wide to pursue OHV activities. OHVs include all-terrain, 4-wheel drive vehicles and dirt bikes. Many of the state's primary OHV areas are found in most of the state's national forests. These include the Upper Tellico and Wayehutta ATV areas located in Nantahala National Forest, the Brown Mountain ORV area in Pisgah National Forest, and Baden Lake ORV area found in Uwharrie National Forest. Policies do not permit cross-country travel; instead travel is limited to existing roads and trails. All trails are signed and blazed for OHV use. Drivers are encouraged to drive responsibly and reduce environmental impacts through the "Tread Lightly!" program initiated in 1985 by the United States Forest Service (USFS) to address concerns about the impacts from increasing numbers of visitors. In 1990, management responsibilities were transferred to the private sector.

Water-Based Activities

North Carolina offers water sport enthusiasts a variety of resources to pursue water-based activities. Aside from the Atlantic Ocean and the natural sounds, almost 40,000 freshwater stream miles and over 300,000 acres of lakes and reservoirs exist in North Carolina (Drake & Bromley, 1997). These resources support flatwater and whitewater canoeing, whitewater kayaking, rafting, sea kayaking, sailing, and powerboating. Windsurfing along with the fast growing sport of kiteboarding, are also popular activities on the state's reservoirs and along the North Carolina coast where wind conditions are ideal. The North Carolina Natural and Scenic Rivers System includes the South Fork of the New River (26.5 miles), the Lumber River (eighty one miles), the Linville River (thirteen miles), and the Horsepasture River (4.2 miles). The South Fork of the New River, the Lumber River, and the Horsepasture River are also included in the National Wild and Scenic River System.

Paddle trails have been developed and maintained along the Roanoke River by the Roanoke River Partners. Paddle trails are also being developed at Cape Lookout National Seashore and other areas throughout the state.

Beach Activities

According to the Travel Industry Association's 2004 report, 15 percent of North Carolina's visitors in 2003 came to visit the beach. And the Cape Hatteras National Seashore was the fourth most popular attraction in the state (North Carolina Department of Commerce—Tourism, Film, and Sport Development, 2004a). Popular activities along North Carolina's 4,000-mile coastline include swimming, sunbathing, shell collecting, surf fishing, and walking for pleasure.

North Carolina has established a Beach Access Program, which works with local governments to identify, improve, and provide access to the oceans and sounds of North Carolina. Currently there are more than 550 beach access sites throughout eastern North Carolina that allow beach access to the public without crossing private property (North Carolina Department of Environment and Natural Resources, 2005). Facilities can be found at most access points and vary from site to site. All areas are accessible for the disabled. Facilities generally fall into three categories:

- Regional facilities provide parking, restrooms, showers, dune crossovers, litter receptacles, water fountains, seating areas, and lifeguards.
- Neighborhood facilities provide limited parking, dune crossovers, and litter receptacles.
- Local facilities provide dune crossovers and litter receptacles.

Paddling

Characterized by long, steep, and rocky channels, spectacular scenery, and high gradients the state's mountain rivers are popular for whitewater canoeing, kayaking, and rafting. Some favorite rivers among whitewater boaters are the Nantahala, French Broad, South Fork of the New, Watauga, Nolichucky, and Tuckaseegee (Benner & Benner, 2002).

Canoeing and kayaking are also possible on Piedmont rivers. Rivers and streams flowing through the Piedmont are generally larger and lack the high gradients and pristine setting of the mountains. Instead, these rivers are usually slower moving and in some cases contain sections of whitewater. Rivers popular with boaters in the central part of the state include the Yadkin, Catawba, Haw, Dan, Cape Fear, and Neuse (Benner, 1987). In addition to the Piedmont rivers, reservoirs constructed by the Army Corps of Engineers provide opportunities for water-based recreation in this part of the state. The larger reservoirs include Jordan Lake, Falls Lake, J.H. Kerr Reservoir, and W. Kerr Scott Reservoir. All areas have a full range of recreation facilities including campgrounds, picnic areas, visitor centers, boat ramps, and marinas. Some of these reservoirs have also become popular destinations for sea kayakers.

The coastal region contains slow-moving rivers and the state's only natural lakes, most of which are state parks. Currently, the State Trails Program is working with local and regional partners and associations in efforts to maintain and enhance the network of 134 paddle trails that travel 1,200 miles through twenty six counties in the eastern portion of the state. Rivers meandering through swamps and marshes characterize the flat terrain of the coastal plain. As these rivers near the sounds, a more tropical landscape emerges. The Trent, White Oak, Lumber, Black River, and Roanoke are popular rivers among boaters in this region (Benner, 1987). The North Carolina Professional Paddle Sports Association has over twenty five members statewide. Many provide guided trips, raft and canoe rentals, equipment, and instructional programs.

Powerboating

The state registered 353,625 boats during 2002, ranking North Carolina twelfth in the nation in boat registration (National Marine Manufacturers Association, 2004). Both inland and coastal resources are available to the state's boaters. The North Carolina Wildlife Resources Commission, Division of Engineering Services (DOES) maintains almost all of the state's boating resources. The primary responsibility of this division is to build and maintain public boating and fishing access areas. The division also maintains waterway markers. Currently the DOES oversees eighty bodies of water and 194 boating access areas throughout the state. Some include restrooms, fish cleaning facilities, and electricity. In addition to these access areas, there are more than 450 private marinas throughout the state (Bradley, 1998). Many offer amenities including fuel sales, restaurants, and supplies. A 265-mile segment of the Intracoastal Waterway, maintained by the Army Corps of Engineers, makes its way through the tidewater region of the state. This waterway follows a protected route through the rivers and sounds of the East Coast.

Diving

North Carolina scuba diving is recognized as some of the best in the world. In Rodale's *Scuba Diving* 1999 reader poll, North Carolina ranked fourth nationally as "best overall dive location" and ranked first nationally as "best wreck diving," "best place to see big animals," "best advanced diving," and "best destination value" in North America. North Carolina diving is popular for three major reasons: (1) The coast's proximity to the warm, clear waters of the Gulf Stream creates comfortable summertime water temperatures, brings a variety of tropical marine species to our dive sites, and allows visibility in excess of 100 feet, (2) the continental shelf extends up to fifty miles outward from the coast, providing a large number of sites in diver accessible depths, and (3) shipwrecks.

Known as the "Graveyard of the Atlantic," North Carolina's coast is renowned for wreck diving. More than 2,000 wrecks are lying on the sea bottom off the North Carolina coast. Most wrecks can be found in depths of forty to 160 feet, with the more popular sites between seventy and 130 feet. Divers can reach these sites on their own, or they can hire charter boats to transport them to sites. Dive shops also offer walk-on charters, conduct classes, and rent equipment. There are more than one hundred dive shops and charter boat operators statewide.

Fishing

North Carolina's waters give anglers unique opportunities to pursue a variety of fish species using different types of fishing tackle. Nationally, fishing ranked sixth among all recreation activities with 41.2 million participants in 2004 (National Sporting Goods Association, 2004). This popularity is also evident in North Carolina. In a recent statewide survey, 50 percent of the respondents indicated they had participated in freshwater fishing and 38 percent in saltwater fishing (North Carolina Comprehensive Outdoor Recreation Plan, 2003). Additionally, over $1.1 billion was spent on fishing related expenses in North Carolina in 2001 (United States Department of the Interior, Fish and Wildlife Service, 2003).

Fishing resources in the Piedmont consist of large rivers, reservoirs, and thousands of farm ponds. Many of these water resources are stocked with hatchery-reared fish. In the reservoirs, crappie, largemouth bass, and striped bass are the most sought after fish, and some cities provide angling opportunities from small reservoirs (200-1,500 acres) and offer amenities such as boat ramps, concessions, and boat rentals.

The mountain region offers great angling on fast-moving mountain streams, rivers, and mountain lakes. The region is best known for its trout fishing, which is supported by over 4,000 miles (1,100 miles are hatchery supported) of trout streams that provide anglers a chance to catch brook, brown, and rainbow trout. A number of commercially operated private trout ponds are also open to the public.

The state's coastal plain and tidewater region extending from Virginia to South Carolina contains a large water resource consisting of slow-moving rivers, natural lakes, farm ponds, and wetlands. Also in this area are the state's sounds: the Albemarle, Bogue, Core, Croatan, Currituck, and Pamlico. Opportunities in this region for anglers consist of offshore fishing, surf and pier fishing, inshore, inlet, and sound fishing. Internationally known for saltwater fishing, the area holds more than fifty saltwater tournaments each year from April to November. Some of these tournaments are part of the Governor's Cup Billfishing Conservation Series that establishes minimum size and recognizes tag and release as part of the requirements for entry. North Carolina is one of the few states in the country that does not require a fishing license for salt-water fishing.

The North Carolina Wildlife Resources Commission Division of Inland Fisheries manages freshwater fishing in public waters, and provides information and management advice for those who use and or own aquatic resources. The North Carolina Department of Environment and Natural Resources Division of Marine Fisheries manages fishing in coastal waters. The North Carolina Wildlife Resource Commission Division of Engineering Services builds and maintains public boating and fishing access areas, and reviews proposed development projects that may negatively affect aquatic habitats (North Carolina Wildlife Resources Commission, 2005).

Human-Made, Resource Dependent Activities

Snow Skiing

North Carolina has eight ski areas. While only 12 percent of North Carolina households participate in downhill skiing and only 1 percent of out of state visitors come to North Carolina to ski (Watson et al., 1999), the sport plays an important economic role in western North Carolina. During the state's 2002-03 ski season, 540,000 skiers contributed $120 million to the state's economy (Millsaps & Groothius, 2003).

Golf

North Carolina has been called "The Golf Capital of the World" due to its broad spectrum of settings, mild year-round climate, and its rich golf history. The state is home to more than 600 public and private golf courses and the Pinehurst Resort and Country Club, the largest golf resort complex in the world (North Carolina Department of Commerce-Tourism, Film, and Sports Development, 2002). In 1998, over 14 million rounds of golf were played in the state, and an estimated $1.3 billion in direct spending was attributed to golfers in North Carolina (Watson et al., 1999).

Moore County, in the Piedmont region of the state, is the "hub" of golf activity. Featured in the Pinehurst area are thirty six championship courses. Some of these courses have held a variety of Professional Golfers Association (PGA) and Ladies Professional Golfers Association (LPGA) events, including the 1994 U.S. Senior Open and the 2001 LPGA championship (the LPGA championship will return to Pine Needles in 2007). In 1999, the U.S. Open, considered by many to be the most prestigious tournament in golf, was played on Pinehurst No. 2. The tournament returned to Pinehurst in 2005, making it the quickest turnaround host since 1946 (North Carolina Department of Commerce-Tourism, Film, and Sports Development, 2002).

Bicycling

According to the North Carolina Department of Transportation, Division of Bicycle and Pedestrian Transportation, 46 percent of all North Carolinians own bicycles. Households with four or more members own at least one bicycle per household (Stutts & Hunter, 2002). To accommodate these riders and others, the state has developed a comprehensive Bicycling Highways System. This system, implemented in 1975, designates, maps, and signs bicycle touring routes throughout the state. These bicycle routes are designed to direct cyclists away from heavily traveled roads to safer, less traveled routes. Currently, there are ten routes statewide encompassing more than 3,000 miles of roads.

Outdoor Resources

Over 2.8 million acres of open space (8.6 percent of the state's land) are protected in North Carolina. These areas include parks, historic sites, state and national forests, wildlife refuges, and other lands held by non-governmental organizations (NGOs) such as the Nature Conservancy and the Triangle Land Conservancy (North Carolina Department of Environment and Natural Resources, 2000a). The majority of this preserved land is owned by the federal government, while the remaining acreage is under the ownership of state and local governments and NGOs (Figure 10.1).

Figure 10.1 Land Ownership in North Carolina.

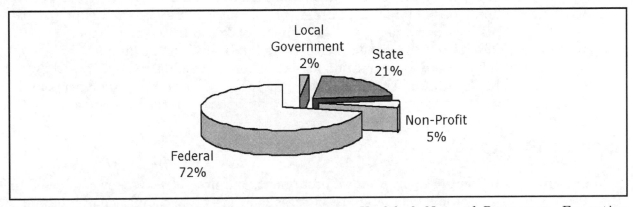

Source: North Carolina Department of Environment, Health & Natural Resources—Executive Summary-Million Acre Plan (2000a)

Urban Open Space

Urban open space can be defined as undeveloped land or land that is largely covered by vegetation. It includes park and recreation areas, farms, greenbelts, trails, flood plains, and cemeteries. Some of these have obvious recreation potential; others, with imagination and proper management, can provide positive experiences for urban dwellers. The existence of natural areas within a metropolitan region greatly improves the quality of life for residents.

Most North Carolina counties, towns, and cities have recreation and parks departments that manage urban open spaces: athletic fields, golf courses, trails, picnic areas, lakes, and swimming pools. These facilities, along with those provided by the private sector and non-profit organizations, offer many "close-to-home" outdoor recreation opportunities.

Wilderness

Designated wilderness contrasts with urban open space on the spectrum of outdoor recreation supply. Here solitude and self-reliance are sought by the outdoor enthusiast and often by "adventure education" programs. The Wilderness Act (1964) and the Eastern Wilderness Act (1975) established the National Wilderness Preservation System. Within North Carolina there are ten federally designated Wilderness areas, totaling over 102,500 acres (Landres & Meyer, 1998).

Wilderness, as defined by the U. S. Congress, is: "Where the earth and its community of life are untrammeled by man, where man himself is a visitor who does not remain" (Wilderness Act, 1964). The wilderness: "Retains its primeval character and influence, and generally appears to have been affected primarily by the forces of nature, with the imprint of man's work substantially unnoticeable; has outstanding opportunities for solitude or a primitive and unconfined type of recreation" (Wilderness Act, 1964).

Forest Resources

The "Old North State" could just as well be nicknamed the "the Old Green State." North Carolina's 19 million acres of forest land are essential to the state's economy and its citizens' lifestyles. This vast acreage supports a number of concentrated and dispersed recreation uses. Forests on farms and other private lands are prime examples of the state's superb supply of outdoor recreation acreage. North Carolina's four national forests: the Pisgah, Nantahala, Uwharrie, and Croatan cover over 1.1 million acres and receive extensive use by the state's population and millions of tourists each year.

Linear Parks

Linear parks are becoming more popular, prominent, and practical as a key component of the state's supply of outdoor recreation resources. They are often comprised of minimal acreage, close to homes, and are readily accessed. Trails, greenways, and riverways are examples of linear parks. The state trails coordinator, along with the staff in the North Carolina Department of Environment and Natural Resources- Division of Parks and Recreation, encourage and coordinate trail development throughout the state. North Carolina has two major long-distance hiking trails. Foremost is the Appalachian Trail, which passes through the mountain region and is the longest marked footpath in the world. It is under the jurisdiction of the National Park Service and the Appalachian Trail

Conservancy, a non-profit agency, which coordinates management efforts among interested parties from Maine to Georgia. The Mountains-to-Sea Trail is the jewel of the state's trail efforts. When completed, it will stretch from Great Smoky Mountains National Park to Jockey's Ridge State Park on the Outer Banks.

Rivers are also linear trails and provide unsurpassed recreation opportunities like float fishing, duck hunting, boating, camping, and nature study. The French Broad River and Yadkin River combine to form 197 miles of the state's trail system (North Carolina Division of Parks and Recreation, 2005). Given the quality of these resources and their recreational use, the North Carolina Natural and Scenic Rivers System was created in 1971.

Reservoirs

Reservoirs are human-made impoundments, which play an important role in water-based recreation since North Carolina's only natural lakes are located in the coastal plain. Examples of these lakes are Lake Mattamuskeet, a national wildlife refuge, and Lake Waccamaw, a state park. The state's other lakes are a result from efforts to provide flood control, hydroelectric power, water supply, and recreation. Ranging across the piedmont and mountain regions are seventeen major dams with reservoirs, creating opportunities for camping, boating, fishing, water skiing, jet skiing, and other related activities.

Statewide Comprehensive Outdoor Recreation Plan

A Statewide Comprehensive Outdoor Recreation Plan (SCORP) has been required since passage of the federal Land and Water Conservation Fund (LWCF) Act of 1965. This is an important requirement since it makes states eligible for LWCF grants. SCORPs are important documents as they provide a framework for addressing problems, needs, and opportunities associated with improving public outdoor recreation. The North Carolina Division of Parks and Recreation is the agency responsible for representing, acting, and creating the SCORP for the state. The contents of the SCORP are created by the planning guidelines of the LWCF Act. The primary requirements are that the report be comprehensive and include an evaluation of the supply and demand of outdoor recreation resources and facilities in the state. The plan must contain a wetlands priority component, a program for implementation of the plan, ample public participation in the planning process, and a description of process and methodology (North Carolina Department of Environment and Natural Resources, 2003).

The North Carolina SCORP has identified five major park and recreation issues to be addressed by 2008: (1) the need to provide improved outdoor recreation services to meet the needs of a growing and changing population, (2) the need to conserve and protect important natural resources and open spaces in a rapidly developing state, (3) the need to ensure a stable and adequate source of funding to provide for the outdoor recreation needs of current and future generations, (4) the need to create effective partnerships between all parties interested in outdoor recreation so they may pursue common interests more effectively, and (5) the need to improve the North Carolina state parks system (North Carolina Department of Environment and Natural Resources, 2003).

Supply and Demand in North Carolina

The supply, demand, and need for outdoor recreation opportunities is basic information managers of federal, state, and local recreation agencies need to assess as well as private recreation ventures. Determining the adequacy of existing resources and the need for new resources should take into account the number and type of recreation facilities currently provided, the number of people who live in the area, and public preferences. From a statewide perspective, it's important for all residents of North Carolina to have access to high quality recreation opportunities.

Supply, as it relates to outdoor recreation, is the collection of natural and human-made resources where people go to recreate. Demand is the long list of outdoor recreation activities in which people wish to participate. Opportunities for most undeveloped outdoor recreation will decline, whereas developed outdoor recreation opportunities are expected to increase due to new parklands acquired by municipal governments and increased involvement by the private sector (English et al., 1993). Population growth and preferences, existing recreation resources, geography, road and transportation systems, natural resources, land ownership, and other factors often help determine the adequacy of existing resources and the need for new ones (North Carolina Department of Environment and Natural Resources, 2003).

As mentioned above, the state's diverse geography and environment combine to provide North Carolinians with a variety of outdoor recreation resources to help support the demands and interests of its population. The vastness of the resources in North Carolina and the providers of each are listed in Table 10.1.

Table 10.1 Outdoor Recreation Acreage by Operator and Site Classification.

Site Classification	Federal	State	Municipal	County	Total
Loacl	0	0	39,189	20,666	59,855
Regional	3,754	175,920	6,481	10,803	196,958
Dispersed Use	2,040,783	362,096	0	0	2,402,879
Total	2,044,537	538,016	45,670	31,469	2,659,692

Source: North Carolina Department of Environment, Health & Natural Resources—Statewide Comprehensive Outdoor Recreation Plan (2003).

North Carolinians engage in a variety of outdoor recreation activities (Table 10.2). More than two thirds of households in the state participate in activities such as walking for pleasure (75 percent), driving for pleasure (72 percent), viewing scenery (71 percent), beach activities (69 percent), and visiting historic sites (62 percent) (North Carolina Department of Environment and Natural Resources, 2003).

Table 10.2. Participation in Selected Outdoor Recreation Activities by Percentage in North Carolina.

Rank	Activity	Percentage of Households Participating
1.	Walking for Pleasure	75
2.	Driving for Pleasure	72
3.	Viewing Scenery	71
4.	Beach Activities	69
5.	Visiting Historical Sites	62
6.	Swimming (lakes, rivers, ocean)	54
7.	Visiting Natural Areas	53
8.	Picnicking	52
9.	Attending Sports Events	52
10.	Visiting Zoos	51
11.	Fishing - Freshwater	50
12.	Use of Open Areas	41
13.	Swimming (pools)	40
14.	Fishing - Saltwater	38
15.	Attending Outdoor Cultural Events	35
16.	Bicycling for Pleasure	32
17.	Other Winter Sports	31
18.	Camping, Tent or Vehicle	29
19.	Softball and Baseball	28
20.	Hunting	28

Source: North Carolina Department of Environment, Health & Natural Resources—Statewide Comprehensive Outdoor Recreation Plan (2003).

The demand for outdoor recreation activities range from moderate to high and is expected to continue to grow. Changes in demand will be reflected in a population that is growing in numbers and age. By 2020 there will be 9.6 million North Carolinians, or a growth rate of 1.3 percent annually (North Carolina Department of Environment and Natural Resources, 2000b). In addition, the number of elderly citizens will increase and will include close to 1 million people age 65 and older. Another third of the population will be at least 45 years old. This factor alone will have a significant impact on park and recreation services, including increased accessibility, safety, and a quality recreation experience. Future demands and support for public funding for these activities can be found in Table 10.3.

Summary

North Carolina provides the outdoor enthusiast with an endless supply of outdoor recreation opportunities and activities. The state's unique geography, climate, and location

Table 10.3. Demands on Outdoor Recreation Activities in North Carolina.

Rank	Activity	Percentage of Households Participating	Future Demands	Support For Public Funding
1.	Walking for Pleasure	75	High	High
2.	Driving for Pleasure	72	Moderate	Low
3.	Viewing Scenery	71	Moderate	Moderate
4.	Beach Activities	69	High	High
5.	Visiting Historical Sites	62	Moderate	High
6.	Swimming (lakes, rivers, ocean)	54	Moderate	Moderate
7.	Visiting Natural Areas	53	Moderate	High
8.	Picnicking	52	High	High
9.	Attending Sports Events	52	Moderate	Low
10.	Visiting Zoos	51	Moderate	High
11.	Fishing - Freshwater	50	High	High
12.	Use of Open Areas	41	Moderate	Moderate
13.	Swimming (pools)	40	High	Moderate
14.	Fishing - Saltwater	38	Moderate	Moderate
15.	Attending Outdoor Cultural Events	35	High	High
16.	Bicycling for Pleasure	32	High	Moderate
17.	Other Winter Sports	31	Low	Low
18.	Camping, Tent or Vehicle	29	High	High
19.	Softball and Baseball	28	Low	Low
20.	Hunting	28	Moderate	Moderate

Source: North Carolina Department of Environment, Health & Natural Resources—Statewide Comprehensive Outdoor Recreation Plan (2003).

combine to make North Carolina one of the most desirable states in the country for outdoor recreation. The land and water resources available for outdoor recreation are many and can be found from the populated urban centers of the Piedmont region to the most remote mountain and coastal areas. North Carolina's mix of outdoor opportunities are both resource dependent and human-made and include both whitewater and flatwater rivers, reservoirs and lakes, thousands of miles of trails, coastline, and greenways. Local, state, and national parks, golf courses, and ski areas add to the mix of diverse settings for outdoor recreation.

Future demand for outdoor recreation resources and activities in North Carolina will be determined by a population that continues to increase and grow older. These two factors will play a significant roll in shaping the future of park and recreation services, including land acquisition, increased accessibility, safety, and a quality recreation experience.

Learning Exercises

1. Issues of access are a major concern for many outdoor recreationists in North Carolina. Select an outdoor recreation activity and explore current and future access to resources.

2. Select an outdoor recreation activity such as skateboarding, jet skiing, or trapping. Who advocates for these user groups in North Carolina?

3. Explore issues of "user conflict" on forest land or rivers in the state. Who is in conflict? Why? What are some solutions?

4. Write a code of ethics for your favorite outdoor recreation activity. Be sure to include behaviors that will speak to the land or water base and other user groups.

5. Visit a magazine rack and compile a list of outdoor recreation themes found in popular magazines.

6. Review the current North Carolina State Comprehensive Outdoor Recreation Plan and prepare a report on one of the issues facing outdoor recreation in the state.

References

Attarian, A. (1991). An investigation of the ecological and social impacts caused by rock climbers. In C. Rademacher and R. Watters (Eds.). *Proceedings of the 1991 International Conference on Outdoor Recreation*, Pocatello, ID: Idaho State University Press (pp. 7-15).

Benner, B. (1987). *A Paddler's Guide to Eastern North Carolina*. Birmingham, AL: Menasha Ridge Press.

Benner, D. & Benner, B. (2002). *A Canoeing & Kayaking Guide to the Carolinas*. Birmingham, AL: Menasha Ridge Press.

Blumenthal, T. (2001). *Mountain biking at ski resorts: An overview*. Retrieved April 21, 2005, from ttp://www.imba.com/resources/bike_management/ski_resorts_overview.html

Bradley, M. (1998, September). *The Economic Impact of Recreational Boats and Boating*. Paper presented at the NC Sports Summit, Raleigh, NC.

Cordell, H.K. (Editor). (1999). Outdoor Recreation in America: A National Assessment of Demand and Supply Trends. Champaign, IL: Sagamore Publishing.

deHart, A. (2005). *North Carolina Hiking Trails*. Boston, MA: Appalachian Mountain Club.

Drake, D. & Bromley, P.T. (1997). *1997 Natural Resources Inventory of North Carolina*. Raleigh, NC: North Carolina Cooperative Extension Service, North Carolina State University.

English, D.B.K., Betz, C.J., Young, J.M., Bergstrom, J.C. & Cordell, H.K. (1993). Regional demand and supply projections for outdoor recreation. *General technical report RM230*. Fort Collins, CO: United State Department of Agriculture, Forest Service, Rocky Mountain Forest and Range Experiment Station.

Ellis, M. (2000, July). A place of extremes. *Our State*, 36-40.

Eastern Wilderness Areas Act (1975). P.L. 93-622, 88 Stat. 2096; 16 U.S.C. 1132.

Gade, O., Rex, A. & Young, J.E. (2002). *North Carolina, People and Environments*. Boone, NC: Parkway Publishers.

Holden, M. (1999). *Horseback Riding Trail Guide to North Carolina*. Winston Salem: John F. Blair Publisher.

International Association of Fish and Wildlife Agencies. (2002). *Economic Importance of Hunting in America*. Washington, DC: Author.

Jahn, L. (2002). *Forests and the North Carolina Economy* (pamphlet). North Carolina State University Raleigh, NC: University Cooperative Extension Service.

Kelley, T. (1995). *The Climber's Guide to North Carolina*. Chapel Hill, NC: Earthbound Sports.

Lambert, Y. & Shull, H. (2002). *Selected Climbs in North Carolina*. Seattle, WA: The Mountaineers Books.

Landres, P. & Meyer, S. (1998). *National Wilderness Preservation System Database: Key Attributes and Trends, 1964 through 1999*. Gen. Tech. Rep. RMRS-GTR-18-Revised Edition. Ogden, UT: U.S. Department of Agriculture, Rocky Mountain Research Station.

Millsaps, S. & Groothuis, P. (2003). *The Economic Impact of the North Carolina Ski Areas on the Economy of North Carolina 2002-2003 Season*. Boone, NC: Department of Economics, Appalachian State University.

Muth, T. (2003). *Mountain Biking North Carolina* (2nd ed.). Helena, MT: Falcon Press.

National Marine Manufacturers Association. (2004, February). *2002 U.S. Recreational Boat Registration Statistics*. Retrieved April 29, 2005, from http://www.nmma.org/facts/local/documents/2002RegistrationsSummary.pdf

National Sporting Goods Association (2004). *2004 Participation*. Retrieved May 3, 2005, from http://www.nsga.org/public/pages/index.cfm?pageid=150

Newman, C. (1995). North Carolina's piedmont: On a fastbreak. *National Geographic, 187*, 114-138.

North Carolina Department of Commerce- Tourism, Film, and Sports Development. (2004a). *Travel Tracker*. Retrieved May 5, 2005, from http://www.nccommerce.com/tourism/TravelTracker/ttreports/ttfeb05.pdf

North Carolina Department of Commerce-Tourism, Film, and Sports Development. (2004b). *2004 Economic Impact of Tourism in North Carolina*. Retrieved April 29, 2005, from http://www.nccommerce.com/tourism/econ/04EconImpact.pdf

North Carolina Department of Commerce-Tourism, Film, and Sports Development. (2002). *North Carolina Official Golf Guide-2002*. Raleigh, NC: Author.

North Carolina Department of Environment and Natural Resources (2005). *DCM adds 350 sites to public beach access database*. Retrieved May 3, 2005, from http://www.nc-coastalmanagement.net/CAMAgram/Summer04/Access.htm

North Carolina Department of Environment and Natural Resources. (2003). *North Carolina comprehensive outdoor recreation plan*. Retrieved May 11, 2005 from http://ils.unc.edu/parkproject/resource/scorp.html

North Carolina Department of Environment and Natural Resources (2000a). *Executive summary-million acre plan*. Retrieved May 11, 2005, from www.enr.state.nc.us/docs/millionsummary.pdf

North Carolina Department of Environment and Natural Resources (2000b). *North Carolina 2000 state of the environment report*. Retrieved May 10, 2005, from http://www.enr.state.nc.us/docs/environchap3.pdf

North Carolina Division of Parks and Recreation. (2005). *Size of the North Carolina State Parks system*. Retrieved May 11, 2005, from http://ils.unc.edu/parkproject/resource/land.html

North Carolina Division of Parks and Recreation. (2000). *1999 Climbing Permit Statistics*. Raleigh, NC: North Carolina Department of Environment, Health and Natural Resources.

North Carolina State University Cooperative Extension-Horse Husbandry. (2005). *Extension Horse Husbandry—Introduction*. Retrieved May 5, 2005, from http://www.cals.ncsu.edu/an_sci/extension/horse/hhmain.html

North Carolina Travel and Tourism Division. (1996). *Rockhounding* (brochure). Raleigh, NC: Author.

North Carolina Wildlife Resources Commission. (2005). *Commission divisions*. Retrieved May 5, 2005, from http://www.ncwildlife.org/fs_index_commission.htm

North Carolina Wildlife Resources Commission. (2003, January). Biennial report. *Wildlife in North Carolina*, 37-58.

North Carolina Wildlife Resources Commission. (1999, January). *Wildlife in North Carolina—Biennial Report*, Raleigh, NC: Author.

Outdoor Industry Foundation (2003). *Outdoor Recreation Participation & Spending Sudy*. Boulder, CO: Author.

Roe C. E. (1992). North Carolina Wildlife Viewing Guide. Helena, MT: Falcon Press.

Sherman, J. (1994) North Carolina bouldering—Carolina dreamin. *Climbing, 189*, 88-96.

Stutts, J. & Hunter, W. (2002). *Bicycling and Walking in North Carolina: Results of a year 2000 Survey*. Chapel Hill, NC: Highway Safety Research Center.

United States Department of the Interior, Fish and Wildlife Service (2003). National Survey of Fishing, Hunting, and Wildlife-Associated Recreation—North Carolina. Washington, DC: Author.

Watson, S., Brothers, G., & Gustke, L. (1999). *The Economic Impact of Golf on North Carolina*. Raleigh, NC: NC Division of Tourism, Film and Sports Development.

Wilderness Act. (1964, September 3). P.L 88-577, 78 Stat. 890; 16 U.S.C. 1, 1, 21 (note), 1, 1, 31-1136.

Young, W. (2001). Deliverance: North Carolina may be bouldering's holy grail. *Rock & Ice, 106*, 70-77.

Chapter 11
Emergence and Development of Outdoor Adventure Education in North Carolina

Maurice Phipps, Ed Raiola, and Debby F. Singleton

What is Adventure Education?

What do you think of when you hear the *term outdoor adventure education?* Whenever we have asked that question, individuals conjure up varying images of what the phrase means. Images have ranged from "Mountain Dew, been there, done that- rappel off a thousand-foot cliff" to group activities that include teamwork and have a ropes or challenge course as part of the experience.

Adventure is a human need. More than a word, it is an atmosphere, an essence, a climate of the mind. Adventure is the curiosity of people to see the other side of the mountain, the impulse in us that makes us break our bonds with the familiar and seek greater possibilities. Although there is not yet consensus on a precise definition of outdoor adventure education, many researchers and practitioners (Bunting, 1990; Hollenhorst, 1986; Ewert, 1989; and Priest, 1990) agree that it contains elements of excitement, uncertainty, real or perceived risk, and effort and that it involves interaction with the natural environment.

Phipps (1985) suggests that the adventure experience is essentially psychological and is attained through physical activities. Bunting sees outdoor adventure education as "environmental communication because, as in interpersonal communication, there is interdependency between the individuals involved. There is interdependency between participants, as well as between the environment and participants" (Bunting, 1990, p. 453-458). She views it as a vehicle for learning about ourselves and about interrelationships.

Cinnamon and Raiola state that outdoor adventure education focuses on education through particular activities. "One of the most important themes in outdoor adventure education is that the participants should be provided with the necessary skills, both mental and physical, to enable them to experience success in using and preserving the outdoors. The emphasis is not on winning or losing, but rather on facing the challenges of the activity. Some of the generally accepted goals are personal growth, skill development, excitement and stimulation, challenge, group participation and cooperation and understanding of one's relationship to the natural environment" (Cinnamon & Raiola, 1991, p. 130).

Historical Developments

In order to understand outdoor adventure education, it is necessary to review its historical roots. The pioneers of this movement were men and women with a vision of the impact that group-focused outdoor learning and living could have on the lives of participants. When we explore the development of outdoor adventure education, we must go back to experiential education, the organized camping movement, conservation education, nature study, and outdoor education. Each has influenced and shaped what we call outdoor adventure education.

To begin, we must understand that outdoor adventure education is a form of experiential education. Experiential education emphasizes direct experience as a resource that increases the quality of learning by combining direct experience that is meaningful to the learner with guided reflection and analysis. It is a teaching and learning approach that allows numerous opportunities for the learner to connect cognitive (head), kinesthetic (body), and affective (spiritual/emotional) aspects. It is a conscious mixing of concrete experience, reflective observation, abstract conceptualization, and active experimentation.

Early Roots

Some of the earliest attempts to use adventure and the outdoors as educational tools can be found in the organized camping movement. In this movement, educators began applying expeditions, camping, and challenge activities in the United States as early as 1861.

Mrs. and Mr. Gunn, who ran the Gunnery School for young boys in Connecticut (1861-1881), were among the first to use the outdoors and adventure as part of an educational program. In August 1861, the whole school went on a two-week, forty-mile trip at the end of the school year. Everyone hiked and then set up a camp to "live simply, doing their cooking and chores, swimming, fishing, and participating in games, songs and stories by the camp fire" (Eells1986, p.6).

Laura Matton was one of many activists and innovators who was concerned with the instruction and personal growth of young women. She taught at private girls' schools in Massachusetts and New York. Having done hiking and camping trips with her family in Canada, she decided to lead an expedition in the summer of 1902 to the New Hampshire wilderness with eight older students from her school. This expedition required that they set up their camp in the forest, chop wood, haul water, and cook for themselves. They hiked mountain trails, swam, and participated in geological field studies and crafts. According to Eleanor Eells (1986), this experiment was so successful that it led to the establishment of a permanent camp and education program. Each succeeding year saw a larger group of female campers.

John Dewey (1938) was applying many of the ideas of earlier philosophers of education. He believed that education should be concerned with living and learning through direct experience and should be directed toward the whole person—physically, mentally, and emotionally. His writings, work, and teaching influenced many school and camping programs from around 1920 to the present.

In the late 1920s and early 1930s, a number of public school programs using the environment and overnight camping were developed. One of the many pioneer leaders in this field was Dr. L. B. Sharp (1930), who began experimenting with education in camp settings. He received his Ph.D. in 1929 from Columbia University and was the first person to receive a doctorate in camping education. While at Columbia he studied with some of the pioneering practitioners of experiential education: John Dewey, William Kilpatrick, Boyd Bode, and Elbert K. Fretwell. These practitioners strongly influenced his thinking on how youth should learn.

Sharp became director of Life Camps, and in 1940 developed a center for advanced leadership training called National Camp. It was through National Camp and its programs that Sharp was able to influence many professional outdoor educators. In 1944 and 1946 he began to use the term *outdoor education* synonymously with public school camping.

Toward the mid-1900s, more sophisticated school and organized camping programs emerged that were strongly influenced by the work of John Dewey and other educators. The nature study movement arose from the inadequacy of rote learning and the sense of isolation from world phenomena and experiences that rote learning provoked. The emphasis was on giving participants actual experience in understanding and appreciating the natural world. Dr. William Gould Vinal, one of the leaders in the nature study movement, invented the term *nature recreation* and emphasized enjoyment and appreciation as important ingredients of nature study.

Another movement, which paralleled the development of nature study, was conservation education. Interest in conservation education arose from concerns about misuse of soil, range, forest, and wildlife resources. One of its principal efforts was to integrate conservation education into school curricula.

Both movements stressed hands-on learning and interaction with the outdoors. Out of the rich history and background of conservation and nature study education developed outdoor education: education *in, about, and for* the outdoors.

The 1950s and early 1960s saw a rapid development of school camping, and the term *outdoor education* began to be applied more generally. The concept was broadened to include experiences not only in residential camps but also on school grounds and in the community. Curricula were developed for kindergarten through high school, and colleges and universities began special programs for educating teachers in the outdoors.

Emergence of Outdoor Adventure Education

From the decade of the 1960s to the present, interest grew in experiential learning and outdoor programs here in the United States. Kurt Hahn (the founder of Outward Bound) and Paul Petzoldt (founder of the National Outdoor Leadership School and the Wilderness Education Association) have each shaped the growth of outdoor adventure education as we now understand it.

Hahn's Outward Bound concept, which began in England, was introduced to America with the establishment of the Colorado Outward Bound School in 1962:

> *What began as a wartime school for survival has evolved into an action-oriented program for personal growth, service to others and physical preparedness. In short, OB is learning about oneself and the world through adventure and service*

to others. Outward Bound has created a sophisticated adventure - based education program to stimulate personal growth (Green and Thompson, 1990 pp. 5-6).

With a descriptive motto of "to serve, to strive and not to yield," Outward Bound has become the largest and most widespread adventure-based education institution in the United States. Outward Bound USA has four U.S. wilderness schools: Outward Bound West, Hurricane Island, North Carolina, and Voyager. The two independent urban programs—New York City Outward Bound Center and Thompson Island Outward Bound Education Center—are specifically designed to address the needs of inner-city youth and the social, cultural, and educational problems of larger cities. Outward Bound also initiated a school reform program called Expeditionary Learning Outward Bound.

The National Outdoor Leadership School (NOLS) was founded in 1965 by Paul Petzoldt, who had been chief instructor for the Colorado Outward Bound School. Petzoldt stated that he was "shocked into the realization that nobody had really trained outdoors men [sic] in America . . . we [OB] couldn't hire anyone that met my standards. I thought the best thing I could do for American youth, if they were going to use the wild outdoors was to prepare better leaders for such experiences" (Petzoldt, 1974). From that desire emerged the National Outdoor Leadership School, which is recognized as a leader in the field of wilderness education and outdoor leadership. NOLS currently has branch schools in Wyoming, Alaska, Washington, Arizona, Africa, Mexico, Chile, and Canada. Since 1965 NOLS has taught wilderness skills, conservation, and leadership to more than 30,000 students.

In 1977, Paul Petzoldt and other leaders from the academic community—concerned about the development of outdoor leadership, the role of education, and the preservation of wild lands—founded the Wilderness Use Education Association (later to be called the Wilderness Education Association-WEA). WEA trains outdoor leaders, promotes stewardship toward the environment, and strongly promotes the development of skills and knowledge for leading and teaching in the outdoors. WEA offers courses through an affiliate system of colleges, universities, and outdoor organizations across the United States.

The Outward Bound movement inspired many educators to use experiential methods. In 1971 Jerry Pieh, then a principal of Hamilton/Windom Junior/Senior High School, wrote a three-year grant to develop a comprehensive, experiential curriculum, applying the Outward Bound concepts to the classroom. He called this new program Project Adventure. The original tenth-grade curriculum focused on integrating the concepts of experiential education and adventure into physical education, English, history, science, theater, arts, and counseling. "No other innovative education proposal spinning off from Outward Bound has enjoyed a greater success with the education establishment than Project Adventure" (J.Miner and J. Boldt,1981, p. 336). Today, Project Adventure is an international organization with offices in Massachusetts, Georgia, Oregon, and Vermont, with international sites in Australia, New Zealand, and Singapore. These offices presently offer training and workshops in the following program areas:

- Physical education
- Health and wellness
- Behavior management through adventure
- Peaceable playgrounds
- Professional development
- Out-of-school time

- Youth and college programs
- Adventure in the classroom
- Customized programs

Since 1974 Project Adventure has published books for the field of adventure education on topics including games, challenge ropes courses, and theory and practice. The organization has been in the forefront of designing and installing challenge ropes courses since 1971.

Historical Overview

Outward Bound, NOLS, Project Adventure, and WEA have evolved from a rich history, and their missions and philosophies have intertwined somewhat. Many of the contemporary outdoor adventure education programs are spin-offs from Outward Bound. Paul Petzoldt and NOLS wanted to focus on the technical skills training for outdoor leadership that was missing at Outward Bound. Project Adventure wanted to take the Outward Bound concepts back to the schools, as Kurt Hahn had originally envisioned Outward Bound doing. The Wilderness Education Association seeks to blend technical skills training with development of leadership, judgment, and decision-making skills.

Outdoor adventure education continues to be an evolving field, shaped by the needs of both participants and the specific environment in which it occurs. These basic concepts and values will continually respond to global, social, and environmental changes.

Benefits of Adventure Education

The benefits of adventure education are many, which explains to some extent why it continues to grow. Schoel, Prouty, and Radcliffe (1988) suggest that self-concept improves through six key elements: trust building, goal setting, challenge/stress, peak experiences, humor/fun, and problemsolving. Ewert (1989) elaborated and integrated psychological, sociological, and physical constructs into the potential benefits of outdoor adventure pursuits. These are shown in Table 11.1.

Table 11.1. Potential benefits of outdoor adventure pursuits

Psychological	Sociological	Educational	Physical
Self-concept	Compassion	Outdoor education	Fitness
Confidence	Group cooperation	Nature awareness	skills
Self-efficacy	Respect for others	Conservation education	Strength
Sensation seeking	Communication	Problem solving	Coordination
Actualization	Behavior feedback	Value clarification	Catharsis
Well-being	Friendship	Outdoor techniques	Exercise
Personal testing	Belonging	Improved academics	Balance

"Activities involving risk require full concentration of attention on the action being performed . . . . This very quality of being fully present where one is, has value for many people" (Miles, 1987, p. 6). Miles states that preoccupation with demands removed in time and space from the present is common in modern life, with its many pressures. Adventure education can provide a powerful experience to get one into the present or to teach by way of metaphor or illustration the ways in which many things may be done differently in the real world. Behavior-oriented practice would also be effective with adolescents and with corporate managers.

In studying the behavior and training of pilots, Helmreisch (1987) developed guidelines for maximizing the impact of training on attitudes. To be effective, training must first be "credible, powerful and active" (p. 19). Irwin and Phipps (1994) compared the Wilderness Education Association's training (which uses mountaineering expeditions) with aerospace training and research (which uses mountaineering expeditions as analogs to space research). The inclusion of adventure aspects in leadership training makes the experience more powerful and, therefore, more effective.

Adventure education offers powerful experiences that—if introduced, experienced, and processed effectively—can have correspondingly powerful effects on people.

Applications of Adventure Education

Applications of adventure education include: recreation, personal growth, therapy, leadership training, and travel. See Figure 11.1.

Figure 11.1.

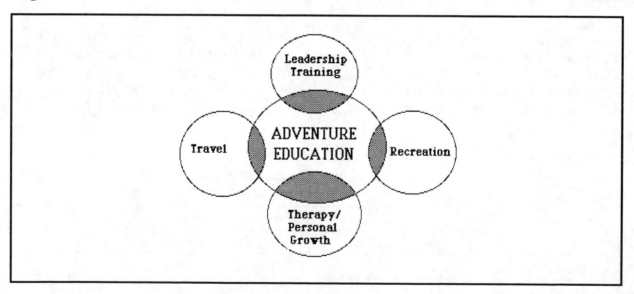

Within these applications, the professional would be required to have a variety of skills, including most of the following;

Leadership)

Instruction) Using appropriate styles and

Processing) techniques for a variety of

Counseling/therapy) populations

Activities (such as rock climbing, caving, canoeing, etc.)

Rescue and First Responder

Administrative and program planning

Populations of students, clients, patients, or guests are varied and may include: the general population (in the form of paying guests), people with disabilities (physical, emotional, and mental), women's groups, youth at risk, disadvantaged youth, youth groups (such as church groups, scouts, etc.), school students, summer camp groups, college students, and corporate groups.

Professional Skills for Adventure Educators

Leadership

The leadership skills needed by an adventure educator fall into two categories: technical and human relation. Phipps and Swiderski (1990) discuss technical skills, such as using hardware in rafting and rock climbing, and human relations or process skills, such as using leadership styles appropriately and attending to the human factors in groups. The amounts of skill needed would depend on the difficulty of the environment, the internal dynamics of the group, and the nature of the activity being done (see Figure 11.2).

Figure 11.2. Outdoor leadership

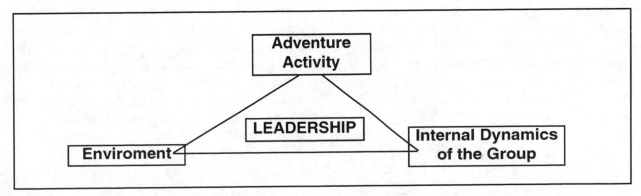

It is the duty of the adventure educator to manage risk by providing as safe a course or workshop as possible. The good judgment of the instructor, which depends on that instructor's knowledge base, is always an underpinning of leadership. An outdoor adventure educator should have sound knowledge, good judgment, the ability to communicate leadership accurately, and facility for group management techniques.

Instructional Skills

To teach concepts (which may vary from stern squirting a kayak on the Nantahala River to conflict management on an expedition in the Slickrock Wilderness Area), an outdoor adventure educator employs skills that enable participants to learn effectively. Research at Nantahala Outdoor Center showed that guest perceptions of instructor effectiveness depended on the following aspects of teaching (Phipps and Claxton, 1997): structure, communication, perception, motivation, arousal levels, feedback, group process, action and practice, and leadership. All of these concepts relate to the experiential learning cycle, which is the foundation on which most teaching and learning is built in adventure education. The experiential learning cycle is shown below in Figure 11.3.

Figure 11.3. The experiential learning cycle

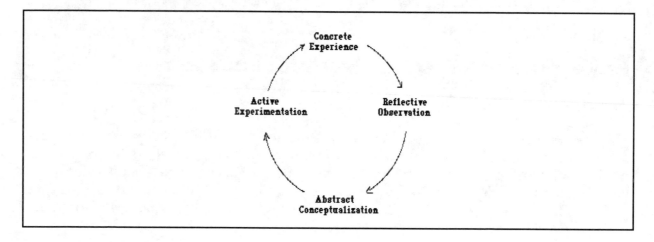

Processing

Processing or de-briefing is the discussion period that usually follows an outdoor adventure education activity. It often relates to briefing information that was given prior to the activity to focus the participants' attention. The instructor can use methods of communication designed to affect future behavior, which consists of the *abstract conceptualization* and *active experimentation* with new ideas. In teaching activities for recreational purposes, often the goal is to address the 'whys' of actions taken so participants gain better judgment. In the development of personal growth or for therapeutic reasons, processing can include: the use of metaphor (Bacon, 1983; Gass, 1993); behavioral techniques, such as reality therapy (Bankie et al. 1984); journaling to bring out personal observations; transference of concepts back to school or the workplace; and many other techniques.

Processing is a complex skill. The facilitator often has to dig out participants' insights while making it as enjoyable as possible and monitoring individual and group behavior that may be very negative. Processing should use reflection about the activity to effect a *positive* influence on future behavior.

Counseling and Therapy Skills

How much instructors need to know and how good their skills should be in order to counsel someone depends on the psychological problem and the person involved. Since adventure education is a powerful medium, it can open up psychological problems that might have been buried for years. Very few adventure educators have a Ph.D. in psychology. Less qualified instructors must understand when and how to lead participants back to safer psychological ground—to a level of discussion the instructor is qualified to handle (Ringer and Gillis, 1995).

Knowledge of counseling and psychological theories is important, and appropriate use of them is critical. Bacon (1983) describes the safe, appropriate use of metaphor and Jung's archetypes by Outward Bound instructors. Clinical techniques like flooding—where patients are 'flooded' with stimuli to which they have an aversion, to help them overcome the aversion—should only be used by qualified therapists. Paul Petzoldt's saying, "Know what you know and know what you don't know," is especially relevant here (Petzoldt, 1981). Adventure educators may need to refer some clients to a qualified therapist.

For instructors with masters degrees or Ph.D.s in therapeutic areas such as counseling and psychology, Adventure Education gives a whole new dimension to work in, taking patients into a totally different environment that can be a great catalyst for change.

Activity Skills

Adventure educators needs sufficient skills in the activities they teach so that they can look after participants and not worry about getting themselves or their participants into trouble. A kayak instructor whose skills are marginal for the French Broad River, for example, should not be trying to teach people on the Ocoee. Instructors with skills in a variety of activities are more employable.

Good performers are not always good instructors. Good demonstrations are often part of teaching, but the most important skill for adventure educators is communication. For the expert rock climber, becoming an instructor involves a completely new set of skills in addition to being able to rock climb. Certification for teaching specific activities (such as top rope climbing, skiing, canoeing, and kayaking) is now common. Some of these certifications may eventually be required by land agencies to gain permits.

Rescue and First Responder Skills

The underlying goal for outdoor leaders and instructors should be exercising enough good judgment and planning to avoid survival situations. Accidents do occur, however; so outdoor instructors should have skills in search, rescue, and wilderness first aid. It has become an industry standard for outdoor leaders to have at least Wilderness First Responder and CPR certification.

For some activities, rescue training is also a "must know." The raft guide on the Chattooga River must know how to unpin a raft or be "live bait," going after someone hurt and face down in the river. The rock-climbing guide on Looking Glass Rock must be able to rappel to a participant needing help and then organize a safe lower to the ground. The backpacking group whose member has wandered away from the campsite in the Great Smokies needs to know how to organize a search and whether or not to bring in professionals to take over. Instructors must train and practice regularly to maintain these skills.

Administrative and Program Planning Skills

Administrative skills help qualify outdoor educators for promotion in some agencies. Effective strategic management is crucial for agencies to survive. According to Ford and Blanchard (1993), the primary administrative functions are programming, staffing, scheduling, budgets, and evaluation. For program planning, the key skills are goal and objective writing, needs assessments, activity selection, planning, risk management, marketing, and evaluation. These skills are the focus of many parks and recreation management degree programs in North Carolina universities and colleges.

Training and Education for Outdoor Instructors

Most places that provide adventure services also provide staff training. Some colleges and universities provide course work in adventure education. Warren Wilson College (near Asheville) and Brevard College have outdoor leadership bachelor's degrees; and Western Carolina University has a concentration in outdoor leadership and instruction as part of the parks and recreation degree. Outdoor pursuits are included to some extent in all physical education bachelor's degree programs in state universities in North Carolina.

The Association for Experiential Education and the American Camping Association accredit agencies for adventure education. Camps are currently looking to these associations for accreditation. The Wilderness Education Association accredits university and college programs and provides national certification of outdoor leaders and instructors (Cockrell, 1991; Drury and Bonney, 1992).

Certifying bodies for instructors are:

- The Wilderness Education Association for outdoor leaders and instructors
- The American Canoe Association for canoeing, kayaking, and river rescue
- Project Adventure for ropes course activities
- Wilderness Medical Associates, SOLO, and the Wilderness Medical Institute for Wilderness First Responders
- American Red Cross for CPR and first aid
- Professional Ski Instructors of America for skiing
- National Ski Patrol for outdoor emergency care
- The American Mountain Guides Association for top rope site manager, rock instructor, and rock guide.

Employment Possibilities

Some outdoor centers (such as Camp Woodson near Asheville, where the instruction is for adjudicated youth) provide year-round employment. Other jobs could be full or part-time (such as Nantahala Outdoor Center, which employs some people year-round and others for the summer only). Most employment at traditional summer camps is seasonal, as is working at ski resorts.

Some outdoor instructors gain full-time employment by doing two different seasonal jobs, such as kayak instructor in the summer and ski instructor or ski patrol in the winter. They may even head to South or Central America during North America's winter season to work in adventure travel. Another alternative for the seasonal worker is to work for a land agency, such as the National Park Service or United States Forest Service, as a rescuer or back country/climbing/river ranger. Many resorts now offer some adventure activities.

Some parks and recreation departments now have positions devoted to outdoor education. Examples are the outdoor programs at Henderson County Parks and Recreation, Raleigh Parks and Recreation, Chapel Hill Parks and Recreation, the 4-H Educational Center in Reidsville, and the Asheville YMCA. The skills required for these jobs are primarily administrative and organizational.

Fulltime employment is also possible in schools. Some public schools include adventure activities as part of various curricula, such as physical education. Asheville Middle School, for example, integrates adventure activities with environmental education. Private schools such as Asheville School provide extracurricular adventure activities. The advantage of working in the teaching profession is that it is a full-time job with benefits and substantial time off in the summers, enabling teachers to work for camps, Outward Bound, etc. Two-year colleges, four-year colleges, and universities have job possibilities both in academic departments (which also have alternate summer possibilities) and in student development departments (most colleges and universities have recreational outdoor programs). Base Camp Cullowhee at Western Carolina University organizes student activities that include rafting, caving, rock climbing, backpacking, etc. The University of North Carolina at Charlotte has the Venture Program and the University of North Carolina at Wilmington has the Discover Outdoor Program. Students often lead these activities.

Of course, if you want to "be all that you can be," the military includes adventure activities in its training.

The types of adventure education jobs available in North Carolina are varied (see Table 11.2.).

Besides these 'front line' jobs, there are positions in administration, marketing, and program planning at centers, camps, resorts, universities, colleges, and other agencies that provide adventure activities. Other positions related to adventure education in the land agencies include rescue teams, back country rangers, climbing rangers, and river rangers. The land agencies that provide these positions in North Carolina are the National Park Service, United States Forest Service, Army Corps of Engineers, and North Carolina State Parks.

Table 11.2. Types of front-line jobs in adventure education in North Carolina

Instructors	Guides	Therapists & Facilitators for	Rescuers & police
Wilderness trip	Wilderness trip leader	Ropes course	Rangers
Kayak/Canoe	Climbing	Adjudicated youth	Ski patrol
Skiing	Rafting	Corporate clients	
Snowboard	Caving	Attention deficit youth	
Caving	Adventure travel	Psychologically disturbed	
Rock climbing			
SCUBA			
Sailboarding			
Mountain biking			
Sailing			
Surfing			
Parasailing			
Hanggliding			

Adventure Agencies in North Carolina

Numerous agencies offer adventure activities in North Carolina, and not all can be mentioned here. For example, probably the largest concentration of summer camps in the nation is in the Brevard/Hendersonville area. Examples of the different types of agencies follow.

Nantahala Outdoor Center (NOC)

Perhaps the largest commercial agency in North Carolina is the Nantahala Outdoor Center (NOC), located in the Nantahala Gorge. The center owns about eighty acres on which it has built shops, restaurants, offices, storage areas, accommodations, an Alpine Tower and Ropes Course, and mountain biking trails. Activities include canoe and kayak instruction for all levels and ages, adventure travel, rafting, a ropes course, mountain and road biking, Alpine Tower, kayak lake tours, and hiking. NOC also hosts a variety of special events, including festivals, bike races, and adventure races. NOC has outposts on the French Broad, Chattooga, Nolichucky, Pigeon, Nantahala, and Ocoee rivers. NOC is the largest whitewater instruction facility in the United States and is internationally known for its leadership in canoeing and kayaking. It is an employee-owned company.

Other Commercial Agencies

North Carolina has numerous other rafting companies and smaller companies offering kayak, canoe, and climbing instruction, including the Vertical Edge Climbing Center in Durham and the Seagull/Seafarer Outdoor Center in Arapahoe. Endless River Adventures, also located in the Nantahala Gorge, was created by former NOC employees. Some companies, such as the Triangle Training Center in Pittsboro and Moonshadow Educational Services in Whittier, specialize in ropes courses. Another company that includes adventure travel is Broadreach in Raleigh. Kitty Hawk Kites, located on the Outer Banks, is the world's largest hang gliding school and has taught over 300,000 people since 1974. In addition to hang gliding, Kitty Hawk Kites offer instruction in kite boarding, guided kayak tours, and parasailing. Another company, Kitty Hawk Sports, offers kayak tours, surf kayaking, kayak ecotours, windsurfing, sailing, and surfing instruction. With an abundance of outdoor recreation possibilities, North Carolina is experiencing growth in adventure activity–based businesses.

Ski resorts in North Carolina do not match resorts in the western U.S. in terms of season length, but with 100 percent snowmaking, they do offer a short season of easily accessible skiing. These resorts are Cataloochee, Sugar Mountain, Appalachian Ski Mountain, Wolf Laurel, Sapphire Valley, Ski Hawksnest, and Ski Beech. Scaly Mountain offers tubing only. Many of the resorts offer year-round activities such as golf, tennis, hiking, mountain biking, festivals, and special events.

North Carolina Outward Bound School

The North Carolina Outward Bound School (NCOBS) has been at the forefront of outdoor adventure education in North Carolina since its founding in 1967. It has an average annual enrollment of 2,800 and an alumni base of more than 30,000 participants. The course curriculum is framed around the core values of self-reliance, compassion, craft, and fitness. Their wide-ranging educational programs fall into four categories:

- *Wilderness adventure programs,* specialized for youth 14-15, young adults 16-18, adult crews, and special courses designed to allow members to focus on particular issues (i.e.. parent-child crews, women's courses, life/career renewal).
- *Professional development and contract-designed courses* that use outdoor adventure programming to develop teamwork, leadership, and effective communication specific to participants' needs.
- *Urban education programs* that bring unique teaching methods to students and teachers in North Carolina, Atlanta, and other major U.S. cities. Both the Kurt Hahn Center for Educational Services and the Atlanta Outward Bound Center partner with public schools and youth-serving community organizations to develop adventure-based education programs.
- *Specialized training courses* are offered for those seeking careers in outdoor adventure education. These courses range in length from three days (Ropes Course Management and Safety) to fifty-five days (Instructor Development Practicum).

Programming is directed at "discovering one's inner resources and the dignity of humankind. NCOBS students, when engaged in dramatic, authentic education experiences, have the opportunity to discover self-respect, strength of character, and the power of teamwork." NCOBS operates from base camps in North Carolina, the Florida Everglades, and Atlanta and also provides international field courses in Mexico and Costa Rica.

The Wilderness Education Association (WEA)

WEA courses are currently run from Western Carolina University (WCU) and Brevard College. WCU runs the Professional National Standard Program (NSP) leadership courses, eight-day Steward courses, and workshops. Brevard College runs the NSP as part of a leadership training immersion semester.

Camps

As mentioned earlier, there are numerous camps that do adventure activities, most commonly canoeing, kayaking, rock climbing, backpacking, and wilderness travel. Some examples are Camp Merriewood at Sapphire Valley, Camp High Rocks at Cedar Mountain, Camp Illahee for Girls at Brevard, and Camp Daniel Boone (Boy Scouts) near Waynesville. There are approximately forty camps in western North Carolina. Some, such as Camp Merriewood, are rich in history and tradition. Girls from this camp were paddling the Chattooga River a long time before *Deliverance*. Camps also exist further east; for example, Camp Hanes YMCA in King.

Therapeutic Camps and Outdoor Centers

A camp of a different nature is Camp Woodson at Swannanoa, a therapeutic wilderness camping program for adjudicated youth operated by the North Carolina Division of Youth Services in western North Carolina. Coastal Horizons Center, Inc. in Wilmington has an outdoor adventure component dealing with substance abuse, crisis intervention, and prevention services.

Project SOAR (based in Balsam, North Carolina) is a therapeutic wilderness program using expedition-style adventures with learning-disordered youths. The course sites include the North Carolina Smokies, Florida Keys, Colorado Rockies, Jamaica, and Alaska.

Summary

North Carolina's natural resources, including mountain, wilderness, estuary, and ocean environments, offer varied kinds of wild country for adventure educators. The state has a rich history in adventure education, with internationally renowned agencies (such as NOC and Outward Bound) and camps that are over sixty years old. The current growth in interest in adventure activities, from participants as well as business ventures, ensures a corresponding growth in the need for adventure education.

Learning exercises

1. Interview an adventure education professional to determine:

a. The professional's academic background;

b. The primary populations served;

c. The philosophy of the agency or organization;

d. Issues that are confronting the agency or organization; and

e. Future direction and changes the agency or organization may experience.

References

Bacon, S. (1983). *The Conscious Use of Metaphor in Outward Bound*. Denver: Typesmith of Colorado.

Bankie, B., Bankie, E., McInnes, J., Oelslager, L., & Phipps, M. (1984). *A Brief Review of Psychological Theories and Counseling Techniques for Outdoor Leaders*. Experiential Education Department, Mankato State University. ERIC document. ED 244752.

Bunting, C.J. (1990). Interdependency: A key in environmental and adventure education. In J. Miles and S. Priest (Eds.), *Adventure Education* (pp. 453-458). State College, PA: Venture Publishing.

Cinnamon, J. and Raiola, E. (1991). Adventure skill and travel modes. In David Cockrell (Ed.), *The Wilderness Educator: The Wilderness Education Association Curriculum Guide* (pp. 129-130). Merrillville, IN: ICS books.

Cockrell, D. (Ed.). (1991). *The Wilderness Educator: The Wilderness Education Association Curriculum Guide*. Merrillville, IN: ICS Books, Inc.

Dewey, J. (1938). *Experience and Education*. NY: Collier Books.

Drury, J. and Bonney, B. (1992). *The Back Country Classroom*. Merrillville, IN: ICS Books.

Eells, E. (1986). *History of Organized Camping: The First 100 Years* (p. 6). Martinsville, IN : American Camping Association.

Ewert, A.W. (1989). *Outdoor Adventure Pursuits: Foundations, Models and Theories*. Columbus: Publishing Horizons.

Ford, P. & Blanchard, J. (1993). *Leadership and Administration of Outdoor Pursuits*. State College, PA: Venture Publishing.

Gass, M. (1993). Enhancing metaphor development in an adventure therapy program. In Michael Gass (Ed.), *Adventure Therapy: Therapeutic Applications of Adventure Programming* (pp. 245-58). Dubuque, IA: Kendall/Hunt.

Green, J., & Thompson, D. (1990). Outward Bound USA. In J. Miles & S. Priest (Eds.), *Adventure Education* (pp. 5-6). State College, PA: Venture Publishing.

Helmreich, R.L. (1987). Theory underlying CRM training: Psychological issues in flight crew performance and crew coordination. In H. Orlady and C. Foushee (Eds.), *Cockpit Resource Management Training* (NASA Conference Publication 2455). Moffett Field, CA: NASA Ames Research Center.

Irwin, C. & Phipps, M. L. (1994) The great outdoors and beyond: Common threads in leadership training on land in the air and in space. In L. McAvoy (Ed.), *The 1994 Coalition for Education in the Outdoors Research Symposium Research Proceedings*.

Lupton, F. (1990). WEA history. In J. Miles and S. Priest (Eds.), *Adventure Education* (p. 90). State College, PA: Venture Publishing.

Miles, J.C. (1987). The value of high adventure activities. In M..F. Meier, T.W. Morash, & G. E. Welton (Eds.), *High-Adventure Outdoor Pursuits: Organization and Leadership* (2nd ed.). Columbus: Publishing Horizons.

Miner, J.L. & Boldt, J. (1981). Outward Bound USA: *Learning Through Experience in Adventure-Based Education* (p. 336). New York: William Morrow.

North Carolina Outward Bound School. (1997). *Course Catalog* (p. 29).

Petzoldt, P.K. (1974). *The Wilderness Handbook*. New York: W.W. Norton.

Phipps, M.L. (1985). Adventure- an inner journey to the self: The psychology of adventure expressed in Jungian terms. *Adventure Education Journal 2* (5)

Phipps, M.L. & Swiderski, M. (1990). The soft skills of outdoor leadership. In J. Miles and S. Priest (Eds.), *Adventure Education*. State College, PA: Venture Publishing.

Priest, S. (1990) Semantics of adventure education. In J. Miles and S. Priest (Eds.), *Adventure Education* (pp. 113-117). State College, PA: Venture Publishing.

Ringer, M., & Gillis, H. L. (1995, May). Managing psychological depth in adventure programming. *Journal of Experiential Education 18* (1).

Schoel, J., Prouty, D., & Radcliffe, P. (1988) *Islands of Healing: A Guide to Adventure-Based Counseling*. Hamilton MA: Project Adventure.

Sharp, L.B. (1930). *Education and the Summer Camp- An Experiment* (p. 41). New York: Teachers College, Columbia University.

Chapter 12
Interpretive Services and Environmental Education in North Carolina

Wayne Williams

The places where people enjoy recreation and leisure include a broad spectrum of natural and cultural resources. The role of the interpreter or environmental educator is to help visitors understand the world they view and, more importantly, to help them appreciate our shared natural and cultural resources. Practically speaking, these professionals provide information to the public. Examples of their work include wildflower walks at state parks, PowerPoint presentations at visitor centers, demonstrations at craft centers, and tours of museum exhibits. Some interpreters dress in period costume and present living history programs at historic and archeological sites; others take rehabilitated wild animals to schools and explain their life histories to students. More recently, resorts and commercial outfitters have begun improving their programming by adding elements of interpretation and environmental education to sea kayak excursions, trail rides, and day hikes.

"Interpretation" and "environmental education" are not synonymous, but they have many similarities, especially in the techniques used. The field of interpretation is a broad umbrella with the common theme of communicating with the public about resources. Many interpreters hold a degree in recreation or leisure services and utilize their knowledge and skills in programming, special events management, and experiential education. Some university recreation and leisure programs offer specific coursework in interpretive methods. Other professionals become interpreters through studying biology, history, archeology, geology, geography, or drama and specializing in interpreting specific types of resources. Majoring in recreation and leisure, and minoring in one of the disciplines listed above, or vice versa, makes for excellent preparation for this type of career.

Environmental educators are more often trained in the natural sciences (biology, ecology, geography, etc.) or have a degree in education with a minor in one of these fields. Environmental educators focus on informing the public about the natural world; they often work in nature centers, zoos, public schools, interactive science museums, or conservation agency outreach programs. Some people trained in environmental education also become park naturalists.

The two fields use communication skills, public speaking, media technology (PowerPoint, film, video, etc.), exhibitry, and marketing to achieve their objectives. Interpreters and environmental educators often look much alike, dressed in park ranger-style uniforms with a nametag and shoulder patches. The differences between these professions lie primarily in objectives. Interpretation serves visitors to parks, museums, historic sites, etc. Visitors "drop in" for a program or sign up shortly before the program takes place. The objective of the interpreter is usually to introduce a subject (the life history of owls, why some flowers bloom in spring and others in summer, farming in Colonial times, the invention of the light bulb, etc.) to visitors and encourage them to continue learning about the subject on their own when their visit ends. Interpretation is also a management tool used to reduce vandalism, encourage volunteerism, increase donations from the public, and enhance the image of the agency (Regnier, Gross and Zimmerman, 1994).

Environmental education often takes place in a school or similar setting with pre-determined educational objectives. Through field trips, students visit sites such as parks and museums for environmental education programs. This type of learning enhances existing school curricula by dovetailing with and building upon classroom experiences. Evaluation often follows to determine whether students absorbed the information presented or learned the skill being taught. Interpretation usually appears to be less formal, however, differences often dissolve when an interpreter presents a program for a school group or an environmental educator participates in a special event for the public at a state park.

Interpretation in North Carolina

Freeman Tilden probably did more to illuminate how successful interpretation works than any other author. He was a creative writer and journalist who published novels, short stories, and his own periodical. *Interpreting Our Heritage* was written at the culmination of his study of interpretive services on behalf of the National Park Service in the 1950s (Dochterman, 2002). In it, he defined interpretation as "an educational activity which aims to reveal meanings and relationships through the use of original objects, by firsthand experience, and by illustrative media, rather than simply to communicate factual information." He also espoused six principles that he felt were the essence of interpretation (Tilden, 1957):

I. Any interpretation that does not somehow relate what is being displayed or described to something within the personality or experience of the visitor will be sterile.
II. Information, as such, is not Interpretation. Interpretation is revelation based upon information. But they are entirely different things. However, all interpretation includes information.
III. Interpretation is an art, which combines many arts, whether the materials presented are scientific, historical, or architectural. Any art is in some degree teachable.
IV. The chief aim of Interpretation is not instruction, but provocation.
V. Interpretation should aim to present a whole rather than a part, and must address itself to the whole man (person—author's addition) rather than any phase.
VI. Interpretation addressed to children (say, up to the age of twelve) should not be a dilution of the presentation to adults, but should follow a fundamentally different approach. To be at its best it will require a separate program.

As the twentieth century came to a close, Tilden's Principles were updated and expanded by Larry Beck and Ted Cable in their book, *Interpretation for the 21st Century*. The newer work adds much to the field with chapters on the Information Age, technology, aesthetics, and passion for the subject. However, *Interpreting Our Heritage*, published in

North Carolina by the University of North Carolina Press in 1957, remains in print; and interpreters across North Carolina apply Tilden's Principles daily in a broad spectrum of programs.

Again, it is important to note that interpretation takes place in a wide range of venues. Interpreters are found at parks, nature centers, museums, historic and archeological sites, and zoos and aquariums. They are employed by all levels of government, non-profit organizations, and businesses. While there are far too many interpretive services to mention here, the following are some typical examples.

One of the first agencies in the state to offer interpretive programs was the National Park Service (NPS), at the Great Smoky Mountains National Park and along the Blue Ridge Parkway. The NPS continues in the forefront of quality interpretive services by offering living history re-enactments at Guilford County Courthouse National Military Park, programs on the physics of flight at the Wright Brothers National Monument, and oceanographic programs at Cape Lookout National Seashore. National park operations in the state are staffed with permanent and seasonal interpretive staff members, and programs and special events are offered at all of the NPS operations within the state.

The United States Forest Service (USFS) and Army Corps of Engineers (ACE) provide interpretive services in the forms of campground programs, wayside exhibits, outreach programs, literature, special events, and visitor centers. Their programming includes historical and archeological material as well as environmental information. Smokey the Bear and Woodsy Owl, two of the best-known interpretive icons, were originally created by these agencies in efforts to reduce wildfires and litter. More about these agencies can be found in the chapter on state and federal recreation services.

As of this writing, few full-time interpreters are employed by North Carolina state parks. Rather, interpretation is but one of several duties of state park rangers, along with law enforcement and maintenance. Despite multitasking, state park rangers offer a wide variety of cultural and environmental programs and outstanding special events. State park rangers have recently been encouraged to complete the requirements for the North Carolina Environmental Education Certification Program (described later in this chapter) to improve their work as park naturalists.

Historical Interpretation

A number of interpretive sites focus primarily on historical and archeological resources in the state. Prominent among these are the historic sites and museums managed by the North Carolina Department of Cultural Resources. The Division of State Historic Sites operates twenty three sites ranging from the Battleship North Carolina to Tryon Palace, a reconstructed Colonial governor's mansion. The Division of State History Museums manages a system of museums including the Maritime Museum and the Mountain Gateway Museum. See more about the Department of Cultural Resources at their Web site: www.ncdr.gov/oah.htm.

The Museum of the Cherokee Indian, located in the town of Cherokee, tells the story of the tribe from the period of the Paleo Indians (11,000 B.C. to 8,000 B.C.) through the Trail of Tears (1838) to the present. This outstanding museum is operated by the Cherokee Tribe. Learn more at their Web site: www.cherokeemuseum.org. The Airborne and Special Operations Museum in Fayetteville is part of the U.S. Army Museum System. This $22.5 million state of the art interpretive facility tells the story of U.S. Army airborne and special operations troops through interactive exhibits, simulations, and displays. Visit their Web site at: www.asomf.org. Other historic sites and museums are managed by non-profit organizations and local governments throughout the state.

Local museums often present a mix of natural and cultural interpretation. One of the best is the Schiele Museum in Gastonia. Originally focused on natural history, the museum has grown to include a recreated Catawba Indian village and a Colonial homestead, an aboriginal studies program, and a planetarium. The public is encouraged to participate in weekend workshops in net making, pottery, and flint knapping. Summer day camp programs feature friction fire making and classic campcraft. Special events are scheduled throughout the year with themes such as dinosaurs and insects.

Environmental Education in North Carolina

The North Carolina Environmental Education Plan (DuBay, 1995) defines environmental education as ". . . an active process that increases awareness, knowledge and skills that result in understanding, commitment, informed decisions and constructive action to ensure stewardship of all interdependent parts of the earth's environment." As stated earlier, environmental education is usually coordinated with school curricula and focuses primarily on natural science topics.

While the majority of the interpretive sites described above involve some environmental education, there are also numerous true environmental education programs in North Carolina. As with interpretation, environmental education is found at all levels of government and in non-profits and businesses.

The Cradle of Forestry, managed by the U.S. Forest Service, is located near Brevard. George Vanderbilt hired Dr. Carl Schenck and Gifford Pinchot to establish on this site the first American school of forestry. The state of the art museum and grounds tell the story of forest conservation from its beginnings, using live interpretation, interactive displays, exhibits, and demonstrations.

The Division of Forest Resources, part of the North Carolina Department of Environment and Natural Resources, operates a system of six Educational State Forests (ESFs). The ESFs feature self-guided trails, exhibits, tree identification signs, and forest education centers. They offer school programs and Investigating Your Environment workshops for teachers during the summer. Project Learning Tree (PLT) is a day-long workshop offered by the Division of Forest Resources that trains teachers, interpreters, and others in techniques for teaching environmental education. PLT is a national program of the American Forest Foundation and includes a 402-page activity guide as part of the workshop. For more information, visit their Web site at: www.dfr.state.nc.us/education/esf.htm.

The North Carolina Wildlife Resources Commission currently operates wildlife education centers in Pisgah Forest and Raleigh, with a third center under construction on Currituck Sound, near Corolla. The centers focus on regional wildlife and the hunting and fishing heritage of the state. The centers offer school programs and special workshops; they feature aquariums, exhibits on enhancing wildlife habitats through plantings, wildlife law enforcement, and environmental education in general. The commission includes a staff of regional wildlife educators who travel the state hosting wildlife education workshops such as Project Wild and Project Wild Aquatic. These educational programs are sponsored by the national Council for Environmental Education in cooperation with state wildlife management agencies. The programs prepare teachers, park rangers, and others to be environmental educators. Each of these free workshops includes a free curriculum guide. For more information, see their Web site: www.ncwildlife.org.

The North Carolina Zoological Park, North Carolina Aquariums, and museums across the state offer environmental education programs for school groups, training programs for teachers, and summer day-camp programs. The North Carolina Museum of Natural Sciences in Raleigh publishes an *Educator's Guide to Museum Services* to enhance visits by school groups. The Museum of Life and Science in Durham and the Western North Carolina Nature Center in Asheville schedule school programs that often feature their collections of wild animals native to the state.

North Carolina Environmental Education Certification Program

In 1995, the North Carolina Office of Environmental Education published a comprehensive plan for environmental education in the state. The fifty four page document includes objectives for in-service teacher education, pre-service teacher education, higher education, library collections, environmental education centers, government agencies, and funding. One outgrowth of this effort is the North Carolina Environmental Education Certification Program.

Under this program, teachers, park rangers, interpreters, museum and zoo employees, and others can earn certification by: attending seven workshops (including Project Learning Tree and Project Wild), gaining fifty hours of structured out-of-doors experiences, spending thirty hours in activities such as visiting museums and environmental education centers, teaching thirty hours of environmental courses, and taking a leadership role in a twenty hour school or community project. The certification program encourages educators, interpreters, and environmental resource managers to increase their skills as stewards of North Carolina's natural resources.

The Future of Interpretation and Environmental Education in North Carolina

The public demand for information on natural and cultural resources continues to grow. As long as this trend persists, there will be a positive and challenging future for professionals in these fields. Organizations such as the National Association for Interpretation (www.interp-net.com/home.html), the Association for Living History, Farm, and Agricultural Museums (www.alhfam.org/), and the North American Association for Environmental Education (naaee.org/pages/index.html) continue to improve the quality of interpretive services through workshops, conferences, and publications for professionals. To pursue a career in these fields, seek an opportunity to become a trained volunteer as a docent (tour guide) or re-enactor at an interpretive site or begin the steps toward certification as an environmental educator.

Learning Exercises

1. Locate the nearest state or national park, museum, historic site, or nature center in your area and inquire about volunteer opportunities.

2. Visit the Web sites mentioned in this chapter and see if there are links to other sites that provide detailed information about interpretation and environmental education. In addition, use search engines to locate additional sites on this topic.

3. Contact a professional at a park, museum, etc. and ask them about their educational background. What combination of courses would they recommend for someone planning to enter the field?

4. Visit a nature center, then visit a historic site. Did you notice a difference in interpretive styles at these sites?

5. Learn more about these fields by scheduling an appointment with one of your professors who might be able to help you find an internship in interpretation or environmental education, or contact the author at: willwe@appstate.edu.

References

Beck, L. & Cable, T. (1998). *Interpretation for the 21st Century*. Champaign: Sagamore.

Dochterman, R. (2002). Freeman Tilden: The writer and wanderer who showed us the way. *Legacy, 5-6:16-25*.

DuBay, D. (Ed.) (1995). *The North Carolina Environmental Education Plan*. Raleigh: Author.

Regnier, K., Gross, M., & Zimmerman, R. (1992). *The Interpreter's Guidebook: Techniques for Programs and Presentations* (3rd ed.). Stevens Point: UW-SP Foundation Press.

Tilden, F. (1957). *Interpreting Our Heritage* (3rd ed.). Chapel Hill: University of North Carolina Press.

Chapter 13

Campus Recreation

Stephanie T. West

A university is charged with the responsibility of promoting the intellectual, cultural, and personal development of its students. The American College Personnel Association has found that learning and personal development are affected by both in-class and out-of-class experiences and that both students and institutional environments contribute to what students gain from college (American College Personnel Association [ACPA], 1996). "Thus, the key to enhancing learning and personal development is not simply for faculty to teach more and better, but also to create conditions that motivate and inspire students to devote time and energy to educationally-purposeful activities, both in and outside the classroom" (ACPA, 1996).

Higher education has traditionally organized its activities into academic affairs, consisting of learning and cognitive development taking place in classrooms as part of a pre-determined curriculum, and student affairs, the part of campus that involves affective or personal development through student activities and residential life. Through these services, universities seek to enhance the value of the undergraduate experience by encouraging students to participate actively on their campuses and support the development of their peers.

Mission on Campus

The purpose of most campus recreation programs is to promote and advance healthy lifestyles through participation and educational opportunities. As such, campus recreation professionals often view their role on campus as health and fitness educators, promoting the benefits of physical activity. By focusing on the average student, rather than the elite athlete, campus recreation programs can meet the athletic, fitness, cultural and social needs of the student body. According to Michael Barron, the director of the Admissions Office at the University of Iowa, "a very high percentage of . . . students have taken part in athletics, cheerleading, or drill team and don't go on to college sports but want to be active" (Slusark, 2005).

Benefits of Campus Recreation

In their efforts to emphasize to college and university administrators the importance of campus recreation to student academic achievement, the National Intramural-Recreational Sports Association (NIRSA) published research by Kerr & Downs Research that showed "participation in recreational sports is a key determinant of satisfaction and success in college" (Downs, 2003, p. 9). Student respondents also cited the following benefits (listed by priority) of a campus recreation program: improves emotional well-being; reduces stress; improves happiness; builds self-confidence and character; improves diversity; teaches team building; and improves leadership skills.

In addition to the positive impacts on participants, student employees receive significant benefits from a campus recreation program. Most schools spend more than half of their campus recreation budgets on student wages for: sports officials, lifeguards, outdoor trip leaders, weight room attendants, scorekeepers, aerobic instructors, personal trainers, climbing wall attendants, ropes course facilitators, facility supervisors, etc. Employees frequently earn minimum wage when getting started but can be paid more than twice that, depending on their skills, abilities, experiences, certifications, and length of employment with the program. Aside from the financial gains, a substantial benefit to student employees of a campus recreation program is the opportunity for student development. While working in campus recreation, student employees receive training and experience in both technical and social skills. Technical skills are job-related skills needed to perform the required duties for that position. For example, officials need to know the rules and mechanics of the sport in which they officiate. Social skills are those inter-personal skills that are often best learned through practice. These include how to calm an irate customer (or player), work together as part of a team, motivate co-workers, solve problems, prioritize tasks, manage time, etc.

While there are many positive benefits to participants and employees of campus recreation programs, as shown above, there may also be indirect benefits for non-participants. For example, providing jobs in campus recreation decreases the number of students looking for employment elsewhere; reducing the stress level of participants may have a positive impact on their interactions with others, including non-participants; and offering positive team-building opportunities for student organizations may decrease the amount of hazing on a campus.

The examples of benefits discussed so far have related to participants and non-participants. However, campus recreation programs also benefit the institution as a whole in terms of recruitment and retention of students, faculty and staff. According to Sybil R. Todd, the vice president for student affairs at the University of Alabama, "We expect to recruit and retain students, faculty, and staff who value a healthy learning environment, and reduce the prevalence and intensity of health-risk behavior among [our] students" (Tudzin, 2004). The campus recreation program at North Carolina Central University also acknowledges this in the closing of their mission statement: "to assist in the recruitment and retention of students, faculty, and staff" (North Carolina Central University [NCCU], 2005). Research has also shown that participation in recreational sports and utilization of campus recreation facilities have a positive effect on student recruitment efforts and retention rates (Maas, 1999; Astin, 1993; Wade, 1991).

State of the art student recreation centers are an integral part of this. To attract and keep the best new students, faculty, and staff, schools must now build facilities that fulfill a wide range of needs (Sharpless & Mave, 2002). The student recreation center is a popular stop among prospective students, faculty, and staff when taking a tour of the campus. In April of 2005, CNN reported that universities are increasingly using campus recreational facilities, or future plans for them, to appeal to prospective students (CNN.com, 2005). According to *The Boston Globe's* Marcella Bombardieri, institutions of higher learning are in a student recreation center war, "a feverish race among schools to lure prospective students and faculty to campus and keep them happy once they arrive" (2004).

Organizational Structure

Within a university, a campus recreation program can report to Academics, Athletics, or Student Affairs (the latter is also known by many other names, including Student Life or Student Development). For instance, the campus recreation programs at Duke University, University of North Carolina-Charlotte, and North Carolina Central University report to academic areas, while the campus recreation programs at Western Carolina University, Winston-Salem State University, East Carolina University, and Appalachian State University report to Student Affairs.

Within the campus recreation program, the organizational structure frequently depends on the number of professional staff. A copy of the organizational chart for UNC-Wilmington can be found in Figure 13.1. From the organizational chart, it is evident that the campus recreation program at UNC-Wilmington reports to the Division of Student Affairs.

Professional staff are responsible for setting policies and procedures within the area they supervise. Participants who fail to adhere to program policies are subject to disciplinary action. Many campus recreation programs create an advisory board to approve the policies and procedures of their programs. At Appalachian State University (ASU), the UREC Council is made up of a diverse group of students who strive to serve their peers in a fair, structured system when dealing with University Recreation policies. They not only help the program shape policies and procedures but also serve as an appeals board for participants who have received disciplinary action. All participants at ASU have the right to appeal to the UREC Council if they feel they have been treated unfairly in any way.

Funding

According to the associate vice president for finance with the Office of the President for the University of North Carolina, non-academic programs at any of the sixteen institutions of the University of North Carolina System are, as a rule, self-supporting (J. Smith, personal communication, June 2, 2005). Instead, campus recreation funding comes directly from mandatory student activity fees (*The UNC Policy Manual*, 2005). In addition, funding can be mandated to cover the repayment of a public bid bonding project for specific campus recreation facilities. In this case, the cost of a facility is spread out over a predetermined period, with the debt retirement typically planned for twenty five to thirty years later.

At East Carolina University, the $118 annual student fee provides for operation of their entire campus recreation program. In addition, students are charged a $76 yearly activity fee that has been designated toward the repayment of the debt for their Student Recreation Center and a separate $8.00 yearly student fee for maintenance and operation of their recreational sports field complex. The following breakdown summarizes their approximate revenue for their Student Recreation Center in a given year, by revenue source:

- Student Activity fees—92 percent of revenue
- Faculty/Staff and spouse memberships—2.25 percent of revenue
- Program/Activity fees/other—5.75 percent of revenue (East Carolina University [ECU], 2005)

Because faculty and staff are not charged the mandatory fees that students pay as part of their tuition requirements, they are usually required to pay a supplemental "membership" fee. As seen from the above example at ECU, membership fees from these users are also a source of revenue for the program. Faculty/staff memberships range from nothing at UNC-Asheville to $48/year at Appalachian State University to $190/year at Duke University. Spouses and dependents of eligible members (students, faculty, or staff) are often treated similarly to faculty and staff; that is, charged a similar membership fee. This is the case at Duke University and East Carolina University. However, other universities treat them in a unique manner. For instance, at UNC-Asheville, spouses and dependents of students, faculty, and staff are charged $25 per person to use the fitness center, while Appalachian State University does not charge spouses or dependents of students to use facilities. Spouses and dependents of ASU faculty and staff, however, are charged the same fee as faculty and staff: $48/year.

Some universities allow alumni to purchase a membership to their facility. For example, at UNC-Greensboro, the membership fee is $200/year. To be eligible for a membership, UNC-G alumni must make a donation to the school in the amount of $50, $100, or $150 if they graduated one year, two years or three years ago, respectively. The fourth year following graduation, and any thereafter, require a donation of at least $200 in addition to the $200 membership fee. In addition to these membership fees, eligible members may purchase a guest pass for themselves or someone else, including someone ineligible for a membership, for about $5 per day. The fee for an alumni membership at UNC-Asheville's newly expanded Health and Fitness Center is only $150 a year, with $75 serving as a tax-deductible gift to the UNCA Alumni Phonathon Fund or any other scholarship fund of choice and the remaining $75 serving as the fee for the fitness center.

Multiple-use facilities—those that house program areas other than campus recreation (such as athletics or academics)—follow different funding guidelines. For instance, facilities in which academic courses are held are eligible to receive state funds for construction and/or operation. The level of state funding provided typically reflects the amount of use of that facility for academic purposes.

Facilities

Facilities operated by campus recreation programs include indoor facilities (such as student recreation centers, gymnasiums, aquatic facilities, and/or fitness centers) and outdoor facilities (including sports fields, outdoor pools, and challenge courses/climbing towers). In the last twenty years, there has been a significant increase in the construction of multi-purpose student recreation centers whose primary purpose is the recreational needs of students. These facilities can include indoor swimming pools, outdoor swimming pools, racquetball/squash courts, an indoor jogging track, multi-use gymnasium sports courts, weight training and cardiovascular fitness areas, classrooms, multipurpose exercise studios, and climbing walls. Operational expenses, program expenses, and student and full-time staff salaries for these facilities are usually supported entirely by the revenue generated through student activity fees and special membership/guest fees. As a result, the priority use schedules at most institutions are typically similar to the one provided by East Carolina University:

■ *First priority:* Programs and services provided by and/or sponsored by the campus recreation program.
■ *Second priority:* Academic classes approved for scheduling by the campus recreation program. Academic programs will provide payment to offset debit service and facility operation and will be financially responsible for special set-ups/strike-downs and any repairs and/or maintenance/housekeeping needs that arise as a direct result of their programs.
■ *Third priority:* Student organizations. No charges will be assessed to student organizations for reserved use unless the reservation creates the need for special set-up and/or strike down or the reservation requires special operating hours or staff supervision, housekeeping needs, supplies, etc.
■ *Fourth priority:* University Affiliates-Groups and individuals related to the mission of ECU such as athletic or academic camps, state, regional, or national events. These programs will be dealt with on a cost recovery basis, making sure that rental charges are passed on for basic costs including debit service, program and facility operations, as well as costs associated with special set-ups/strike-downs and special staffing needs.
■ *Fifth priority:* Programs sponsored by student organizations and/or academic departments for the community outside of ECU. Sponsored programs have the same financial responsibility as University Affiliates.
■ *Sixth priority:* Non Affiliate-Profit making or not-for-profit organizations and/or activities with no affiliation to ECU. Charges for reserved facilities for non-affiliate groups will be set in such a fashion as to reduce debit service, program and facility operations costs, as well as generate revenue. These rental charges will include all staffing and personnel charges, housekeeping and housekeeping supplies, utilities, and pro-rated maintenance/repair charges (ECU, 2005).

Program Areas

Intramurals—Taken literally, intramurals means "within the walls." An intramural sports program, therefore, consists of athletic competitions within a campus, that is, between students attending the same institution. Intramural sports offer a variety of recreational and competitive activities for all skill levels. They offer participants the opportunity to meet new people, socialize with friends, and enhance their physical well-being through participation in team and individual/dual sports. With most programs providing one game a week and no practice, intramurals can easily fit into anyone's schedule (games are typically played in the evenings, Sunday through Thursday). While students comprise the majority of participants, faculty and staff are also often encouraged to participate. Otherwise eligible participants with certain intramural playing restrictions include those individuals who have benefited from advanced training and coaching opportunities in the same or related intramural sport. These include current members of a sport club team, former members of an intercollegiate team, and former professional players. Restrictions include prohibited participation for a specific number of years following involvement in one of the above categories, limits on the number of restricted players allowed on a team, and prohibited participation by a restricted player in less-than-advanced skill levels. Eligible participants may also be restricted from playing if they have been ejected and/or suspended for inappropriate conduct.

There are typically five "major" team sports provided by an institution: flag football, volleyball, soccer, softball and basketball. In addition, other team sports, such as indoor soccer, sand volleyball, 3 on 3 basketball, 4 on 4 flag football, wallyball, and ultimate frisbee, may be offered. Individual and dual sports frequently include badminton, tennis, table tennis, racquetball, golf, billiards, swimming, track, and bowling. Non-traditional activities, such as flickerball, pickleball, oozeball, dodgeball, team handball, fantasy football, tug-of-war, innertube water polo, 2 on 2 indoor soccer, and 1 on 1 basketball might also be provided. The schedule is determined by each campus recreation program and is influenced by the demand for participation, facility availability, and funding availability.

In addition to selecting the sports to be provided, campus recreation professionals also choose the divisions, skill levels, and formats that will be offered for each sport. Divisions consist of men, women, and/or CoRec (a combination of men and women), while skill levels typically include advanced, intermediate, or beginner. Because intramural programs target all students, not just the elite athlete, it is common for schools to deemphasize the focus on skill by providing alternative labels, such as colors (black, white, and gold classes) to differentiate the levels of play. The availability of various levels of play allows participants at different skill levels to compete against similarly skilled opponents. This enhances the opportunity for participants by providing more evenly matched contests in which predetermined winners are less likely.

Available formats include league play or tournament play and can take place throughout the semester or be limited to one day. Most team sports have a regular season, employing a round robin format. Because it is common to have a large number of teams that participate, teams are often placed into leagues with three to five other teams. Following the regular season, teams participate in a single-elimination tournament. Depending on time and facility availability, all teams might advance to the tournament or only the teams with a certain standing following league play will advance, such as those who finished first in their league or those with a .500 record or better.

Rather than awarding championship teams with trophies, campus recreation programs usually award championship t-shirts to tournament winners in each division and skill level. To discourage teams or players from "sandbagging," that is, signing up to participate in a lower skill level so as to increase their likelihood that they win, winners in lower skill levels might receive certificates, t-shirts designed with fewer colors, or t-shirts that indicate the skill level in which they won.

Many colleges and universities also have a year-long competition based on a point system among the various participant "units" in a wide variety of intramural sports activities.

Units receive points to recognize their participation, achievement, and sportsmanship in the intramural sports program. Units typically consist of fraternities or sororities, residence halls, campus organizations, and/or independents, that is, those students not aligned with any other organizations that wish to participate together. At UNC-Chapel Hill, winners of the "All-University Championships" receive their name on a plaque and an opportunity to participate in an end of year tournament.

Extramurals—As intramurals consists of athletic contests between teams within a campus, it stands to reason that extramurals involves athletic contests between teams from different campuses. In this case, teams from different campuses typically compete in a tournament. While many schools send their best teams to represent their school at an extramural tournament, schools may elect to send any of their teams. Extramural tournaments are particularly common in flag football and basketball but can occasionally be found within other sports. The most famous extramural tournament is the National Invitational Flag Football tournament held each year in New Orleans between Christmas and New Years. The winners in each division (men's, women's and CoRec) are considered to be the national champions in flag football.

Sports Clubs—Sports clubs are registered student organizations consisting of students, and sometimes faculty and staff, with a common interest in a sport. Depending on the institution, sports clubs may be competitive, instructional, recreational, or a combination of these. A sports club program provides a compromise between an institution's intercollegiate athletic program and its intramurals program. In contrast to intramural sports, participation is limited to members, who are typically required to pay dues and maintain a specific level of participation throughout the year.

Whereas varsity athletic teams are administered by university professionals, sports clubs are developed, governed, and administered by students. Thus, the key to a successful sports club is its student leadership and membership base. Once a sports club has been recognized by the institution, a campus recreation professional helps to oversee them and advise their administration. In addition, campus recreation programs typically support their sports clubs financially or through the provision of reserved facility space for their practices and/or contests. Failure to follow institution requirements, such as paperwork or policies, can result in the loss of institutional support or recognition. Common sports clubs found within North Carolina universities and colleges include: badminton, baseball, crew, cycling, equestrian, fencing, field hockey, golf, ice hockey, in-line hockey, lacrosse, martial arts, rugby, sailing, skiing/snowboarding, softball, swimming, tennis, triathlon, ultimate frisbee, volleyball, water polo, water ski, soccer, table tennis, and wrestling.

Outdoors—As part of a comprehensive program, campus recreation programs also offer an outdoor adventure-related component that provides outdoor recreation equipment and activities or trips for eligible participants. Outdoor recreation equipment can either be purchased or rented for short-term use. Equipment usually available for rent includes: backpacks, tents, sleeping bags, lanterns, stoves, camping pads, coolers, cooking sets, and canoes/kayaks. Rental fees range from less than a dollar per day for items like stoves, lanterns and coolers to $18 per week for a four person tent. Popular activities include: backpacking, camping, canoeing/kayaking, caving, climbing, challenge courses, fishing, fly-fishing, horseback riding, mountain biking, orienteering, sea kayaking, skiing and whitewater rafting. The Mars Hill College Outdoor Center even takes students for a soak in Hot Springs, North Carolina.

Professionals in these areas are also often responsible for indoor rock climbing walls, outdoor climbing tours, and challenge courses. Most rock climbing walls offer opportunities for top-rope climbing and bouldering. Services provided at rock climbing walls include equipment, belaying, and instruction. Ropes and harnesses are usually provided free of charge, while shoes and chalk bags are provided at a small fee. For example, shoes at UNC-G cost $2/day or $20/semester. Appalachian State University also provides simulated ice climbing with their rock climbing wall. Student workers at the rock climbing wall are responsible for ensuring safety, checking out equipment, providing instruction, and/or belaying participants. In addition to opportunities for open climbing and instruction, many climbing walls also host climbing competitions for climbers in various stages of skill development (beginner, intermediate, and advanced). Those wishing to further their climbing skills can also take part in trips to nearby outdoor climbing sites. Challenge courses led by campus recreation professional and student staff are frequently used by campus groups (such as athletic teams, freshman cohorts, and department staff) to develop group cohesion and teamwork. In addition, many challenge courses are a source of revenue for campus recreation departments that allow them to be rented by non-campus organizations.

In addition to the programs listed above, several North Carolina institutions provide specialized programs for campus freshmen. These programs have been designed to help facilitate students' transition into college by pushing their personal limits and teaching them to work closely with a diverse group of people in a dynamic environment. For example, First Ascent, Appalachian State University's wilderness orientation program, provides students with challenging opportunities focused on fun, friendships, and teamwork in which students share a common bond to last throughout their college experience. A similar program, Wilderness Adventures for First Year Students (WAFFYS), is offered by UNC-Chapel Hill.

Aquatics—As the name indicates, the Aquatics program area provides aquatic-related recreation opportunities. Professionals in this area are responsible for managing facilities, staff, and programs. Typical facilities include indoor and outdoor swimming pools, diving wells, and open water areas (such as lakes). Typical programs offered include lap swimming, open swimming, lessons (swimming, diving, scuba diving, kayaking/canoeing), clubs (swimming, water polo, synchronized swimming, diving, scuba diving), aqua-aerobics, and lifeguard/Water Safety Instructor training. The indoor swimming pool is the most likely campus recreation facility to house both athletics and academics.

To accommodate all these needs, universities often schedule academic classes in the morning and athletics in the afternoon, with campus recreation programs taking place in the evening. In addition, most pools are capable of meeting multiple uses through the use of moving bulkheads or floating lane lines. This way, lap swimming can be offered in the middle of the pool, while swim lessons occur in the shallow end and aqua aerobics takes place in the deep end.

During the weekends, natatoriums (swimming facilities) are often rented by local swim teams for home meets. This allows the campus recreation program to generate revenue in a facility that might receive little use otherwise. To facilitate this opportunity, many large natatoriums are built with a second smaller pool so that regular patrons may still swim while the other pool is being rented or used by athletics. Additional trends in natatoriums or pool construction include water slides, lazy rivers, spray devices, and zero depth entry points (where entry to the pool is via a gradual slope, similar to entering the ocean from the beach).

Fitness and Wellness—The mission of fitness and wellness components of a campus recreation program—to encourage members of the university community to live a healthier lifestyle—is typically met by offering quality classes and workshops that educate, motivate, and stimulate physical and mental growth in a comfortable and enthusiastic atmosphere. The objective of the Fitness and Wellness program at North Carolina State University is "to offer essential knowledge and energy to all participants so that they may set and achieve personal fitness goals at their own level" (North Carolina State University, 2005).

Most fitness/wellness programs include group fitness classes, such as aerobics, yoga, spinning, Pilates, kickboxing, and dance. Some universities offer all classes free of charge, such as Appalachian State University, Duke, and UNC, while others, such as East Carolina University, charge for the majority of their classes. In addition to providing exercise classes, most universities provide instructor training programs, including certification workshops and exams, for potential instructors. Since most classes are taught by currently enrolled students, an instructor training program helps to ensure an adequate pool of certified and knowledgeable instructors.

The wellness component of a campus recreation program varies from group wellness workshops and seminars to individualized fitness level testing and personal training. Incentive programs are also incorporated into many campus recreation programs as part of their role in motivating members of the university community to be physically active.

Other—Many campus recreation programs also offer activities that do not fall within one of the program areas listed above. A unique program area provided by East Carolina University is their adapted recreation program. The "A Real Integrated Sports Experience" (ARISE) program provides University community members with and without disabilities the opportunity for involvement in a variety of unique sports, fitness, and recreational activities as a means to enhance their physical, intellectual, social, and emotional well-being (ECU, "ARISE," 2005). The program features modified sport and recreational activities and instruction in an integrated setting. Programs provided include adapted climbing, hand crank bicycling and skiing clinics; adapted open climbing, camping, and therapeutic horseback riding; wheelchair basketball; and rugby and goalball for the visually impaired (those who are not visually impaired may also participate by wearing a blindfold).

Employment Opportunities

Part-Time Employment—As mentioned previously, most schools spend more than half of their allocated budgets on student wages for part-time employment. Available positions include: sports officials, lifeguards, outdoor trip leaders, weight room attendants, scorekeepers, aerobic instructors, personal trainers, climbing wall attendants, ropes course facilitators, and facility supervisors. Employees frequently earn minimum wage but are also given many opportunities for training, experience, and professional development.

Experienced student employees may also have the opportunity to participate in other administrative responsibilities, such as scheduling facilities or programs and hiring, supervising, training, and scheduling student staff.

Graduate Assistantships—While fulfilling the academic requirements of a master's degree, many students work as graduate assistants for campus recreation programs. These students typically receive a monthly stipend for working twenty hours a week for about nine months a year, September to May. While stipends vary by institution, the average pay comes out to about $10-$12 per hour. Benefits that might be included with the graduate assistantship include health insurance and/or a tuition break. This may include the actual cost of tuition or the application of in-state tuition rates for out-of-state students. Job responsibilities of graduate assistantships are often similar to that of professional staff but vary by institution. A listing of available graduate assistantships for campus recreation programs can be found at NIRSA's job Web site, Bluefishjobs.com.

Full-Time Employment—Securing a professional position at a campus recreation program can be a worthwhile challenge. Competition for entry-level positions is intense, with many positions receiving applications from forty to sixty qualified individuals. This is partly due to a high interest in this profession; the opportunity to combine recreation with the development of college students is especially appealing to individuals who participated in this system as an undergraduate and graduate student. In addition, positions in campus recreation are challenging, provide significant variety, and are very rewarding.

Because campus recreation programs follow an academic calendar, positions are most frequently posted in March, near the time of the annual NIRSA conference, with interviews to be held April-June, for positions beginning early August, just in time to prepare for the upcoming academic year. As with graduate assistantships, available positions are almost always posted on NIRSA's job Web site, Bluefishjobs.com. While most program areas within campus recreation only require a bachelor's degree, most applicants will have a master's degree and experience in campus recreation as a graduate assistant. The key to gaining an entry-level position is a strong graduate assistantship at a reputable institution. Additional experience can be a valuable substitute for those who do not have a graduate assistantship in campus recreation. Program areas most likely to hire someone without a master's degree and/or experience in campus recreation are outdoor recreation and fitness/wellness, where traditional applicants are less likely to be the norm. Because of the competitive nature of campus recreation positions, it is important for candidates to follow application directions precisely. Most application procedures include submitting a résumé, a cover letter, and a list of three references. On occasion, actual reference letters or academic transcripts are required.

Assessment and Evaluation

Campus stakeholders—including students, parents, administrators, and accreditation bodies—are now demanding that campus recreation programs demonstrate both the value and effectiveness of programs and services (Student Voice). As a result, assessment has taken on increased importance and is no longer optional.

The role of assessment is to provide reliable data and evidence to senior administrators concerning the value of programs and services and the impact of recreation services on students. This is typically accomplished through examining the usage of campus recreation programs and facilities, satisfaction with these services, and the ability of the programs to meet academic, social, emotional, and health-related outcomes. Although student satisfaction measures are capable of assessing student fulfillment, it is critical that assessments are conducted on the impact of various policies and programs on learning and personal development. Campus recreation programs should be evaluated periodically to determine how students learn and what they know, thereby improving institutional productivity (ACPA, 1996). Related to the improvement of institutional productivity, assessment and evaluation are important tools in determining the effect of campus recreation on student recruitment and retention rates. In particular, campuses are beginning to examine first-year cohorts to determine if any relationships exist among grade point averages (GPAs), drop-out rates, and student engagement in campus recreation programs. Research by Belch, Gebel and Maas (2001) found that although non-users of a student recreation center (SRC) at a large university entered college with higher high school GPAs and ACT/SAT scores than users of the SRC, SRC users persisted at a greater rate. In addition, users earned slightly higher GPAs and more first-year credit hours.

Key issues often analyzed for determining the success of campus recreation programs include: 1) progress toward institutional or departmental goals; 2) areas of success and strength, as well as areas of opportunity; 3) identification of unmet student needs; and 4) cost effectiveness and applicability of programs (Student Voice). Results of the assessment can then be used to improve and enhance programs, aid day-to-day and long-term decision-making and planning, gain support for new programs and services, and allow for benchmarking with other campuses.

Summary

Although each campus recreation program is unique, many programs share common characteristics in terms of mission, funding, organizational structure, and program areas, facilities, and activities offered. Career opportunities continue to grow as campuses increase their campus recreation programs to assist with campus recruitment and retention and to facilitate student learning by improving their programs' abilities to meet the needs of students, faculty, and staff. Assessment and evaluation have been critical thus far in improving the positioning of recreation programs on a campus and must be continued and improved upon to sustain their progress. Given this, it is likely that recreation programs will continue to be an integral component on campuses in North Carolina and beyond.

Learning Exercises

1. Compare and contrast the following programs: intramurals, extramurals, and sports clubs.

2. Spend time with both a campus recreation professional and a professional from another area (such as municipal recreation, military recreation, or non-profit recreation) within a similar program area (such as aquatics, athletics, informal recreation, wellness, or outdoors). Compare and contrast the job responsibilities for these individuals.

3. Spend time with a campus recreation professional at your institution and prepare a report that identifies the facilities and programs available, participation patterns, and funding strategies of that program.

4. Locate an organizational chart for a campus recreation program at a small college and one at a larger university. Compare and contrast the two administrations.

5. Interview a campus recreation professional and prepare a one-page report that details their academic and professional preparation. Conclude the report with a recommendation of what you should do to prepare if you want to assume a similar position.

For more information

National Intramural-Recreational Sports Association (NIRSA)

In 1950, campus recreation programs from eleven historically black colleges organized the National Intramural Association, now known as the National Intramural-Recreational Sports Association (NIRSA) (NIRSA, 2005). Today, NIRSA is a non-profit membership organization serving more than 4,000 professionals, students, and associate members in the recreational sports field throughout the United States, Canada, and other countries. Although NIRSA represents colleges, universities, United States military bases, correctional institutions, and municipalities, 94 percent of NIRSA's 740 Institutional members come from college and university recreational sports programs. NIRSA's member institutions represent nearly seven million college students, of whom an estimated 5.5 million participate in recreational programs. Visit nirsa.org for more information.

REFERENCES

American College Personnel Association. (1996, February 14). *The student learning imperative: Implications for student affairs.* Retrieved May 26, 2005, from http://www.acpa.nche.edu/sli/sli.htm.

Astin, A.W. (1993). *What Matters in College?: Four Critical Years Revisited.* San Francisco: Jossey-Bass.

Belch, H.A., Gebel, M. & Maas, G. (2001). Relationship between student recreation complex use, academic performance, and persistence of first-time freshmen. *The National Association of Student Personnel Administrators Journal, 38*(2): 254-268.

Bombardieri, M. (2004, December 18). *BU shapes up its recruiting: Campus officials hope $90m athletic center will lure top students.* Retrieved May 29, 2005, from http://www.boston.com/news/local/massachusetts/articles/2004/12/18/bu_shapes_up_its_recruiting/.

CNN,com. (2005, April 1). Recreation centers used to woo students. Retrieved April 8, 2005, from http://www.cnn.com/2005/EDUCATION/04/01/campus.rec.centers.ap/index.html.

Downs, P. (2003). The value of recreational sports in higher education. *Recreational Sports Journal, 27*(1), 5-64.

East Carolina University. (2005). *ARISE.* Retrieved May 30, 2005, from (http://www.ecu.edu/cs-studentlife/recserv/index.cfm?load=ari).

East Carolina University. (2005). *Frequently asked questions.* Retrieved May 26, 2005, from http://www.ecu.edu/cs-studentlife/recserv/index.cfm?load=fac-faq.

East Carolina University. (2005). *Student Recreation Center facility use policies.* Retrieved May 26, 2005, from http://www.recserv.ecu.edu/index.cfm?load=facpol.

Maas, G. (1999). *Relationship between campus recreation participation and measures of college success.* Presented at the 50th Annual Conference of the National Intramural-Recreational Sports Association, Milwaukee, WI.

North Carolina Central University. (2003). *Campus rec.* Retrieved May 26, 2005, from (http://www.nccu.edu/studentlife/campusrec/guidelines.shtml.

North Carolina State University. (2005, February 15). *Our mission*. Retrieved May 30, 2005, from http://www.ncsu.edu/imrec/Fitness/Mission.htm.

Sharpless, Jr., P.M. & Maves, M. (2002, March). Higher education- The market that just doesn't stop! *The WBC Bulletin*. Retrieved May 26, 2005, from http://www.wbcnet.org/MAR02.HTM.

Slusark, J. (1995, April 13). UI joins trend in bulking up rec space. *The Daily Iowan*. Retrieved May 29, 2005, from http://www.dailyiowan.com/media/paper599/news/2005/04/13/Metro/Ui.Joins.Trend.In.Bulking.Up.Rec.Space-922284.shtml.

Student Voice. *Campus recreation impact study*. Retrieved May 29, 2005, from http://www.studentvoice.com/pdf/Arizona_SV_CampusRec.pdf.

Tudzin, C. (2004, September 2). Redone Rec Center Wows AU Students. *The Crimson White*. Retrieved May 29, 2005, from http://universitybusiness.com/page.cfm?p=161.

The University of North Carolina. *The UNC policy manual*. Retrieved June 2, 2005 from http://www.northcarolina.edu/content.php/legal/policymanual/contents.htm.

Wade, B. K. (1991). A profile of the real world of undergraduate students and how they spend discretionary time. Paper presented at the Annual Meeting of the American Educational Research Association (Chicago). ERIC Document Reproduction Service No. ED 33 7776.

** The author also wishes to acknowledge Mr. David Gaskins, Associate Director of Programs at East Carolina University's Recreational Services, for his feedback and advice in the development of this chapter.

Chapter 14

Coastal Recreation Resource Management

Jim Herstine, Jeffrey M.Hill, and Robert B.Buerger

The coastal zone of North Carolina is one of the most exciting, intriguing, dynamic, fragile and yet resilient areas in the southeastern United States. Its natural resources play an important role in the overall safety and well-being of individuals living near the ocean. It is a highly productive area that is accessible to millions of North Carolinians and non-North Carolinians alike. North Carolina's coastal zone offers countless recreational opportunities and experiences as well as priceless aesthetic moments. The area also provides unique habitat for numerous plants and animals.

How many of us either own a primary or secondary residence in the North Carolina coastal zone or rent a house, a hotel room, or a motel room in order to spend our vacation there? Who isn't awestruck by the spectacular beauty of a North Carolina coastal sunrise or sunset? How many of us love to paddle, sail, or power boat the crystal clear waters of the Atlantic Ocean off the coast of North Carolina or the waters of North Carolina's sounds, bays, estuaries, and creeks? Whose heart and pulse rate don't jump at the sight of a line of brown pelicans in flight, floating gently and effortlessly on the currents of the wind just inches above the ocean waves, or the frequent breaching of a pod of dolphins as they make their way along the North Carolina coast? How many of us swim, surf, wakeboard, hunt, camp, fish, water-ski, kayak, or canoe the lands and waters of North Carolina's coastal zone? The answer is: Almost too many to count. Unfortunately, due to our very love of the natural resources of the coastal zone of North Carolina, we are in danger of totally losing these precious resources. At the very least, we risk squandering our ability to experience and enjoy these diverse activities. North Carolina's coastal and ocean resources are under increasing pressure from population growth and development. The challenge facing us is to not love the coastal zone natural resources of North Carolina to death!

Introduction

The coastal zone of North Carolina has approximately 320 miles of oceanfront beach; over 4,000 miles of estuarine, sound, and riparian shoreline; and over 2 million acres of sounds, creeks, tidal marshes, and wetlands. The area includes twenty coastal North Carolina counties (North Carolina Division of Coastal Management, 2002) (See Figure 14.1). It is home to numerous commercial, residential, industrial, and public entities and operations and is a significant source of tourism, commercial, retail and recreational revenue and expenditures. The economic impact of tourism in the twenty North Carolina coastal counties in 2001 was $1.76 billion (North Carolina Division of Coastal Management, 2002a). Since the beginning of recorded time, the coastal zone of North Carolina has served vitally important economic, commercial, developmental, residential, ecological, and recreational roles and responsibilities. It is and has been a hotbed of recreational activities, services, facilities, and experiences, including fishing, hunting, swimming, boating, shelling, sunbathing, bird-watching, hiking, and camping. The value and importance of the coastal zone of North Carolina cannot be overstated.

Figure 14.1 Twenty North Carolina coastal counties (Beaufort, Bertie, Brunswick, Camden, Carteret, Chowan, Craven, Currituck, Dare, Gates, Hertford, Hyde, New Hanover, Onslow, Pamlico, Pasquotank, Pender, Perquimans, Tyrrell, Washington) (North Carolina Division of Coastal Management, 2002a)

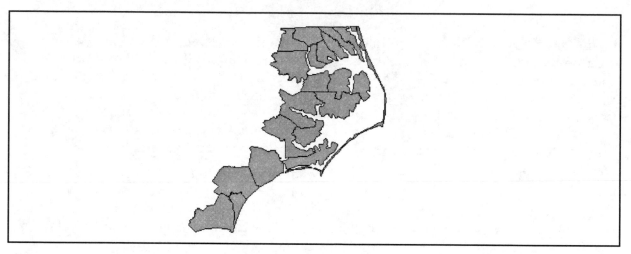

North Carolina's coastal zone is comprised of numerous diverse yet integrated natural resources and ecosystems, including the ocean's waters and reefs; the fishes, birds, reptiles, and mammals living in and on the waters and reefs; the barrier islands; the ocean surf zone; the oceanfront dry and wet beach areas; the beach dune systems; the vegetation growing on the dune systems; the maritime forests and shrub thickets; the birds, reptiles, and mammals living in the maritime forests and shrub thickets; the fresh and saltwater marshes; the waters of the sounds, bays, rivers and creeks; and the upland areas immediately adjacent to these to natural resources.

One of the greatest challenges facing North Carolina lawmakers, policy-makers, and citizens is the utilization, protection, management, and sustainability of these vital coastal zone natural resources and ecosystems. This challenge is spurred on by the increasing and competing demands upon the lands and waters of the coastal zone of North Carolina occasioned by population growth and economic development. These and other impacts have resulted in the loss of living marine resources, wildlife, and nutrient-rich areas; permanent and adverse changes to ecological systems; decreasing open space for public access and use; and coastal and estuarine shoreline erosion.

Coastal recreation resource management

The concept of coastal recreation resource management is relatively new and is best understood as a response to the multiplicity of challenges facing the North Carolina coastal zone. Coastal recreation resource management is a field of study designed to develop, refine, and disseminate knowledge, techniques, tools, and procedures for the proper management and protection of those natural resources in the coastal zone of North Carolina that support and sustain recreational activities, services, facilities, and experiences. It concentrates on the human dimensions of natural resource management. Coastal recreation resource management involves understanding, planning and managing human recreational activity in such a manner as to facilitate and enhance the total recreational opportunity and experience while simultaneously protecting the natural resources of the coastal zone.

Coastal recreation resource management is unique in that it focuses on the management of recreational activities, services, facilities and experiences as they relate to other coastal resources. It deals with the relationships and conflicts that can and do exist between the needs and interests of the recreational user and the non-recreational user (such as governmental agencies, developers, non-profit organizations, special interest groups, commercial operations, and private citizens). The goal of coastal recreation resource management is to provide individuals with the understanding, knowledge, skills, tools, and techniques necessary to plan and implement sound recreational activities, services, facilities, and experiences in the North Carolina coastal zone while at the same time protecting the finite, fragile, and unique natural resources upon which recreation in the North Carolina coastal zone depends.

Historical background

Early efforts to manage coastal zone natural resources were historically quite diffuse and uncoordinated and normally either single-resource-oriented (maritime forests, marine aquatic life, wetlands, ocean reefs, colonial nesting water-birds, etc.) or single- issue oriented (water quality, erosion, water quantity, dredging, etc.). Often multiple federal and state agencies had jurisdiction and authority over the same resource or the same issue. Unfortunately, seldom did these agencies agree on or even understand the policies and procedures in place for managing the coastal zone natural resources.

Only in recent years has the nation collectively and the state of North Carolina individually begun to think in terms of a more systematic and coordinated approach to managing coastal zone natural resources. In fact, effective coastal management in general in the United States traces its modern organized beginnings to the passage of the federal Coastal Zone Management Act (CZMA—U.S. Code Title 16, Chapter 33, Sec. 1251—1465) in 1972. The opening statement in the CZMA of 1972 declares that *"Congress finds that there is a national interest in the effective management, beneficial use, protection and development of the coastal zone."* The Coastal Zone Management Act of 1972 authorized the creation of the National Coastal Management Program (CZMP) to be administered at the federal level by the Coastal Programs Division (CPD) within the National Oceanic and Atmospheric Administration's Office of Ocean and Coastal Resource Management (OCRM). The CPD is authorized and responsible for advancing national coastal management objectives and maintaining and strengthening state coastal management capabilities.

The Coastal Zone Management Act of 1972 stresses the ecological, cultural, historic, and esthetic fragility and values of the coastal zone while at the same time identifying the need to manage and protect the natural resources of the coastal zone from use and development pressures and demands. The Coastal Zone Management Act of 1972 altered the balance between federal government and the states by calling upon the coastal states themselves to exercise their full authority over local issues and take the lead in the effective protection and use of the land and water resources of the coastal zone. The approach behind the CZMA of 1972 is to encourage the coastal states to cooperate with the federal government in developing land and water use programs for the coastal zone in order to establish unified policies, procedures, standards, methods, and processes for dealing with natural resource use issues in a manner that also transcends local interests. The CZMA of 1972 calls for a national policy to (1) preserve, protect, develop, and restore or enhance coastal zone natural resources; (2) encourage and assist the individual states to effectively exercise their responsibilities in the coastal zone through the development and management of state coastal management programs to achieve wise use of the land and water resources of the coastal zone; and (3) promote coordination and cooperation among citizen, governmental, and non-governmental entities, agencies, and organizations in effectively identifying and carrying out coastal zone management procedures and policies. As mentioned above, however, the National Coastal Management Program leaves day-to-day management decisions to each individual state.

The Coastal Zone Management Act of 1972 provides federal grants for planning, land acquisition, policy development, and regulatory activities. As such, the CZMA of 1972 is an institutional or enabling act that requires the individual states to do nothing. It is not a regulatory act. There are no laws or regulations that the states can "break" by not adhering to the CZMA of 1972. Rather, the intent of the CZMA of 1972 is to make it so lucrative through the incentives of its grant program for the states to adopt and administer coastal management programs that all of the coastal states will place themselves under the umbrella of the Coastal Zone Management Act of 1972. This strategy has worked well, because currently thirty four out of thirty five eligible states and territories have approved coastal management programs covering 35,376 miles of national shoreline (99.9 percent).

North Carolina's immediate response to the federally implemented Coastal Management Act of 1972 and its appeal for states to individually implement coastal management programs was the adoption of the North Carolina Coastal Area Management Act (CAMA) in 1974. This act was a direct recognition by the state legislature that the coastal lands and waters of North Carolina are among the state's most valuable natural resources and offer the citizens of North Carolina incalculable benefits from recreational opportunities and tourism.

The North Carolina Coastal Area Management Act provides both the direction and the means for the operation of North Carolina's coastal management program in accordance with the goals and objectives of the federally mandated Coastal Zone Management Act of 1972. The administrative arm of CAMA is the Division of Coastal Management (DCM) in the Department of Environment and Natural Resources (DENR). The Division of Coastal Management, under authority from the Coastal Resources Commission (CRC), is responsible for implementing the North Carolina Coastal Management Program for the protection, orderly development, and management of the state's twenty coastal counties (See Figure 14.1). The North Carolina Division of Coastal Management became operational in

1978 and works to protect, conserve, and manage North Carolina's coastal resources through an integrated program of planning, permitting, education, and research.

The goals of North Carolina's coastal management program under CAMA include:

1. Providing a management system capable of preserving and managing the natural ecological conditions of the estuarine system, the barrier dune system, and the beaches, so as to safeguard and perpetuate their natural productivity and their biological, economic, and esthetic values;
2. Ensuring that the development or preservation of the land and water resources of the coastal area proceeds in a manner consistent with the capability of the land and water for development, use, or preservation based on ecological considerations;
3. Ensuring the orderly and balanced use and preservation of our coastal resources on behalf of the people of North Carolina and the nation; and
4. Establishing policies, guidelines, and standards for:
   a. Protection, preservation, and conservation of natural resources including but not limited to water use, scenic vistas, and fish and wildlife; and management of transitional or intensely developed areas and areas especially suited to intensive use or development, as well as areas of significant natural value;
   b. The economic development of the coastal area, including but not limited to construction, location and design of industries, port facilities, commercial establishments, and other developments;
   c. Recreation and tourist facilities and parklands;
   d. Transportation and circulation patterns for the coastal area including major thoroughfares, transportation routes, navigation channels and harbors, and other public utilities and facilities;
   e. Preservation and enhancement of the historic, cultural, and scientific aspects of the coastal area; and
   f. Protection of present common-law and statutory public rights in the lands and waters of the coastal area (North Carolina Division of Coastal Management, 2002c).

The North Carolina Coastal Area Management Act (CAMA) requires a joint and coordinated effort between state and local government to be successful. CAMA's primary management tool is local land-use planning. The North Carolina Coastal Area Management Act was one of the first attempts in the United States to combine local-level planning with state-level regulations to protect natural resources. The local-level planning component of CAMA is a concrete realization that a state-mandated regulatory program alone would not effectively address long-term coastal management issues and concerns in North Carolina. Local-level planning was envisioned as the best method for addressing long-term growth and development issues in coastal North Carolina while providing local coastal communities and governments a substantial role and responsibility in the coastal management process.

A land-use plan is a collection of maps and policies that serves as a coastal community's blueprint for action and growth. The North Carolina CAMA requires each of the twenty coastal counties to develop a local land-use plan in accordance with guidelines established by the Coastal Resources Commission (CRC). These guidelines establish a common format for the local plans and set forth issues that must be addressed during the planning process. Each plan is certified by the CRC and contains local policies that address specific growth and development issues that are important to the local government. Typical issues include protection of productive coastal resources, such as farmland, fisheries stocks, and maritime forest resources; severe storm mitigation techniques; desired types of economic growth; and general natural resource protection.

The North Carolina Division of Coastal Management assists the local coastal communities in the land-use planning process by providing staff technical expertise and by awarding grants each year for local planning and management projects. The local land-use planning process also provides one of the best opportunities for public citizen involvement in the North Carolina Coastal Management Program through public hearings and public meetings (North Carolina Division of Coastal Management, 2002b).

Stakeholders

Many groups, organizations, agencies, and individuals have a stake in the coastal zone of North Carolina. Coastal management policy and implementation are more often than not the result of critical political and social interfaces between these stakeholders. It is imperative that coastal recreation resource managers be able to identify the stakeholders in any coastal management issue. Managers must also be able to comprehend the policies, goals, and objectives of the stakeholders in each coastal recreation resource management issue and concede that these issues will, by necessity, be managed and decided within a political process.

The list of stakeholders in North Carolina coastal recreation resource management typically includes:

1. the North Carolina state government and its various state coastal management agencies;
2. the coastal North Carolina local governments and their corresponding city and county agencies;
3. the federal government and its various federal coastal management agencies;
4. coastal special interest groups and organizations;
5. the coastal development community;
6. coastal tourists;
7. coastal residents;
8. coastal retail companies and corporations;
9. the commercial fishing industry;
10. recreational fishermen;
11. oceanfront beach users such as swimmers, surfers, sun-bathers, etc.; and
12. the coastal marine trades industry and businesses.

We will identify the most important stakeholders and highlight their role and responsibility in the coastal management process. The first and most politically influential stakeholder is the state government of North Carolina itself. North Carolina government has demonstrated its interest in coastal management through adoption of the Coastal Area Management Act and creation of the Division of Coastal Management within the Department of Environment and Natural Resources. North Carolina's stake in coastal management is primarily directed at controlling its own destiny and managing coastal management initiatives within its jurisdiction by ensuring that any federal coastal policies remain flexible and allow North Carolina discretion over policy implementation. The state of North Carolina is also interested in encouraging and guiding the coastal local governments through wise land-use planning of coastal zone natural resources, policies, and programs.

North Carolina state government includes numerous agencies and programs that are "players" in coastal management. We will identify the most influential and highlight their sphere of influence and primary goals and objectives.

1. *Department of Environment and Natural Resources*—lead stewardship agency for the preservation and protection of North Carolina's outstanding natural resources.
   a. *Albemarle-Pamlico National Estuary Program (APNEP)*—focuses not just on improving water quality in the Albemarle-Pamlico Estuary, but on maintaining the integrity of the whole system: its chemical, physical, and biological properties as well as it economic, recreational, and aesthetic values. Important components of the program are the consideration of water quality, fisheries resources, land and water habitats, and the interaction of humans with the natural resources of the estuarine system.
   b. *Boating Access Design, Construction, and Maintenance and Waterway Marking Programs*—housed within the Wildlife Resources Commission. These programs operate and maintain over 185 public boat access areas that allow free, twenty four hour access to eighty different bodies of water. They also maintain over 1,200 buoys and navigational aids.
   c. *Clean Water Management Trust Fund (CWMTF)*—established in 1996 to help local governments, state agencies, and conservation non-profit groups finance projects to protect and restore surface water quality. The CWMTF provides grants to enhance or restore degraded waters; protect unpolluted waters; and contribute toward a network of riparian buffers and greenways for environmental, educational, and recreational benefits.
   d. *Coastal Reserve Program*—authorized in 1989 to protect unique coastal sites. The North Carolina Coastal Reserve is comprised of ten sites. Four of these are designated as the North Carolina National Estuarine Research Reserve, which includes Currituck Banks, Rachel Carson, Masonboro Island, and Zeke's Island sites. Other sites are Kitty Hawk Woods, Emily and Richardson Preyer Buckridge, Buxton Woods, Permuda Island, Bald Head Woods, and Bird Island. The Coastal Reserves operate as living laboratories for research, education and management.
   e. *Coastal Resources Commission (CRC)*—a fifteen-member group created when the North Carolina General Assembly adopted the Coastal Area Management Act (CAMA) in 1974. The CRC establishes policies for the North Carolina Coastal Management Program and adopts implementing rules for both CAMA and the North Carolina Dredge and Fill Act. The commission designates areas of environmental concern, adopts rules and policies for coastal development within those areas, and certifies local land-use plans.
   f. *Customer Service Center (CSC)*—a single source of information regarding all programs of the Department of Environment and Natural Resources. The center, through its 1-STOP permit assistance program, helps individuals determine what environmental permits are needed for a particular project as well as permit decision timelines.

g. *Division of Air Quality*—works with the state's citizens to protect and improve outdoor, or ambient, air quality in North Carolina for the health and benefit of all.

h. *Division of Coastal Management (DCM)*—works to protect, conserve, and manage North Carolina's coastal resources through an integrated program of planning, permitting, education, and research. Carries out the state's Coastal Area Management Act, Dredge and Fill Act and the federal Coastal Zone Management Act of 1972 in the twenty coastal counties, using rules and policies of the North Carolina Coastal Resources Commission.

i. *Division of Environmental Health*—This agency's[GESS2] mission is to safeguard life, promote human health, and protect the state's environment. The division accomplishes its mission through the practice of modern environmental health science; through the use of technology, rules, and public education; and, above all, through its dedication to the public trust.

j. *Division of Land Resources*—mission is to allow development within the state of North Carolina while preventing sedimentation pollution.

k. *Division of Marine Fisheries*—responsible for the stewardship of the state's marine and estuarine resources.

l. *Division of North Carolina Aquariums*—established to promote awareness, understanding, appreciation, and conservation of the diverse natural and cultural resources associated with North Carolina's ocean, estuaries, rivers, streams, and other aquatic environments.

m. *Division of Parks and Recreation*—mission is to conserve and protect representative examples of natural beauty, ecological features, and recreational resources of statewide significance; to provide outdoor recreational opportunities in a safe and healthy environment; and to provide environmental education opportunities that promote stewardship of North Carolina's natural heritage.

n. *Division of Pollution Prevention and Environmental Assistance*—mission is to protect the environment and conserve natural resources by providing technical assistance on the elimination, reduction, reuse, and recycling of wastes and pollutants.

o. *Division of Soil and Water Conservation*—cooperates with federal agencies and local partners to administer a comprehensive statewide program to protect and conserve North Carolina's soil and water resources.

p. *Division of Water Quality*—responsible for statewide regulatory programs in surface water and aquifer protection. Mission is to preserve, protect, and enhance North Carolina's surface water and groundwater resources through quality monitoring programs, efficient permitting, responsible management, fair and effective enforcement, and excellence in public service.

q. *Division of Water Resources*—administers programs for river basin management, water supply assistance, water conservation, and water resources development. Administers two environmental education outreach programs: Stream Watch and Project WET.

r. *Ecosystem Enhancement Program*—in 2003, the United States Army Corps of Engineers (USACE), the North Carolina Department of Environment and Natural Resources, and the North Carolina Department of Transportation signed a memorandum of agreement establishing procedures for a unique program designed to improve watershed functions through the development of specific plans and projects in advance of the occurrence of permitted impacts from transportation projects. The program's mission includes restoring, enhancing, and protecting North Carolina's wetlands, streams, and streamside buffers.

s. *Environmental Management Commission (EMC)*—a nineteen-member commission that is responsible for adopting rules for the protection, preservation and enhancement of North Carolina's air and water resources.

t. *Office of Environmental Education*—promotes environmental education throughout North Carolina. Serves as a clearinghouse linking people to Environmental Education (EE) materials, facilities, programs, and professionals across North Carolina.

u. *Natural Heritage Program*—mission is to inventory, catalogue and support conservation of the rarest and the most outstanding elements of the natural diversity of North Carolina.

v. *Natural Heritage Trust Fund*—a supplemental funding source for state agencies to acquire and protect North Carolina's ecological diversity and cultural heritage and to inventory the natural areas of the state.

w. *Parks and Recreation Trust Fund (PARTF)*—offers matching grants to local governments in North Carolina to provide parks and recreational projects for the general public.

x. *Storm-water Management Program*—requires developments to protect sensitive Outstanding Resource Waters (ORW) or High Quality Waters (HQW) by maintaining a low density of impervious surfaces, maintaining vegetative buffers, and transporting run-off through vegetative conveyances.

y. *Wetlands Restoration Program*—seeks to increase wetland and riparian area acres and functions. The program was established to restore wetland, stream, and non-wetland riparian areas throughout North Carolina.

2. *North Carolina Sea Grant*—through research, education, and outreach programs, North Carolina Sea Grant works with individuals, groups, government agencies, and businesses to develop an understanding of North Carolina's coastal environment and to promote sustainable use of marine resources.

Second on the list are the local governments of the coastal zone of North Carolina themselves. After state government, coastal local governments have the most direct and influential stake in coastal recreation resource management in North Carolina. Coastal counties, towns, and cities stand to *lose* the most (loss and degradation of the coastal natural resources, loss of tourist dollars and depletion of the residential and commercial tax base), **and** *gain* the most (protection and conservation of the coastal natural resources, increases in tourism spending, and expansion of the residential and commercial tax base) as a result of the coastal management decision-making process. Coastal local governments are the ones most eminently and directly impacted by coastal management decisions at all levels. The natural resources and economies of the coastal counties, towns, and cities are the very reasons many coastal management decisions are made in the first place.

The coastal counties, towns, and cities exert their most consistent influence on coastal management issues in North Carolina through the land-use planning process. By 1997, seventy two coastal cities and towns had joined the twenty CAMA coastal counties in adopting land-use plans. By 1999, all twenty coastal counties, and many of the towns and cities, had updated their land-use plan four times, improving the quality of the plan with each revision and update. These land-use plans, approved and certified by the Coastal Resources Commission, form the basis upon which all coastal management issues are decided at the local level.

In addition to the land-use planning process, coastal counties, towns, and cities also influence and guide coastal management issues and policies through parks and recreation departments and emergency management programs. Parks and recreation departments provide direct services to local residents and tourists and also administer the public beach and coastal waterfront access programs. The local government emergency management departments work with citizens to protect them from the effects of natural and technical disasters through strategies involving prevention, off-scene response, recovery, and on-scene response.

The most significant stakeholders at the local government level include:

1. *Planning Department*—provides guidance and direction in the adoption of policies and regulations to encourage orderly growth and development and long-term community development.
2. *Parks and Recreation Department*—provides direct coastal recreation activities, services, facilities, and experiences, including public access to beaches and waterfronts.
3. *Emergency Management Department*—protects citizens from the effects of natural and technical disasters such as hurricanes, nor'easters, other severe storms, and industrial catastrophes.

The third major stakeholder, the federal government, claimed and expressed its interest and stake in coastal zones through the passage of the Coastal Zone Management Act of 1972 and its recent re-authorizations. The federal stakeholders who play the greatest role in coastal recreation resource management are:

1. *Environmental Protection Agency (EPA)*—mission is to protect human health and the environment. The agency's strategic plan is built around the themes of air and global climate change, water, land, communities, and ecosystems as well as compliance and environmental stewardship.
2. *Federal Emergency Management Agency (FEMA)*—mission is to lead the effort to prepare the nation for all hazards and effectively manage federal response and recovery efforts following any national incident. FEMA initiates proactive mitigation activities, trains first responders, and manages the National Flood Insurance Program.
3. *National Oceanic and Atmospheric Administration (NOAA)*—conducts worldwide research and gathers data about the oceans, atmosphere, space, and sun, and applies this knowledge to science and service that touch the lives of all Americans. NOAA warns of dangerous weather, charts our seas and skies, guides our use and protection of ocean and coastal resources, and conducts research to improve our understanding and stewardship of the environment that sustains us all.
   The Office of Ocean and Coastal Resource Management—responsible for administering the Coastal Zone Management Act and is a leader on United States coastal, estuarine, and ocean management issues.
4. *National Marine Fisheries (NMF)*—mission is stewardship of living marine resources through science-based conservation and management and the promotion of healthy ecosystems. Is responsible for the management, conservation and protection of living

marine resources within the United States Exclusive Economic Zone (water three to 200 miles off-shore).

5. *Department of the Interior (DOI)*—mission is to protect and provide access to the nation's natural and cultural heritage. The department has five major goals: resource protection, resource use, recreation, serving communities, and management excellence.

    a. *National Park Service (NPS)*—mission is to promote and regulate the use of the . . . national parks . . . whose purpose is to conserve the scenery and the natural and historic objects and the wildlife therein and to provide for the enjoyment of the same in such a manner and by such means as will leave them unimpaired for the enjoyment of future generations.

    b. *U.S. Fish and Wildlife Service (USFWS)*—working with others to conserve, protect and enhance fish, wildlife, and plants and their habitats for the continuing benefit of the American people.

6. *U.S. Army Corps of Engineers (USACE)*—mission is to provide quality, responsive engineering services to the nation including: planning, designing, building, and operating water resources and other civil works projects (navigation, flood control, environmental protection, disaster response, etc.); designing and managing the construction of military facilities for the Army and Air Force; and providing design and construction management support for other Defense and federal agencies.

7. *U.S. Coast Guard (USCG)*—mission is to protect the public, the environment, and United States economic interests in the nation's ports and waterways, along the coast, on international waters, or in any maritime region as required to support national security.

In addition to state, local, and federal government stakeholders, numerous national, state, regional, and local special interest groups and organizations are also important players in coastal management in North Carolina. Typically, these special interest groups are environmental organizations whose stake in the coastal zone involves protecting, conserving, and enhancing coastal natural resources. However, other special interest groups who are active stakeholders in coastal management issues and policies lean toward development. Some of the most influential and visible coastal special interest groups and organizations in North Carolina are:

1. *Atlantic Intracoastal Waterway Association*—concerned with the protection, preservation, operation, and maintenance of the Atlantic Intracoastal Waterway.

2. *American Shore and Beach Preservation Association*—purpose of the association is to bring together for cooperation and mutual helpfulness the many agencies, interests, and individuals concerned with the protection and proper utilization of the shores of the nation's oceans, lakes, and rivers and in all legitimate ways to foster sound, farsighted, and economical development and preservation of the lands which will aid in placing their benefits within the reach of the largest possible number of people in accordance with the ideals of a democratic nation.

3. *Cape Fear River Assembly*—mission is to provide for the highest quality of life possible for the residents of the Cape Fear River Basin, through the proper management of the Cape Fear River, its tributaries, and adjacent land uses.

4. *Cape Fear River Watch*—mission is to protect and improve the water quality of the Lower Cape Fear River through education, advocacy, and action.

5. *Environmental Defense*—dedicated to protecting the environmental rights of all people, including future generations. Among these rights are clean air, clean water, healthy food, and flourishing ecosystems.
6. *Homebuilders Associations*—purpose is normally to promote the home development, home building, and home remodeling industries.
7. *Audubon North Carolina*—mission is to conserve and restore ecosystems, focusing on birds, other wildlife, and their habitats for the benefits of humanity and North Carolina's biological diversity.
8. *North Carolina Coastal Federation*—mission is to provide citizens and groups with the assistance needed to take an active role in the wise stewardship of North Carolina's coastal water quality and natural resources.
9. *North Carolina Coastal Land Trust*—enriches the coastal communities of North Carolina through the acquisition of open space and natural areas, conservation education, and the promotion of good land stewardship.
10. *North Carolina Shore and Beach Preservation Association*—is committed to the conservation, restoration, and preservation of North Carolina's renewable resource, our ocean beaches.
11. *Partnership for the Sounds*—promotes ecotourism in the Albemarle-Pamlico Region by appealing to those who enjoy and appreciate the sustainable use of an area's natural, cultural, and historic resources.
12. *Regional Association of Realtors*—normally strive to be the premier, innovative resource for technology, services, and information for real estate professionals so that they may better serve the public. Promote private property rights; monitor and propose regulation and legislation to ensure the availability and affordability of insurance for both residential and commercial property owners; and work with the National Association of Realtors, the North Carolina Association of Realtors, and the North Carolina Real Estate Commission to promote ethically and legally sound representation for the consumer.
13. *The Nature Conservancy*—mission is to preserve the plants, animals, and natural communities that represent the diversity of life on Earth by protecting the lands and waters they need to survive.

Although the various federal, state, and local government agencies and the special interest group stakeholders are important, the impact that other, less publicized stakeholders can and do have must not be overlooked. These other stakeholders include the individual realtors and developers who build and sell within the North Carolina coastal zone and attempt to influence development rules, regulations, and policies. There are also the visitors and tourists from both in-state and out-of-state who come to the North Carolina coast and stay at areas and facilities; surf, swim, fish, boat, and recreate in the coastal zone; and put billions of dollars into the coastal economy. And of course, we cannot forget the residents of the twenty coastal counties themselves. The residents pay taxes, work, and recreate in North Carolina's coastal zone and directly influence coastal management issues and policies through their voting power and by serving on local boards and commissions. Other stakeholders include the thousands of retail companies, corporations, and coastal marine trades industry and business representatives who pay taxes, vote, and supply goods, services, and jobs for both visitors to and residents of North Carolina's coastal zone alike. These stakeholders have a significant interest in coastal management issues and policy considerations and are often quite vocal and definitive in their response to coastal management decisions and plans. Last, but certainly not least, are the commercial and charter boat owners and operators who influence coastal recreation resource management through legislative lobbying and their direct impact on commercial and recreational fisheries stocks. It is imperative that coastal recreation resource managers discover who the coastal management stakeholders are in their area, how they are likely to react to given situations, and what course of action they are expected to pursue relative to coastal management issues and policies.

Pressures

As discussed earlier, the North Carolina coastal zone is fragile but amazingly resilient. The coastal zone ecosystem as a whole is a dynamic and regenerative force—if left alone, natural mechanisms maintain an equilibrium between living things and the natural environment. However, there are limits to the extent to which the coastal ecosystem can withstand assaults to its integrity. Most of these limits are imposed upon the coastal zone by pressures that are both natural and anthropogenic.

To effectively and efficiently manage the coastal resources of North Carolina, we need to understand the pressures impacting coastal recreation resource management. Some of these pressures have been present since earliest times. Others have emerged and developed as a result of modern influences and practices.

The coastal zone of North Carolina is one of the most popular destinations in the southeastern United States. The price of this popularity is an ever-growing list of pressures, exerted daily, that place an enormous strain upon the area's natural resources. Some of the pressures are natural; others result from human activity. The natural pressures include waves, wind, coastal storms (including nor'easters and hurricanes), barrier island migration, inlet movement, and sea level rise. Some of the more significant anthropogenic pressures include population growth, population density, requirements for infrastructure (such as housing, schools, hospitals, parking space, shopping centers and malls, restaurants, and recreational amenities), commercial development, water and waste disposal, and "hard structures" (groins, jetties, bulkheads, and rip-rap on the estuarine shorelines and ocean beaches).

The natural pressures, although part of the natural processes of the coastal zone, do change the coastal zone ecosystem and impact coastal recreation resource management. Managers must understand these natural pressures and how they impact North Carolina's coastal zone natural resources. Barrier islands constantly migrate toward the mainland. Inlets open and close as well as shift laterally up and down the coast. Sea level rises and, in the process, inundates parts of the coastal zone. The coastal landscape changes as wind and waves move sand up and down the beach and back and forth over sand dunes. Salt spray from ocean winds transforms the shape of trees and shrubs and even kills some of them. Sand moves on and off of the oceanfront beach in response to wind and waves. All of these natural pressures have bearing upon what coastal recreation resource managers can accomplish.

The pressures exerted by humans in the North Carolina coastal zone often interfere with and exacerbate the natural processes. For example, the rapid increase in the number of individuals recreating in, living in, and moving to the coastal zone places significant strains on coastal natural resources and interferes with natural processes such as sand movement and barrier island migration. These individuals require roads, houses, motels, hotels, restaurants, shopping centers, retail stores, hospitals, schools, jobs, offices, spas, health clubs, and other infrastructure and recreational amenities. These requirements place tremendous demands upon finite and limited coastal natural resources.

Population density is another measure of the stresses and pressures placed on coastal areas. The carrying capacity of the North Carolina coastal zone is in danger of being exceeded as more and more individuals are moving into the area. Compounding the issue is the fact that during the summer vacation months, the numbers and density of population in the North Carolina coastal zone can increase dramatically. It is not uncommon for many coastal communities to experience population numbers that double, triple, and even quadruple during summer vacations. This places enormous stresses and strains on the location's natural resources and infrastructure such as potable water, roads, and solid waste management and disposal.

Anthropogenic pressures also include "hard structures" such as groins, jetties, bulkheads and rip-rap. Groins are normally made out of wood, rock, or concrete and are placed perpendicular to the shoreline to control erosion by blocking sand as it travels laterally up and down the oceanfront beach. Jetties are placed on the ends of barrier islands at the mouths of inlets to stabilize the inlets and keep them from migrating. Jetties are typically constructed from large rocks and extend several hundred feet out into the ocean and are also designed to control shoreline erosion by blocking sand as it travels laterally along the beach. Bulkheads are made out of wood, plastic, concrete, or a synthetic material and are placed parallel to the shoreline to stop shoreline erosion. Rip-rap, made out of large stone or rock, is placed parallel to the shoreline to stop shoreline erosion. Bulkheads and rip-rap are not designed to stop sand as it moves laterally along the shoreline, but to stop the shoreline from eroding due to wind and waves pounding at the beach.

Hard structures such as groins, jetties, bulkheads, and rip-rap are presently illegal on the oceanfront in North Carolina. However, they can be used to manage shoreline erosion along North Carolina's creeks, rivers, sounds, bays, and estuaries. The major problems cited with hard structures are: (1) They interfere with the natural movement of sand in the water, thereby robbing the system of valuable sand resources; and (2) They cause erosion on properties on either side of the structure itself and, in the case of bulkheads and rip-rap, in front of them as well.

Management practices, knowledge, and techniques

There are numerous management practices, knowledge, and techniques available to coastal recreation resource managers in North Carolina. It is not possible to present each of these in great detail. Some of the most effective, useful, and operative ones will be discussed briefly.

Acquisition and restoration

The acquisition of new coastal land and water resources, as well as the restoration of that which has been degraded or lost, is a valuable tool. One of the best methods for protecting the vanishing habitats of coastal plants, fisheries, and animals is to acquire the lands and waters upon which they depend before development and other pressures destroy them. Most federal, state, local, and non-profit coastal recreation resource managers in North Carolina use this management practice. The most common obstacle they face is a lack of funding to restore, purchase and acquire the coastal resources they target. Managers can try to obtain funding from the Parks and Recreation Trust Fund, the Clean Water Management Trust Fund, the National Estuarine Research Reserve Program, and the Natural Heritage Trust Fund. They can also work with other managers to form collaborative partnerships that are capable of combining their limited resources into one fund that can be used to restore, purchase, and acquire the targeted property. This is a common practice for organizations such as The Nature Conservancy, the North Carolina Coastal Land Trust, Audubon North Carolina, and the North Carolina Coastal Federation.

Comprehensive land-use planning

The ability of the coastal recreation resource manager to understand and to work effectively through the local land-use planning process in the twenty coastal North Carolina counties is an indispensable skill. Many North Carolinians believe that the land-use planning component of the state's Coastal Management Program is the most significant element of CAMA. The North Carolina Coastal Area Management Act requires each of the twenty coastal counties to have a local land-use plan in accordance with guidelines established by the Coastal Resources Commission. The land-use planning requirement under CAMA allows the state to establish the basic framework for coastal management in North Carolina while allowing each individual coastal county to determine how that framework is to be completed. An analogy would be that the State of North Carolina has provided what the skeletal bone structure will look like and the individual coastal counties have placed the muscle, meat and flesh on the skeleton to give the visible appearance. The local land-use planning process sets priorities for resource allocation, protection, conservation, and utilization. At the local level, land-use plans guide individual projects as well as a broad range of policy issues, such as the development of regulatory ordinances, the allocation of green and open space, and public investment programs. The local land-use planning process helps shape the policies and guidelines that direct CAMA permit decisions and the growth and development of coastal North Carolina.

Environmental education and awareness

Educating the public and making them aware of the value, dynamics and fragility of the North Carolina coastal zone is a major objective of coastal recreation resource management. Residents and tourists alike are usually uninformed about the consequences of their actions and the negative impacts their decisions can have on coastal resources. How many times have you observed people walking up the side of a tall sand dune to get to its top for a better view of the ocean, totally unaware that their steps were destroying the dune vegetation and creating ruts in the side of the dune that would cause it to erode? Who would suspect that a helium-filled balloon released into the air over coastal waters will probability find its way into a sea turtle's stomach, causing its death due to starvation? What is wrong with allowing a dog to run free and untethered along a clear strand of ocean beach where water-birds are nesting? Why should personal water-craft not be allowed to freely navigate the shallow tidal creeks and coastal wetlands of North Carolina's sounds and estuaries? What is the purpose of a "prescribed burn?" If the shoreline in front of my oceanfront residence is eroding away and the ocean's waters threaten my home's structure, why can I not build a bulkhead to protect it? These and other, similar questions are asked each day by residents and tourists in North Carolina's coastal zone. Coastal recreation resource managers can provide an extremely valuable service by educating individuals about the North Carolina coastal zone and making them aware of the consequences of their actions and inactions regarding coastal resources. This can be accomplished through public meetings, workshops, forums, brochures and other educational materials, videos, research, and the local land-use planning process.

Federal consistency

Federal consistency is an important but often overlooked benefit of North Carolina's participation in the national Coastal Management Program. In essence, it requires activities and projects of the federal government within the coastal zone of North Carolina to comply with the state's enforceable coastal management policies, even if those activities do not require CAMA permits under North Carolina law. This applies to any activity that *takes place* in the coastal zone or *affects* any land use, water use, or any natural resource within North Carolina's coastal zone (even if the activity occurs outside the coastal zone). This includes any activity that is federal, requires a federal license or permit, receives federal money, or is a plan for exploration, development, or production in any area leased from the Outer Continental Shelf Lands Act. To be approved, such activities must comply with the key elements of North Carolina's Coastal Management Program.

The federal consistency stipulation essentially gives the state of North Carolina final authority in determining whether or not federally sponsored projects and activities can occur. Examples of the federal consistency requirement in action include the proposed jetties at Oregon Inlet in Dare County, the rock revetment at the Fort Fisher State Historic Site, the relocation of the Cape Hatteras Lighthouse, and dredging of the Atlantic Intracoastal Waterway in North Carolina. Before the federal government could perform any of these proposed projects, it submitted a consistency determination to the state of North Carolina under the Coastal Zone Management Act. In the case of the jetties at Oregon Inlet, the state determined that the project was inconsistent with North Carolina policies and regulations that make hard structures on the oceanfront illegal in North Carolina. The state also determined that the rock revetment at the Fort Fisher State Historic Site was inconsistent with state policies and regulations banning hard structures on the oceanfront; however, a variance to CAMA was granted by the state of North Carolina to the federal government that allowed the project to proceed. Both the relocation of the Cape Hatteras Lighthouse and the dredging of the Atlantic Intracoastal Waterway were determined to be consistent with the state's coastal management program and were therefore authorized.

Coastal recreation resource managers employed by the federal government, or working for an agency or organization impacted by federal projects and activities in the North Carolina coastal zone, should understand the federal consistency requirement. In essence, this provision of the Coastal Zone Management Act of 1972 allows the state of North Carolina to convey to the federal government what the federal government can and cannot do within the boundaries of the North Carolina coastal zone. The federal consistency requirement truly makes coastal management in North Carolina a state and not a federal program. The federal consistency requirement holds up in all situations except those involving national defense and national security.

Managing uses and conflict

One of the most useful things to understand about coastal recreation resource management is the difference between conflict and competition over coastal resources. Conflict is usually defined as a situation in which an actor or stakeholder is engaged in opposition to someone who is pursuing what are, or at least appear to be, incompatible goals. The objective of this conflict is often the pursuit of power and resources in order to neutralize, injure, or even eliminate one's opponent or rival stakeholder.

Conflict in the coastal zone of North Carolina has always existed; however, it has increased in recent years, due to several factors. For one, the pressures discussed in the previous section of this chapter (population growth, population density, infrastructure requirements, barrier island migration, shoreline erosion, etc.) have forced an increase in conflict over sparse and finite coastal natural resources. Another cause of conflict is the increase in recreational users. Besides recreators, more people are living and working in the coastal zone; yet there are limited amounts of private and public land, fisheries, and other available natural resources. Water quality in the coastal zone, which is so important to all users, is deteriorating rapidly. In sum, usage of all the finite resources in North Carolina's coastal zone is increasing.

Conflict can be a positive factor if managed properly. For example, conflict tends to clarify issues by bringing new information to light. Conflict helps people understand what the coastal issues are, who the specific stakeholders in coastal issues are, and what each stakeholder wants. Another benefit of conflict is that it sometimes integrates groups involved in the coastal conflict and forges new alliances. Conflict integrates groups by helping groups with the same interests and objectives come together and by allowing opposing groups to better understand each other. Conflict can force needed social change; for example, the new laws and regulations that evolve out of conflict are more equitable to all stakeholders involved in the conflict.

Competition offers a somewhat different perspective than conflict. Competition can be defined as a situation in which two or more stakeholders who are willing to co-exist pursue the same or similar goals with the same power and resources. Neither has a substantial advantage over the other stakeholder, yet each wants to accomplish the same or a very similar objective.

Competition in the coastal zone is normally thought of as more positive than conflict, particularly in determining how coastal resources are utilized. Resources tend to be utilized more efficiently if there is competition for them because the competitors are not interested in the depletion of the resource in order to eliminate, injure, or neutralize the competitor. Resources also tend to have greater value if there are several competing uses for them. For example, the ocean and the oceanfront beach are more valuable because there is competition for them from users interested in sun-bathing and shelling on the dry sand, fishing in and from the surf area, swimming in the sea, entering the sea from the shoreline, and surfing in the waves. Another benefit of competition over conflict is that resources tend to cost less to consumers if there is competition for them—i.e., there is no monopoly on the resources.

The coastal recreation resource manager must understand that conflict over resources usually starts as competition. It is mainly when the competition escalates into conflict that problems arise and the issue must be successfully managed. When competition in the coastal zone of North Carolina moves into conflict, it presents the coastal recreation resource manager with some unique challenges. For one, it is often difficult for the manager to fully understand the nature of the conflict. Understanding requires figuring out who the stakeholders in the conflict are and what each stakeholder hopes to accomplish. The manager is also faced with challenges associated with objectivity in managing conflict in the coastal zone. Many coastal recreation resource managers may not be as objective in managing coastal conflict as they should be, since they probably consider themselves environmentalists opposed to the wide and rapid spread of development in North Carolina's coastal zone. This lack of objectivity may cloud managers' thought processes and bias them toward a specific perspective in a conflict. It is also often difficult for managers to know how they want the conflict to be resolved. Resolving a conflict is often a matter of knowing what you want to accomplish and then managing the issues to reach that conclusion. They frequently do not know who the "winners" and "losers" should be, or even if there should be "winners" or "losers." An example is a conflict in which surfers, surf fishermen, and ocean swimmers all want access to the same beach and water at the same time. Who should "win" this conflict? This challenge presents an ideal opportunity for the manager to employ the tools of negotiation and collaboration to resolve the conflict successfully. A final challenge facing managers is accepting that some conflicts may never be resolved and are not manageable. Some parties to a conflict may be "in the game until the end," and no matter what solutions are proposed, the conflict will continue.

A useful tool for coastal recreation resource managers to employ to better understand and manage conflict in the coastal zone is a matrix that identifies the **types of user conflicts** and the **categories of user conflicts** in coastal recreation. This matrix distinguishes among three *types* and three *categories* of user conflicts. The types of user conflicts are:

1. conflict between recreation users and other types of users;
2. conflict between different recreation users; and
3. conflict between same recreation users with different technology.

The categories of user conflicts are:

1. conflict between two land-based uses;
2. conflict between a land-based use and a water-based use; and
3. conflict between two water-based uses.

By using this matrix, the manager can fully identify the stakeholders in a coastal conflict and gain insight into their motivations and constraints. The following table provides examples of these different forms of coastal resource conflict:

Table 14.1 Conflict matrix

	Conflict between recreation users and other types of users	Conflict between different recreation users	Conflict between same recreation users with different technology
Conflict between two land-based uses beach access	Oceanfront home development vs. public beach	Beach sun-bathing vs. dogs freely roaming the horses on the beach	Riding ATVs on the beach vs. riding horses
Conflict between a land-based use and a water-based use	Beach sun-bathing and menhaden trawling	Personal watercraft in the marsh vs. bird-watching in the marsh	Kite-flying vs. parasailing
Conflict between two water-based uses	Commercial fishing vs. recreational fishing	Surfing vs. swimming	Power boaters vs. sail boaters

Negotiation

Because conflict and competition are natural, frequent occurrences in the coastal zone, coastal recreation resource managers must master the skills and principles of successful negotiation. Negotiation is not a competitive sport. Rather, it is a conflict management technique that can be summarized as: "I win some; I lose some; you win some; you lose some." The parties involved negotiate about interests and about things that people really want and need, not about what they say they want or need. The negotiator must develop options for mutual gain.

Five basic principles should guide managers as they negotiate solutions to conflicts in the coastal zone. First, *be hard on the problem and soft on the people*. When negotiating, managers must do all they can to maintain or enhance the self-image of stakeholders while pushing them to look seriously at the problem to be solved. Second, *focus on needs and interests, not positions*. Understand each stakeholder's position in the conflict, but draw attention to that person's needs or interests. Third, *emphasize common ground*. The manager should be able to see what common needs and interests exist and use those commonalities to negotiate a solution to the conflict. This creates the "I win some, I lose some, you win some, you lose some" scenario. Fourth, *be inventive about options*. Think outside the box and be creative in negotiating the solution. And, fifth, *make clear agreements*. The manager must be sure to make the solution agreed upon crystal clear to each of the stakeholders so there are no misunderstandings or misconceptions later on (Conflict Resolution Network, 2005).

Trends, issues, and challenges

Coastal recreation resource management in North Carolina has a challenging yet bright future. This section will examine some of the trends, issues, and challenges managers are currently facing and will continue to face. Some of these have confronted coastal managers for decades; others are just beginning to make their presence known. Many will be short term; others will be here for the long term and will compound the decision making of managers for years to come. All of these issues require the successful manager to understand them and be equipped to manage them. The most significant issues facing coastal recreation resource managers in North Carolina include:

1. *Beach nourishment/shoreline protection*—Should beach nourishment be an allowable practice on North Carolina's oceanfront beaches? Who should pay for the beach nourishment project? If it is allowed, what criteria should be implemented in order to ensure that the project does not harmfully impact endangered species such as colonial nesting water-birds and sea turtles or marine life on the beach itself and in the ocean surf zone? Where will the sand come from for the project? How will it be determined that the sand that is placed on the beach through the project will be consistent and compatible with the sand already on the beach? How can public access to the beach be guaranteed, and who will pay for and provide such access?

2. *Cumulative impacts*—A single project alone may not have much of a detrimental effect on coastal resources. However, what are the cumulative impacts of ten or twenty or thirty similar projects on coastal resources? One homeowner who drains or fills one hundred square feet of coastal wetlands may have absolutely no negative impact on the ability of the coastal wetlands to perform their vital functions. However, three hundred homeowners who drain or fill one hundred square feet of coastal wetlands in the same general area would have a severe and detrimental effect on the coastal wetlands. An example often cited refers to an acre pond of water. If only one individual throws a rock into the acre pond of water, it would really have no negative impact on the pond at all. In fact, it would probably be impossible to tell that the rock had even been thrown into the pond. But, if every individual who came to the shores of the pond threw a rock into the acre pond, it would not take very long for the pond to fill up with rocks and become a rock quarry. Coastal recreation resource managers must constantly guard against the negative impacts of cumulative activities. Do not be drawn into the misleading statement that "it's only one." One quickly becomes two; two become three; and, before you know it, the cumulative impacts of repetitive actions have damaged or destroyed the coastal resource.

3. *Ecosystem management*—An ecosystem is defined as a geographic area including all the living organisms, their physical surroundings, and the natural cycles that sustain them. Ecosystem management is often defined as an approach to maintaining or restoring the composition, structure, and function of natural and modified ecosystems for the goal of long-term sustainability. It is based on a collaboratively developed vision of desired future conditions that integrates ecological, socioeconomic, and institutional perspectives, applied within a geographic framework defined primarily by natural ecological boundaries (Meffe and Carroll, 1997). Ecosystem management ultimately is not a geographic place but an approach to problem solving. In essence, ecosystem management involves stakeholders in the North Carolina coastal zone deciding how to manage human behavior (Meffe, et Al., 2002). It is adapting management to fit the needs of a specific landscape, such as the North Carolina coastal zone. Coastal recreation resource managers must understand ecosystem management and strive for its implementation in the decisions impacting the North Carolina coastal resources. They must move beyond just looking at what is happening in the area immediately adjacent to projects and activities and anticipate the ecosystem implications of actions. This will require managers to develop a comprehensive approach to coastal management that encompasses all systems operating in the North Carolina coastal zone.

4. *Loss of public trust areas*—One of the most significant, yet least appreciated, consequences of coastal zone development is the extensive loss of public trust areas due to permitting of residential piers, commercial piers, bulkheads, marinas, etc. in public trust waters. Public trust areas in the coastal zone of North Carolina include the coastal waters and submerged lands that every North Carolinian has the right to use for activities such as boating, swimming, or fishing. The following is a breakdown of the lands and waters considered public trust areas in North Carolina: 1) all waters of the Atlantic Ocean and the lands underneath, from the normal high water mark on shore to the state's official boundary three miles offshore; 2) all navigable natural bodies of water and the lands beneath, to the normal high water mark on shore (a body of water is considered navigable if you can float a canoe in it); 3) all water in artificially created bodies of water that have significant public fishing resources and are accessible to the public from other waters; and 4)   all waters in artificially created bodies of water where the public has acquired rights by prescription, custom, usage, dedication, or any other means (North Carolina Division of Coastal Management, 2002d). Every time a pier, marina, or bulkhead is permitted by the North Carolina Division of Coastal Management and constructed by a North Carolina property owner, some portion of the coastal public trust area is lost.

5. *Non-point source pollution*—Non-point source (NPS) pollution, unlike pollution from industrial and sewage treatment plants, comes from many diffuse sources. It is synonymous to storm-water run-off and is caused by rainfall, snowmelt, or irrigation waters moving over and through the ground. As this run-off moves, it picks up and carries with it natural and human-produced pollutants, finally depositing the pollutants into the lakes, rivers, sounds, coastal waters, bays, and even our underground sources of coastal drinking water. Non-point source pollutants include excess fertilizers, insecticides, and herbicides from agricultural lands and residential properties; bacteria and nutrients from livestock, pet wastes, and septic systems; salt from irrigation practices and acid drainage from abandoned mines; sediment from improperly managed construction sites, crop and forest lands, and eroding stream banks; and, oil, grease, and toxic chemicals from urban run-off and energy production. For the most part, non-point source pollution is a land-based, anthropogenic problem. Major sources of NPS pollution in coastal waters include agriculture and urban run-off. Other significant sources include septic systems, forestry practices, marinas and recreational boating, physical changes to stream channels, and habitat degradation, especially the destruction of wetlands and vegetated areas near streams and rivers (U.S. Environmental Protection Agency, 2005a).

Most experts agree that non-point source pollution is the leading cause of water quality problems in the North Carolina coastal zone. The pollutants in NPS pollution impact North Carolina coastal waters in different ways; however, in all cases they have harmful effects on drinking water supplies, wildlife, fisheries, and recreation. Managers can take an active role in reducing or eliminating non-point source pollution in coastal North Carolina. Educating the public and making the public aware of NPS pollution and its sources is one role that coastal recreation resource managers can play. Coastal recreation resource managers can also push for more stringent federal, state, and local zoning and erosion control regulations that manage and control non-point source pollution. They can ensure that federal, state, local, and private lands themselves are properly managed to reduce soil erosion. Finally, coastal recreation resource managers as individuals can play an important role in reducing and eliminating non-point source pollution by practicing conservation and by changing their own everyday habits that contribute to NPS. These would include disposing of used oil, antifreeze, paints, and other household chemicals properly (not in storm sewers or drains); cleaning up spilled brake fluid, oil, grease, and antifreeze (not hosing them into the streets where they can eventually reach local streams and rivers); controlling erosion on one's own property by planting ground cover and stabilizing erosion-prone areas; applying lawn and garden chemicals sparingly and according to directions; and keeping litter, pet wastes, leaves, and debris out of street gutters and storm drains that eventually lead to coastal waters (U.S. Environmental Protection Agency, 2005b).

6. *Public beach and waterfront access*—North Carolina currently has one of the most successful and most comprehensive public beach and coastal waterfront access programs in the United States. The public beach and waterfront access program officially had its start in North Carolina in 1981 when CAMA was amended by the North Carolina General Assembly to provide matching grants to local governments for oceanfront beach access. The North Carolina Coastal Area Management Act was amended again in 1983, expanding the public access program to include estuarine beaches and waterways. The CAMA public access program provides for the construction of low-cost public access facilities; the replacement of aging access facilities; the acquisition of land for access sites; and the acquisition of land for the revitalization of urban waterfronts. Approximately $1 million is awarded annually to coastal local governments; the funds come from the state's Parks and Recreation Trust Fund. Coastal local governments are responsible for the construction, operation, and long-term maintenance of these public access facilities. Over 280 public access facilities have been funded and constructed to date. Coastal recreation resource managers must meet the challenge of providing enough public beach and coastal waterfront access to meet the demand for these services. The fact that so many of North Carolina's beach and waterfront areas are owned by private entities makes the need for public access critical. Managers must work closely with coastal local governments, the United States Army Corps of Engineers, and the North Carolina Division of Coastal Management to ensure that all North Carolinians have free, unrestricted access to public beach and waterfront areas.

7. *Sustainability of coastal resources*—Sustainability refers to the capacity to meet the needs of the present without compromising the ability of future generations to meet their own needs. In the North Carolina coastal zone, so many people are placing so many demands upon the coastal resources that we are in danger of depleting some of the most fragile of these resources (fisheries stocks, coastal wetlands, habitat for plants, animals and fisheries, and potable water). The challenge for managers is to help North Carolina's residents and visitors realize that unless we begin to conserve our natural resources now, they will not be available for future generations. The concept of sustainability is catching on in the North Carolina coastal zone. Practices are being developed and implemented to produce sustainable coastal North Carolina communities. Unfortunately, these practices are not well known at this time. Managers can have a positive influence by educating the public, practicing sustainability in resource management, and supporting politicians and decision-makers who are proponents of sustainability of coastal resources.

8. *Water quality*—Water is the single most important resource that defines the coastal zone of North Carolina. Unfortunately, as previously discussed, the high quality of

North Carolina's coastal water is in danger of being lost. Without water, especially high quality water, there will be no coastal recreation resource management. There will be no clean ocean, rivers, sounds, bays, creeks, and estuaries in which to swim and boat. The fisheries stocks that spend so much of their early growing period in the coastal wetlands and estuaries will disappear as their habitats are degraded. The beauty of the North Carolina coastal zone will quickly disappear. Coastal recreation resource managers must do all that they can to ensure the high quality of North Carolina's coastal waters. This includes working with local governments to clean up old and inefficient sewage treatment facilities; lobbying to eliminate or reduce the number of 2-stroke engines operating on the coastal waters; practicing and encouraging viable storm-water run-off management practices; protecting larger and more diverse natural, vegetative buffers along our creeks and rivers; and working with developers, private citizens, and local governments to reduce nitrogen and phosphorous emissions that eventually find their way into North Carolina's coastal waters.

9. *Water quantity*—Many coastal experts believe that water quantity (more specifically, the lack of usable and potable water) will soon be the top issue facing coastal recreation resource managers and coastal management officials in North Carolina. Usable and potable water is currently the most scarce and least accessible resource in North Carolina's coastal zone. There are many reasons this is true. The very nature of the coastal zone makes usable and potable water scarce and inaccessible. So much of the water in and surrounding the coastal zone is salt or brackish, not freshwater. Rising sea levels, combined with demands upon groundwater, are putting tremendous pressures on the underground aquifers. The growing numbers of individuals who live in, work in, recreate in, and visit North Carolina's coastal zone place phenomenal demands on the availability of potable water for drinking, bathing, sewage treatment, etc. A solution to this challenge must be found, and it must be found quickly. Management must take a lead in educating the public about this problem and seeking solutions that are both short term and long term. Short-term solutions might include:
   1. educating people about turning off the water while brushing teeth or soaping up in the shower;
   2. making sure lawn irrigation systems are efficient and well-maintained; and
   3. collecting rainwater coming from roofs and building tops.

   Long-term solutions might include:
   1. producing economical methods for converting seawater into freshwater; and
   2. developing the technology to use the water in the polar ice caps.

In summary, it is evident that coastal recreation resource managers need to be aware of the challenge of securing and maintaining a supply of usable and potable water for North Carolina's coastal zone.

Career opportunities in North Carolina

Individuals who develop the skills, knowledge, techniques, and tools of coastal recreation resource management in North Carolina will be qualified for professional positions in many areas, including:

- **For-profit companies and corporations** such as E. I. Dupont, Weyerhaeuser, Georgia Pacific, and Carolina Power and Light—natural resource manager, environmental educator, compliance officer, planner
- **National parks**—park ranger, natural resource manager, environmental educator
- **National seashores**—park ranger, natural resource manager, environmental educator
- **National wildlife refuges**—park ranger, natural resource manager, environmental educator
- **Non-governmental organizations (NGOs)** such as the North Carolina Coastal Federation, Cape Fear River Watch, North Carolina Audubon, the Nature Conservancy, the Cape Fear River Assembly, and the North Carolina Coastal Land Trust-natural resource specialist, field biologist, planner, environmental educator
- **North Carolina Division of Coastal Management**—field representative, permit manager, planner
- **North Carolina Division of Marine Fisheries**—field biologist
- **North Carolina State Natural Areas**—park ranger, natural resource manager, environmental educator
- **North Carolina State Parks**—park ranger, natural resource manager, environmental educator
- **North Carolina State Recreation Area**—park ranger, natural resource manager, environmental educator
- **North Carolina Wildlife Resources Commission**—enforcement officer, field biologist
- **Retail stores and coastal outfitters**—sales representatives, trip leaders, environmental educators
- **United States Army Corps of Engineers**—enforcement officer, planner, field biologist, permit officer

Learning exercises

1. Understanding the needs and interests of the various stakeholders in each coastal recreation resource management issue is vitally important. With this in mind, identify the stakeholders who would be involved in developing policies and procedures to manage the use of personal watercraft (PWCs) along the Cape Hatteras and Cape Lookout National Seashores and provide a short position statement for each of the stakeholders.

2. Non-point source pollution is one of the major problems facing the North Carolina coastal zone. What exactly is non-point source pollution, and why is it a problem for coastal recreation resource management? What are some of the harmful pollutants introduced by non-point source pollution into the waters and wetlands of the coastal zone? What can be done to reduce, prevent, and/or eliminate non-point source pollution? Develop a non-point source pollution position paper for the North Carolina coastal zone.

3. You are a member of the governor's Blue Ribbon Commission on Coastal Recreation Resource Management. You have been charged by the governor and the state legislature to recommend the course of action to be followed by the state regarding coastal recreation resource management. Specifically, you have been asked to discuss the pros and cons of a management strategy stressing "controlled sustainable development" for the coastal zone and to recommend whether North Carolina should adopt "controlled sustainable development" or an alternative planning and management strategy as its guiding philosophy.

4. Take the three *categories* of user conflicts in coastal recreation resource management and identify an example of the *type* of user conflict that might be involved for each of the three categories. Complete the following: 1) Identify what the conflict might be; 2) Identify who should manage the conflict; and 3) Identify how the conflict could/should be managed.

Contacts/sources for additional information

1. Atlantic Intracoastal Waterway Association
   Web site: www.atlintracoastal.org/
2. Audubon North Carolina
   Web site: www.ncaudubon.org/
3. Audubon Society
   Web site: www.audubon.org/
4. Cape Fear River Assembly
   Web site: www.cfra-nc.org/
5. Cape Fear River Watch
   Web site: www.cfrw.us/
6. Crystal Coast Canoe and Kayak Club
   Web site: www.ccckc.org/
7. Environmental Defense
   Web site: www.environmentaldefense.org/
8. National Marine Fisheries Service
   Web site: www.nmfs.noaa.gov/
9. National Oceanic and Atmospheric Administration
   Web site: www.noaa.org/
10. National Park Service-Cape Hatteras National Seashore
    Web site: www.nps.gov/caha/
11. National Park Service-Cape Lookout National Seashore
    Web site: www.nps.gov/calo/
12. North Carolina Big Sweep
    Web site: www.ncbigsweep.org/
13. North Carolina Coastal Federation
    Web site: www.nccoast.org
14. North Carolina Coastal Land Trust
    Web site: www.coastallandtrust.org/
15. North Carolina Conservation Network
    Web site: www.ncconnet.org/p.asp?WebPage_ID=139
16. North Carolina Division of Coastal Management
    Web site: dcm2.enr.state.nc.us/
17. North Carolina Division of Marine Fisheries
    Web site: www.ncfisheries.net/
18. North Carolina Sea Grant Program
    Web site: www.ncseagrant.org/
19. North Carolina Shore and Beach Preservation Association
    Web site: www.ncshoreandbeach.org/
20. North Carolina Sierra Club
    Web site: ncsierraclub.org/sierra-nc.asp
21. Pamlico-Tar River Foundation
    Web site: www.ptrf.org/
22. Partnership for the Sounds
    Web site: www.pamlico.com/pfs/
23. Partnership for the Sounds
    Web site: www.albemarle-nc.com/pfs/

24. The American Shore and Beach Preservation Association
    Web site: www.asbpa.org/
25. The Nature Conservancy
    Web site: www.nature.org/
26. United States Army Corps of Engineers
    Web site: www.usace.army.mil/
27. United States Coast Guard
    Web site: www.uscg.mil/
28. United States Fish and Wildlife Service
    Web site: www.fws.gov/

References

Beatley, T., D. Brower, J., & Schwab, A.K. (2002). *An Introduction to Coastal Zone Management*. (2nd ed.). Washington, DC: Island Press.

Conflict Resolution Network. (2005). *Negotiation skills*. Retrieved May 25, 2005, from http://www.crnhq.org/windskill10.html.

Dennis, S. (2001). *Natural Resources and the Informed Citizen*. Champaign, IL: Sagamore.

Environmental Health Center. (2000). *Coastal Challenges: A Guide to Coastal and Marine Issues*. Washington, DC: National Safety Council.

Kaufman, W., & Pilkey, O.H., Jr. (1983). *The Beaches are Moving: The Drowning of America's Shoreline*. Durham, NC: Duke University Press.

Meffe, G.K., & Carroll, C.R. (1997). *Principles of Conservation Biology* (2nd ed.). Sunderland, MA: Sinauer Associates.

Meffe, G.K., Nielsen, L.A., Knight, R.L., & Schenborn, D.A. (2002). *Ecosystem Management: Adaptive, Community-Based Conservation*. Washington, DC: Island Press.

North Carolina Division of Coastal Management. (2002a). *CAMA counties*. Retrieved April 2, 2005, from http://dcm2.enr.state.nc.us/cama_counties.htm

North Carolina Division of Coastal Management. (2002b). *CAMA handbook for development in coastal North Carolina*. Retrieved April 14, 2005, from http://dcm2.enr.state.nc.us/Handbook/section2.htm

North Carolina Division of Coastal Management. (2002c). *CAMA land-use planning: All about it*. Retrieved April 27, 2005, from http://dcm2.enr.state.nc.us/Planning/about.htm

North Carolina Division of Coastal Management. (2002d). *The Coastal Area Management Act*. Retrieved April 18, 2005, from http://dcm2.enr.state.nc.us/Rules/cama.htm

U. S. Environmental Protection Agency. (2005a). *Polluted run-off (non-point source pollution). What is non-point source (NPS) pollution? Questions and answers*. Retrieved May 20, 2005, from http://www.epa.gov/owow/nps/qa.html

U. S. Environmental Protection Agency. (2005b). *Polluted run-off (non-point source pollution). What you can do to prevent NPS pollution: Urban storm-water run-off*. Retrieved May 12, 2005, from http://www.epa/gov/owow/nps/whatudo.html

Chapter 15

Outdoor Recreation and Natural Resource-Based Non-Profit Organizations

Eric Frauman

In North Carolina, a large number of non-profit organizations serve the needs of people across the state. Not to be confused with government or public agencies or commercial for-profit organizations, non-profit organizations operate without direct support of public funds (e.g., taxes) and are not required to generate a profit for owners or investors. Non-profit organizations are generally tax exempt and generate income from a variety of sources including: donations, user fees, grants, fundraising, and membership fees. While the intention of this chapter is to focus on one type of non-profit organization there are five commonly recognized types. They include: 1) service-oriented organizations such as the YMCA and Boy Scouts whose primary function is assisting the public through recreation and leisure service offerings (see chapter four in this text), 2) professional development entities such as the National Recreation and Parks Association (NRPA) and North Carolina Recreation and Park Society (NCRPS), 3) private clubs such as a property owners association (POA) that benefit its members (see chapter sixteen in this text), 4) foundations or "friends groups" such as the Blue Ridge Parkway Foundation and Friends of the Blue Ridge Parkway that benefit a government agency (e.g., National Park Service) by raising funds for them, and 5) special interest groups such as The Nature Conservancy and Pisgah Climbers Coalition whose focus is generally specialized to serve the needs and desires of its members.

Non-profit organizations commonly exist to meet needs in situations where the public sector or for-profit sector is unable or unwilling to operate. With public agencies and for-profit businesses simply not able to meet all the demands and needs of the public, there are an increasing number of non-profit opportunities for professionals who have natural resource conservation and/or recreation management organizational skills. From internship to entry-level positions to executive director roles, more and more opportunities are becoming available to those who have a desire to help non-profit organizations around the country meet the needs of both humans and non-humans alike. The purpose of this chapter, therefore, is to describe some of the special interest types of non-profits operating in the state. Natural resource conservation as well as recreation-based organizations will specifically be examined. Additionally, a more comprehensive list of Web sites that highlight some of the non-profits operating in the state and nation will be provided.

Natural Resource-Based Non-Profit Organizations

Within natural resource-based organizations (sometimes known as environmental organizations) is great variation in focus and mission. Even with the name of the organizations come variation in that some are referred to as conservancies (e.g., Rails-to-Trails Conservancy), others trusts (e.g., Trust for Public Land), with still others known as associations (e.g., National Parks Conservation Association), funds (e.g., World Wildlife Fund), and societies (e.g., The Wilderness Society). Many are also members of networks (e.g., North Carolina Conservation Network), alliances (e.g., Land Trust Alliance), or federations (e.g., North Carolina Coastal Federation) that work together for common goals while receiving any or all of the following benefits: coordinated trainings, public relations, and lobbying, resource publications, digital libraries, grant assistance, assistance with management of contracts with state and federal government conservation programs, and liability insurance. While a discussion of entire range of this type of non-profit is not appropriate for this text, it is possible to briefly describe what many of these organizations have in common.

One overriding commonality is conserving and protecting natural resources. Many of these organizations utilize the land trust process to conserve and protect natural resources. According to the Land Trust Alliance, over thirty five land trusts throughout North Carolina work on the front lines with communities to help them save their heritage (http://www.lta.org). Community-based land trusts are experts at helping interested landowners find ways to protect their land in the face of ever-growing development pressure. They may protect land through donation and purchase, by working with landowners who wish to donate or sell conservation easements (permanent deed restrictions that prevent harmful land uses), or by acquiring land outright to maintain as open space. Land trusts have been extraordinarily successful, having protected more than 9.3 million acres of open space across the nation, according to the *National Land Trust Census (http://www.lta.org/aboutlt/census.shtml).*

While some organizations in the state are more focused on land and others have a greater focus on water conservation, many have a broader mission that encompasses both, as well as a focus on protecting ecological diversity (i.e., preserving plant and/or animal habitats and ecosystems). Moreover, many of these organizations work closely with other non-profits and local, state, and federal agencies that have similar interests. For instance, it is not uncommon for a non-profit organization to purchase and manage a natural resource (e.g., piece of land) until a governmental agency can secure the monies to buy the land from the non-profit. A fairly new initiative in the state is the creation of One North Carolina Naturally (http://www.onencnaturally.com). Its three-part mission is to:

1. Lead in developing and implementing a comprehensive statewide conservation plan that involves the public, governmental agencies, private organizations, and landowners.
2. Maintain functional ecosystems, biological diversity and working landscapes through the stewardship of land and water resources.
3. Implement a plan that will conserve and restore the state's natural heritage and sustain a healthy life for all North Carolinians and visitors *(http://www.onencnaturally.com/pages/mission.html).*

Additionally, many of these non-profits advocate for their causes via environmental education efforts, fundraising special events (e.g., festivals), recreational activities such as organized hikes, paddle trips, cleanups, flora and fauna inventories, and letter-writing efforts to Congress.

Examples of Natural Resource Non-Profits Operating in North Carolina with a State Focus

1. The Eno River Association. Located in Durham, their mission is to "conserve and protect the natural, cultural and historic resources of the Eno River basin" (http://www.enoriver.org). Since 1966, the Association has worked actively to protect the lands and waters along the Eno River and its tributaries and has resulted in more than 4,900 acres of protected lands (http://www.enoriver.org/eno/About/index.html). The Eno River Association also engages in a variety of other activities, from environmental education to advocacy. Excerpts from their Web site include:
   Our "Eno River Watch" volunteer water quality program gathers volunteers from the community four times a year to do water quality sampling on the river. We engage in advocacy for the protection of the river and the environmentally responsible development of our community, especially those lands nearest to the river and her tributaries. We host both a winter and spring hike series along the Eno River, to educate the community on the flora, fauna and history of the river. The Association also produces the fun and amazing Festival for the Eno. Now in its third decade, the Festival attracts over 30,000 people to the banks of Eno River for a three day festival full of live music, craft artists and delicious food. All proceeds from the Festival for the Eno go toward the protection of Eno River conservation lands (http://www.enoriver.org/eno/About/index.html).
2. Blue Ridge Rural Land Trust (BRRLT). Located in Boone, their mission is to "preserve rural communities and culture in northwestern North Carolina through the preservation of the land resource upon which they depend" *(http://www.brrlt.org/)*. Since its beginning in late 1997, BRRLT has protected through conservation easements and purchased 5,558 acres in Alleghany, Ashe, Avery, Watauga, and Wilkes counties *(http://www.brrlt.org/)*.
3. North Carolina Rail-Trails (NCRT). Located in Durham, NCRT monitors the state's rail system and actively pursues corridor retrieval and conversion to public recreation trails throughout the state. NCRT provides coordination between local, state and federal agencies, allied state and national organizations, and project funding sources *(http://www.ncrail-trails.org/DEPOT.HTM)*.
4. Catawba Lands Conservancy. Based in Charlotte, they focus on land that protects ecological diversity (i.e., natural habitats), water quality, and open space (e.g., farmland). Many of their properties possess all three of these traits, and each is valuable to the property itself while providing a public benefit for the entire Charlotte region *(http://www.catawbalands.org/what.php)*.
5. North Carolina Coastal Land Trust. Located in Wilmington, the Coastal Land Trusts' mission is to "enrich the coastal communities of our state through acquisition of open spaces and natural areas, conservation education, and the promotion of good land stewardship" (http://www.coastallandtrust.org/pages/about_us.html). The Coastal Land

Trust is active throughout the coastal plain of North Carolina including its beaches, river corridors and marshes, sandhills and savannas, public parks, and greenways.

6. The Bald Head Island Conservancy (BHIC). Located on Bald Head Island, their mission is "to protect, preserve and promote the natural environment of the Smith Island complex" (http://www.bhic.org/about/mission.shtml). They focus on Bald Head, Middle and Bluff Islands, all of which are bounded by the Cape Fear River and the Atlantic Ocean. The BHIC sponsors and facilitates scientific research to benefit the barrier islands, and it provides diverse activities to enrich and enlighten the islands' many visitors and residents. The Smith Island Land Trust complements their efforts by preserving significant properties in perpetuity, ensuring that land within the island complex will be forever protected in its natural state *(http://www.bhic.org)*.

Examples of Natural Resource Non-Profits Operating in North Carolina with a Regional or National Focus

1. National Committee for the New River (NCNR). NCNR is located in West Jefferson. Their land trust program began in the early 1990s and has grown throughout the years. Rapid development in northwestern North Carolina and southwestern Virginia has increased the need for permanent protection of open space. NCNR has helped to protect over 1,800 acres for a total of 24 miles along the river and its tributaries, and is currently working on many additional projects in the New River Basin *(http://www.ncnr.org/landtrust.html)*.

2. North Carolina Nature Conservancy. With eight offices located throughout North Carolina, the mission of the Nature Conservancy is to "preserve the plants, animals and natural communities that represent the diversity of life on Earth by protecting the lands and waters they need to survive (http://www.nature.org). The NC Chapter of the Nature Conservancy has protected over 105 sites across the state *(http://www.nature.org/wherewework/northamerica/states/northcarolina/)*. The larger national organization has over 1 million members, works in all fifty states and twenty seven countries, and has protected more than 117 million acres of land and 5,000 miles of river around the world (http://www.nature.org).

3. Southern Appalachian Highlands Conservancy (SAHC). Located in Asheville, SAHC has helped ensure the protection of more than 21,000 acres throughout the mountain region. Their mission "is to protect the world's oldest mountains for the benefit of present and future generations. To this end, our volunteer-based organization works with individuals and local communities to identify, preserve, and manage the region's important lands" *(http://www.appalachian.org/index.htm)*.

4. Audubon North Carolina. Located in Chapel Hill, the mission of the National Audubon Society's North Carolina State Office is to "conserve and restore natural ecosystems, focusing on birds, other wildlife, and their habitats for the benefit of humanity and North Carolina's biological diversity" *(http://www.ncaudubon.org/nccas_home.html)*.

5. Sierra Club North Carolina. Located in Raleigh, Sierra Club has local chapters in thirteen communities throughout the state. Their mission is to "1. Explore, enjoy and protect the wild places of the earth. 2. Practice and promote the responsible use of the earth's ecosystems and resources. 3. Educate and enlist humanity to protect and restore the quality of the natural and human environment. 4. Use all lawful means

to carry out these objectives" *(http://www.sierraclub.org/inside/)*. With a member-ship of over 750,000, they are one of the largest grassroots environmental organizations in the world. Priority issues include clean air and water, ending commercial logging, slowing sprawl, wildland protection, and forest protection and restoration.

6. Trout Unlimited (TU). With fourteen chapter organizations in North Carolina, Trout Unlimited's mission is to "conserve, protect and restore North America's trout and salmon fisheries and their watersheds" *http://www.tu.org/site/pp.asp?c=7dJEKTNuFmG&b=277832)*. TU accomplishes their mission on local, state, and national levels with a dedicated volunteer network. TU's national office, based just outside of Washington, D.C., and its regional offices employ professionals who testify before Congress, publish a quarterly magazine, intervene in federal legal proceedings, and work with the organization's 142,000 volunteers in 450 chapters nationwide to keep them active and involved in conservation issues *(http://www.tu.org/site/pp.asp?c=7dJEKTNuFmG&b=277832)*. TU has a broad spectrum of large projects in place that include managing for the pacific north-west salmon, water access in the west, brook trout and Atlantic salmon in the east, watershed restoration, and protecting public lands that border waterways *(http://www.tu.org/site/pp.asp?c=7dJEKTNuFmG&b=310256)*.

7. Appalachian Voices. A regional organization based in Boone, their mission is to protect and restore the ecological integrity, economic vitality, and cultural heritage of the central and southern Appalachian Mountains. Appalachian Voices' members, donors, volunteers, staff, and board work to fight air pollution, end mountaintop removal mining, protect public lands, and promote private lands stewardship. As the only organization dedicated exclusively to defending the central and southern Appalachians, they believe these four interconnected campaigns represent the major threats to the region. They are member-based and promote individual and community involvement in the important environmental decisions facing our neighbors throughout the region (http://www.appvoices.org/about.asp).

8. Trust for Public Land. With a regional office located in Charlotte, the Trust for Public Land (TPL) is a "national, nonprofit, land conservation organization that conserves land for people to enjoy as parks, community gardens, historic sites, rural lands, and other natural places, ensuring livable communities for generations to come" (http://www.tpl.org/tier2_sa.cfm?folder_id=170). Since 1972, TPL has worked with landowners, communities, and national, state, and local agencies to complete more than 2,700 land conservation projects in forty six states, protecting nearly 2 million acres. TPL's Conservation Initiatives include:

- Parks for People: Working in cities and suburbs across America to ensure that everyone, especially children, can enjoy close-to-home access to a park, play-ground, or natural area;
- Working Lands: Protecting the farms, ranches, and forests that support land-based livelihoods and rural ways of life;
- Natural Lands: Conserving wilderness, wildlife habitat, and places of natural beauty for our children's children to explore;
- Heritage Lands: Safeguarding places of historical and cultural importance that keep us in touch with the past and who we are as a people;
- Land and Water: Preserving land to ensure clean drinking water and to protect the natural beauty of our coasts and waterways (http://www.tpl.org/tier2_sa.cfm?folder_id=170).

Recreation-Based Non-Profit Organizations

As with natural resource-based organizations there is great variation in focus across recreation-based organizations operating throughout the state. While some organizations in the state are more focused on land-based recreation and others have a greater focus on water-based recreation, many have a mission that encompasses both recreation opportunities as well as a focus on protecting the sites used. Many of these organizations work closely with other non-profits and as with natural resource-based organizations, local, state, and federal agencies that have similar interests. Additionally, many of these non-profits advocate for their causes via public education efforts, fundraising special events, and workshops and clinics with groups interested in learning more about their respective organization and the activities they engage in (e.g., school, church, Boy Scouts).

From rockclimbing to caving to scuba diving, there are numerous non-profits operating in the state to meet the needs of recreationists. While some have a nationwide reach and others are more community focused, these organizations continue to proliferate as more and more people are recognizing that the benefits of membership go a long way in addressing concerns such as safety and access as well as creating opportunities for networking, socializing, and comradery. Moreover, because of the aforementioned issues, many of the public agencies (e.g., United States Forest Service) that manage the natural resources recreationists seek access to are requiring greater responsibility of users in order to engage in their chosen activity.

Examples of Recreation-Based Non-Profits Operating in North Carolina with a State Focus

1. Pisgah Commercial Climbers Association (PCCA). Located in Hendersonville, PCCA's mission is to "preserve the future of climbing in Pisgah National Forest by addressing group impact, access, and safe climbing practices" *(http://www.pisgah-climbers.org/)*. PCCA was created in 2000 by a group of local rock climbers and commercial operators interested in limiting their impact on the environment while promoting safe rock climbing practices in the Pisgah National Forest. The PCCA is open to any interested parties, recreational or commercial users of Pisgah, and any associated local manufactures and retailers that supply equipment to these groups (http://www.pisgahclimbers.org/).
2. Nantahala Hiking Club. Located in Franklin, the Nantahala Hiking Club is one of the member-maintaining clubs of the Appalachian Trail Conference (ATC) (http://www.maconweb.com/nhc/). The club has the responsibility of the Appalachian Trail in Western North Carolina from the Georgia state line at Bly Gap approximately sixty miles northward to the Nantahala River at Wesser NC. The NHC was recognized formally by ATC as a club in 1968 and has approximately 300 members (http://www.maconweb.com/nhc/).
3. Nantahala Racing Club (NRC). Located in Almond, the NRC is dedicated to the promotion and development of the whitewater canoe and kayak sport. The NRC assists athletes of every age level and ability in their preparation for national and international competition, including U.S. Team Trials, National Championships, World

Championships, World Cup, and the Olympic Games
(http://www.nrcrhinos.com/history.htm).

4. Carolina Canoe Club (CCC). Based in Raleigh, they were formed in 1969 and now have over 700 members (http://www.carolinacanoeclub.com/welcome.html). While there are scheduled trips throughout the year, CCC has significantly increased its role in education. Instruction is offered for all skill levels from beginner to advanced with weekly rolling sessions. The CCC also conducts rescue and safety classes, including Basic Rescue and Swiftwater Rescue. In addition, the Club offers ACA Instructor and Swiftwater Rescue Instructor classes on an "as needed" basis. The CCC has become increasingly active in the area of river conservation and in promoting the development of whitewater facilities. As described on their Web site, "If we don't, who will?" (http://www.carolinacanoeclub.com/welcome.html).

5. Flittermouse Grotto of Western North Carolina (FMG). Located in Asheville, FMG is an affiliate of the National Speleological Society. Their organizational purpose is to "promote the conservation of caves, safety in their exploration, and to promote fellowship between those interested in caving" (http://www.caves.org/grotto/flittermouse/).

6. Blue Ridge Bicycle Club (BRBC). Located in Asheville, the club's mission is to "bring together a community of mountain and road cyclists, who work together to provide opportunities for safer and more enjoyable recreational cycling in Western North Carolina. We strive to improve public awareness of cycling by serving our communities through educational activities, advocacy of cycling causes, and maintenance on road bike pathways and mountain bike trails"
(http://www.blueridgebicycleclub.org/). BRBC is affiliated with the International Mountain Bike Association, League of American Bicyclists, and Bicycle Alliance of North Carolina. They have scheduled rides for all abilities and ages, advocate for road and mountain bike causes, and work closely with local, state, and federal agencies to promote recognition, access, and safety
(http://www.blueridgebicycleclub.org/).

Examples of Recreation-Based Non-Profit Organizations in North Carolina that have a National or Regional Focus

1. The Appalachian Trail Conference (ATC). The ATC is a volunteer-based organization dedicated to the preservation and management of the natural, scenic, historic, and cultural resources associated with the Appalachian Trail, in order to provide primitive outdoor-recreation and educational opportunities for Trail visitors (http://www.appalachiantrail.org/). ATC is governed by an all-volunteer, twenty seven member board. Today, about fifty year-round and seasonal employees report to the executive director. The ATC staff is organized largely along the lines of its program clusters. Senior managers for public affairs, trail management, development, accounting, and the land trust work with a corresponding oversight committee of board members (http://www.appalachiantrail.org/about/atc/index.html). ATC is both a confederation of the thirty clubs with delegated responsibility for managing

sections of the Trail and an individual-membership organization. As caretaker of the Trail its founders originally built, ATC seeks to:

- Protect the footpath itself, the surrounding public land that buffers it, and all the natural, scenic, and historical resources on that land or otherwise with it;
- Provide for the public's safe and enjoyable use of the Trail and its facilities; and
- Strengthen itself as an organization, so that it can meet those two goals *(http://www.appalachiantrail.org/about/atc/index.html).*

2. American Canoe Association (ACA). The ACA has eleven affiliate clubs across North Carolina. The mission of the American Canoe Association (ACA) is to "promote the health, social and personal benefits of canoeing, kayaking and rafting and to serve the needs of all paddlers for safe, enjoyable and quality paddling opportunities" *(http://www.acanet.org/mission.htm).* The ACA strives to communicate the benefits of canoeing, kayaking, and rafting as lifetime recreation and keeps participants informed about paddlesport opportunities and activities, thus helping to "grow" the sport. ACA is the nation's recognized leader in the fields of paddlesport instruction and education *(http://www.acanet.org/mission.htm).* Currently there are more than 4,500 ACA-certified canoe and kayak instructors in the U.S. and more that 240 ACA instructor trainers. ACA's Conservation and Public Policy department is one of only a few national paddlesport public policy advocates and resources. The department helps ensure clean, accessible recreational waterways, from whitewater to flatwater to coastal resources *(http://www.acanet.org/mission.htm).* ACA's Events and Programs department provides high-quality paddlesport events of all types to ACA members and the general public, introducing thousands of new paddlers to the sport each year *(http://www.acanet.org/mission.htm).* In conjunction with the United States Coast Guard and other groups, the ACA develops and distributes safety materials, which reach millions of novice paddlers each year. The ACA is also one of the leading national organizations involved in enforcing the Clean Water Act *(http://www.acanet.org/mission.htm).* At the time of this writing, the ACA is creating a national water access land trust program, with local management and oversight, to ensure that recreational waterways remain accessible *(http://www.acanet.org/mission.htm).* The ACA sanctions over 700 events each year, providing event organizers with comprehensive assistance including insurance/risk management, technical assistance, loaner equipment, and event promotion and funding *(http://www.acanet.org/mission.htm).*

3. American Hiking Society (AHS). With an office located in Winston-Salem, AHS acts as a national voice for America's hikers by promoting and protecting foot trails and the hiking experience (http://www.americanhiking.org/inside/index.html). Examples of its work include:
   a. Working with elected officials as well as land managers at the Bureau of Land Management, National Park Service, Forest Service, and similar state and local agencies, to create and protect trail systems nationwide.
   b. Protecting and conserving trails through its National Trails Fund, supporting the volunteer-based organizations that construct and maintain trails.
   c. Serving as a clearinghouse for 170 local hiking clubs nationwide while also providing them with technical, organizational, and financial assistance through our Alliance of Hiking Organizations.
   d. Recruiting and deploying volunteer trail-maintenance crews all across America

to repair trails and construct new ones as part of Volunteer Vacations.

    e.   Fostering new and responsible hikers through National Trails Day, an annual celebration with thousands of events across the nation to encourage people to discover, enjoy, and protect their local trails *(http://www.americanhiking.org/inside/index.html)*.

4.   International Mountain Bike Association (IMBA). With nineteen affiliated bike clubs located throughout the state, IMBA's mission is to "create, enhance and preserve trail opportunities for mountain bikers worldwide" *(http://www.imba.com/)*. IMBA encourages low-impact riding, volunteer trailwork participation, cooperation among different trail user groups, grassroots advocacy and innovative trail management solutions *(http://www.imba.com/about/history.html)*. IMBA's worldwide network includes 32,000 individual members, more than 450 bicycle clubs, more than 130 corporate partners and about 200 bicycle retailers. Since its inception in 1988, IMBA and its affiliated clubs have . . .

- Spent more than $4 million keeping trails open for mountain bikers;
- Donated more than 1 million volunteer hours of trailwork;
- Built more than 5,000 miles of new trails;
- Given out more than 1,000 free tools to help volunteer trailwork efforts;
- Led more than fifty five IMBA Trailbuilding Schools; and
- Supported more than 450 IMBA affiliated clubs (http://www.imba.com/about/history.html).

5.   National Speleological Society (NSS). In North Carolina there are two local chapters (grottos) of the NSS, one located in Asheville and the second in the Research Triangle Park *(http://www.caves.org/io/iolookup.php?state=NC)*. These groups sponsor trips, offer training, teach and practice cave conservation, and generally provide a framework for studying caves. Most grottos will welcome new members who are interested in caves and committed to cave conservation. With over 12,000 members and 200 grottos, the National Speleological Society does more than any other organization to study, explore, and conserve cave and karst resources; protect access to caves; encourage responsible management of caves and their unique environments; and promote responsible caving *(http://www.caves.org/)*.

6.   The Access Fund. The Access Fund is a national organization whose purpose is to keep climbing areas open and to conserve the climbing environment *(http://www.accessfund.org/)*. North Carolina has four affiliate organizations of the Access Fund including the Boone Climbers Coalition, Carolina Climbers Coalition, Pisgah Commercial Climbers Association, and Southeastern Climbers Coalition. To finance its many projects, the Access Fund seeks corporate and individual support in the outdoor industry. Membership, corporate sponsorship, and retail sponsorship programs are the primary sources of monies used. To date, over one hundred outdoor industry members and other companies have become corporate sponsors; 250 outdoor retailers, climbing gyms, and regional climbing organizations have become Access Fund partners; and over 10,000 members from every state in the nation and over a dozen other countries have become individual members (http://www.accessfund.org/about/history.php). The Access Fund is involved in projects at hundreds of climbing areas around the country, working to reverse or prevent closures, reducing climbers' environmental impacts, and educating land managers and the general public as to the special concerns and needs of climbers. The Access

Fund collaborates with some of the country's foremost environmental organizations on issues such as the use of fixed anchors in wilderness areas, the preservation of lands threatened by development, the role of local stewardship in protecting public lands, and the protection of nesting peregrine falcons and other cliff-dwelling wildlife (http://www.accessfund.org/about/overview.php).

Some North Carolina Natural Resource Non-Profit Organizations Listed at eco-usa.net (http://www.eco-usa.net/orgs/nc.shtml)

Audubon North Carolina (http://www.ncaudubon.org/)
Audubon Society of Forsyth County (Winston-Salem) (http://www.forsythaudubon.org/
Bald Head Island Conservancy (http://www.bhic.org/)
Blue Ridge Rural Land Trust (http://www.brrlt.org/
Carolina Bird Club (http://www.carolinabirdclub.org/)
Carolina Butterfly Society (http://www.carolinabutterflysociety.org/)
Catawba Lands Conservancy (http://www.catawbalands.org/what.php)
Conservation Trust for North Carolina (http://www.ctnc.org/)
Eno River Association (http://www.enoriver.org/)
Foothills Conservancy of North Carolina (http://www.foothillsconservancy.org/)
High Country Conservancy (http://www.highcountryconservancy.org/)
Land Trust for Central North Carolina (http://www.landtrustcnc.org/)
Land Trust for the Little Tennessee (http://www.ltlt.org/)
National Committee for the New River (http://www.ncnr.org/)
North Carolina Coastal Land Trust (http://www.coastallandtrust.org/index.jsp)
North Carolina Rail-Trails (http://www.ncrail-trails.org/)
North Carolina Wildflower Preservation Society (http://www.ncwildflower.org/)
Open Space Protection Collaborative (http://www.openspaceprotection.org/)
Pacolet Area Conservancy (http://www.pacolet.org/)
Piedmont Land Conservancy (http://www.piedmontland.org/)
Riverlink (http://www.riverlink.org/)
Sandhills Area Land Trust (http://www.sandhillslandtrust.org/)
Sierra Club - North Carolina Chapter (http://nc.sierraclub.org/sierra-nc.asp)
Southern Appalachian Highlands Conservancy (http://www.appalachian.org/)
Tar River Land Conservancy (http://www.tarriver.org/)
Triangle Land Conservancy (http://www.tlc-nc.org/)

Some National Natural Resource Non-Profit Organizations Found at eco-usa.net (http://www.eco-usa.net/orgs/national.shtml)

Environmental Defense (http://www.environmentaldefense.org/home.cfm)
Friends of the Earth (http://www.foe.org/)
Greenpeace USA (http://www.greenpeace.org/usa/)

Izaak Walton League of America (http://www.iwla.org/)
Keep America Beautiful (http://www.kab.org/)
Land Trust Alliance (http://www.lta.org/)
League of Conservation Voters (http://www.lcv.org/)
National Audubon Society (http://www.audubon.org/)
National Parks Conservation Association (http://www.npca.org/)
National Wildlife Federation (http://www.nwf.org/)
Natural Resources Defense Council (http://www.nrdc.org/)
Nature Conservancy (http://www.nature.org/)
Rails-to-Trails Conservancy (http://www.railtrails.org/)
Sierra Club (http://www.sierraclub.org/)
Trust for Public Land (http://www.tpl.org/)
Wilderness Society (http://www.wilderness.org/)

Some National Recreation-Based Non-Profit Organizations Found at GORP (http://gorp.away.com/gorp/nonprof/main.htm)

The Access Fund (http://www.accessfund.org/) is a national, non-profit organization dedicated to supporting climbers' interests in the United States while preserving America's diverse climbing resources.

American Alpine Club (www.americanalpineclub.org/) founded in 1902 is a national organization in the United States devoted exclusively to mountaineering and climbing. Club activities emphasize adventure, scientific research and education.

Amercian Birding Association, Inc. (www.americanbirding.org/)
P.O. Box 6599, Colorado Spring, CO 80934, (800) 850-2473

National Audubon Society. (http://www.audubon.org/)
American Canoe Association (ACA) (http://www.acanet.org/mission.htm). The American Canoe Association (ACA) is a national organization providing a wide variety of services to those who canoe, kayak, or raft. The ACA is also a national advocate for waterway protection and boating access.

American Hiking Society information from the Hiking and Walking Home page (www.americanhiking.org/).

The American Whitewater Affiliation (http://www.americanwhitewater.org/). The AWA is a national boating organization with a membership of approximately 30,000 individual and local kayak and canoe club affiliates. The association's home page includes tons of useful information of interest to whitewater enthusiasts.

Appalachian Mountain Club (AMC) (http://www.outdoors.org/). America's oldest non-profit outdoor recreation/conservation organization.

Continental Divide Trail Society (http://www.cdtsociety.org/). Promotes development and management of the Continental Divide National Scenic Trail as a quiet nonmotorized trail.

Inner City Outings (http://www.sierraclub.org/ico/). Inner City Outings (ICO) is a non-profit volunteer organization dedicated to providing wilderness adventures for youth who would not otherwise have them.

SeaLegs, The Handicapped Sailing Experience (http://www.adaptiveadventures.org/links/sailinglinks.html). This is a non- profit organization dedicated to making the joys of sailing available to everyone. The program enables people with physical or sensory 'challenges' to experience the freedom of sailing.

Sierra Club Home Page (http://www.sierraclub.org/) is a great source of information on this organization. The site also includes listings of the club's outings, book offerings, and a directory of local chapters.

Volksmarch and Walking Index (http://www.ava.org/). This is an association of over 550 walking and hiking clubs nationwide. They host non-competitive walking events that are free and open to the public.

Watchable Wildlife (http://www.watchablewildlife.org/). The Watchable Wildlife Program is a cooperative, nationwide effort to help meet a growing national interest in wildlife and the outdoors.

Learning Exercises

1. Visit a non-profit natural resource conservation or recreation-based organization state or regional office. Arrange to meet with and interview the executive director or a board member. Include in your interview questions related to internship and employment opportunities with them or similar organizations, their overall operation and relationship with public agencies and other non-profits, and how they perceive they impact the surrounding region and communities. An alternative exercise is to arrange a phone interview. After collecting this information, present an oral report to your class.

2. Investigate a national level non-profit natural resource conservation or recreation-based organization via the Web. Identify its history/origin, mission statement, organizational structure, membership fee structure, number of members served, and three to five top issues or concerns it has or is currently working on. After collecting this information, present an oral report to your class.

3. Go to a state, regional, or national level non-profit natural resource conservation or recreation-based organization via the Web, and take action on an issue they are currently working on by sending a letter to a member(s) of Congress whom heads up the senate or house committee responsible for it. Report on the issue to your class.

4. Arrange to volunteer for five to ten hours with a non-profit natural resource conservation or recreation-based organization in the area. Make it a fact finding and experiential learning activity. Write a one to two page report on the experience.

References

All references were drawn from the Web sites listed throughout the chapter in May, 2005.

Chapter 16

Property Owners' and Community Associations in North Carolina: The Next Generation of Recreation Services

Kevin Riley and Paul L. Gaskill

Not-for-profit Property Owners' Associations (POAs) and Home Owners' Associations (HOAs) are becoming more prevalent throughout the United States. These organizations attempt to ensure that the common interests of the inhabitants of residential communities, subdivisions, or resorts are met. As part of the quality of life in a residential subdivision, these associations have determined that recreational opportunities must be provided. Their responsibilities have expanded to include the construction and operation of recreational facilities or resources such as lakes, pools, spas, golf courses, and trail systems. As the provision of recreation services has increased, so has the diversity of property owners' association duties and responsibilities. The purposes of this chapter are: 1) to examine the scope of the industry in the U.S. with a focus on North Carolina; 2) to discuss the history and background of this trend; 3) to review the legal and statutory foundations of these associations; 4) to identify the various trade associations involved in the industry, and 5) to present several case studies highlighting examples of POAs and HOAs from the mountains to the coast of North Carolina.

Scope of the Industry

From a national perspective, home owners'/property owners' associations (HOAs/POAs) are experiencing rapid growth. For example, in the last fifteen years the number of HOA/POA communities has nearly doubled. According to the Community Association Institute (2005), over 54 million people reside in 274,000 HOAs/POAs in the United States. Of these, approximately 35-40 percent live in condominiums (21.6 million), while 55-60 percent (33 million) live in single-family dwellings. The typical community association resident reports a household income of $45,000 or more a year, lives in a single family home, has at least a college degree, and is approximately forty eight years old *(www.cai.org)*.

In 2004, it was estimated that 53 percent of North Carolinians lived in HOAs; this percentage represents 1.6 million homes. In the last fifteen years, North Carolina has added almost 3,500 associations to the HOA-NC membership. The major cities in the state—Charlotte, Raleigh, Wilmington, and Greensboro—have a total of over 500 HOAs in their respective counties (HOA-NC, 2005).

Another component of the HOA/POA industry is timeshare properties. A timeshare unit (condominium or single family dwelling) is rented for an entire week for each of the fifty two weeks in the year. In 2004, it was reported that the United States had over 132,000 timeshare units in more than 1,600 resort properties. North Carolina ranks sixth nationally in the number of timeshare properties with a total of fifty nine developments. The average number of timeshare units at each resort is eighty three. The average price for a week at a timeshare unit in the United States is $14,500, with an average maintenance cost of $385 per week. Almost five million timeshare weeks are owned in the United States. The typical owner is fifty three years old, owns another home, and is married and college educated with a median household income of $85,000 (ARDA, 2005).

Benefits of Living in an HOA/POA

According to a study by the Community Association Institute Research Foundation (1999), people choose to live in HOAs/POAs for many reasons. The overall maintenance (e.g., trash pickup, snow removal, landscaping, street lighting, and street and sidewalk repair) and appearance of the community are the major variables for a majority of the members wanting to live in this type of community. Other reasons contributing to the success of this type of community are: financial attributes (i.e., home repair, property fees, resale value); location of the community; and responsiveness of the community association related to governance of the property (i.e., the association keeps members informed about current issues via newsletters and enforcement of covenants). Some residents are satisfied with the various recreation amenities that are available to them, such as swimming pools, tennis courts, golf courses, and playgrounds. Others take comfort in having in-house security, social activities, clubhouses, trails, marinas, lakes, and ponds. The survey suggested that residents of HOAs/POAs are more likely to be very positive about their community than non-association members. Finally, the study also indicated 40 percent of the residents would not consider selling their home even if they were offered over 15 percent of the market value.

According to the Community Associations Institute (CAI, 2005), this high level of satisfaction could be related to HOA/POA efforts in master planning the communities to allow them to meet the demand of the future. These efforts allows a more efficient use of land development compared to overdeveloped communities that build one home at a time with limited foresight. Good planning makes community housing more affordable for first-time homebuyers, retirees, and moderate-income families.

History and Background

For centuries, humans have congregated in common areas to seek shelter, security, and the resources necessary for their survival. Housing has always been one of the most important of these quests, and people have actually pooled their physical and financial resources to secure adequate housing since the time of ancient Rome. Many attributes that people sought in a residence were unaffordable to the individual but could be obtained by the collective.

Throughout American history, villages, towns, and cities provided the vast majority of these required services, supported by the tax dollars and volunteer contributions of the citizens. Neighborhoods within these governmental entities often had to meet the specific needs of their residents through the volunteer labors of the inhabitants. Neighborhood services often included self-policing, beautification, maintenance, and recreation.

For decades the development of condominium residences has been another housing trend addressing the collective need of homeowners in America. The term "condominium" actually derives from the Latin word for co-ownership and is a housing practice that has existed since the Middle Ages. The concept is often predicated on the owners' desire to gain access to common facilities (pools, spas, tennis courts, club houses, etc.) while delegating all or some of their home maintenance duties to others, often for an annual fee. Condominium owners may also become involved in the governance of the overall development through participation in property owners' or homeowners' associations (Freedman & Alter, 1992).

As America suburbanized throughout the latter half of the twentieth century, subdivisions were also created that provided for the needs of their residents in the same fashion that urban neighborhoods had once done. Legally, subdivisions are pieces of real property that have been divided into two or more units according to a development plan. They generally include common areas or facilities that belong to the owners collectively and are intended for the exclusive use and enjoyment of the property owners. In order to ensure that the common interests of the residents of the subdivision are addressed, not-for-profit property owners' associations or homeowners' associations have been formed. The members of these property owners' associations are either legal residents or property owners of the subdivision. Originally, property owners' associations were charged with the duties of establishing by laws and covenants, collecting dues or fees from residents, placing liens on delinquent property owners, foreclosing on property owners, maintaining water systems, roadways, and common areas, and often providing snow removal. Today, however, as common areas and facilities have expanded, property owners' associations have assumed a myriad of new tasks and responsibilities.

Many of these responsibilities include the construction and operation of recreation facilities and programs. Examples include, but are not limited to: lakes, pools, spas, golf courses, racquetball courts, tennis courts, trails (hiking, biking, greenways), fishing and camping areas, fitness centers, marinas, club houses and social centers, playgrounds, skate parks, game rooms, multipurpose fields, recreational vehicle storage areas, and concession stands. As facilities were constructed, many POAs began to establish recreation programs for the residents. For example, instructional activities in a variety of programs as well as youth league swimming or soccer teams were organized.

Legal and Statutory Foundations

The legal foundations of property owners' associations for both condominiums and subdivisions in the United States date back to the 1950s. From the federal perspective, associations generally seek Internal Revenue Service not-for-profit (501(c)(3) status. IRS Publication 4220 presents the general guidelines for organizations that seek tax-exempt status from federal income taxes. This publication describes the eligibility requirements, responsibilities, benefits, and application procedures for each applicant. The three key components in determining not-for-profit status include: 1) evidence of *organization* (statement of purpose, articles of incorporation, by laws); 2) *operational guidelines* consistent with the IRS; and 3) a succinct statement of *exempt purpose*. Preparing for tax-exempt status enables the homeowners' or property owners' association to review and refine its articles of incorporation, operational by laws, and procedures. A Board of Directors must also be established and show proof of quarterly board meetings and annual membership meetings. Annual financial statements must be submitted to the Internal Revenue Service.

With respect to board member liability, the federal Tort Claims Act provides a limited waiver of the federal government's sovereign immunity when its employees are negligent within the scope of their employment. The act also specifies that a tort claim can only be filed against the government in accordance with the law of the place where the act or omission occurred. In allowing suits, the federal Tort Claims Act enabled the establishment of state Tort Claims Acts which vary from state to state and define the degree to which liability issues will impact the association. The conclusion is evident: Agents of a homeowner's association (board members, volunteers, employees) may be sued pursuant to the state tort law.

Every state has its own set of state statutes that establish, authorize, and define the roles of homeowners'/property owners' associations. These statutes have a variety of titles, many referred to as subdivision or platting acts. In North Carolina, for example, Chapter 47F, the North Carolina Planned Community Act of the *North Carolina General Statutes*, authorizes the establishment of community associations. This act also describes the rights and responsibilities of the association. The state in which the subdivision is located will determine the specific contents of these criteria. Essentially, these associations have become quasi-governmental agencies, often providing some or all of the same services to homeowners that municipalities provide to the tax-paying public.

In other interrelationships with the local government, property owners' associations can work hand in hand with Recreation and Park Departments in planning park spaces and recreation programs. For example, in Lewis and Clark County, Montana, subdivision planning has been addressed in their Parks, Recreation, and Open Space Plan. This type of master plan is common throughout the United States. In this instance, the county has outlined the requirements for open space and recreational improvements within subdivisions and has offered professional planning assistance for these areas. These examples illustrate that the government/private developer relationship need not be adversarial; rather, it can function to benefit all citizens of a geographic area. In other communities, Recreation and Park Departments have entered into agreements with privately owned subdivisions and offered professional recreation programming assistance to property owners' associations engaged in the provision of recreation and leisure services to their residents.

Landowner liability is another important issue with which property owner's associations need to be familiar. Again, most states have enacted landowner liability statutes, also called recreational use statutes, which serve to limit the personal liability that landowners assume when their property is used for recreational purposes. For example, the *North Carolina General Statutes*, Chapter 38A, states:

> *Except as specifically recognized by or provided for in this Chapter, an owner of land who either directly or indirectly invites or permits without charge any person to use such land for educational or recreational purposes owes the person the*

same duty of care that he owes a trespasser, except nothing in this Chapter shall be construed to limit or nullify the doctrine of attractive nuisance and the owner shall inform direct invitees of artificial or unusual hazards of which the owner has actual knowledge. This section does not apply to an owner who invites or permits any person to use land for a purpose for which the land is regularly used and for which a price or fee is usually charged even if it is not charged in that instance, or to an owner whose purpose in extending an invitation or granting permission is to promote a commercial enterprise.

Recreational use statutes have a significant impact on property owners' associations that operate recreation facilities and programs. Generally, the association owes the invitees the same standard of care that the government would owe to its patrons, and hence the statute would afford no legal protection under the law from landowners who have paid dues or membership fees. However, if no fees are charged, the association would enjoy immunity from any user who is an invitee of the association or of homeowners in the subdivision. As an example, in *Clontz v. St. Marks Evangelical Lutheran Church*, both the church and the landowner were sued for damages when a patron at a church festival was injured. Since neither the church nor the landowner received any financial remuneration and neither was willfully or wantonly negligent, the suit was dismissed.

Risk Management Considerations

POA/HOA board members and officers are obviously held to a high standard of care and can be held liable for decisions and actions since they are agents of the property owners' association. Minimizing the risk of lawsuits is not always easy, but it can be done. Developing and implementing a comprehensive risk management plan is the key to avoiding and/or successfully defending the association in the event a lawsuit is filed. This plan needs to be based on the legal duties of the association, which include the duty to warn of unknown risks, to advise of inherent risks, to inspect the POA properties and facilities, to maintain and repair all facilities, and to generally keep all areas safe.

The risk management plan should contain procedures to ensure the following actions are taking place. These include, but are not limited to:

1. Review of the articles of incorporation, by laws, and restrictive covenants to assure that the actions and practices of the association are consistent with the legal foundations. If they are not, the board needs to take immediate action to modify either the practice or the bylaws.
2. Knowledge of and adherence to all industry standards, particularly those standards that may become more stringent over time through court decisions. State and local housing codes must also be reviewed to assure that the POA is in compliance.
3. Review and modification of all safety and security documents that have an impact on the safety of residents. Consult with a law enforcement agency or private security consultant and document such contact.
4. Secure the services of a qualified attorney familiar with the legal issues involved with property owners' associations.
5. Procure adequate liability insurance for all board members, officers, and employees. Routinely review all insurance coverage to see if the policies afford adequate protection. Update all policies as needed.

6. If inadequacies are discovered in any facility or program, promptly execute corrective measures.

7. Perform a background and performance review of all employees to assure that they themselves do not pose a security risk.

8. Make all residents aware of all safety codes, rules, and regulations and make sure all are enforced. Create a vehicle that allows all residents easy access to the board to report all incidents or evolving safety or liability concerns.

9. When possible, make sure new facilities have safety built in, through both design and construction.

10. Conduct a routine safety audit that outlines the frequency of inspections and document all information.

11. Make sure all routine maintenance on all facilities is performed according to a master maintenance schedule. Document the completion of all maintenance tasks.

12. Develop and implement an accident and injury reporting system that is employed regardless of the severity of the injury.

13. Enforce the use of waivers and informed consent agreements. These can be very effective tools in avoiding liability and making participants assume responsibility for risks associated with an activity. By using these documents, the participant enters into a contractual agreement (indirectly in the case of an informed consent agreement) not to hold the service provider liable. Be aware that even the best waivers may not hold up in court.

14. Review all of the position descriptions of all employees to make sure that the employees are acting within the scope of their duties at all times. When discrepancies are discovered, modify the position description immediately.

15. Provide routine in-service training for all employees and board members and officers. Standards for the credentialing of employees and board members are rising. The Community Associations Institute, for example, a trade association that represents over 250,000 property owners' associations, provides training programs, conferences, and workshops leading to the CAI Professional designation. One of these professional designations is for the Community Insurance and Risk Management Specialist (CIRMS). It is advised that at least one board member of the property owners' association seek and complete this professional designation. Raise association dues to finance these educational efforts as necessary.

16. Use public recreation agencies as consultants to develop a risk management plan that will reduce the risk for property owners' associations.

17. Hire a private property management organization to conduct a risk management assessment for the POA.

18. For the smaller POA, contact a larger POA that has established risk management plans and model their approaches and philosophies.

Trade Associations

Three associations oversee the rights of HOA/POA residents and property managers: Homeowners Association North Carolina (HOA-NC), the Community Associations Institute (CAI), and American Resort Development Association (ARDA). These associations assist individual communities within North Carolina and throughout the United States by being clearinghouses of information.

HOA-NC is the only state-affiliated HOA clearinghouse in the United States. It is responsible for maintaining a statewide directory that enables individual HOA board and community members to stay informed about current issues and fine-tune the governance of their community. This association provides a Web site and newsletter from which HOA members can glean information on issues such as liability, government mandates, and management strategies. In addition, HOA-NC is leveraging product and service discounts for all North Carolina associations and their residents, this being yet another benefit of being connected to this association (HOA-NC, 2005).

The Community Associations Institute (CAI) is the only national organization dedicated to fostering responsive, competent community associations. Its mission is to assist community associations in promoting harmony, community, and responsible leadership. It believes giving board members, managers, and homeowners increased knowledge will in turn create a better-managed association. This allows the owners of the property to increase harmony among their neighbors, which will produce a safer community. Its pledge is to provide a friendly and accessible forum to develop relationships, increase one's knowledge, and help shape the future of HOA/POA communities. CAI offers many resources, including educational courses for association managers, publications and other professional guides, and a directory of certified risk management and insurance specialists. It also conducts research for best practices in community associations nationally (CIA, 2005).

The American Resort Development Association (ARDA) is a trade association representing the vacation ownership and resort development industries. Today over 1,000 association members share ideas and resources. ARDA members range from privately owned companies to state and regional associations to major corporations in the United States. The mission of ARDA is to foster and promote the growth of the industry and to serve its members through education, public relations and communications, legislative advocacy, and ethics enforcement. ARDA is uniquely positioned within the vacation ownership industry to provide an aggressively proactive image campaign and to lobby Congress on behalf of its membership. ARDA's mission at the state level is particularly concerned with education, legislative advocacy, and membership development. North Carolina is only one of twelve state or regional associations in the nation. The state/regional committees assess dues and legislative contributions as necessary to accomplish their agenda for the benefit of all within the state or region (ADRA, 2005).

Case Studies

Because of the trend nationally and specifically in the state of North Carolina, recreation professionals need to address the recreation demands of the residents of their associations. As more and more services, programs, and facilities are offered, the recreation professional will need to assist the associations in the provision of recreational services. After all, these communities are marketing recreation opportunities as incentives for individuals purchasing property within the association.

The purpose of this section is to describe the current recreation opportunities and programs that three HOAs/POAs offer North Carolina residents. Examples from each region in the state (Mountain, Piedmont, and Coastal) will be used. These large-scale associations have been selected to depict the need for the recreation professional to be prepared to manage these unique communities.

Mountain Region

Mountain Air Resort, located in Burnsville, North Carolina, is a POA that has over 425 built home-sites with plans to expand to 850 sites in the future. POA members have two different fee structures: maintenance and recreation. The maintenance fee is associated with the cost of maintaining the homeowner's property (painting, tree removal, and basic home repair). The recreation fee allows members to join the Private Equity Club. This fee allows club members to interact with the recreation staff. Typically, the club members make suggestions about programs and services, and their needs are met by the recreational staff. The club offers three divisions of recreation services: nature, recreation, and education. The nature program provides interpretive nature hikes, junior naturalist programs, and canoe trips. The recreation department is responsible for overseeing the summer camp for children ages five to twelve, an outdoor pool, a movie theater, a multipurpose room, and a room dedicated for yoga. Most of the educational programs are lecture-based and focus on various topics, such as travel, history, and culture.

There are numerous other recreation amenities at the resort such as an eighteen hole golf course, the Golf Learning and Performance Center with short game and long game practice areas, a planned golf library, and golf swing video analysis. There are also eight and a half miles of hiking trails, three park sites, and an airport runway.

Piedmont

The Point, located just outside of the Charlotte area, is a POA that offers an upscale country club lifestyle in a very casual setting. The Point is situated on the shores of Lake Norman, the largest inland lake in North Carolina. It is designed to look like the waterside town of Nantucket. Typical home sites average one acre, providing plenty of green space for each member. POA members have a fee structure similar to Mountain Air Resort's, and The Point also offers a Private Equity Club. Luxury amenities include golf, tennis, swimming, and boating.

The Point's range of recreational facilities is extensive. The eighteen hole championship golf course, designed by Greg Norman, has thirteen holes that play along or over the lake. The family golf program caters to all skill levels, enhancing the quality of the club membership and allowing everyone to participate in the sport of golf. The Family Activity Village features a swimming complex, racquet club, and fitness center. The Swim Complex has a Junior Olympic lap pool for both recreational swimming and swim meets. It also has a splash pool with waterslides and a tot pool. The Tennis Casino features spectator viewing areas for the four lighted clay courts and two lighted hard surface courts. Other services include professional tennis instructors, locker rooms, and a tennis pro shop. The fitness building has state of the art aerobic and strength training equipment along with regularly scheduled recreational fitness classes.

The Point is situated on Lake Norman, a 32,510-acre lake. This is ideal for outdoor recreation activities such as fishing, sailing, canoeing, water skiing, camping, picnicking, and swimming (Private Communities, 2005).

Coastal

Landfall, located in Wilmington, North Carolina, is a 2,200-acre gated community umbrella association with twenty two sub-associations (two condominium associations and nine villa communities). Currently 1,000 homes have been constructed on its 1,800 lots. Each of the twenty two sub-associations has its own POA governance, and each sub-association must comply with Landfall's Council of Associations governance. The council works closely with its members, and the residents sponsor and initiate the many recreational programs that are offered. Landfall works with the local Wilmington government by allowing various sports associations to use its recreation fields.

The major social event sponsored and organized by the POA members is the Fourth of July celebration. This all-day event requires advanced planning, dedicated volunteers, and lots of hard work. In 2001 more than 800 residents participated in the celebration. The affair has activities for residents of all ages, such as golf and tennis competitions, children's games, a two-generation softball game, and an old-fashioned parade.

According to the CAI (2005), one of the sub-associations, the Great Oaks Club, encourages environmental involvement by protecting and conserving native trees, plants, and wildlife. Other activities include educational workshops and seminars related to environmental issues (preserving and protecting the natural environment and wildlife).

Landfall's country club offers its 1,034 members a twenty seven hole golf course, fourteen tennis courts, an Olympic-size swimming complex, and a state of the art fitness club. The club offers various recreational programs such as aerobics, nutrition education, and bodybuilding. Tennis players can play day or night. The tennis center has a fully stocked pro shop offering tennis, fitness, and swimming apparel and accessories. The fitness center includes a weight training room, an aerobics room, and a massage therapy room; it also has men's and women's locker rooms and saunas. The weight room has free weights and a full range of cardiovascular equipment, including treadmills, recumbent and upright bicycles, and stair steppers. Both a multipurpose recreation facility and the Temple Garden area can be rented by members for private social events such as weddings and family reunions *(www.landfall.org)*.

Summary

The phenomenal growth of homeowners' and property owners' associations in North Carolina and across the country reflects of a variety of societal factors. Increased affluence, the desire to live in a more natural environment, the need to raise children in a safer and more crime-free setting, the ability to engage directly in self-governance, and the opportunity to have access to quality recreation and leisure facilities and services are all variables contributing to this trend.

The aging of the population of the United States is perhaps the most significant of all of the demographic factors influencing this service sector revolution. The authors firmly believe that these trends will not only continue but will accelerate as Americans seek to ensure that their lives possess both quality and quantity. There is ample evidence to suggest that this is indeed "the next generation of leisure and recreation services" in America.

Learning Exercises

1. Locate and interview a board member or director of a North Carolina propert own-
    ers' association and ask some or all of the following: a) What types of recreation facil-
    ities are available on your property? b) What type of programs are offered for owners
    and their guests? 3) Do you provide these services or facilities yourself, or do you
    contract with an outside management company? 4) What types of fees are charged to
    the owners of property for these services?

2. Conduct an investigation about the differences between a property owners' associa-
    tion and a property management company that is contracted by a POA to provide
    services and programs.

3. Arrange for an on-site visit to a subdivision/property with a property owners' associ-
    ation representative. Go on a tour of the area, noting the different amenities and the
    quality of the facilities offered. Is there a staff employed to plan and program activi-
    ties and events for the property owners?

4. Conduct an investigation of current newspaper and other articles from periodicals
    (see Chapter 18 for guidance) that are related to legal issues or risk management
    practices involving POAs and property management companies. Discuss how these
    issues will affect the industry.

Resources

American Homeowners Resource Center (AHRC)
P.O. Box 97
San Juan Capistrano, California 92693
Telephone: (949) 366-2125

American Resort and Development Association
1201 15th Street NW, Suite 400
Washington, D.C. 20005-2842
Telephone: (202) 371-6700
Fax: (202) 289-8544
www.arda.org

Community Association Institute
225 Reinekers Lane, Suite 300
Alexabdria, Virginia 22314
Telephone: (703) 548-8600
Fax: (703) 684-1581
www.ciaonline.org

CAI Carolinas Chapter
3209 Steepleton Way
Greensboro, North Carolina 27410
Telepone: 336-288-7186
Fax: 336-288-2493
http://www.cai-nc.org

Homeowner Associations of North Carolina
One Copley Parkway, Suite 205
Morrisville, North Carolina 27560
Telephone (919) 462-3232
Fax (919) 462-0030
www.hoa-nc.com

Landfall Country Club
800 Sun Runner Place
Wilmington, North Carolina 28405
Telephone (910) 256-8411
info@countrycluboflandfall.com

Mountain Air
P.O. Box 1037
Burnsville, North Carolina 28714
Telephone: (828) 682-3600 or
Toll Free: (866) 316-3429
homes@mountainaircc.com

PrivateCommunities.com
Division of Private Communities Registry, Inc.
Voice: (772) 234-0434
Toll Free: (800) 875-3072
FAX: (772) 231-8443

The Point
1913 Brawley School Road
Mooresville, North Carolina 28117
Telephone: (704) 663-3030 or
Toll-free: (877) 542-3030

References

American Resort and Development Association (2005). Retrieved from www.arda.com on May 11, 2005.

Clontz v. Saint Marks Evangelical Church, 578 S.E.2D 654, 2003.

Community Association Institute (2005). Retrieved from www.ciaonline.org on May 13, 2005.

Community Association Institute Research Foundation (1999). "National Survey of Community Association Homeowner Satisfaction." Alexandria, VA: Community Association Institute Research Foundation

Francis T. v. Village Green Owners' Association, 723 P. 2d 573 (Cal., 1986).

Freedman, W. & Alter, J.B. (1992). *The Law of Condominia and Property Owners' Associations*. New York: Quorum Books.

Homeowners Association of North Carolina (2005). Retrieved from www.hoa-nc.com on May 10, 2005.

Internal Revenue Service Publication 4220, Tax Exempt Organizations.

Landowner Liability, Chapter 38A, *North Carolina General Statutes*, (1995).

North Carolina Planned Community Act, 47F, *North Carolina General Statutes*, (1998).

Chapter 17
Formulas for Success: Library Resources and Strategies for Students Majoring in Recreation Curricula in North Carolina

Glenn Ellen Starr Stilling

Library research is required for one or more assignments in practically every recreation or leisure studies course. It is a necessary activity for college students—something that becomes associated with college, as do writing papers, taking tests, and giving in-class presentations. Both librarians and college faculty are well aware, however, that we live and work in an information society. Some of the information learned in college courses today will be superseded by the time students enter the workforce. It is vital, therefore, to have strong research and critical thinking skills. These skills, which are part of information literacy, take you beyond merely fulfilling assignments and passing tests. They can help you excel when library research is a stated requirement; do even better work on assignments for which use of outside resources is optional; gather essential data for tasks such as researching a community in which you're applying for a job; generate ideas for an on-the-job meeting, project, or report; and deal with practical matters such as purchasing a car or researching matters regarding your health.

The American Library Association Presidential Committee on Information Literacy (January 10, 1989, Washington, D.C.) says, "Ultimately, information literate people are those who have learned how to learn. They know how to learn because they know how knowledge is organized, how to find information, and how to use information in such a way that others can learn from them. They are people prepared for lifelong learning, because they can always find the information needed for any task or decision at hand."

A person who has become information literate can do the following:

- Determine the extent of information needed
- Access the needed information effectively and efficiently
- Evaluate information and its sources critically
- Incorporate selected information into one's knowledge base
- Use information effectively to accomplish a specific purpose
- Understand the economic, legal, and social issues surrounding the use of information, and access and use information ethically and legally." (Association of College and Research Libraries, 2000).

By using the sources and strategies outlined in this chapter (keeping in mind—as a goal for yourself—the definition and characteristics of an information literate person) and by making the gathering and consideration of outside information one of your basic problem-solving skills, you will be well prepared for success in the Information Age.

Library services

Most people who use libraries think first of the materials and facilities libraries provide—books, periodicals, space for studying, and computers for finding information, typing papers, and designing PowerPoint presentations. Most people are accustomed to interacting with librarians to check out a book or figure out where a periodical is located. There are other services librarians offer, however, that can make library research more fruitful as well as less stressful and time-consuming.

Reference services

Reference librarians are specialists both in finding the information you need and in explaining how to use the sources that get you to the information (for instance, the library catalog; databases of references to periodical articles; reference books; and Web search engines and directories). Another important thing to keep in mind is that they genuinely enjoy answering questions and showing people how to use library resources. Never feel that you're interrupting a librarian, that you should already know how to find the information you need, or that you must spend hours looking on your own before you ask for help.

Be aware, however, that reference librarians may ask *you* several questions about the project or paper you're working on. They may ask you where (and how) you've already searched, what type of course you're in, how many sources (and what types of sources) you're required to use, how recent the sources need to be, and how long the paper or project must be. Librarians are not being nosy when they ask these questions. They are trying to match, as carefully as they can, the library's information retrieval systems and the materials the library owns with *your* information needs. Librarians don't want to weight you down with too many ways to search or too much information. They don't want to duplicate searching you've already done. They also don't want to give you too little information, or information that's not specialized enough for your project. In fact, you can help the librarian meet your needs even better by coming to the reference desk prepared. Bring with you the syllabus or assignment sheet for your course, and having in mind answers to the questions mentioned above.

Reference service is available most hours your library is open. You can simply ask your question of the librarian at the Reference Desk. The help you get will be either brief or detailed, depending on whether other people are waiting for help. Keep in mind that you can always go back to the librarian and ask for more help. Reference service is also available by telephone. Most libraries offer reference service by e-mail; many will help you through online chat during certain hours. Check your library's Web site for something called "e-mail reference" or "ask a librarian" to find out.

Many college and university libraries also offer in-depth, one-on-one reference assistance by appointment. These appointments are an excellent way to maximize your time and efforts when you have a large, challenging project or assignment. Generally, you'll fill out a form (either on the library's Web site or at the Reference Desk) describing your assignment and the topic you've chosen. You'll then be scheduled for an appointment with a particular librarian. Keep in mind that the librarian helping you will require advance notice of a day or two. The librarian will research your topic in advance and, during the appointment, show you library catalog searches, periodical database searches, reference books, and other sources and strategies for researching your topic effectively.

Instruction services

Most college and university libraries also provide workshops or instruction sessions. These sessions are usually held in a classroom or computer lab in the library. They are usually arranged for your class by your professor. If your class has been assigned a research paper or project that will require some fairly extensive library research, your professor might call the reference staff and request a session in which a librarian teaches your class the library sources and strategies that will be most useful for your assignment. The library might also offer open workshops that you can attend on how to use particular databases or on how to find information in certain subject areas.

Interlibrary loan

With a little advance planning, you can easily obtain books, journal articles, and other information that you need but your library does not own. You don't have to drive to another library or purchase it from a bookstore or on the Web. If a database search, or the bibliography of a book or article, lists a promising source that the library does not have, ask a reference librarian about interlibrary loan. You'll have to fill out a form (usually on the library's Web site or from within a database) for each item you want. The library will either borrow the item from another library that owns it (for books, theses, dissertations, microfilm, or government documents) or get the other library to make a photocopy or fax (for articles from periodicals). The process can take from a couple of days to a couple of weeks or more, depending on how many libraries own the item and how busy their interlibrary loan departments are. Many libraries don't charge for this service, or charge only a very small fee. Books, theses, dissertations, government documents, or microfilm borrowed on interlibrary loan can usually be used for two or three weeks; photocopies or faxes are yours to keep.

How do you find out if your library offers e-mail reference service, chat reference, or reference by appointment? How do you find out about your library's specific procedures for interlibrary loan? Check the library's Web site or contact the Reference Desk.

Formats of information

Libraries own (in print or electronic format)—or can obtain for you—information in a variety of published or unpublished formats. Part of the research process is deciding which formats the information you need might appear in. Sometimes your instructor specifies the format(s) you are to use. In any case, format can be an important factor in your research, since materials in different formats (books, journal articles, government publications, court cases, newspaper articles, Web sites) often are retrieved through different databases.

Here are some of the formats of materials your library offers:

- **Reference books**—works such as general encyclopedias, specialized encyclopedias, directories, statistical compilations, atlases, quotation books, and book-length bibliographies. These works—in print or electronic format—are designed to be consulted for brief bits of information (an article, a biographical sketch, an address, a statistical table) rather than read cover-to-cover.
- **Circulating books**—These are fiction or nonfiction books that can be checked out. The range of topics and authors for which your library will have is based mainly on your college or university's curriculum. For instance, colleges that don't offer degrees in recreation and leisure will have far fewer books and journals in their library for those areas. Remember, in your research, that you may need to search your topic more broadly when you're looking for books than you do when searching for references to periodical articles. A periodical database will probably list articles specifically about therapeutic recreation with prison populations, whereas a library catalog may only list books on therapeutic recreation in general. You should browse through those books on therapeutic recreation, looking at the table of contents and the index to see if there are chapters or sections on prison populations.
- **Articles in periodicals**—Depending on your topic, you might be able to find articles in scholarly journals (such as *Journal of Leisure Research, Journal of Park and Recreation Administration, or Annals of Tourism Research*), professional or industry journals (*Ski Area Management, Ranger* [Association of National Park Rangers]), newsletters (*Sports, Parks & Recreation Law Reporter*), newspapers (*News and Observer* [Raleigh], *New York Times, USA Today*), or theme-oriented popular magazines (*National Parks, Outside, Outdoor Life*).

When your information needs or your course assignments require the use of periodicals, there are three basic steps you will usually follow to find them. *First*, you'll need to decide which indexes to periodicals (we'll call them as periodical databases, since the ones that will be discussed in this chapter are Web-based) are most likely to list articles on your topic. *Second*, do searches for your topic and print out the article references (or the full text of the articles, if available). *Third*, if the full text of the articles wasn't right there in the database, check to see (1) if the library subscribes to the journals or magazines your articles were published in, (2) if yes, whether the library has the particular volumes containing those articles, and (3) where in the library those volumes are located.

This checking on whether the library owns the journal or magazine is done in the *library catalog*. You may discover that, rather than print volumes, the library has an electronic subscription to the periodical you need—or that you can find a full-text version of the article in a different database from the one you searched. If you're unable to locate a needed periodical in your library, you can initiate an interlibrary loan request.

The process of searching for information

The remaining sections of this chapter will explore search strategies and specific resources (including reference books, circulating books, databases, and Web sites) for finding information on topics related to recreation and leisure. The topics are based on some of the assignments given in recreation and leisure courses in North Carolina colleges and universities, as described in course syllabi. Please keep in mind that the resources and strategies described in this chapter are *not* the only ones available to you. The reference librarians at your college or university can make additional suggestions. Also remember that the descriptions of how the databases and other resources work, and the numbers of references found in each search, are based on searches done in June 2005. Since each example is based on a real search, you can practice it on your own, following the steps given. As you read each example, assume you're at a computer and connected to the database.

Finding information in books

Reference books

Two different types of books might have information on recreation and leisure topics: reference books (which themselves fall into different categories) and circulating books.

- **Specialized encyclopedias** (whether one volume or multi-volume in length) give you concise introductions to, and overviews of, the topics within their scope. The articles often conclude with a selected bibliography, leading you to more information on the topic. For example, an encyclopedia of education would discuss adventure and experiential education; a psychology encyclopedia would have articles on counseling techniques as well as client conditions relevant to therapeutic recreation; and an encyclopedia on government agencies would tell you about the functions and structure of the National Park Service. Suppose your Group Dynamics and Leadership professor has given you have an assignment to teach a game. You must also submit a card that gives the directions for the game, number of people required, and where you found your information. Your library might have in its reference collection Marilyn S. Mohr's *The New Games Treasury* (Houghton Mifflin, 1997), or some other encyclopedia of games. There you would find all the necessary information (including history and variations) for a card game such as "Go Fish" or an outdoor game such as "Statues" or " Red Lion." You will find two recreation and leisure encyclopedias especially valuable sources for definitions of, and concise introductions to, concepts in your field; most of the articles will also give you references for further reading. They are: *Encyclopedia of recreation and leisure in America* (two volumes, Charles Scribner's Sons, 2004) and *Encyclopedia of leisure and outdoor recreation* (Routledge, 2003).
- **Directories** are useful lists of basic information about businesses, organizations, people in a particular profession, and more. If you're looking for camps—whether for an internship, a job, or for mailing out a survey—the annual *Guide to ACA-Accredited Camps,* published by the American Camping Association, will help. It lists camps in order by state, then by name. For each camp, it gives the director's name, address,

phone and fax numbers, Web site, year established, a description, and a list of activities offered. It has indexes listing the camps by special groups (such as behavioral problems, gifted and talented, or youth at risk) and by specific philosophies (such as Christian, African-American culture, and Jewish tradition). You can use the ACA Web site (*http://www.acacamps.org*) to search for camps in some of these same ways.

If your assignment is to report on professional or trade associations related to a particular area of recreation, the annual *Encyclopedia of Associations* is essential. It lists associations of all types. They are arranged by broad categories; but the keyword index will help you find the associations having, for example, "fitness" or "canoeing" in their name. If your library subscribes to the SBRnet (Sports Business Research Network) database, you'll find excellent links to the Web sites of sports- and activity-related organizations.

- **Statistical compilations** can be helpful for a variety of purposes. Although statistics can be found in other places—such as databases (*Statistical Universe* from LEXIS-NEXIS is an example), Web sites (*Sports Business Research Network* is especially useful), and articles in periodicals—reference books such as *Statistical Abstract of the United States* should not be overlooked. *Statistical Abstract* is an annual compilation (with a detailed index) of a wide variety of statistics on all aspects of the United States and its people. The statistics come mainly from publications of federal government agencies, but other sources are used as well. Find what you need by using the detailed index. You might need to know, for example, how much land is set aside for parks and recreation in North Carolina. The 2004 edition of *Statistical Abstract of the United States*, Table 1250, tells you that as of 2002, North Carolina had 168,000 acres devoted to parks and recreation; received 12,758,000 visitors that year, and took in revenues of $3,703,000 (which paid for 11.9 percent of operating expenditures).

If you need statistics on participation in various sports and activities, Alison Wellner's *Americans at Play: Demographics of Outdoor Recreation and Travel* (New Strategist Publications, 1997) is valuable. You'll discover, for example, that watersports are among Americans' favorite outdoor recreation activities. Swimming is ranked fifth in the National Survey of Recreation and the Environment, which showed that 44 percent of Americans sixteen or older swam in a pool in the last twelve months and 39 percent swam in the ocean, a lake, or a river (page 187). Additional, more recent data on participation rates can be found in *Statistical Abstract of the United States*, the *SBRnet* database, and the National Sporting Goods Association's annual reports on sports participation for each sate. Also useful is the National Survey of Fishing, Hunting, and Wildlife-Associated Recreation (which provides both national- and state-level data) at http://www.census.gov/prod/www/abs/fishing.html.

- **Atlases** can be helpful for visual representations of data or statistics, as well as for their customary purpose of locating places or geographical features. The *North Carolina Atlas: Portrait for a New Century* (University of North Carolina Press, 2000) is an impressive reference book, featuring (besides the wide array of figures) detailed text, a thorough index, and a bibliography at the end of each chapter. Chapters relevant for recreation and leisure include "The Natural Environment" (2), "Agriculture, Forestry, Fishing, and Mining" (7), "Trade, Finance, and Tourism" (10), and "Outdoor Recreation" (19). An example of the data this atlas provides is Figure 19.7, "Selected Federal and State Outdoor Recreation Areas." It shows, within the counties, symbols for national parks, parkways, and seashores; national forests; state forests; educational state forests; the zoo; the Intracoastal Waterway; and the Appalachian Trail.

Searching the Library Catalog for books

Circulating books, according to library terminology, are books that can be checked out. Your library's catalog probably offers all of the following ways to search for circulating books on topics of interest.

■ **Known item searches**. Suppose you have a partial or complete reference for a particular book on your topic. For known item searches, your library catalog probably offers three choices—author, title, and author/title. Let's say your professor suggested three books that you should peruse for your paper on evaluation in recreation: (1) a recent book (a new edition, actually) by Robert Manning; (2) *Research and Evaluation in Recreation, Parks and Leisure Studies,* by Richard Kraus and Laurence Allen; and (3) Karla Henderson's *Evaluating Leisure Services.*

For the first book, you try an Author search, typing in: **manning robert** (notice that you must put the last name first, and you don't need to capitalize). There are several Robert Mannings, and you don't want to check each one separately. The best strategy is to Limit your search. First, you Limit by Words in the Title, typing in: **evaluation**. The catalog finds no matches. You wonder if the professor had the title slightly wrong, so you try another Limit by Words in the Title, this time typing in: **recreation**. This search finds the book for you: Robert E. Manning's *Studies in Outdoor Recreation: Search and Research for Satisfaction* (1999).

For the second book, you decide to do a Title Search. You type in: **research and evaluation in recreation**. It's not necessary to type in the entire title when you have a lengthy title. The catalog will find all titles that begin with the words you typed in. The professor remembered the title correctly, and the catalog found the book.

For the third book, you try an Author/Title search, which combines both author and title in the same search. Please note that not all library catalog systems offer this option. In the Author blank, you type in: **henderson** (always use the author's last name). In the Title blank, you type in: **evaluating** (always select a less common word from the book's title). The catalog finds the book in one easy step, and you only need one search word in each blank. This kind of search is especially helpful when your author has a common name or has published many books, or when the book title is a fairly common one.

■ **Subject Searches**. Searching by subject is one of the two ways of finding books on a topic when you don't have an author or title of a particular book. Subject searching uses Library of Congress Subject Headings, which are the standardized index items chosen by the catalogers at the Library of Congress. If the search terms you type in don't match the terms used by the Library of Congress for your topic, you might get a message "no matches found." Another possibility is that you'll get a message that some other word or phrase is used instead, and you'll be able to click on that word or phrase to re-execute your search. If you do get a match, you'll probably be able to scroll through a list of subject headings that begin with your search term.

Suppose you're planning to lead an outing at the Outer Banks and are looking for interesting information to incorporate in your program. A Subject search for **beaches** would turn up a large number of listings of subject headings, in alphabetical order, all beginning with the word Beaches. Scanning through the listings, you would see the subject heading Beaches—North Carolina—Guidebooks. Clicking on this heading shows you the book *North Carolina Beaches* by Glenn Morris (University of North Carolina Press, 1998).

- **Keyword searching** is another important way to find books on a topic. With this type of searching, you try to anticipate words or phrases that will be used for your topic and combine them, if necessary, using parentheses and using the Boolean operators **OR** and **AND**. Keyword searching finds your words in a book's title, its Library of Congress Subject Headings, or (if the book has one) its contents note (the latter is usually a paragraph describing the book's topic or a list of all its chapter titles and authors). Keyword searching is not as precise as Subject searching. It often finds some books that are not on your topic (even though your search words appear in the record), as well as some that are. In online searching terminology, items that contain your search words but don't relate to your topic are called *false drops*.

Suppose you want to find books about interpretation in the field of recreation. Your keyword search might look like this:

(interpretation or interpreter*) and (recreation* or leisure or park or parks)

Notice the asterisks used in the search statement. In most databases, and in Web search engines, the asterisk is a *truncation character* that lets you search for word variants by typing in just the stem (the part that's the same in all the variants). For example, **recreation*** will find the words **recreation** or **recreational** without typing both search words. Be careful using truncation, however. Consider whether the stem you type in might find search words that are not relevant to your topic. Notice that the example above uses **park or parks** rather than **park***. That's because **park*** would retrieve words such as **parking, parka,** and the name **Parker**.

The Keyword search we typed will find books containing—in the title, the subject headings, or the contents note—the word **interpretation** as well as the word **recreation**; or the word **interpreter** as well as the word **parks**; and so forth.

Look at Figure 17.1. This catalog record was retrieved by the Keyword search; and the book looks right on target. The word **interpretation** appears in the book's title, and the word **parks** appears in the Subject field (i.e., the Library of Congress Subject Headings that were assigned to the book). Since this book is on target—it's just what you need—you might decide to re-execute your search using one of the two Library of Congress subject headings that relate to interpretation. It looks as if the Library of Congress calls the topic of interpretation in national parks **National parks and reserves-Interpretive programs**. It calls interpretation in other outdoor areas **Natural areas-Interpretive programs**. Both of these subject headings are hot links in the library catalog. Thus, if you're more interested in interpretation in natural settings other than national parks, clicking on **Natural areas-Interpretive programs** would put you into a search listing books containing a substantial amount of information on this topic (a guarantee you don't get with keyword searching).

Figure 17.1

Author	Ham, Sam H
Title	Environmental interpretation : a practical guide for people with big ideas and small budgets / Sam H. Ham
Publisher	Golden, Colo. : North American Press, c1992

LOCATION	CALL #	STATUS
ASU MAIN STACKS	QH75 .H36 1992	NOT CHK'D OUT
NC ARBORETUM	QH75 .H36 1992	LIB USE ONLY
WCU GENERAL	QH75 .H36 1992	NOT CHK'D OUT

Description	xxvi, 456 p., [5] p. of plates : ill. (some col), maps ; 23 cm
Bibliography	Includes bibliographical references and index
Subject	Natural areas -- Interpretive programs
	Show similar items
	Environmental education
	National parks and reserves -- Interpretive programs
	Show similar items

But let's look at two other examples from the Keyword search. The book in Figure 17.2 is a false drop. It deals with leisure—but not with interpretation as a special kind of leisure service. In this book title, the word **interpretation** has a different meaning.

Figure 17.2

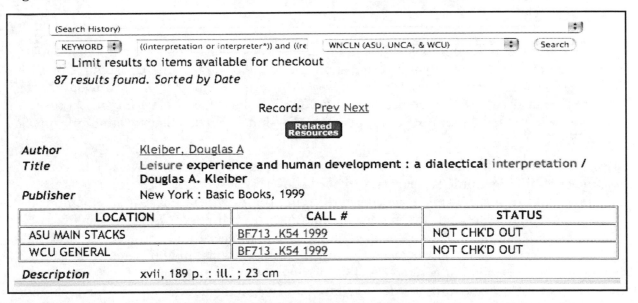

Now look at Figure 17.3. In this book, **park** turns up in the Title and **parks** in the Subject field of the catalog record. This example shows one of the beauties of Keyword searching. The word **interpretation** matched in the Contents field, because one of the book's chapters is about interpretation in parks. Only Keyword searching will find your search words in the Contents field; but be aware that, as of 2005, only a small percentage of books in most library catalogs have contents notes. It's not very likely that a researcher would have found this book without doing a Keyword search, because most researchers wouldn't be patient enough to browse the library's book stacks in the call number area for parks, checking the books' index and tables of contents for information on interpretation.

Figure 17.3

Author	Sharpe, Grant William
Title	A comprehensive introduction to park management / Grant W. Sharpe, Charles H. Odegaard, Wenonah F. Sharpe
Publisher	Champaign, Ill. : Sagamore Pub., c1994
Edition	2nd ed

LOCATION	CALL #	STATUS
ASU MAIN STACKS	SB481 .S5 1994	NOT CHK'D OUT
WCU GENERAL	SB481 .S5 1994	NOT CHK'D OUT

Description	viii, 559 p. : ill. ; 24 cm
Bibliography	Includes bibliographical references and index
Subject	Parks -- Management
	Show similar items
Contents	An overview of park management -- Structure -- Policy -- Recreation laws and liabilities -- Politics -- Fiscal management -- Personnel management -- Citizen involvement -- Planning, land acquisition and development -- Park facilities -- Maintenance and safety -- Environmental impact -- Vandalism -- Conflicts -- Law enforcement -- Fire management -- Interpretation -- Care of visitors -- The park manager

Finding books beyond your library: The *WorldCat* database

What happens when you're writing a major project or research paper—one that counts for, say, 20 or 30 percent of your grade—and you'd like to know what books have been published on your topic *other than* the ones your library owns? The *WorldCat* database, available in all NC LIVE libraries (more on NC LIVE later), is perfect for such a task. We'll see what else is available on interpretation—but first some background information on *WorldCat*.

WorldCat, whose official name is OCLC Online Union Catalog, is the world's largest database of bibliographic records (i.e., records describing written materials). It is the database that thousands of libraries use to create their own catalogs. When member libraries purchase a new book, they download a record from *WorldCat* if the book is already there; if not, one of their catalogers will create a record and add it to *WorldCat*. As of June 2005, *WorldCat* had records for over 58 million items, in 400 languages (the majority in English), owned by over 53,548 libraries in the United States, Great Britain, and ninety four other countries. It is updated daily, and it includes all records created by the Library of Congress (even for not-yet-published books, since publishers send the Library of Congress preliminary information on their books a few months in advance). *WorldCat* is also the database that thousands of libraries use to fill interlibrary loan requests. Besides books, *WorldCat* contains records for periodicals (that is, for the journals and magazines as a whole—not, as a general rule, for the articles within them), government publications (from U.S. as well as state agencies), maps, videotapes, DVDs, sound recordings, dissertations, masters and undergraduate honors theses, manuscripts, and computer files. *WorldCat* lists the holdings of large, prestigious libraries (such as Harvard, Duke, and the Smithsonian), specialized libraries, and many small, hometown libraries.

When you search *WorldCat* and find a book that interests you, clicking on "Libraries worldwide that own item" will show you which libraries own the book (listing those in North Carolina first). Thus, if you want to borrow the book through interlibrary loan, you'll know how likely it is that the book can be gotten for you (if several libraries in North Carolina or the Southeast own it, your chances are great; if only one library in the U.S. owns it, not so good). It's likely that you can type in your interlibrary loan request for the book while in *WorldCat*, just by clicking on ILL or ILLIAD and filling in an online form. Before you do this, however, check the list of libraries carefully to be sure your library isn't shown.

Let's see what *WorldCat* offers on interpretation for natural areas. We'll use the same Library of Congress Subject Heading that we discovered in our Keyword search in the Library Catalog (refer back to Figure 17.1). In the Advanced Search mode, change the field on the first search blank, using the pull-down menu, to Subject Phrase. Type in: **natural areas**. Do the same for the second search blank and type in: **interpretive programs**. The Boolean operator between them is already set for AND. Subject Phrase, in this database, means Library of Congress Subject Heading. For a subject heading that contains a dash, as does **Natural areas—Interpretive programs**, the search must be entered on two search blanks, using AND between them. We'll also set Language to English, Type to Books, and Year to 1990-2005. The search retrieves sisty six items. See Figure 17.4 for an illustration of how to type in the search and set the limits:

Figure. 17.4

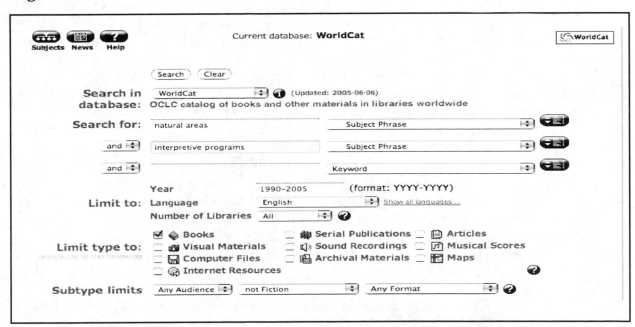

Here are a few promising items found in the search:

- 1999 *Interpretive sourcebook: changing seasons, changing centuries* (259 pages; a compilation of papers from the 1999 National Interpreters' Workshop. The subject headings indicate it deals with interpretation in historic sites, natural areas, national parks, and other types of parks.)

- a 1998 dissertation on evaluating interpretive programs
- a 1999 book called *Explaining Our World: An Approach to the Art of Environmental Interpretation* (a large number of libraries own it, so it would be easily obtained through interlibrary loan)
- a 1998 children's book, *Leapfrogging Through Wetlands*, containing activities for discovering wetland ecology
- a 1994 book called *The Interpreter's Guidebook: Techniques for Programs and Presentations* (this is the third edition, so it undoubtedly has been useful and successful)

Searching periodical databases for articles in journals, magazines, or newspapers

Many of the assignments you'll be given in a recreation and leisure course will require you to use articles in periodicals—sometimes exclusively, sometimes along with other sources of information. As a recreation professional, you will undoubtedly continue to rely on scholarly and professional journals. There are quite a few periodical databases that can be used for recreation and leisure research. In this chapter, we will explore only the most relevant ones.

Several of the databases we'll discuss are available to you through the NC LIVE (North Carolina Libraries for Virtual Education) program. A special appropriation by the General Assembly, along with (for independent colleges) funding from the Duke Endowment and Cannon Foundation, enables NC LIVE to provide computer equipment, technical support, and subscriptions to seventy three databases. These benefits are freely available to the users of all University of North Carolina System libraries, community college libraries, the State Library, all public libraries, and independent college and university libraries. NC LIVE is intended to level the playing field so that geographical isolation, or level of community or institutional funding, is not a barrier to the access of information. These seventy three NC LIVE databases can be searched from any of the types of libraries listed above, and often from home as well, by connecting to your college library's Web site. Be sure to enter the databases through the *library's* Web site. This way, you'll be *authenticated* as an eligible user of the database and won't be asked for an NC LIVE password. Remember that after you graduate, you can still use NC LIVE databases as long as you're a North Carolina resident. Your local public library can give you details on how to do this. For more details on the NC LIVE project, visit www.nclive.org/about.phtml.

- **Sport Discus**. This international database, covering articles 1975 to current, contains over 700,000 records and is updated quarterly. It lists journal articles, magazine and newsletter articles, books, book chapters, conference proceedings, Web sites, and theses and dissertations. Over 70 percent of the database consists of periodical articles, and 25 percent of the items are research level. Besides all aspects of sports and fitness, it also covers recreation and leisure. The reading level of each item is rated basic, intermediate, or advanced, and many of the records include abstracts (brief summaries of the items). The database is produced by SIRC (Sport Information Resource Center) in Ottawa, Canada and is based on that library's holdings. An added bonus to Sport Discus is its indexing of the University of Oregon's Kinesiology Publications. This program publishes and disseminates, in microfiche or electronic (full text) format, theses and dissertations on recreation, play, dance, health, fitness, physical education, exercise and sport sciences, and related fields. The works chosen by this program are reproduced on microfiche. Over one hundred university libraries and research institutions subscribe to the microfiche. To learn more about Kinesiology Publications, visit http://kinpubs.uoregon.edu/. For more information on *Sport Discus*, visit www.sirc.ca/products/sportdiscus.cfm.

Example #1: You need to find information on therapeutic recreation in prisons. First, you check the Thesaurus for each of the two concepts—therapeutic recreation and prisons—to see what index terms (like Library of Congress Subject Headings) Sport Discus uses for the concepts. You click on Thesaurus, type in: **prison**, and click Go to Term. Prison is indeed the Subject Heading used by Sport Discus. Do the same for: **therapeutic recreation**. That term is also used in the database. Now, click on Searches. Type in: **prison-** in the first blank and **therapeutic-recreation** in the second. In *Sport Discus*, type in the Subject Headings you found in the Thesaurus with a dash at the end (if one word) or a dash between words (if a phrase). Set both search blanks to Subject. Click on Search Limits and set Lanugage to English. Then, execute the search. This search retrieves twenty one items in publications such as *World Leisure Journal, Journal of Leisurability, Parks and Recreation,* and *Therapeutic Recreation Journal*. In one of the items retrieved by the search, you'll notice the Subject Heading: **Correctional recreation**. Do a new Subject search, using this phrase and limiting to English. You'll find 126 items.

Example #2: You need to find articles on a topic of your choice, but only in journals specified by your instructor. Suppose your assignment is to write four two-page summaries of articles dealing with leisure and women. The articles must be from 1995 or later, and you have a list of seven journals that the articles can come from.

Sport Discus can easily handle such a requirement, but your search must be done in several steps. (Note that these steps are based on the Ovid Technologies WebSPIRS version of *Sport Discus*.)

First, you must check to see whether Sport Discus indexes any (or all) of the seven journals you can use. Click on Index. In the Index to Search menu, select Journal Name. Type in the name of a journal. Then, click on Go to Term. If you see your journal in the list, with a number after it (indicating the total number of articles indexed from that journal), you'll be able to decide whether you want to search for your topic within this journal. Now, continue to search the other journals in the list.

Second, search the online Thesaurus to see which index terms are used for women and related concepts. Notice that *Sport Discus* uses the singular term, **woman**. Notice also that there are several related terms listed in the Thesaurus. Your search will retrieve more sources if you include them. Typing in the main Subject Heading, **woman**, does not automatically include all the related terms; you must type them in if you want to search them.

Now you're ready to do your searches.

For each of the journals from your list that *Sport Discus* indexes, do a search this way:

journal of leisure research (set search blank to Journal Name)

and

(woman- or femininity- or sex-role or gender-identity or feminism)(set search blank to Subject)

and   **py=1995-2005**

Limit Language to English.

This search retrieves twenty two items. From among them you can mark and print, say, five or six records that interest you. It's always wise to print more records than your paper requires, since some may not turn out to be as useful or interesting as you expected. Follow the same steps shown above for other journals, if you want or need to.

A couple of promising items from these searches are:

■ "Women and adventure recreation: reconstructing leisure constraints and adventure experiences to negotiate continuing participation," in *Journal of Leisure Research,* 2002
■ "Just recreation: ethics, gender, and equity," in *Journal of Park and Recreation Administration*, 1997

■ **Leisure, Recreation, and Tourism Abstracts.** This international database, covering 1974 to current, indexes over 400 journals as well as books, technical reports, and conference proceedings. It contains information on leisure, recreation, tourism, sports, hospitality, facilities management, and natural resources and environment. The aspects of these topics that it encompasses are history, theory, research, specific groups, policy, economics, sociological approaches, psychological approaches, attitudes and perceptions, and participation trends. Clearly, you can consult this database for many topics besides tourism.

Example #1: You need to find information on heritage tourism. A Subject Terms search of just that phrase, limited to English, retrieves 213 items. Some interesting choices include:

■ "Exploring the sustainability of mining heritage tourism," in *Journal of Sustainable Tourism,* 2004
■ "Links between tourists, heritage, and reasons for visiting heritage sites," in *Journal of Travel Research*, 2004
■ "Managing heritage tourism," in *Annals of Tourism Research,* 1999
■ "Heritage, tourism, and places: A review," in *Tourism Recreation Research*, 2000. (This review article, citing sixty four other articles, shows that relationships among heritage, tourism, and geography can be harmonious, in conflict, or potentially sustainable.)

Example #2: A Subject Terms search of **recreation** and **north carolina** retrieves sixty items. Below are some interesting items found:

- "An application of the Kuhn-Tucker model to the demand for water trail trips in North Carolina," in *Marine Resource Economics*, 2003
- "Using performance measurements to explore the influence of service quality dimensions on customers' perceptions of overall value of a nature based tourism outfitter," in *Journal of Quality Assurance in Hospitality & Tourism*, 2001
- "The impact of recreation on a barrier island: a case study on Masonboro Island," in *Coastal Management*, 2000

- **Ingenta.** This large database, which covers 1988 to current for most journals, is an interdisciplinary, table-of-contents index to over 26,000 periodicals, most of them in English. Over 5,400 of these periodicals have some full text articles. It is updated daily. Over half the journals are science and technology related; one third are social sciences, and the remainder deal with the humanities or general topics. The database can be searched by author, journal title, keyword, or all fields at once. Some of the periodicals it indexes which are useful for recreation and leisure are: *Adapted Physical Activity Quarterly, Annals of Tourism Research, CRM* (formerly *Cultural Resource Management*), *Current Issues in Tourism, Journal of Leisurability, Journal of Leisure Research, Journal of Park and Recreation Administration, Journal of Retail and Leisure Property, Journal of Tourism Studies, Leisure Manager, Leisure Sciences, Leisure Studies, Managing Leisure, Schole, Therapeutic Recreation Journal*, and dozens of periodicals devoted to specific activities such as baseball, bicycling, hunting, cross-country skiing, golf, hang gliding, mountain biking, canoeing, climbing, and more.

Example #1: You must select a "contemporary issue" related to administration of recreation and write a paper on that topic. To help select an issue, you decide to browse the tables of contents of the last three or four years of *Managing Leisure*. Click on Browse Publications. In the By Words in Title blank, type in: **managing leisure**. You must choose to browse in Online Articles or in Fax/Ariel (these are two separate databases). Since you have no way of knowing which to choose, try Online Articles first. *Managing Leisure* happens to be in this part of the database, so Ingenta displays for you, from most recent back to 1995, a list of all the issues. You simply click on an issue number and date to see the author, title, and page numbers of each article in the issue (i.e., the table of contents). After browsing a few issues, your list of potential topics includes spectator loyalty to teams, visitor wayfinding in recreation areas, positioning parks and recreation departments within a community's economic development strategy, inclusion of disabled people in recreation centers, and ski resort operators' perceptions of sustainability standards.

Example #2: You must write a major report on issues related to risk, liability, and security in recreation. At this point, you haven't decided on a more specific aspect of the topic. You limit the search to 1997-2005 and type in the following Keywords:

(risk or liabilit* or negligen* or legal or law or security) and (park or parks or recreation)

Your search retrieves 243 items in the fax/ariel part of the database and 705 in online articles (most of the latter are false drops related to scientific and medical topics). There are plenty of promising articles in the fax/ariel results. One big advantage of *Ingenta* is its interdisciplinary nature, as the following references show:

- "Examining legal rules to protect children from injuries in recreational and sport activities," in *Journal of Safety Research*, 2005
- "Sharps discarded in inner city parks and playgrounds—risk of bloodborne virus exposure," in *Communicable Disease and Public Health*, 2004
- "Blowing snow: The National Park Service's disregard for science, law, and public opinion in regulating snowmobiling in Yellowstone National Park," in *Environmental Law Reporter News and Analysis*, 2004
- "Security issues in public recreation centers," in *Journal of Legal Aspects of Sport*, 2002.
- "Rural landowner liability for recreational injuries: myths, perceptions, and realities," in *Journal of Soil and Water Conservation*, 2002

- **ERIC**. This NC LIVE database, which covers 1966 to current, is the world's largest source of education information. *ERIC* (*Education Resources Information Center*) is sponsored by the U.S. Department of Education. It provides over 1.1 million references, with abstracts, for journal articles (from over 750 journals) as well as other, largely unpublished materials in education and related fields. *ERIC* is an international database, but a large percentage of the sources it lists concern education in the United States. The *ERIC* database has two main divisions: *CIJE* (for journal articles) and *RIE* (for *ERIC* documents). *ERIC* documents, which have a record number beginning with ED in the database, are items such as reports on projects that received grant funding; papers presented at conferences; workbooks; and literature reviews, including the highly useful *ERIC* Digests. Over 90 percent of the *ERIC* documents were reproduced on microfiche as part of the *ERIC* Collection and are available in many college libraries. The U.S. Department of Education has made over 107,000 ERIC documents, produced between 1993 and 2004, available free as PDF files. The *ERIC* database has some very useful special fields that you can include in your search. One is the Intended Audience field, which allows you to limit your search to materials written for practitioners, teachers, parents, policymakers, researchers, students, or staff. Another is the Publication Type field, allowing you to limit your search (in the EBSCOhost version's terminology) to Reports—Research/Technical (which will give you research-based articles and documents), Reports—Descriptive, or Reports—Evaluative/Feasibility. A few of the topics that are well represented in *ERIC* include: adventure education, therapeutic recreation, camping, outdoor education, parks, recreational activities, recreational facilities, and Outward Bound. Although a version of the *ERIC* database is freely accessible from the *ERIC* Web site (*http://eric.ed.gov/*), you should use the EBSCOhost version provided through NC LIVE, because it has links to numerous full-text journal articles via *Academic Search Elite* (another NC LIVE EBSCOhost database).

Example #1: Your assignment is to design a self-administered survey or questionnaire, pilot it with at least ten people, and write about how you designed it, administered it, and analyze the results. You plan to survey people's reactions to an outing in a park, and you'd like to read about—or see—other park surveys. In the EBSCOhost version of *ERIC*, using Advanced Search, you type in: **(questionnaires or surveys or needs assessment)** and set the first search blank to Default Fields. In the second search blank you type: **park** and set the search to Descriptors (All). Set the Date Published to 1980-2005. The search retrieves forty six items. Some interesting references include:

- "Incorporating environmental behavior, ethics and values into nonformal environmental education programs," in *Journal of Environmental Education*, 1997
- "Interpretive motivations and preferences of campfire program participants on the Blue Ridge Parkway," in *Legacy*, 1995
- "The citizen survey process in parks and recreation." American Alliance for Health, Physical Education, Recreation and Dance, Reston, VA. American Association for Leisure and Recreation, 1986. (This 127-page guide includes chapters on every stage of the process of designing a survey, testing and administering it, and writing the report. Libraries with the ERIC microfiche collection will own this document.)

Example #2: You need to write reports on five recent journal articles for your Therapeutic Recreation course.

In Advanced Search, type in: **therapeutic recreation** in the first search blank. Set the search blank to the Descriptors (Major) field. This will assure that therapeutic recreation is a major concept in the articles retrieved. Then, at Journal or Document, choose Journal. This finds journal articles only—no *ERIC* documents. Finally, set the Date Published to 2000-2005. This search retrieves twenty nine articles. As you decide which articles to read, use the criteria in the section below on distinguishing journal articles from magazine articles. Even though you checked "journal" on your search, *ERIC* includes some publications that would not be considered scholarly journals. Some interesting results from this search are:

- "Inclusive fitness strategies: Building wellness among developmentally disabled adults," in *Parks & Recreation*, 2002
- "Social cognitive theory: A framework for therapeutic recreation practice," in *Therapeutic Recreation Journal*, 2002
- "An evaluation of therapeutic horseback riding programs for adults with physical impairments," in *Therapeutic Recreation Journal*, 2001

- **PsycINFO**. This NC LIVE database, covering material published since 1887 and updated monthly, is the best source for scholarly information on psychology and related areas (including psychiatry, medicine, sociology, education, pharmacology, and nursing). It indexes over 1,500 journals in over twenty languages, as well as dissertation abstracts, book chapters, and books in English. Because the *PsycArticles* database is also provided by NC LIVE and is embedded within *PsycINFO*, your searches may include the full text of articles from fifty journals published by the American Psychological Association. In fact, you can try limiting your search to just articles from those journals. *PsycINFO* includes articles on the following topics: recreation; recreation therapy; summer camps; specific types of recreation (such as clubs, children's recreational games, dance, gambling, football, television viewing, travel, and vacationing); leisure time; hobbies; and wilderness experience.

Example: Suppose you need comprehensive information on the role of recreation and leisure in the lives of the elderly. Your first step in searching *PsycINFO* would be to check its online Thesaurus to see what terms it uses for the two concepts—recreation and elderly. Since you need lots of information, you'll write down both broad and specific terms from the Thesaurus. Here are the steps to use in the search, once you've selected your search terms. Please note that these apply to the Ovid WebSPIRS version of *PsycINFO*. First, click on Change, near the word Limits at the top of the screen. Apply these limits to your search: Set All Journals to Yes, Language to English, and Publication Year to 1985-2005. Click OK to set these new limits. Next, type in this search statement, setting both search blanks to Descriptors:

(leisure or recreation) and (aged or geriatric patients or elder care or nursing homes)

It's very important *not* to leave the search set to (Terms Anywhere); this would cause a large number of false drops to appear in your results, due to the word *aged*. You would get, for example, articles studying the recreation habits of college students *aged* 18-25. When you execute the search, it retrieves sixty eight articles. Besides articles in leisure studies and therapeutic recreation journals, the results include highly relevant articles from journals such as *Activities, Adaptation and Aging, Journal of Music Therapy, American Journal of Alzheimer's Disease and Other Dementias, Aging and Mental Health, Journal of Applied Gerontology, Journal of Aging and Identity, Archives of Gerontology and Geriatrics, Physical and Occupational Therapy in Geriatrics,* and *Journal of Aging and Health.*

■ **ABI/INFORM Complete**. This NC LIVE database, updated weekly, indexes 1,800 scholarly and trade journals dealing with every aspect of business—including banking and accounting, computers, economics and finance, health care, human resources, management, marketing, and communications. This database should be consulted, therefore, for recreation and leisure topics related to finance, employee relations, management, travel and tourism, or commercial recreation. Three hundred fifty of the journals are published outside the United States; and for over 600 of the journals, the articles published since 1991 are full text (meaning the entire articles are included in the database and can be printed, e-mailed, or saved to disk). You can search all parts of the database at once (labeled Multiple Databases); you can select just one part from the drop-down menu; or you can limit your search to full text articles and/or scholarly journals only.

Example: For your Organizational Behavior course, you must present an in-service workshop to the class, as if they were the staff of a recreation agency. Your topic is: How can work teams learn to manage and resolve conflict?

First, check the online thesaurus of the database (note that it's called Topic Guide; it's a tab at the top of the screen) to see what index terms are used for the two concepts in this topic, conflict and teams. Then, set the first two search blanks to Subject. Set the Date Range to after 01/01/1990. Type in your search this way:

(conflicts or conflict resolution) and (teams or teamwork)

You have a total of 113 articles to choose from. A few useful examples include:

- "Want collaboration? Accept—and actively manage—conflict," in *Harvard Business Review*. 2005
- "Learning to manage intergroup dynamics in changing task environments: an experiential exercise," in *Journal of Management Education*. 2004
- "Workplace conflict, bullying, and counterproductive behaviors," in *International Journal of Organizational Analysis*, 2003 (full text)
- "Illustrating a constructive approach to conflict management," in *Training Journal*, 2002 (full text)

- **Business and Industry**. This international database, covering 1994 to current and updated daily, provides references (many with the full text of the article) from over 1,000 business magazines, journals, newsletters, and general press publications (such as *USA Today* and *Atlanta Journal Constitution*). Articles deal with public and private companies, industries, products, and markets for both manufacturing and service industries. It indexes regional publications, such as *Crain's Chicago Business*, as well as industry publications, such as *Sporting Goods Business*.

Example: For your Commercial Recreation paper, you must write an industry analysis. You have selected the health club industry. One section of your paper must discuss issues and trends in the industry. This section can include consumer demographics, new products and services, legislation, competition from other countries, and predictions for the industry. You plan to skim through recent articles to figure out what the issues and trends are.

By doing a search for: **health club*** in the Words and Phrases blank and browsing the results, you discover that the index term that this database uses for health clubs is: **physical fitness facilities**. Use this information to refine your search to better fit your assignment. Again using the Words and Phrases blank, type in:

physical fitness facilities and

(trend* or demographic* or innovat* or forecast* or prediction* or outlook* or concept*)

Before executing the search, set these limits: Geo region: USA and Date: 01/01/2000 to 06/07/2005. This search retrieves 240 items. Some useful examples include:

- "Meditate on this: A nationwide chain of yoga studios," in *New York Times*, March 2005
- "New fitness gyms target out-of-shape, over-30 males," in *Knight Ridder-Tribune Business News*, January 2005
- "Health clubs are pumping up growing neighborhoods; Gyms cater to fitness buffs in Fort Greene, Williamsburg; larger players may follow," in *Crain's New York Business*, October 2004
- "Bally's loses hardbodies: Health clubs go real to lure Average Joe," in *Advertising Age*, May 2004
- "Yoga USA: from fringe activity to full-blown craze, yoga and other types of alternative fitness have hit the mainstream," in *Sporting Goods Business*, March 2004

- "Club throws weight around Manhattan; Popular, fast-growing Curves fitness chain for women appeals to franchisees, landlords," in *Crain's New York Business*, August 2003
- "Coming of age: entering its formative years, the fitness industry is growing into itself," in *Sporting Goods Business*, July 2003 (2022 words)

- **InfoTrac OneFile.** This NC LIVE database from Gale Group indexes over 6,325 periodicals (over 3,000 of them full text) in a wide range of subject areas, representing the humanities, social sciences, sciences, business, and general interest publications. Indexing goes back to 1980, and the database is updated daily. It is important to remember that there are two other databases available through NC LIVE—EBSCOhost's *Masterfile and Academic Search Elite*—whose structure, purpose, and usefulness are similar to *InfoTrac OneFile's*. Due to space constraints, these databases will not be discussed in depth—but they should be kept in mind for the same types of topics and assignments that are appropriate for *InfoTrac OneFile*.

Because of its interdisciplinary nature, its varied and sophisticated search features, and its wealth of full text articles, this database will be illustrated with three different examples.

Example 1: For your Disabling Conditions and Therapeutic Recreation course, you must write a paper giving the etiology, interventions, and characteristics of a disease or disability. Your topic is **multiple sclerosis**. Go into Subject Guide. Type in: multiple sclerosis. Your search finds 6,048 periodical references, but you have the option to Narrow by Subdivision. Click this link to display numerous subtopics, in alphabetical order. They include -Care and treatment, -Causes of, -Complications, -Demographic aspects, -Drug therapy, -Genetic aspects, and -Research. By selecting some of these subtopics, you can view a variety of articles—many of them full text—in periodicals such as *Inside MS, The Lancet, Science News, Family Practice, British Medical Journal, JAMA, Townsend Letter for Doctors and Patients,* and *Real Living with Multiple Sclerosis.*

Example 2: For your Group Dynamics and Leadership course, you must read a book and write a book review on it. The book must deal with a person you consider a leader, and the person's leadership must have been influenced by age, gender, race, class, sexual identity, or disability. You decide to write about Betty Ford, a First Lady who overcame substance abuse and championed the need for treatment and facilities for those troubled by this problem. You hope that your search will find a published book review that will lead you to a book focusing on this particular aspect of her life. In Advanced Search, type in: **ford, betty** in the first blank and set it to search by Subject. In the second blank, type in: **review*** and leave it set to search Keyword. This search finds four different reviews of the book *Betty: Glad Awakening*, by Betty Ford with Chris Chase.

Example 3: A frequent assignment in recreation courses is to write a paper, an annotated bibliography, or several separate reports on individual journal articles about a contemporary trend or issue in recreation and leisure. Here's a quick, useful approach to such an assignment. First, it's valuable to know the titles of five important recreation journals that are available full text in *InfoTrac OneFile: Journal of Leisure Research, Journal of Park and Recreation Administration, Journal of Physical Education, Recreation* and *Dance, National Parks, and Parks and Recreation.* By using the following formula, you can search all five of these journals at once and also find articles that are full text. Let's use the topic of preservation of wilderness. To keep the search simple (and to find articles that might use some word or phrase other than *preservation*), we'll search only for the *wilderness* concept.

■ Leave the *first* search blank set for Keyword. Set the *second* search blank for Journal Name.
■ Type in: **(wilderness or wild lands)** and **(recreation or parks or leisure)**
■ Limit to: Articles with text, and refereed publications
■ Set date for after January 1, 1990

This search finds twenty four articles. Remember that you can use the same search formula for your own topic; just substitute keywords for your topic in the first search blank.

How to recognize a journal article

If your assignment requires that you use one or more journal articles—or that you use only journal articles—there are certain characteristics you can look for in order to make your decision.

If you're just beginning your database search, you might be able to structure the search so that most or all of your results will be journal articles that will fit your assignment. Here are some examples:

■ *Limit the search to peer-reviewed or scholarly articles. InfoTrac OneFile, Academic Search (EBSCO),* and *ABI/INFORM* are among several databases that allow you to do this. *Sport Discus* allows you to do this by limiting the level of the source to Advanced. You must also limit the publication type to Article.

Be careful to sort through your search results, however. Your search may find articles that are book reviews, feature articles (reviewed by the journal's editorial board but not by outside referees), or other types of brief articles which, although they were published in peer-reviewed journals, may not meet the criteria of your assignment.

If you've already done a search (but haven't limited it to journal articles) and you're browsing through the results, here are some criteria to help you recognize the journal articles:

■ Article topics may be very narrow and specific.
■ Article titles may contain a semicolon and subtitle.
■ Journal titles may be long (example: *Journal of adventure education and outdoor learning*).
■ Journal titles may contain a semicolon and subtitle (example: *Event management: An international journal*)
■ Journal titles may contain "academic" words such as Journal, Review, Research, Annals, International, Studies, Science, Progress, Society, World, or Quarterly.
■ Articles are often lengthy.

If you're looking at the full text of an article, either online or in print, here are some common characteristics that usually indicate the article was published in a journal:

- Journal articles are intended for professors, college students, researchers, or professionals working in the field or discipline studied by that journal.
- Journal articles are generally written by scholars or experts on the topic, rather than by journalists.
- The writing style may be scholarly or technical, using specialized terms that aren't defined but would be understood by the intended audience.
- Journal articles contain citations (footnotes and/or bibliography)—possibly a large number of them—documenting the source(s) of the information provided.
- The journal may look formal and serious, with few illustrations or advertisements.
- The author's "credentials" (degrees, job title, place of employment, and other recently published works) are probably listed with the article.
- Many journal articles are screened by outside experts on the topic and/or by an editorial board before being accepted for publication. These journals are called *refereed* or *peer-reviewed*.
- Journals may be published quarterly, monthly, or even less often.
- Journals may be published by a professional association (such as the Association of Experiential Education) or at a college or university.
- Topics of journal articles are usually discussed in depth and detail.
- Journal articles may contain statistics.
- Journal articles may be based on a research study; if so, they will describe the study's methods, results, and conclusions.

Major journals in recreation, leisure, parks, outdoor education, interpretation, and tourism

This list includes the major journals that you'll see frequently in searches of the databases discussed in this chapter. It also includes some journals that have a smaller circulation and are not indexed by many databases, as well as some that have ceased publication but are important to know about because they are devoted to an important topic in recreation and leisure. Finally, there are some major professional magazines listed, as well as some e-journals that make their articles freely available to everyone. Please note that earlier titles have not been tracked for most journals, so the beginning date usually indicates the date the journal started publication under its current title. Be aware that the indexing and full text information is current as of early June 2005 but could change at any time. Some databases will not have the full text of the most recent issues of a journal due to a publisher's embargo.

Annals of leisure research
1998-current. Published 1x/year. Peer reviewed. International. Published in Australia. Covers recreation, tourism, outdoor recreation, the arts, entertainment, sports, culture, and play. Indexed in *Leisure, Recreation and Tourism Abstracts*.

Annals of tourism research
   1973-current. Published 4x/year. Peer reviewed. Indexed in *Ingenta*.

Australian journal of outdoor education
   1995-current. Published 2x/year. Peer reviewed. Publishes articles on topics concerning both Australia and other countries. See complete tables of contents and some sample articles at http://www.wilderdom.com/ajoe/.

Event management: an international journal
   2000-current. Published 4x/year. Peer reviewed. Indexed in *Sport Discus*.

Environment and behavior
   1969-current. Published 6x/year. Peer reviewed. Indexed in *Academic Search Elite, ERIC, InfoTrac OneFile, Leisure, Recreation and Tourism Abstracts,* and *PsycNFO*. Full text in *Academic Search Elite* since 1994.

International journal of heritage studies
   1994-current. Published 4x/year. Peer reviewed. Indexed in *Leisure, Recreation and Tourism Abstracts*.

International journal of hospitality and tourism administration
   2000-current. Published 4x/year. Peer reviewed. Indexed in *Academic Search Elite, Ingenta,* and *Leisure, Recreation and Tourism Abstracts*.

International journal of tourism research
   1999-current. Published 2x/year. Peer reviewed. Indexed in Ingenta and *Leisure, Recreation and Tourism Abstracts*. Full text in *ABI-INFORM* since 1999 (delayed one year).

International journal of wilderness
   1995-current. Published 3x/year by the University of Idaho Wilderness Research Center. Peer reviewed. Indexed in *Leisure, Recreation and Tourism Abstracts*.

Journal of adventure education and outdoor learning
   2000-current. Published 2x/year by the Institute for Outdoor Learning, UK.

Journal of ecotourism
   2000-current. Published 3x/year. Peer reviewed. Indexed in *Ingenta* and *Leisure, Recreation and Tourism Abstracts*.

Journal of environmental education
   1971-current. Published 4x/year. Peer reviewed. Indexed in *Academic Search Elite, ERIC, InfoTrac OneFile, PsycINFO,* and *InfoTrac OneFile*. Full text in *Academic Search Elite* since 1999 and *InfoTrac Onefile* since 1999.

Journal of environmental psychology
   1981-current. Published 4x/year. Peer reviewed. Indexed in *Leisure, Recreation and Tourism Abstracts* and *PsycINFO*.

Journal of experiential education

1978-current. Published 3x/year by the Association of Experiential Education. Peer reviewed. Indexed in *Academic Search Elite* and *ERIC*. Full text in *Academic Search Elite* since 2001.

Journal of hospitality and leisure marketing

1992-current. Published 8x/year. Peer reviewed. Indexed in *Academic Search Elite, Leisure, Recreation and Tourism Abstracts,* and *Sport Discus.*

Journal of hospitality, leisure, sport & tourism education

2002-current. Published 2x/year by the Hospitality, Leisure, Sport & Tourism Network, UK. Peer reviewed. Indexed by *Leisure, Recreation and Tourism Abstracts* and *Sport Discus.* All articles freely available online at *http://www.hlst.ltsn.ac.uk/johlste/about.html*

Journal of interpretation research

1996-current. Published 2x/year by the National Association for Interpretation. Indexed in *ERIC*.

Journal of leisure research

1969-current. Published 4x/year by the National Recreation and Park Association. Peer reviewed. Indexed in *Academic Search Elite, ERIC, InfoTrac OneFile, Leisure, Recreation and Tourism Abstracts, PsycINFO,* and *Sport Discus.* Full text in *ABI-INFORM* since 1994, *Academic Search Elite* since 1992, and *InfoTrac OneFile* since 1993.

Journal of leisurability

1980-2000. Ceased publication; formerly published 4x/year. Indexed in *Leisure, Recreation and Tourism Abstracts* and *Sport Discus.*

Journal of park and recreation administration

1983-current. Published 4x/year by the American Academy for Park and Recreation Administration. Peer reviewed. Indexed in *ERIC, InfoTrac OneFile, Leisure, Recreation and Tourism Abstracts,* and *Sport Discus.* Full text in *InfoTrac OneFile* since 1994.

Journal of physical education, recreation and dance (JOPERD)

1930-current (under various earlier titles). Published 9x/year by the American Alliance for Health, Physical Education, Recreation and Dance. Peer reviewed. Indexed in *Academic Search Elite, ERIC, InfoTrac OneFile, Leisure, Recreation and Tourism Abstracts,* and *Sport Discus.* Full text in *InfoTrac OneFile* since 1993.

Journal of sustainable tourism

1993-current. Published 4x/year in the UK. Peer reviewed. Indexed in *Ingenta* and *Leisure, Recreation and Tourism Abstracts.*

Journal of tourism studies

1990-current. Published 2x/year in Australia. Indexed by *InfoTrac OneFile* and *Ingenta*.

Journal of travel and tourism marketing

1992-current. Published 4x/year. Peer reviewed. Indexed in *ABI-INFORM, Leisure, Recreation and Tourism Abstracts*, and *Sport Discus*.

Journal of travel research

1972-current. Published 4x/year. Peer reviewed. Indexed in *ABI-INFORM, InfoTrac OneFile*, and *Leisure, Recreation and Tourism Abstracts*. Full text in *ABI-INFORM* since 1992.

Journal of vacation marketing

1995-current. Published 4x/year. International. Peer reviewed. Full text in *ABI-IN-FORM* since 2001.

LARNET: The cyber journal of applied leisure and recreation research

Published by North Carolina Central University. International. Peer reviewed. All articles are freely available. View abstracts and full text at *http://www.nccu.edu/larnet/abstracts.html*.

Legacy: The journal of the National Association for Interpretation

1990-current. Published 6x/year. Peer reviewed.

Leisure / Loisir

2000-current. Published 4x/year by the Canadian Association of Leisure Studies. Peer reviewed. In English and French. Indexed in *Leisure, Recreation and Tourism Abstracts*. View tables of contents of the issues, with abstracts, at *http://www.unbf.ca/kinesiology/leisure/journal/evolution/leisureinfo/leisuretable. html*

Leisure management

1981-current. 10x/year. Indexed in *InfoTrac OneFile, Leisure, Recreation and Tourism Abstracts*, and *Sport Discus*.

Leisure sciences

1977-current. Published 4x/year. Peer reviewed. Indexed in *Leisure, Recreation and Tourism Abstracts, PsycINFO*, and *Sport Discus*.

Managing leisure

1995-current. Published 4x/year. Peer reviewed. International. Indexed in *Leisure, Recreation and Tourism Abstracts* and in *Sport Discus*.

National parks

1980-current. Published 6x/year by the National Parks and Conservation Association. Indexed in *Academic Search Elite, ERIC*, and *InfoTrac OneFile*. Full text in *Academic Search Elite* since 1990 and in *InfoTrac OneFile* since 1993.

Natural resources journal

1961-current. Published 4x/year. Peer reviewed. International and interdisciplinary. Indexed in *Academic Search Elite* and in *LegalTrac*.

Palaestra: Forum of sport, physical education & recreation for those with disabilities

1984-current. Published 4x/year. Indexed in *Academic Search Elite, ERIC, InfoTrac OneFile,* and *Sport Discus*. Full text in *InfoTrac OneFile* since 1990. View tables of contents (with some full text feature articles) of issues since 1999 at *http://www.palaestra.com/contentscomplete.html*.

Park science

1980-current. Published 2x/year by the U.S. National Park Service. Articles are reviewed by an editorial board. Indexed in *Leisure, Recreation and Tourism Abstracts*. All articles are freely available as PDF files at http://www2.nature.nps.gov/parksci/.

Parks and recreation

1966-current. Published 12x/year by the National Recreation and Park Association. Indexed in *Academic Search Elite, ERIC, InfoTrac OneFile, Leisure, Recreation and Tourism Abstracts,* and *Sport Discus*. Full text in *Academic Search Elite* since 1996 and *InfoTrac OneFile* since 1992.

Ski area management

Beginning date uncertain. Published 6x/year by the National Ski Areas Association. Indexed in *Leisure, Recreation and Tourism Abstracts* and in *Sport Discus*.

Schole: a journal of leisure studies and recreation education

1988-current. Published 4x/year by the Society of Park and Recreation Educators. Peer reviewed. Indexed in *ERIC, Leisure, Recreation and Tourism Abstracts, PsycINFO,* and *Sport Discus*.

Society and natural resources

1968-current. Published 10x/year. Peer reviewed. Indexed in *Academic Search Elite* and *Leisure, Recreation and Tourism Abstracts*. Full text in *Academic Search Elite* since 1997 (one-year delay)

Sports, parks, and recreation law reporter

1987-current. Published 4x/year. Peer reviewed. Indexed in *Sport Discus*.

Therapeutic recreation journal

1968-current. Published 4x/year by the National Therapeutic Recreation Society. Peer reviewed. Indexed in *ERIC, Leisure, Recreation and Tourism Abstracts, PsycINFO,* and *Sport Discus*.

Tourism and hospitality research

1999-current. Published 4x/year in the UK. Peer reviewed. International. Indexed in *ABI-INFORM* and *Ingenta*. Full text in *ABI-INFORM* since 2001.

Tourism management
1982-current. Published 8x/year. Peer reviewed. International. Indexed in *Ingenta* and in *Leisure, Recreation and Tourism Abstracts*.

Tourism recreation research
1977-current. Published 3x/year in India. Peer reviewed. Indexed in *Sport Discus*.

World leisure journal
2001-current. Published 4x/year by the World Leisure and Recreation Association. Peer reviewed. International. Indexed in *Leisure, Recreation and Tourism Abstracts* and in *Sport Discus*. More information at http://www.worldleisure.org/.

North Carolina General Statutes

If you need to find state laws regarding recreation and parks, there are several different ways to do so:

- *Consult your library's print copy* of the *General Statutes*. The index volume can be very helpful; and in some situations it's easier to browse through a print volume than to search for what you need in the online version. It can be a little difficult to search for the *General Statutes* in your Library Catalog in order to get the call number and location. To save yourself some time, ask a reference librarian to show you where the *General Statutes* are located. They'll probably be in the library's Reference or Ready Reference area. If you do search your Library Catalog, try a Title search for: **General statutes of North Carolina annotated**
- *Use the searchable version on the North Carolina General Assembly Web site at:* http://www.ncleg.net/gascripts/Statutes/Statutes.asp. This version conveniently lists each of the 168 chapters, in order, with a link to the text of that chapter. You can search for a word or phrase (such as recreation or natural and scenic rivers). You can search within all 168 chapters, or you can designate a particular chapter to search within. You can have your search show the matches by chapter, by article, or by section (perhaps the most useful) of the *General Statutes*. Each match can be viewed as an html, pdf, or rich text file. You can also search by citation, if you already have it; for example, 100-13 is the section authorizing the state to charge user fees in parks.
- *Use the searchable version in the LEXIS-NEXIS Academic database.* If your library subscribes to this database, this version is easy to search. Your results can be printed or e-mailed to yourself. Here's the path to the searchable *General Statutes*, once you're in this database:

Academic Search Forms: Legal Research> Codes & Regulations> State Codes> North Carolina

Web pages to assist your research

You'll find that there are many Web pages—prepared by librarians, by recreation management faculty, or by others—that can help you with various information-gathering tasks related to recreation and leisure. Here are just a few examples:

- **Selected Resources for Research in Recreation and Leisure Studies**. This detailed page, prepared by a librarian at the University of North Carolina at Chapel Hill, lists a number of sources and research strategies not included in this chapter. *http://www.lib.unc.edu/reference/socsci/recleist.html*
- **Outdoor Recreation Research**. This page was compiled by Yu-Fai Leung, a professor in the Parks, Recreation, and Tourism Management program at North Carolina State University. The page is a useful, well-organized collection of links to Web sites for: recreation areas; all the state parks systems; specific outdoor recreation activities; academic programs in recreation in the United States as well as other countries; outdoor-recreation-related government agencies in the United States and elsewhere; professional organizations; research methods; and recreation-related periodicals and book publishers. *http://www4.ncsu.edu/~leung/recres2.html*
- **Outdoor Education Research and Evaluation Center**. This impressive, content-rich site is maintained by James Neill, a former Outward Bound instructor. It is part of his Wilderdom.com site. It organizes and annotates links to a vast range of information resources about outdoor education. *http://www.wilderdom.com/research.html*
- **Recommended sources and strategies for finding information for grant proposals**. This Web page was designed for the RM 3610, Administration of Recreation Services II course at Appalachian State University. It is maintained by Glenn Ellen Starr Stilling, a librarian at Appalachian State University. *http://www.library.appstate.edu/reference/classguides/rm3610.html*
- **Finding an internship site**. This Web page was designed for the RM 3315, Career Development course at Appalachian State University. It is maintained by Glenn Ellen Starr Stilling, a librarian at Appalachian State University. *http://www.library.appstate.edu/reference/classguides/rm3315.html*
- **Finding job openings on the Web and in print sources**. This Web page was designed for the RM 4210, Senior Seminar course at Appalachian State University. It is maintained by Glenn Ellen Starr Stilling, a librarian at Appalachian State University. *http://www.library.appstate.edu/reference/classguides/rm4210.html*

The Planning Process for Library and Database Research

Now that you've read about library services and been introduced to a variety of databases and other sources for finding information, you are probably wondering how to sketch out a plan for researching a topic of your own. This final section of the chapter will outline a comprehensive process; you can adapt it, if you need to, for shorter, smaller projects. We will use the same topic as an example throughout this outline of the research process.

Step 1: Write your topic as a short sentence or phrase.

Example: **Managing or preparing for risk and liability**

Step 2: Decide how thorough your research needs to be.

A. *Brief* (only a few, good, very relevant sources).
B. *Intermediate* (the instructor requires a large number of sources; you're very interested in the topic; or you want to do really well on the assignment).
C. *Extensive* (it's a major paper; it counts a large percentage of your course grade; you are vitally interested in the topic; or it's a difficult topic to research).

Step 3: Break the topic into concept groups; or, if it's a simple topic, just list words and phrases that describe it.

Example:

A	B	C
risk	parks	management
liability	recreation departments	planning

Examples of phrases for some simple (or broad) topics: multiple use; Outward Bound; serious leisure; user fees, watchable wildlife.

Step 4: Decide which concepts you really need to include in your search strategy.

Unless you think you'll be overwhelmed with information, it's best to start small and simple. Two concepts (three at the most) are usually enough. So, to keep things simple, we'll only use concepts A and B for this outline. Besides, concepts such as *managing* or *planning* can be hard to search for. It would be difficult to think of all the different words the articles might use for this part of the topic; and if you don't think of the best ones, your search might miss some useful articles. When we do the search for concepts A and B, we'll turn up articles that discuss managing or planning for risk, along with articles on other aspects of risk and liability in parks and recreation. So, we'll just skim the article references, looking for those that relate to managing or planning. If we find ourselves with an unmanageably large number of references—too many to browse through—we'll go back and redo the search, adding in Concept C.

Step 5: List words and phrases that might be used for each of your concepts.

Example:

A	B
risk	park
legal	parks
liability	recreation
negligent	
negligence	
security	
surveillance	
waivers	

Be aware that you probably won't need to use *all* the words in your list. You may end up choosing other words, based on checking a database's online thesaurus before executing the search. In addition, as you go through the references found in a search, you may see other words (in an abstract, or in the index terms assigned to an article) that you hadn't thought of. Be sure to add these to your list as you discover them and redo some of your searches, using these new words. Finally, be aware that you'll sometimes drop a concept from your search because of the nature of the particular database you're searching. For instance, if you search a law database, such as *LegalTrac* or *LEXIS-NEXIS Academic* (the sections called *Legal News* and *Law Reviews*), you may be able to drop Concept A.

Step 6: Decide what formats of information you could use for your topic, and make a list. Sometimes your instructor specifies that you can use only certain formats (such as journal articles). If this is not the case, be open-minded in choosing your formats—and consider checking with a reference librarian for suggestions. Two formats that are frequently overlooked are circulating books and reference books.

Example: journal articles

books (probably just a chapter or section)

magazine or newsletter articles

reference books (recreation or law)

newspaper articles

Web sites

Step 7: List the disciplines (or subject areas)—both broad and specific—that are relevant for your topic.

Example: Sports

Law

Recreation and leisure

Business

Step 8: List databases, reference books, experts, etc. that you will consult for information.

You can choose from the sources listed in this chapter. Depending on your topic, however, there may be other databases or sources that would be useful to you. In addition, individual libraries—as well as the NC LIVE project—add new databases practically every year; and databases may change their name, search commands, focus, and the particular journals they index. Consult your library's Web site, or ask a reference librarian, for other suggestions.

Example: Sport Discus

LEXIS-NEXIS Academic (*Legal News; Law Reviews*)

Library Catalog

InfoTrac OneFile

Ingenta

Step 9: Plan a basic search strategy that you will alter or adjust for each database you search.

Example:

(risk or liable or liability or negligen* or legal or waiver*) and   (park or parks or recreation)

Step 10: Conduct searches in the chosen databases.

As a preliminary step, you might prioritize the databases, so that you start with the ones you think will give you the most information. You might find plenty of information in the first two or three and not need to look further. If, however, your searches don't turn out as you expected and you don't know what the problem is, ask a reference librarian for assistance.

Step 11: Find the sources listed in the printouts from your searches.

Check your Library Catalog for books and for journals that were not full text. It's also possible that an article that wasn't full text in the database in which you found the reference listed may actually be available full text in a different database (one provided by NC LIVE or subscribed to by your library). Again, librarians can help you figure this out.

Here are some recommendations for making your research easier and more efficient:

- **Start early**. Your searches might turn up some highly relevant, extremely promising articles or books that are not available in your library. They can be gotten for you—possibly free—through interlibrary loan, but the process usually takes a few days to two weeks.
- **Check out books and print or photocopy articles** as soon as you finish your searches, rather than waiting until close to the time when the assignment is due. If you wait, books you need might get checked out (and maybe even kept overdue) by someone else; journals might get misplaced in the library or sent to the bindery; and some of the articles you selected from your searches might turn out to be unhelpful or disappointing, requiring you to do more searches. Checking on your sources now can avoid, or at least allow time to deal with, these potential difficulties.
- **Read your articles and other sources a little at a time**, rather than all at once and right before the paper is due. This gives the information time to sink in—and gives you better ideas, since you're under less pressure and have more time to process the information. You might even discover an exciting new angle on the topic and decide to search for some more information on that angle.
- **Skim through the footnotes and bibliography of each article**, book, or other source that you use from your searches. These references might include useful items that didn't turn up in the searches. Many people assume that database searches will find everything you need. In fact, there are periodicals that aren't indexed in any databases. Another possibility is that an article you find in a bibliography didn't turn up on any searches because the words you searched under didn't match with the words that the databases used to index that particular article. The best research uses a combination of searches and bibliography-scanning.

Learning Exercises

1. Check your library's Web site to see if the library has each of the databases listed in the section on Searching Periodical Databases. If you're not sure how to do this, ask a librarian for assistance.

2. Search your library's catalog to find out if it has the following: (a) two specialized encyclopedias: *Encyclopedia of Recreation and Leisure in America,* and *Encyclopedia of Leisure and Outdoor Recreation*; (b) the soil survey for your home county; and (c) a subscription to the *Journal of Leisure Research*. Where is each item located in the library? What years of *Journal of Leisure Research* does your library have?

3. Following the steps described above, do a Keyword search, followed by a Subject search, to find out how many books your library has on multiple use of parks, forests, or public lands. Then, search this same topic in *WorldCat*, using the same Library of Congress Subject Headings that you discovered in your library catalog. How many books in English does *WorldCat* list?

4. Following closely the steps described above, search *ERIC* for journal articles on the topic of risk management and the outdoors. Select three articles that look interesting, and print off the references. Check to see if the articles can be found in your library.

5. Following all of the steps described in Exercise 3 above, do two searches in *InfoTrac OneFile* to find full text articles on the topic of fees. First, try the search with **fees** in Keyword. Next, search **fees** in Text word. How many articles did each search find? How many of the articles found in your second search had a significant amount of information on fees? Hint: To see where *fees* matches in the article text, go to Edit on your browser menu, and select Find. Type in **fees**. Click on Next.

References

American Library Association. Presidential Committee on Information Literacy. *Final Report*. American Library Association, 1989. *http://www.ala.org/ala/acrl/acrlissues/acrlinfolit/infolitoverview/introtoinfolit/introinfolit.htm*

Association of College and Research Libraries. "Information Literacy Competency Standards for Higher Education." Chicago: Association of College and Research Libraries, January 18, 2000, 3.

Chapter 18
The Future of Recreation and Leisure Services in North Carolina

Paul L. Gaskill and Ben Tholkes

In the early years of twenty first century, futurists predict a number of changes that will affect our society and how recreation and leisure are experienced. This chapter will incorporate information from previous chapters in the text with some of these predicted changes. The particular focus is on those changes that will most greatly affect North Carolina.

Simplicity versus Extravagance

As people become more aware of diminishing renewable resources, there will be increased emphasis on simplicity. Simplicity will take the form of moderation, self-discipline, and spiritual growth, rather than conspicuous consumption. Material accumulation will be de-emphasized by many, and renewed emphasis will be placed on getting maximum use out of everything. With growing concern over toxins and pollutants, many will seek alternatives to fossil fuels and chemicals for transportation, agriculture, heating, etc. Increased efforts will be directed at developing ways to recycle waste into useful products. In a sense, we will see a back to nature movement. This philosophy is already evident in some areas of North Carolina where individuals and groups are producing their own organically grown food, giving greater consideration to the long-term impact of development, and coordinating efforts to protect natural resources. The rise in the number of land trusts and grassroots conservation efforts is also indicative of this environmental movement.

The implications to North Carolina recreation and leisure professionals are that there will be increased use of outdoor recreation areas as people seek to enjoy the mountains, rivers, forests, and beaches they are trying to protect. Accommodating increased numbers of users, even environmentally conscious ones, while protecting the resource will be a difficult task. Recreation agencies, whether natural resource based or not, will need to operate and maintain their facilities and programs in an increasingly environmentally responsible manner.

At the opposite end of the spectrum is the continued growth of large entertainment-oriented commercial endeavors such as Carowinds. Enhanced technology makes it possible to offer experiences that were unimagined a few years ago. The excitement and immediate gratification of innovations such as virtual reality draw large numbers of participants. For these ventures to attract new and returning customers, they must constantly develop rides and shows that are bigger, brighter, faster, and more thrilling than the previous ones.

Whether recreationists favor simple experiences or more extravagant ones, they are likely to have several things in common. Individuals are interested in experiencing new things and they expect those experiences to deliver quality. There is growing interest in stimulating high risk activities, whether those take place on a remote rock face or in the midst of a hundred fellow screamers on the newest amusement ride.

Fitness and Health

Current trends indicate that the fitness industry is here to stay. North Carolinians are pursuing healthier lifestyles, as witnessed by the growth in public recreation and park fitness offerings, YMCA/YWCA memberships, fitness center rosters, and sales of consumer goods. Activities such as hiking, cycling, skiing, backpacking, water sports, swimming, sailing, and windsurfing are experiencing record participation. While some of these fitness pursuits entail traveling to a destination, most are close to home and are both convenient and affordable.

Futurists see fitness as an absolute necessity in the years to come. With the changing work place and the need to be more self-sufficient in the home, individuals will need to maintain healthy lifestyles to survive. Physically fit individuals will engage in domestic chores that were previously performed by hired help. Examples will include taking personal responsibility for the maintenance of lawns, converting yard space into much needed vegetable/flower garden spaces, trimming trees, painting, or cutting and splitting firewood. Exercise or workout routines will be integrated into these life activities, so that both developing fitness and completing chores will be accomplished simultaneously.

Although the home fitness center will survive into the next millennium, there will be more interest in personal fitness services. These will be purchased at *longevity centers*, businesses that will be a combination of fitness center, spa, and resort. Personal trainers will counsel patrons on weight loss, aerobic training principles, effects of substance abuse, and nutrition. The focus will be on education and lifelong learning, and many of the fitness development approaches will also teach personal skills like self-defense techniques. Many areas of North Carolina, such as the mountains and the coast, will see the emergence of longevity centers as destination attractions. Statewide programs like the Be Active North Carolina program sponsored by the Blue Cross/Blue Shield Foundation will also contribute to the wellness education and fitness of North Carolinians.

As fitness and wellness practices become more prevalent early in this century, the longevity of North Carolinians will rise. Senior adults currently account for over 14 percent of the total population of the state, and this is expected to reach 18 percent by the year 2010. This increase in senior adults will create new demands for comprehensive leisure services in public, private, and therapeutic recreation agencies.

Travel and Tourism

The natural beauty of North Carolina's mountains and beaches provide two powerful tourism magnets. Residents of metropolitan areas in the state, such as Charlotte and the Research Triangle, are frequent visitors to the high country and the coastal areas. In ever increasing numbers, tourists from outside the state visit North Carolina as well. This trend is expected to continue as technology, such as the Official North Carolina Travel and Tourism Web site, makes information more easily accessible to visitors. As much of North Carolina's available beachfront is used up, other areas of the state, particularly the western mountains, will continue to gain in popularity.

Eco-tourism is expected to increase in popularity along with heritage tourism as travelers seek to learn while vacationing (Marshall, 1996). Other factors contributing to growth in these areas are the aging of the tourist population and the public's increasing environmental awareness (Ayala, 1996). North Carolina's rich heritage and numerous historic sites make it an ideal destination for the education-seeking traveler. Protection of the very environment that attracts so many visitors will continue to be critical. As user numbers increase, the impact on the environment is greater; therefore, it is essential that use is carefully managed.

The same features that make North Carolina a tourist destination also attract individuals to retire to mountain and beach areas, or to purchase vacation homes. As the percentage of older adults increases, recreation professionals will be called upon to provide additional services geared to this population's needs. Opportunities for social interaction will be important as individuals enter a community. Those who purchase vacation homes will look for organized leisure opportunities in the community. As noted in a previous chapter, property owner's associations are beginning to assume the bulk of these responsibilities, and this trend will continue as the new century unfolds.

In 1994, Governor Hunt and Cherokee tribal leaders signed a compact allowing the establishment and operation of a casino on the Cherokee Indian Reservation. If gambling attracts the interest that it has in other areas of the country, it will have a significant impact on the number and type of visitors drawn to the southwestern area of the state. Current visitors come to the Cherokee area to enjoy the mountain scenery and the Native American culture; and although these visitors are likely to continue to come, others, primarily interested in gambling, are expected to swell the numbers. Possible positive changes resulting from casino gambling include expansion of tourist-related business such as hotels and restaurants; the creation of new jobs due to casino employment and related businesses; and year-round rather than seasonal economic growth from tourist dollars.

There are also a number of negative changes that have emerged since the Harrah's/Cherokee casino opened for business. Traffic problems in and around the Cherokee/Great Smoky Mountain National Park area have increased, along with water and sewer problems, increases in crime, displacement of tourists from Cherokee shops to the casino, and the transfer of employees from current businesses to the casino.

Family Structure

As the U.S. population continues to grow, longevity increases, and affordable housing becomes more scarce, a rise in multigenerational households is anticipated. Increasing numbers of older adults will move in with their children rather than retirement communities or nursing homes. Generation Xers and their young children will also move back home. With more adults in the household to share housekeeping, babysitting, and child-rearing responsibilities, leisure opportunities should increase, particularly for young parents. Recreation professionals will need to give greater attention to intergenerational programming so that grandparents and grandchildren can participate together.

In some respects the nuclear family is rebounding with higher rates of marriage and family formation. Paralleling this is the decline in the divorce rate. Parents are looking for quantity time that is also quality time. Family oriented-recreation programs, such as the YMCA's Indian Guides and Indian Princesses, will receive increased attention.

Although often marrying later in life, singles will seek viable avenues through which to develop meaningful relationships. At the same time, the traditional American family is being redefined with more single parent households and with many grandparents bearing the primary responsibility for raising their grandchildren. Family will continue to broaden beyond that of blood relationships to include groups of interdependent people. Although this framework will provide a social and support network for its members, there will be a need for more opportunities for unattached individuals to meet and bond with others. Recreation programs that provide social benefits and enable individuals to meet others with similar interests will grow in popularity. Internet-and computer-based dating services will continue to see increased use.

Effects of Technology

According to Marvin Cetron in *The Futurist,* all the technological knowledge we work with today will represent only 1 percent of the knowledge that will be available in the year 2050. As the pace of technological growth quickens, so too does the pervasive effect of these technologies on our lives.

In North Carolina, the effects of technological innovation and change are already evident. Employers are downsizing companies and laying off employees in record numbers. While this may increase entrepreneurship, as some futurists have asserted, it also creates a decentralized work force that is in need of re-training and technological education. With traditional jobs fading, those with high level technological skills will replace service and factory workers in the more flexible workplace. Workers who have thus mastered the virtual office can telecommute to their paid jobs while residing in any area of the state they choose.

Jobs will therefore have less externally controlled variables, and job elements such as work hours and intensity will be controlled by the worker, not the employer. With a strong need to develop and maintain professional skills, continuing education and training will become an integral part of the typical work day. In addition, these jobs may demand tremendous mental concentration, but in general will not be physically engaging.

These future trends, some of which have already begun, have real implications for leisure services in North Carolina. Decentralized workers will be moving to rural areas of the state to enjoy the quality of life that small towns have to offer. Many will work alone in their homes or offices, and may lack significant social contacts. Artificial contacts such as video phones and virtual reality may suffice for the short term, but are impersonal medium.

Leisure service organizations in North Carolina therefore have to consider many of these attributes of their future consumers. Their users will be highly educated, and will need to be provided programs that challenge and engage their intellects. They will have a real need for substantive social interaction, so opportunities for developing affiliations with other individuals in structured or unstructured activities must become an agency priority.

Further, the telecommuter will have flexible work hours which will challenge the leisure service providers in the state to move offerings to non-traditional times or locations. This will entail the development of a network of opportunity that, much like the work environment, is decentralized to meet the changing needs of the leisure service consumer. With respect to marketing and promoting these new services, it is evident that the agency needs to use the primary medium of its constituents: the computer. Home pages and current on line events need to be posted if this audience is to be reached and served. Electronic bulletin boards are also consistent with the dominant environmental ethics of the audience, and far fewer pieces of paper will be used over time. Continuing to serve the current user population while effectively reaching this emerging techno-user group will emerge as a major challenge to leisure service organizations in North Carolina within the next decade.

Summary

There are a tremendous number of changes that will affect future resources, facilities, and participants in North Carolina. Ultimately, future leisure service consumers in the state will expect high quality services from all sectors of the leisure service industry. The public sector will be held accountable for tax supported services and will be increasingly privatized in the years ahead. Non-profits and commercial agencies will become more specialized and highly competitive. All agencies will be expected to consider individual leisure needs and devise program delivery systems that address these needs. Jobs and career opportunities will be plentiful in this new era, because diversified leisure interests and favorable demographic data give way to diversified leisure service settings and entrepreneurship possibilities. Young professionals with a solid grounding in history, human behavior, and programming/management indeed have a bright future as we progress through the new millennium in North Carolina.

An angler logs on to her lap top computer in Raleigh in May 2006. She accesses the U.S. Forest Service Web site for the Pisgah National Forest, and is able to obtain complete topographic information and descriptions of fly fishing streams in each section of the Pisgah. Descriptions of each stream with topographic map location, detailed highway directions, and parking areas are all provided, including pictures of some of the most accessible fishing areas. After securing fishing license and permit information, she secures a back country permit from the Forest Service and pays via her Internet debit account.

After purchasing some new fishing lures from an on line catalog, she decides to investigate fishing guide services that would take her to areas with which she is unfamiliar but hold promise as fertile fly fishing streams. Browsing the Web pages, she decides to secure the services of a local guide service and makes her reservation. Because several of these areas are very remote, she decides to purchase a personal locator devise (PLD), which will pinpoint her exact location in the Pisgah at all times by satellite. She then decides to spend a night in a hotel before returning to Raleigh, and makes her reservation directly using the High Country Host Web pages as her source of information.

En route to her wilderness experience, she is in constant communication with her office via cellular phone. After reaching her destination, the peace and tranquility of the fishing experience have allowed her to clear her mind and think of a new solution to a nagging problem in her office. She logs on to her lap top and sends a fax to her office via satellite before the idea is forgotten. Upon her return to Raleigh the next day, she is psychologically and emotionally refreshed and ready for the next series of professional challenges. Perhaps she will go fly fishing again next week.

Index